The Slovak-American Cookbook

Edited by the First Catholic Slovak
Ladies Association

**ALLEGRO
EDITIONS**

The First Catholic Slovak Ladies Association,
a fraternal benefit society, was founded in 1892.
www.fcsla.org

Published by Allegro Editions

Cover image adapted from the work of Dr. Joseph G. Cincik

ISBN: 978-1-62654-079-8

Printed and bound in the United States of America

Dedicated to . . .

Our Mothers and Grandmothers

In grateful remembrance.

TRADITIONAL CHRISTMAS EVE SUPPER MENU

Oplatky (Christmas Wafers)

Wine

Mushroom Soup

Bobalky

Honey

Pagach

Fish Beans Peas Sauerkraut

Mixed Dried Fruits or Stewed Prunes

Assorted Fresh Fruits

Nut and Poppyseed Rolls

Coffee

Mixed Nuts

Rozky

The traditional Christmas Eve Supper is prepared with home grown crops. The meal, therefore, varies in different parts of Slovakia. Varieties of soups are served. For example, some people serve mushroom soup, others serve sauerkraut soup with mushrooms poured over a serving of mashed potatoes, which were combined with browned onions. Another soup served in another part of Slovakia is the lima bean and prune soup. The dried fruits are grown on their own soil.

TRADITIONAL EASTER BREAKFAST

Sausage

Hard Cooked Eggs

Sweet Butter

Baked Ham

Beet Horseradish

Paska

Sirok (Egg Roll)

Home Baked Twist Nut and Poppy seed Rolls

Coffee

TABLE OF CONTENTS

Appetizers

COCKTAILS, CANAPES & HORS D'OEUVRES

Canapes and Hors d'oeuvres are served as snacks at cocktail and buffet parties and their festive appearance lends a party atmosphere to any gathering.

Appetizers may precede a simple, well prepared dinner, in the living room with a cocktail. The cocktail may be tomato juice, citrus fruit juice, seafood juice, or it may be the conventional alcoholic appetizer. Most cocktails should be chilled thoroughly before serving. The snacks should be bite-sized and well seasoned, to stimulate the appetite.

- FRUIT & VEGETABLE JUICE COCKTAILS -

CITRUS FRUIT JUICE COCKTAIL

⅜ cup lemon juice
¾ cup orange juice
1½ cups chilled carbonated water
½ cup sugar
1⅛ cups grape juice

Place the mixture in a cocktail shaker and shake vigorously. Serve at once in iced glasses. Garnish each cocktail with a sprig of fresh mint. Serves 6.

Agatha Filush, Benton Harbor, Mich.

GRAPEFRUIT-GINGER COCKTAIL

2 cups diced grapefruit
2 cups diced fresh pineapple
1 tablespoon preserved ginger
1 tablespoon ginger syrup

Mix and chill thoroughly. Serve in Sherbet glasses, or orange cups. Decorate with a green cherry.

Margaret DeSilva. Chicago. Ill.

GRAPEJUICE FLOAT

3 cups grape juice
½ cup lemon juice
1 cup apple cider

1½ cups gingerale
Sugar to sweeten
Orange sherbet or orange ice

Combine grape juice, lemon juice and apple cider. Sweeten to taste. Just before serving add gingerale. Fill glasses about 3/4 full, drop a scoop of orange sherbet or orange ice on top. Serve immediately. All ingredients should be cold. (Serves 6.)

Loretta Kasovsky, Chicago, Ill.

TOMATO JUICE

2 cups tomato juice
2 tablespoons minced onion
2 tablespoons chopped parsley
2 tablespoons lemon juice

¼ teaspoon salt
½ teaspoon Worcestershire sauce
½ teaspoon sugar
½ teaspoon celery salt

Combine ingredients, chill 1 hour, strain and serve.

CHILLED JUICES

Place shaved ice in cocktail glasses and fill with one of the following chilled juices:

1. **Equal parts tomato and sauerkraut juice**
2. **Coca-Cola with fresh lime juice**
3. **Grapefruit juice topped with minted cherries**
4. **Equal parts prune and pineapple juice**

Justine Kasovsky. Chicago. Ill.

-FRUIT CUP COCKTAILS -

AVOCADO AND GRAPEFRUIT COCKTAIL

3 grapefruits
1 avocado
6 minted cherries

Cut grapefruit in halves, remove pulp carefully. Separate the membrane from pulp. Dice the pulp and mix with diced avocado. Chill. Serve in grapefruit shells that have been fringed or cut in scallops, garnish with minted cherries. If grapefruit is tart, sprinkle some sugar over the pulp.

Loretta Kasovsky, Chicago, Ill.

MELON BALL COCKTAIL

Melon Balls
Lime or lemon juice
Mint leaves

With a french ball cutter, or with a teaspoon, scoop out balls from watermelon, cantaloupe, honey dew melon, or any melon in season. Arrange in cocktail glasses. Squeeze over the balls juice of fresh limes or lemons. Chill thoroughly and garnish with mint leaves. At Christmas, cut up maraschino cherries for garnish.

Margaret Valacak, Benton Harbor, Mich.

RASPBERRY-MELON CUP

1½ cups fresh raspberries
1 cup sugar
3 cups diced watermelon

Cover fresh raspberries with sugar and let stand in refrigerator about one hour. Then force through coarse sieve. Heap watermelon in cocktail glasses, or sherbets and pour raspberry puree over melon. Yield: 6 servings.

Helen Valacak, Benton Harbor, Mich.

SUNGOLD COCKTAIL

Cantaloupe, peach, apricot and pineapple mixed together in diced form, serve ice cold in cocktail glasses. Serve with 1 tablespoon orange and lemon juice mixed for each cocktail glass. (Mix juices together and then measure - tablespoon for each glass.)

Justine Uhlarik, Chicago, Ill.

- SEA FOOD COCKTAILS -

SHRIMP COCKTAIL

Clean shrimp, removing black line from back. Arrange in cocktail cups with 4 tablespoons finely chopped celery to 1 can of shrimp. Serve chilled with cocktail sauce and a wedge of lemon.

CRABMEAT COCKTAIL

For each serving, use ¼ cup flaked or larger pieces of cooked crabmeat with Cocktail Sauce, or combine crabmeat from 1 8-ounce can, (removing flat bones) and ½ cup finely chopped celery. Serve well chilled with cocktail sauce and wedge of lemon.

Anna K. Hruskovich, Whiting, Ind.

-COCKTAIL SAUCES-

SHRIMP APPETIZER SAUCE

½ cup chili sauce
2 tablespoons lemon juice
Dash of tobasco sauce
Pinch of salt

1 teaspoon finely grated onion
¼ cup catsup
1 teaspoon Worcestershire sauce
½ cup horseradish

Combine all ingredients and chill. Serve with shrimp or raw oysters.

Vincentian Sisters of Charity, Bedford, Oh.

SEAFOOD SAUCE

1 cup mayonnaise
2 tablespoon catsup
2 tablespoons chili sauce

1 tablespoon tarragon vinegar
1 teaspoon lemon juice

Mix all ingredients together and chill.

Gertrude Kolar, Chicago, Ill.

- CANAPES -

Canapes consist of bite sized tidbits of savory spreads on cracker or toast base. There are hot and cold canapes. Fillings may be prepared a day or two in advance and refrigerated in covered containers until needed. Canapes may be simple or elaborate in appearance. In either case they must be made neatly and attractive.

The foundation for cold canapes usually consist of bread. It may be toasted or plain and lightly buttered. Use very sharp cutting utensils to assure even shapes.

Garnishes should be carefully placed and then allowed to remain. Borders and lines should be perfect as possible.

BEET AND ANCHOVY CANAPE

2 large cooked beets
6 anchovies
2 hard-cooked eggs
1 lemon

1 sprig parsley
6 slices toast
Lettuce

Cut cooked and seasoned beets in slices ¼-inch thick. Place one slice of beet on lettuce leaf and place anchovy in center; surround with chopped egg and sprinkle with finely chopped parsley. Garnish with triangles of toast and ⅛ of lemon.

Loretta Kasovsky, Chicago, Ill.

PEANUT BUTTER AND BACON

Spread prepared toast with crunchy peanut butter. Sprinkle with crumbled crisp bacon. Trim with minced parsley.

Emily Jurinak, Chicago, Ill.

DEVILED HAM

Mash deviled ham with a little horseradish, grated onion, and coarse black pepper to taste. Spread on toast base.

Emily Jurinak, Chicago, Ill.

SMOKED TURKEY

Mash the paste, if necessary, blend in a little mayonnaise to make easy to spread. Spread on prepared toast base. Dip the edges all around in mayonnaise, then in minced parsley or pimento.

Emily Jurinak, Chicago, Ill.

COTTAGE CHEESE AND CHIVES

Mix together chilled cottage cheese and finely minced chives. Season with a little salt and pepper. Serve as an appetizer or as a salad on lettuce leaf.

Pauline Knapcik, Chicago, Ill.

CHEESE CRACKER SPREAD

8 ounces cream cheese
2 to 4 ounces blue cheese
Drop of onion juice or few drops of Worcestershire sauce

Mix together with enough milk to make it a spreading paste. Serve with crackers for snacks.

Vincentian Sisters of Charity, Bedford, Oh.

- HOT CANAPES -

CHEESE PUFFS

½ pound freshly grated American cheese
1 slightly beaten egg
1 teaspoon soft butter
Pinch of salt
1 teaspoon mustard (optional)

Toast bread or rounds on one side. Spread other side with above mixture. Place under broiler and brown.

Anna Kochis, Sr., Hammond. Ind.

TOASTED BACON MUSHROOM ROLLS

12 slices bread
1 can cream mushroom soup
6 slices bacon

Trim bread and spread with mushroom soup. Roll each slice. Cut bacon strips in half and wrap around each bread roll. Fasten with toothpick. Broil 4 minutes or until golden brown. Serve immediately with tomato slices, potato chips and olives.

Mary Skurka, Whiting, Ind.

LIVERSAUSAGE APPETIZER

Cut sliced bread into rounds or ovals. Spread with butter and a little mustard. Cover thickly with mashed liver sausage to which a little grated onion has been added. Place under broiler, 400°F about 1 inch from flame. Broil about 7 to 10 minutes, or until hot and puffy. Decorate with slice of stuffed green olive and serve hot.

Margaret Jurinak. Chicago. Ill.

PARTY SNACK

12 slices bread
1 can mushroom soup

Trim bread and spread with mushroom soup. Roll each bread into a rectangle; fasten with toothpick. Place in broiler until golden brown. Serve immediately with sliced tomatoes, potato chips and olives.

Mary Skurka, Whiting, Ind.

- HORS D'OEUVRES -

Hors d'oeuvres are made of the nippy, high-flavored foods that stimulate appetites. An endless variety of food combinations go into their making, but it is well to limit the different foods blended into one recipe. Hors d'oeuvres should be small and dainty, if they are to be eaten with the fingers. In this connection, toothpicks and cocktail picks are invaluable aids. Trays of hors d'oeuvres may be passed at afternoon parties, buffet suppers or they may be served on individual plates in place of salads at informal dinners and supper parties.

Hors d'oeuvres and canapes may be served together in a special dish divided into compartments, or on a large platter or tray. Place those of the same type together. Keep the darker colors on the outside.

You may cut a cantaloupe, grapefruit, apple, or other fruit of similar shape in half, place the halves flat sides down on the tray, and stud them with hors d'oeuvres on toothpicks and surround them with canapes.

Here are some suggestions for the Hors D'Oeuvres Platter:

- Tiny onions alternated with pieces of cocktail sausages
- Rolled chipped beef
- Wrap stuffed olives in bacon and broil
- Squares of cheese alternated with halves of stuffed olives
- Tiny broiled sausages seasoned with tartar sauce
- Roll pineapple chunks in softened cream cheese, then in finely chopped mint
- Serve shrimp in bowl or on appetizer sticks and accompany with cocktail sauce.

CHEESE·STUFFED CELERY

Use only the crisp, white stalks or celery hearts. Wash and leave tips on stalks, or remove tips from coarser stalks and let stand in ice water for crisping. Dry, then fill grooves with the following filling:

½ package cream cheese
2 tablespoons mayonnaise
4 chopped stuffed olives
2 tablespoons crushed nuts and about ¼ teaspoon salt
Dash of nutmeg (optional)

Gertrude Kolar, Chicago, Ill.

EGG-STUFFED CELERY

Prepare celery as above and fill with following filling: 1 hard-cooked egg that has been finely chopped and mixed with 2 tablespoons mayonnaise, seasoned with salt and pepper to taste. Stuff and decorate with finely chopped parsley or paprika.

Gertrude Kolar, Chicago, Ill.

STUFFED OR DEVILED EGGS

4 hard-cooked eggs   **1 teaspoon vinegar**
2 tablespoons grated cheese   **1 tablespoon butter, melted milk**
¼ teaspoon dry mustard   **Salt and pepper to taste**

Cut eggs in halves lengthwise. Remove yolks, mash or force through sieve. Add cheese, seasonings, vinegar, butter and enough milk to moisten. Fill egg whites and put halves together. Wrap in waxed paper and chill to serve cold. These eggs may be served warm with hot vegetables.

Theresa Krasula, Chicago, Ill.

SAVORY DILL FRANKS

Spread two ¼-inch slices cooked frankfurts with a mustard-piccalilli-mayonnaise spread. Put a slice of dill pickle between and fasten with wooden pick.

Catherine Otrembiak, Chicago, Ill.

CHICKEN LIVERS

Season chicken livers with salt and pepper, wrap in a piece of bacon, and fasten with toothpick. Broil until bacon is crisp.

PICKLED HERRING

Pickled herring may be served in small squares on toothpicks. Pickled herring may also be served as an appetizer with pickled onion and marinated in sour cream. Serve on lettuce leaf and garnish with parsley, tomato slice and celery stick.

MARINATED BEEF APPETIZER

1 pound steak or boneless beef, cooked
1 sliced onion
Salt and pepper to taste
1 ounce lemon juice
1 cup sour cream
Lettuce and garnish of vegetable

Slice cooked beef into strips (julienne strips). Add onion, salt and pepper. Sprinkle lemon juice over meat mixture and blend in sour cream. Mix well and serve on lettuce leaf, garnish with parsley or tomato slice.

SAUSAGE SQUARES

Spread wafer-thin slices of bologna sausage or any preferred sausage with cream cheese, seasoned a little with horseradish. Place four or five slices together, chill until firm, cut with sharp knife into one inch cubes and serve on toothpicks.

Beverages

- COOLING SUMMER DRINKS -

Four Steps to Successful Fruit Juice Beverages

1. *Sweetening:* Use a sugar syrup for sweetening, since a syrup gives a smoothness not obtained with granulated sugar. (In the summertime it is well to keep a covered jar in the refrigerator.)

2. *Blending:* When combining two or more fruit juices or beverages, always have one predominate in flavor.

3. *Ripening:* Store the combined mixture in the refrigerator for at least half hour or longer to improve the flavors. Add the carbonated flavor just before serving.

4. *Serving:* Serve well chilled. When possible use ice cubes made of the predominate fruit flavor. If plain ice cubes are used, allow for dilution of melting ice.

SUGAR SYRUP

1 cup sugar
1 cup water

Combine sugar and water and boil at least 5 minutes. Cool, keep chilled. Store in covered jar any left over syrup for later use. This recipe makes 1 cup of syrup.

Helen Kocan, Whiting, Ind.

CRANBERRY PUNCH

2½ cups cranberry Juice
1½ cups orange Juice
Quartered orange slices
Fresh mint

Combine fruit juices. Chill an hour, then serve in tall glasses over ice cubes, or cubes made of cranberry juice. Garnish with orange slices and mint.

Loretta Kasovsky, Chicago, Ill.

PEACH RASPBERRY FLOAT

1 cup crushed fresh peaches
6 tablespoons sugar or sugar syrup
1 cup red raspberries
6 cups milk
1 pint vanilla ice cream or peach ice cream

Blend peaches with sugar or syrup. Pour into tall, chilled glasses. Add raspberries, reserving a few for garnishing. Slowly pour in the cold milk. Top with vanilla ice cream and garnish with red raspberries. Serve immediately. Six servings.

Helen Kubasak, Burbank, Cal.

RASPBERRY SHRUB

1 pint raspberries	Sugar syrup to taste
1 cup water	1 quart sparkling water
Juice of three lemons	Sprigs of mint or orange slice

Wash raspberries, add water and heat to a boiling point. Boil for about 5 or 6 minutes. Force through sieve. Add lemon juice and sweeten to taste with sugar syrup. Place in refrigerator for at least half hour to ripen. When ready to serve add sparkling water and pour over ice cubes. Garnish. Serves four.

Helen Kubasak, Burbank, Cal.

GINGER ALE PUNCH

Juice of four lemons	Sugar or syrup to taste
1 pint grape-juice	1 quart ginger ale

Mix fruit-juices and sugar or syrup. Just before serving, add ginger ale.

Justlne Uhlarik, Chicago, Ill.

GRAPE JUICE PUNCH

1 cup sugar syrup	Juice of one orange
1 pint water	1 pint grape juice
Juice of three lemons	

Mix ingredients in order given. Chill and serve.

Mary Vevurka, Chicago, Ill.

LEMON PUNCH

Juice of six lemons	½ cup mashed strawberries
Juice of three oranges	½ cup crushed pineapple
1 quart water	Syrup, made of sugar and water

Mix fruit-juice, sweeten to taste with syrup, add water and crushed fruit. Garnish with very thin slices of orange.

Anna Kochis, Sr., Hammond, Ind.

EGGNOG

1 egg
Pinch of salt
Milk
1 tablespoon honey, or more if desired
2 tablespoons brandy

Add salt to the egg and beat well. Add honey. Fill the glass with ice-cold milk. Add Brandy, stir and drink. Use extra large glass for these measurements.

Rev. Daniel Romancik, Chicago. Ill.

MINT JULEP

4 ounces gin
1 teaspoon powdered sugar
6 sprigs mint
1 teaspoon lemon juice

Dissolve sugar in small amount of water. Add four sprigs of mint and bruise, but do not crush it. Stir with ice until glass is frosted, add gin, sugar and lemon juice. Decorate with mint.

Helen Kocan, Whiting, Ind.

WHISKEY MINT JULEP

Fill glass with finely chopped ice and put aside
Four ounces of Bourbon
10-12 mint leaves
1 teaspoon sugar

Place fresh mint in mixing glass and sprinkle with one teaspoon sugar. Muddle to extract flavor from mint. Add splash of club soda and bourbon. Stir lightly and strain into iced glass. Frost glass by working spoon up and down in glass. Garnish with fresh mint and cherry. Serve with transparent green straws. Handle glass with towel to keep frosted.

Margaret Czabala, Chicago, Ill.

MULLED CIDER

Thoroughly mix ¾ cups of firmly packed brown sugar, one teaspoon cloves, one teaspoon allspice, one teaspoon cinnamon, and ¼ teaspoon salt. Add spices to cider and heat thoroughly. This drink is best when served steaming hot in earthen mugs.

Justine Zubo, Chicago, Ill

RUM SOUR

1½ ounces Jamaican Rum
¼ teaspoon sugar
Juice of half lemon

Shake well with cracked ice. Strain into chilled cocktail glass. Garnish with maraschino cherry and slice of orange.

Ann Hruskovich, Whiting. Ind.

HOT TODDY

1 lump sugar	2 ounces whiskey
Hot water	Cinnamon
2 cloves	

Place sugar in glass and dissolve in small amount of hot water, using muddler to dissolve. Add 2 cloves and cinnamon to taste. Add whiskey and fill the glass with hot water. Stir well and decorate with slice of lemon and nutmeg if desired.

Helen Kocan, Whiting, Ind.

MULLED WINE

1 quart red table wine	1 stick cinnamon
1 lemons	Sugar to taste
10 whole cloves	

Cut gashes into the skins of the lemon and insert whole cloves. Roast lemon for three minutes in hot oven. Heat wine with roasted lemon and stick cinnamon. Add sugar to taste and serve in warm punch bowl with lemon cut in slices for garnishing. Makes 8 to 10 punch cups.

Agnes Lukso, Chicago, Ill.

TOM AND JERRY

6 eggs	1½ ounces Jamaican Rum
6 teaspoons powdered sugar	Hot milk, or water
1 teaspoon all spice	Grated nutmeg
¾ ounce Brandy	

Separate eggs and beat whites to stiff froth. Add sugar and all spice. Mix thoroughly. Beat yolks until thin and mix with whites. Stir well. Pour approximately two tablespoons of mixture into mug. Add brandy and rum to each mug and fill with milk or water and sprinkle with nutmeg.

Agatha Filush, St. Joseph, Mich.

WALDORF FIZZ

8 lemons	1 pint gin
6 raw eggs	1 pint light honey

Wash lemons and cut in real thin slices into a bowl. Break in the whole eggs and let stand in cool place at least four hours. Strain and squeeze this through a cloth, then stir in the honey and gin. Keep in a fruit jar in refrigerator. When serving put an ice cube in a ten or eleven ounce glass, pour in ¼ cup of the basic mixture and fill glass slowly with Canada Dry, stir and serve. Very refreshing.

Mary Kinsock, Whiting, Ind.

THANKSGIVING SPECIAL COCKTAIL

¾ ounce Apricot Nector Liqueur
¾ ounce Apricot Flavored Brandy
¾ ounce French Vermouth
¼ teaspoon Lemon Juice

Shake well with cracked ice and strain into 3 ounce cocktail glass. Serve with a cherry.

Helen Kocan, Whiting, Ind.

PINK SQUIRREL

1 ounce Creme De Cacao (White)
1 ounce Creme De Almond
2 ounces whipping cream

Shake well with fine crushed ice, use blender or mixer if desired, until foamy or creamy. Serve in 3 ounce glasses or champagne glass. Makes one serving.

Variation: 1 part Creme De Menthe (Green) and one part White Creme De Cacao may be used with the whipped cream.

Julia Machacek, Chicago, Ill.

Bread, Rolls & Coffee Cakes

- YEAST BREADS -

BRAN BREAD

4 cups flour
1 cake yeast
1½ tablespoons shortening
1 teaspoon salt

3 to 4 tablespoons sugar
1 cup Kelloggs All-Bran
1 cup lukewarm water

Dissolve yeast in lukewarm water, add 1 tablespoon sugar. Set aside for 5 minutes. Add to sifted flour and mix well. Add all-bran. Let rise until doubled in bulk. Brush top with melted butter. Punch down and let rise again. Roll dough for 3 - 5 x 9" pans and let rise. Bake at 350°F for 30 minutes.

Johanna Silvay, Bethlehem. Pa.

RYE BREAD

1st Step:
1 small potato, grated
4 cups water
1 tablespoon salt
2 tablespoons sugar

Combine ingredients in saucepan and boil for 15 minutes.

2nd Step:
2½ cups rye flour

Sift into large mixing bowl. Add above boiling ingredients over the flour. Mix well with wooden spoon. Cool for 30 minutes.

3rd Step:
2 cakes yeast
1 cup warm water
1 teaspoon sugar

Dissolve yeast in warm water and sugar. Let stand for 5 minutes. Add this mixture to the 2nd step. Mix well until it becomes slightly smooth. Mixture will be lumpy, work until lumps are loose. Cover and set in warm place overnight.

4th step

Next day add these ingredients to the third step:

1 tablespoon caraway seed
2 tablespoons sugar
1 teaspoon salt

10 cups white flour
2 cups warm water
2 tablespoons melted shortening

Knead until batter is stiff. Add 2 tablespoons-shortening or bacon fat. Knead again until blended. Sprinkle top slightly with flour. Cover with cloth. Let rise until doubled in bulk. Turn out on floured board. Divide dough into 4 parts. Shape into loaves. Let rise again in bread pan. Bake at 350°F for 1 hour.

Mary Skurka, Whiting, Ind.

RYE BREAD

5½ cups Bohemian rye and wheat flour
¾ cup scalded milk
1 cup boiling water
1 tablespoon salt
1 ounce yeast combined with one tablespoon sugar
1 tablespoon caraway seed

Pour boiling water over caraway seed and salt. Add milk. When lukewarm, add dissolved yeast. Gradually add flour, beating thoroughly until too stiff to work with wooden spoon. Turn out onto floured board and knead about five minutes, adding enough white flour to form a medium dough. Place in greased bowl, brush top with melted shortening. Allow to rise until double in size. Turn out onto board and knead again for 5 minutes. Allow to rise again until double in size. Turn out onto board and knead slightly. Shape to fit large sized bread tin. Brush with melted butter. Allow to stand in warm place until doubled in bulk. Bake at 400°F about 40 minutes, reduce heat to 350°F and bake about 20 minutes longer. Remove from tin and place on cake rack to cool. This bread will remain fresh several days.

Theresa Krasula, Chicago, Ill.

WHITE BREAD

2 cups milk, scalded
2 tablespoons salt
2 tablespoons lard
2 tablespoons sugar

1 pint water
2 cakes compressed yeast
12 cups flour

To the scalded milk, add salt, lard and sugar. Add cold water and cool to lukewarm. Crumble yeast into the mixture and stir until dissolved. Add enough flour to make a soft dough. Knead in the remaining flour, kneading until dough is smooth and elastic. Set dough aside in bowl and let rise until double in bulk, about 2 hours. Turn out on board and knead lightly. Set aside to rise about 1½ times its size. Punch down, and shape into 4 loaves. Place in greased loaf pans. Let rise again. Bake at 400°F for 15 minutes, then reduce temperature to 375°F and bake 30 minutes longer. Do not bake over 45 minutes.

Anna B. Russell, Cleveland, Oh.

PRUNE BREAD

2 cakes yeast
1 cup warm water
5 cups flour
2 tablespoons sugar
1½ tablespoons salt

½ cup milk, scalded
2 eggs, beaten
1 pound prunes, cooked, drained
and chopped

Dissolve yeast in water. Sift 4 cups flour and salt together. Add yeast, lukewarm milk and eggs to sifted dry ingredients. Mix thoroughly. Cover and let rise until double in bulk. Add prunes and mix. Place remaining 1 cup flour on well floured board. Add dough and knead until smooth and elastic. Shape into loaves, place in greased bread pans. Cover and let rise until doubled in bulk. Bake in hot oven, 400°F for 40 to 50 minutes. When cool, ice with confectioners' sugar, flavored with orange juice.

Mary Molson, Whiting, Ind.

-SWEET DOUGH & HOLIDAY BREADS -

BRAIDED BREAD

1 cake yeast
1 cup scalded milk
6 cups flour
1 small can evaporated milk
1 cup warm water

2 teaspoons sugar
1 tablespoon butter, melted
2 egg yolks, beaten
¾ tablespoon salt

Dissolve yeast with sugar in lukewarm milk. Set aside to rise. Sift flour in deep bowl. Add warm evaporated milk mixed with water and melted butter. Add beaten egg yolks, salt and yeast mixture. Knead very well. Cover and set in warm place. Do not permit dough to stand in draft. Let dough rise 2 hours. Roll out on floured board, divide into portions for braided bread. Cover, let stand for 15 minutes. Braid, place in buttered pans. Allow to rise until doubled in bulk. Brush with melted butter. Bake at 350°F for 10 minutes, then raise temperature to 375°F and bake for one hour. Yield: 2 loaves (6 x 10").

Helen Kocan, Whiting, Ill..

SWEET BREAD DOUGH

1 cake compressed yeast
1 pint lukewarm milk
8 cups flour
1 cup soft butter

1 cup sugar
4 eggs
1 teaspoon salt
Grated rind of ½ lemon

Crumble yeast into bowl, add 1 cup milk and 1 cup flour. Set aside to rise in warm place. Cream butter, add sugar and eggs and mix well. Add remaining flour, and salt alternately with yeast mixture and remaining milk. Add lemon rind. Knead until dough is smooth and elastic. Set aside in warm place until doubled in bulk. Form into desired shapes, or can be braided into loaves. Allow dough to rise again in pan. Bake at 325°F for 30 minutes, then raise temperature to 350°F and bake for another 30 minutes. Brush top with beaten egg yolk to which a little milk has been added.

Anna Stanek, Whiting, Ind.

SWEET BREAD OR DOUGHNUT DOUGH

1 cake yeast	¼ cup sugar
½ cup warm water	1 teaspoon salt
½ teaspoon sugar	2 cups warm water
½ cup crisco	8 cups flour
1 egg	

Dissolve yeast in ¼ cup warm water and ½ teaspoon sugar. Cream crisco with sugar until creamy. Add beaten egg, salt and warm water. Add dissolved yeast and sifted flour. Knead until dough is smooth and elastic. Set aside in warm place to rise until doubled in bulk. Punch down and let rise again. Shape and let rise in pans. Bake at 400°F for 50 to 60 minutes for bread. For Doughnuts, shape and deep fat fry until golden brown.

Anna Pavlik, Greensburgh, Pa.

THREE KINGS BREAD

⅞ pound butter	2½ cups flour
2 cups sugar	2 teaspoons baking powder
6 eggs separated	1½ cups white raisins

Cream butter, add sugar and beat until sugar is dissolved. Add yolks one at a time, beating after each addition. Sift flour and baking powder, then gradually add alternately with raisins, stirring well. Beat egg whites, fold in well. Pour into greased loaf pan and bake at 350°F for 45 minutes.

Anna Dzurovsak, Hammond, Ind.

BOBALKY

One pound braided bread dough recipe, see page 33.

Pinch off portion of dough, roll out on floured board by hand to make roll about half inch in diameter. Place on cookie sheet. Cut with edge of teaspoon into small pieces. Let rise for 10 minutes. Bake at 375°F for 15 minutes, or until lightly brown. When cool, break and place in colander. Pour boiling water over bobalky. Cook 1½ cups ground poppy seed in ¾ cup water for 10 minutes. Boil 3 cups milk, add 1 cup sugar, or according to taste, pour over poppy seed and mix. Add to bobalky. Mix well.

Sophie Greshko, Whiting, Ind.

PAGACH

1 cup scalded milk	1 cup warm water
1 cake yeast	1½ pounds all-purpose flour
1 tablespoon butter	2 egg yolks, slightly beaten
1 tablespoon sugar	2 teaspoons salt

Dissolve yeast in half cup warm water. Pour half cup scalded milk over butter and sugar. Cool to lukewarm. Add dissolved yeast. Sift flour and salt into deep bowl, add eggs and yeast mixture with remaining milk and water. Knead well. Cover with cloth and set aside in warm place to rise until doubled in bulk, about two hours. Turn out on floured board. Divide dough into three portions. Cover each portion with bowl and let rest for ten minutes. Take one piece at a time, turn over, flatten in the center with back of hand. Place filling in center and draw up and pinch edges together. Again place bowl over dough for ten minutes. Heat oven to 375°F, turn dough over with filling and press carefully with back of hand all around, then roll out slowly, so the filling will not break through, to 12-inches in diameter. Place both hands under pagach and put in the bottom of the oven for ten minutes, then turn over on the rack (in center of oven) and bake for another ten minutes. When done, wrap in damp cloth. Let it stand for ten minutes. Brush lightly with sweet cream, then with golden brown butter on both sides. Cut to desired size. Sprinkle with sugar. Follow the same method for the other two pieces. Each portion is for one pagach.

PAGACH FILLING

Sauerkraut

½ pound sauerkraut	2 tablespoons sugar
2 tablespoons butter	Pinch of salt and cinnamon

Wash sauerkraut in half cup of water, squeeze dry. Chop fine. Saute in browned butter and seasonings until brown. Cool to lukewarm.

Potato Filling - see page 93.

Cabbage Filling - see page 93.

Cheese Filling - see page 93.

Sophie Gresko, Whiting, Ind.

- RAISED ROLLS -

CINNAMON ROLLS

1 cake yeast
¼ cup milk
1 teaspoon sugar
4 cups flour
3 egg yolks
½ teaspoon salt
1¾ cups milk

Filling:
¼ pound butter
4 tablespoons powdered sugar
1 teaspoon vanilla
1 teaspoon cinnamon

Dissolve yeast in ¼ cup milk, add 1 teaspoon sugar. Set aside in a warm place for 5 minutes. Add yolks, flour, salt and milk. Knead until dough is smooth. Roll dough into oblong. Spread with filling, sprinkle with cinnamon. Roll up tightly, beginning at wide side. Seal well by pinching edges of roll together. Cut roll into 1-inch slices. Place in buttered pan and let rise until double in bulk. Bake at 350°F for about 30 minutes.

Filling: Cream butter and powdered sugar, add vanilla.

Apolonia Blahunka, Whiting, Ind.

HOT CROSS BUNS

1 cup milk, scalded
¾ teaspoon salt
½ cup sugar
½ cup shortening

1 cake yeast, softened in ¼ cup
  warm water
4½ cups flour
3 egg yolks

Add scalded milk to salt, sugar and shortening. Cool to lukewarm. Add softened yeast and 1½ cups flour. Beat well and let rise until very light. Add egg yolks and remaining flour. Knead lightly. Let rise until doubled in bulk. Roll out to one-inch thickness and cut into rounds. Set these close together on a greased pan and let rise. Glaze the surface of each bun with a little egg white diluted with water. With a sharp knife cut a cross on top. Bake about 20 minutes in a hot oven (400°F). Just before removing from the oven, brush with sugar and water. Fill the cross with plain frosting. A cup of raisins may be added to the dough, if desired.

Veronica Radocha, Coaldale, Pa.

ICE BOX ROLLS

1 cup warm water
½ cup sugar
1 cake yeast
4½ cups flour

½ cup butter
½ teaspoon salt
3 well beaten eggs

Dissolve yeast in warm water with 1 teaspoon sugar for 15 minutes. Cream butter and sugar. Add beaten eggs, salt, water and dissolved yeast. Mix together with flour. Knead well. Let rise once before you chill dough. Place in refrigerator overnight. Roll out in circle and cut in pie shaped pieces. Roll up each piece, beginning at wide end, and shape into crescent. Place on baking sheet and let rise 2 or 3 hours. Bake at 375°F for 12 to 15 minutes.

Theresa Sabol, Whiting, Ind.

ICE BOX ROLLS

½ cup crisco
¼ cup sugar
½ cup boiling water
1 cake yeast

1 egg, well beaten
Scant teaspoon salt
3 cups unsifted flour

Dissolve yeast in ½ cup cold water. Cream sugar and shortening. Add boiling water and cool. Add yeast and beaten egg, salt and flour. Knead lightly. Place in greased bowl, cover and place in refrigerator until ready to use. About 1½ to 2 hours before serving, remove from refrigerator. Turn on floured board and roll into round sheet, to the size of a 9-inch pie pan. Cut pie-shaped pieces and roll from wide end. Let rise about 3 hours. Bake at 350°F for 15-20 minutes.

Millie Rey, Chicago, Ill.

ORANGE ROLLS

1 cake yeast
¼ cup lukewarm water
1 cup milk, scalded
1 teaspoon salt
¼ cup sugar
¼ cup butter
1 egg beaten
3½ cups all-purpose flour

Orange Filling:
½ cup sugar
¼ cup butter
2 tablespoons honey (optional)
Grated rind of small orange
2 tablespoons orange juice

Add sugar, salt and butter to scalded milk. Cool to lukewarm. Crumble yeast into warm water. Add milk mixture and beaten egg and stir well. Add flour and knead until smooth and satiny. Let rise in warm place about 2 hours. Punch down and let rise again about 45 minutes, or until doubled in bulk. Turn onto lightly floured board, knead slightly. Roll to about 1/3 inch thick. Spread with orange filling, roll up like a jelly roll and pinch ends to hold in filling. Place on waxed paper and cut into slices, one-inch wide. Put cut side down in well greased muffin pan. Cover with damp cloth, let rise until double in bulk. Bake 5 minutes in 400°F oven, reduce temperature to 375°F and continue to bake 15 to 20 minutes. When done turn pan upside down to let orange mixture run down on rolls.

Mary Kinsock, Whiting, Ind.

PARKER HOUSE ROLLS

6 tablespoons butter
4 tablespoons sugar
1½ teaspoons salt
2 cups scalded milk
1 cake yeast

¼ cup luke warm water
1 egg well beaten
Grated rind of half lemon
About 6½ cups of flour

Add butter, sugar, salt, to scalded milk. Cool. Soften yeast in water, add with egg and rind to milk. Stir enough flour, gradually, to make soft dough. Softer than bread dough. Beat thoroughly. Cover, let rise until doubled in bulk. Turn onto floured board, if necessary, work in additional flour. Let rise until doubled in bulk. Toss on floured board and knead. Roll out to 1/3 inch thickness. Lift dough from board, allow to shrink back. Cut with biscuit cutter. Brush with melted butter, fold over in half, and place on greased baking pans. Brush tops with melted butter, let rise. Bake at 425°F about 15 minutes. Yield 36 rolls.

Mary V. Hajdu, Braddock, Pa.

PARKER HOUSE ROLLS

2 rounding teaspoons butter
½ cup sugar
1 teaspoon salt
1 cup boiling water
1 cup cold water

1 cake yeast, dissolved in
    ½ cup warm water
2 eggs, beaten
7 cups unsifted flour

Combine first five ingredients. Stir until well blended. When lukewarm, add dissolved yeast and eggs. Stir in flour. Do not knead. Cover mixture with damp cloth. Place in refrigerator. About 4 hours before ready to serve, remove portion of dough and roll thin. Cut round or oblong with cookie cutter, brush with melted butter and fold. Place on greased baking pan and let rise 3 to 4 hours. Bake at 375°F to 400°F for 15 minutes. Note the following variations made from this dough: Cinnamon rolls, coffee cake or any desired rolls, pan them, cover with waxed paper, place in refrigerator. To bake for breakfast, remove from refrigerator the night before. In the morning bake rolls in 15 to 20 minutes. This is an inexpensive recipe and a variety of rolls always on hand. This dough will keep for a few days in refrigerator.

Eleanor Kochis, Whiting, Ind.

PASCHA

¾ pound butter or oleo
1 cup sugar
4 eggs
10 cups flour (approximately)

1 teaspoon salt
1 quart milk
2 packages dry yeast
2 tablespoons sugar

Allow ½ pound butter or oleo to soften. Add one cup sugar to the softened oleo and cream thoroughly. Beat four eggs and add to mixture and mix well. Heat your milk to lukewarm. Prepare yeast mixture by adding 2 tablespoons sugar to the dry yeast and pouring ¼ cup of the lukewarm milk. Allow to rise. Sift flour into the creamed mixture, salt and lukewarm milk, and the raised yeast. Knead and work well, adding flour when necessary. The softer the dough, the lighter the bread will be. The consistency is good when the dough leaves the side of the bowl and does not stick to your hands. Raisins may be added if desired. Lastly, add ¼ stick melted butter or oleo and knead well. This keeps your pascha soft. Allow to rise until double in bulk, about 2 hours. Punch dough down and allow it to rise second time. Shape into loaves and place in greased pans. Let rise for ½ hour and bake at 400°F for about 40 minutes. Conventional individual bread pans will yield 5 loaves.

Josephine Valyo, Garden City, L.I., N.Y.

PECAN ROLLS

1 cup milk, scalded
½ cup sugar
1 teaspoon salt
½ cup butter, or margarine
1 ounce yeast
3 eggs, well beaten

4½ cups flour (about)
½ cup soft butter
1½ cups brown sugar
1 cup pecans
⅔ cup maple syrup

Place milk, sugar, salt and butter in bowl and stir until butter is melted. Cool to lukewarm. Add crumbled yeast and let stand for 20 minutes. Add eggs, and gradually flour. Beat until smooth. Turn out on floured board and knead until smooth and elastic. Let rise until double in bulk. Divide dough into two parts. Roll each piece into rectangle about ½-inch thick, spread half of butter on each piece and sprinkle with brown sugar. Roll like jelly roll. Cut each roll into 12 pieces. Place in two well buttered 8x8 inch pans. Sprinkle nuts over top and let rise until double in bulk. Just before baking, dribble 1/3 cup of syrup on each pan of rolls. Bake at 400°F for 30 minutes.

Mary Kovacik, Whiting, Ind.

POTATO ROLLS

1 cup raw diced potatoes
2 cups water
½ cake yeast
4 cups sifted flour

1½ teaspoons salt
1 tablespoon sugar
3 tablespoons fat

Boil potatoes in water until tender. Drain and put through sieve. Save 1 cup potato water, if necessary add more water to make 1 cup of liquid. Soften yeast in lukewarm potato water. Sift 3½ cups flour with salt and sugar. Rub in fat with finger tips. Add dissolved yeast and potatoes. Knead until it springs back when pressed with finger. Add remaining ½ cup flour, if needed. Place in greased bowl, brush with fat and cover. Let rise until doubled in bulk. Pinch off small pieces and shape lightly into round balls. Place 3 balls together in greased muffin tins, cover and let rise until double in bulk. Bake for about 25 minutes in moderately hot oven 350°F to 400°F Serve hot.

Louise Zaremba, Joliet, Ill.

REFRIGERATOR ROLLS

½ cake yeast
2 cups sifted flour
⅛ teaspoon salt

1½ teaspoons sugar
¾ cup milk
½ cup butter

Crumble yeast into sifted dry ingredients and mix well. Add cold milk to make soft dough. Turn onto a lightly floured board and knead until smooth and elastic. Roll into long narrow strip ⅓-inch thick. Divide butter into 5 portions. On half of strip place 1 portion thinly sliced hard butter. Fold over unbuttered half and press down firmly. Place in refrigerator for 10 minutes. Repeat 4 times. After last rolling, wrap in waxed paper and chill overnight. Next day, cut dough into portions. Roll out each portion about ½ inch thick. Shape into crescents, twists, pocketbooks, or any other desired shapes. Place on baking sheet. Brush with milk and melted butter. Sprinkle with salt, or poppy seed if desired. Place shaped rolls in refrigerator, cover with waxed paper, and chill from ½ to several hours. Bake at once in hot oven, 400°F 18 to 20 minutes. Yield: 16 rolls.

Anna Yanega, Lansford, Pa.

RICH REFRIGERATOR ROLLS

1 ounce yeast
¼ cup sugar
1 cup milk
1 teaspoon salt

½ cup butter or margarine
3 eggs, beaten
5 cups flour, approximately

Crumble and combine yeast with sugar, let stand 15 to 20 minutes. Scald milk, add butter and salt. Cool to lukewarm. Add yeast and beaten eggs. Add flour, beating thoroughly. Knead until smooth and satiny. Place in greased bowl, brush top with melted butter. Place in refrigerator. About 2 hours before serving time, shape into rolls. Roll dough to ½ inch thickness. Cut strips 6-inches long. Holding strips by both ends, stretch lightly and tie into a loose knot. Place on a greased baking sheet, cover and let rise about 2 hours. Bake in hot oven, 425°F for 15 to 20 minutes. Yield: 32 rolls.

Mary Kovacik, Whiting, Ind.

RICH YEAST CRESCENTS

1 cup shortening
1 cake yeast
2 tablespoons sugar
1 teaspoon salt

3½ cups flour
½ cup scalded milk
2 eggs, slightly beaten

Cut shortening and yeast into sifted sugar, salt and flour until well blended and like a coarse meal. Add cooled milk and eggs and mix thoroughly. Shape lightly and chill about 2 hours, or over night. Roll out dough to ⅛-inch thickness on board which was sprinkled with powdered sugar. Cut into 5 circular pieces, about 10 inches in diameter. Cut each circle into 8 pie-shaped wedges. Spread lightly with thick jam and roll, beginning at the wide end. Shape into crescent and place on greased baking sheet. Bake at 400°F for 15 minutes.

Mary Salat, Chicago, Ill.

RICH ROLLS

1 pound butter	**1 cake yeast**
5 cups sifted all-purpose flour	**4 beaten egg yolks**
½ cup lukewarm milk	**Grated rind of 1 lemon**
½ cup sugar	**1 cup each sugar & ground nuts**

Cut butter into flour until mixture resembles cornmeal. Combine milk, sugar, and stir in crumbled yeast. Dissolve. Add to flour mixture with egg yolks and rind. Knead lightly until smooth. Cover, let rise until doubled. Pinch off balls of dough, size of walnuts. Roll each in sugar and nut mixture. Flatten with rolling pin, form into crescents. Bake on greased cookie sheet at 400°F, 20 minutes or until golden.

Mrs. Martin Dolak, Youngstown, Oh.

- BISCUITS -

BUTTERMILK BISCUITS

2 cups flour	**¼ teaspoon soda**
3 teaspoons baking powder	**¼ cup shortening**
1 teaspoon salt	**¾ cup buttermilk, or sour milk**

Cut shortening into dry ingredients until mealy. Add milk and stir. Knead lightly for 20 seconds. Roll out to about ½-inch thickness. Cut with floured biscuit cutter. Place on ungreased cookie sheet. Bake in very hot oven, 450°F for 10 minutes.

Barbara Bires, Pittsburgh, Pa.

HOT BISCUITS

2 cups sifted flour	**2 tablespoons melted shortening**
4 teaspoons baking powder	**⅞ cup milk or water**
1 teaspoon salt	

Sift together flour, baking powder and salt. Add melted shortening to milk or water and stir into flour mixture, making a soft dough. Toss onto slightly floured board, roll out about 1 inch thick. Cut with biscuit cutter. Place on ungreased baking sheet. Bake at 450°F about 15 minutes. Serve piping hot with butter, jelly, honey or syrup.

Justine Kasovsky, Chicago, Ill.

MORNING ROLLS

3 cups flour
½ cup melted shortening
2½ teaspoons baking powder
½ cup sugar

¼ teaspoon salt
2 eggs, beaten
⅔ cup canned milk

Sift together dry ingredients. Combine milk, eggs, cooled melted shortening and add to flour mixture. Roll out on lightly floured board to ¼ inch thickness. Spread over dough any filling, but not jelly. Roll as for jelly roll. Cut with scissors ½ inch slices and place on baking sheet. Bake at 375°F for 25 to 30 minutes.

Anna Kikta

PAGAČKY

(Biscuits with Cracklings)

3 cups flour
½ cup sugar
3 teaspoons baking powder
1 teaspoon salt

2 cups cracklings, finely ground
2 eggs
½ cup milk or more to make
   soft dough

Mix flour with cracklings until well blended. Add rest of ingredients and mix well. Form into patties and place on buttered cookie sheet. Bake at 350°F for about 20 minutes. Cracklings: Leftovers after rendering leaf lard.

Marie Hornik, Chicago, Ill.

- YEAST DOUGH COFFEE CAKES -

BABOVKA

1 cake yeast
1 tablespoon sugar
4 eggs, separated
1 teaspoon vanilla
½ cup lukewarm milk

¼ pound butter
¼ pound sugar
Flour
1 teaspoon salt
¼ pound blanched almonds

Combine yeast, lukewarm milk and 1 tablespoon sugar. Set aside to rise. Add enough sifted flour to mixture to make a spongy dough. Allow to rise again. Cream butter and sugar. Add beaten yolks and continue to beat. Combine creamed mixture with yeast. Add 10 ounces flour, salt and vanilla. Fold in stiffly beaten whites and almonds. Allow to rise in warm place until doubled in bulk. Bake at 350°F for about 45 minutes.

Mary Druso, Bedford, Oh.

BRAIDED ALMOND ROLL

1 cake yeast
2 tablespoons warm water
1 cup warm milk
¼ cup melted butter
½ cup sugar
1½ teaspoons grated lemon rind

⅛ teaspoon almond extract
2 eggs, well beaten
3 cups sifted flour
1 egg yolk
1 tablespoon blanched almonds

Dissolve yeast in warm water, add to warm milk. Add melted butter, sugar, lemon rind and almond extract and mix well. Stir in eggs and flour. Knead until smooth. Allow to rise until doubled in bulk. Knead again, divide dough into three parts. Roll each portion into a long strip. Braid strips into roll. Place on buttered pan, cover with floured towel and allow to rise until doubled in bulk. Brush with beaten egg yolk. Sprinkle top with thin slivers of almonds. Bake in moderate oven for 30 to 40 minutes.

Mary Osadjan, Chicago, Ill.

COFFEE CAKE RING

1 cake yeast
3½ cups sifted flour
3 eggs
½ cup brown sugar
⅓ cup sugar
⅔ cup warm milk
½ cup melted shortening
2 tablespoons margarine
1 teaspoon salt
1 teaspoon cinnamon

ICING:
½ cup confectioners' sugar
2 teaspoons milk
½ teaspoon vanilla

TOPPING
Pecan halves
Maraschino cherries
Chopped nuts

Dissolve yeast and sugar in warm milk. Add one cup flour and beat until smooth. Let rise until doubled in bulk. Punch down and roll ½ inch thick into a rectangle that measures about 10x20 inches. Spread with margarine. Sprinkle sugar and cinnamon. Roll like jelly roll. Shape into circle on greased cookie sheet. With sharp scissors cut almost through, spacing cuts about 1½ inches apart and turn each division upward to show filling. Let rise until doubled. Bake in moderate oven for 25 to 30 minutes. Spread icing on top and decorate with nuts and cherries.

Mary Druso, Bedford, Oh.

ENGLISH COFFEE CAKE BRAIDS

1¼ cups milk, scalded	2 eggs, slightly beaten
¼ cup shortening	4½ cups flour
¼ cup sugar	2 teaspoons cinnamon
1 teaspoon salt	1½ cups seedless raisins
1 cake yeast	

Combine milk, shortening, sugar and salt. Cool to lukewarm. Crumble yeast into this mixture. Add eggs and mix well. Add flour sifted with cinnamon. Add raisins. Knead until dough is smooth and elastic. Place in greased bowl, brush top with melted butter. Cover with towel and let rise until doubled in bulk, about 2 hours. Punch down. Let rise again. Divide dough into two equal parts. Roll each part into three strips. Braid the strips into loaf form and place on greased baking sheet. Allow to rise until light. Bake in moderate oven for 30 minutes. When slightly cooled, brush top with icing, sprinkle with nutmeats. Yield: Two 4x12-inch braids.

Icing: 1 cup powdered sugar, add about 1½ tablespoons top milk.

Veronica Radocha, Coaldale, Pa.

FORM COFFEE CAKE *(10-inch Tube Pan)*

1 large cake yeast	1 cup granulated sugar
1 cup lukewarm milk	4 eggs
1 cup all-purpose flour	Grated rind of lemon
¾ teaspoon salt	¼ teaspoon nutmeg
½ cup butter	2½ cups flour

Dissolve yeast in warm milk. Sift 1 cup flour and salt, and combine with yeast mixture. Beat until smooth. Let rise until double in bulk. Cream butter and sugar until light. Add eggs, one at a time and beating after each addition. Add lemon rind and nutmeg. Add yeast mixture and blend. Add 2½ cups flour and beat until smooth. Grease tube pan. Decorate bottom of pan with pecan nuts. Turn dough into pan and let rise until doubled. Bake at 350°F for one hour.

Lillian Cherney, Chicago, Ill.

FRUIT FILLED PASTRY

1 small cake yeast	2 cups fruit preserves or
2 teaspoons sugar	plum butter
½ cup warm milk	1 pound chopped nuts
6 egg yolks	6 egg whites
1 cup soft butter	¼ cup sugar
3 cups flour	1 teaspoon vanilla

Combine yeast, sugar and milk, stir until yeast is dissolved. Stir in egg yolks and soft butter. Add flour to make soft dough. Divide dough into 3 portions. Roll one section to fit bottom of pan that measures 9x12x2 inches. Spread with 1 cup preserves or plum butter. Sprinkle with ⅓ of nuts. Roll second portion of dough to fit over the first layer. Spread with remaining preserves or plum butter. Sprinkle with ½ of remaining nuts. Roll out last portion of dough to fit over second layer and seal edges. Put in warm place to rise for 1 hour. Bake in moderate oven for about 25 minutes, or until light brown. Remove from oven. Beat egg whites to a light foam. Add vanilla and sugar gradually and continue beating until whites stand in peaks. Pile meringue on top of cake and sprinkle with remaining nuts. Return to oven for about 15 minutes, or until light brown.

Mary A. Bosko, Homestead, Pa.

PASKA *(Easter Bread)*

BASIC DOUGH:

8 cups flour
2 tablespoons salt
1 cup warm water
1 tablespoon sugar
¼ pound butter
½ cup sugar
2 cups milk, boiling point
1 cake yeast
3 eggs

CHEESE DOUGH:

1 cake yeast, 1 ounce
1 pound dry cottage cheese
1 cup yellow raisins
4 egg yolks
1 cup sugar, or less, to taste
1 teaspoon salt
1 teaspoon lemon rind
1 teaspoon baking powder
½ cup milk
3 cups flour, sifted

Basic Dough: Crumble yeast in ½ cup water and 1 tablespoon sugar. Set aside for 5 minutes. Pour boiling milk over sugar and butter, add balance of water. Cool to lukewarm. Sift flour into bowl, add salt, eggs, milk mixture and yeast. Knead dough until smooth and elastic. Cover. Let rise until doubled in bulk, about 2 hours, in a warm place.

Cheese Dough: Crumble yeast in warm milk to which 1 tablespoon sugar has been added and let stand 5 minutes. Mix cottage cheese with spoon until smooth. Add raisins and yeast mixture. Add unbeaten egg yolks, remaining sugar, salt, lemon rind, baking powder and flour, and knead well. Set aside to rise until doubled in bulk, about 2 hours. When basic dough has doubled in size, turn out onto lightly floured board and shape into four parts. Let stand on board, covered, for about 15 minutes. Take one part of dough and lightly punch around the edge so that the center is elevated. Take cheese dough and place around the elevated center, then lightly make an opening in the center. Join edges of center with the outside edges, press carefully so that the cheese dough is completely covered. Place into 9-inch tube pan and let rise for about 30 minutes. Cover dough to prevent drying. Just before placing into oven, brush top with egg yolk. Bake for 10 minutes at 325°F, increase temperature to 350°F and bake for 40 minutes. Yield: 4 Paskas. For 2 Paskas, cut recipe in half.

Anna Norko, Perth Amboy, N.J.

PATICA

2½ cups milk
1 cup sugar
¼ pound butter, or margarine
3 eggs, well beaten
3 ounces yeast
½ cup warm water
9 cups flour
4 teaspoons salt

FILLING:
2 pounds walnuts, ground
1 cup honey
1 cup sugar, white or brown
Hot milk

Heat milk to lukewarm, add sugar and butter and blend well. Add eggs. Dissolve yeast in warm water. Combine milk and yeast mixtures. Add sifted dry ingredients and knead until smooth. Allow to rise until doubled in bulk. Turn out on floured board, divide dough into two large balls. Let rise one hour. Cover table with large cloth, stretch dough until very thin. Spread filling, raise cloth by one side and roll. Butter 10 inch tube pan, coil dough around and around in pan. Let rise for one hour. Bake at 250°F for 2 hours, or until done.

Filling: Combine first three ingredients, add enough milk for spreading consistency.

Pauline Suca, Joliet, Ill.

POPPY SEED BUCHTA

1 cake yeast
3 tablespoons sugar
⅓ cup butter
⅓ cup milk, scalded
1 teaspoon salt
½ teaspoon vanilla
2 eggs, beaten
2½ cups sifted flour (about)

POPPY SEED FILLING:
1 can prepared poppy seed filling,
or ¾ cup poppy seed, ground
and cooked with ½ cup milk
4 tablespoons sugar
2 tablespoons butter
½ teaspoon vanilla

Soften yeast in one tablespoon of sugar. Add remaining sugar, salt and butter to scalded milk. Stir until well blended. Cool to lukewarm. Add yeast, eggs and vanilla. Blend. Add flour to make soft dough. Turn onto lightly floured board and knead until smooth and elastic. Place in a lightly greased bowl, cover with damp cloth and let rise until dough is doubled in bulk. Turn out on lightly floured board and roll into rectangle about 12x18 inches. Cut into three equal parts. Divide the filling into three portions. Spread evenly over each part of dough. Roll as for jelly roll, beginning at widest side. Braid rolls loosely to form twist and place in greased loaf or tube pan. Brush top with melted but nut hot fat. Allow to rise until doubled in bulk. Bake about 40 minutes in 350°F oven. Remove from pan and while warm, brush top with thin confectioners' sugar frosting.

For unprepared poppy seed filling: Place poppy seeds and milk in pan. Cook slowly until milk is absorbed. Add sugar, butter and vanilla. Blend well. Cook mixture to consistency of jam.

Anna K. Hruskovich, Whiting, Ind.

SOUR CREAM COFFEE CAKE

3 cups flour
½ pound butter, melted
4 egg yolks
½ pint sour cream

1 cake yeast, combined with little milk
1 teaspoon salt
3 tablespoons sugar

Dissolve yeast in lukewarm milk. Add melted butter and rest of ingredients and mix well. Let dough rise. Roll out dough and use any desired filling. Bake at 375°F for 40 to 45 minutes.

Mary Slifcak, Cleveland, Ohio

TEA RING

½ cup sugar
¼ cup butter
2 eggs
1 teaspoon salt
1 cup scalded milk
2 small cakes yeast
¼ cup lukewarm water
4¾ cups all-purpose flour

FROSTING:
1 cup confectioners' sugar
2 tablespoons cream
2 tablespoons soft butter
¼ teaspoon vanilla

Pour scalded milk over butter, sugar and salt and stir well. Crumble yeast into water. Cool milk mixture to lukewarm, add dissolved yeast. Add eggs and blend well. Gradually stir in sifted flour to make soft dough. Knead until smooth. Place into greased bowl, cover and let rise until doubled in bulk. When dough is light, roll into rectangle about ¼ inch thick. Brush with melted butter and spread with poppy seed or almond filling. Roll as for jelly roll and place on greased baking sheet. Form into a ring and cut almost through with scissors, spacing cuts about one inch apart. Turn slices slightly. Cover and let rise until doubled in bulk. Bake at 375°F for about 30 minutes. While warm, frost with white frosting.

Frosting: Blend together until smooth, spread and sprinkle ground toasted almonds over top.

Mary Prischak, N.S. Pittsburgh, Pa.

TWIN COFFEE RINGS

1 cup milk, scalded
½ cup shortening
2 teaspoons salt
1 cake yeast, or 1 package
   granulated yeast
1 egg, beaten

1 teaspoon grated lemon rind
4 cups flour
½ cup brown sugar
2 teaspoons cinnamon
1 cup broken nut meats

Combine milk, shortening, sugar and salt. Cool to lukewarm. Soften yeast in this mixture. Add egg, lemon rind and flour. Mix to make soft dough. Knead until smooth. Place in greased bowl and brush top with melted butter. Cover and let rise until doubled, about two hours. Punch down. Let rise again. Divide into two parts. Roll each into rectangle about ½ inch thick. Brush with melted butter, sprinkle with brown sugar, cinnamon and nutmeats. Roll lengthwise and shape into ring. Place on greased cookie sheet. Snip at 1½ inch intervals. Cover, let rise until doubled in bulk. Bake in moderate oven for about 30 minutes.

Albina Sloboda, Coaldale, Pa.

ZLATE HALUŠKI (Golden Nuggets)

1 pound sweet yeast dough
Melted butter
¾ cup sugar

1 teaspoon cinnamon
½ cup finely chopped nuts

Roll out dough. Cut with floured cookie cutter, or medium sized glass. Dip each round in butter, then in sugar, cinnamon and nut mixture. Place in well greased pan, one by one until all used up. Sprinkle with more butter and nut mixture. Cover and let rise until light. Bake in moderate oven 35 to 40 minutes. When cool, each golden nugget can be separated. It is delightful with coffee.

Irene Menzezoff, Long Island, N.Y.

- COFFEE CAKES-REFRIGERATED YEAST DOUGH -

BUTTER RING

6 cups flour
2 tablespoons sugar
¼ teaspoon salt
¼ pound butter, or margarine
1 cup milk

3 egg yolks, beaten
¼ cup milk, scalded and cooled
2 teaspoons sugar
2 cakes yeast

Sift together flour, sugar and salt. Work in butter as for pie crust. To the beaten yolks, add yeast which has been combined with 2 teaspoons sugar and ¼ cup milk. Add flour and milk alternately, blending thoroughly after each addition. Chill overnight in refrigerator. Divide dough into six sections. Roll each piece into long strip. Twist two strips together. Shape into ring and let rise about 2 hours. Bake at 350°F for 25 minutes, or until done. When cool, spread powdered sugar frosting and sprinkle with fine ground nuts. Yield: 3 rings.

Mary Uhely, Los Angeles, Ca.

COFFEE CAKE WITH SOUR MILK

1 cake yeast
4 tablespoons sugar
2 cups buttermilk, or
   sour milk, cooled
2 cups flour
4 tablespoons sugar
½ cup melted butter, cooled

3 egg yolks
3 cups flour
½ teaspoon baking soda
1 teaspoon salt
Lemon rind
Chopped nuts and raisins

Combine yeast, 4 tablespoons sugar, buttermilk and flour. Set aside for 20 minutes. To this mixture add melted butter, sugar, and yolks. Blend well. Gradually add sifted flour, baking soda and salt. Mix well. Add lemon rind raisins and chopped nuts. Place in refrigerator overnight. Next day roll out and place dough on greased pan. Let rise for 2 hours. Bake at 350°F for one hour.

Theres Kulostak, Chicago, Ill.

CONTINENTAL COFFEE CAKE

2¼ cups all-purpose flour
¼ teaspoon salt
½ pound butter, or 1 cup
3 egg yolks, beaten
½ ounce yeast
¼ cup milk, scalded
3 tablespoons sugar

FILLING:
3 egg whites
1 cup sugar
1 package dates, cut fine
1 cup nut meats, chopped

Sift flour and salt. Combine with butter and egg yolks. Add sugar to scalded milk and cool. Add yeast. Mix flour mixture together with yeast mixture. Wrap in waxed paper and place in refrigerator overnight, or at least 6 hours. Divide dough into two parts. Roll into rectangle about 12x18 inches. Spread with meringue. Sprinkle dates and nuts. Roll up like jelly roll, sealing ends. Bake on lightly greased cookie sheet in moderate oven for about 35 minutes.

Yield: 2 large coffee cakes. Filling: Beat egg whites very stiff, add sugar gradually and continue beating.

Violet Matlon Brown, Whiting, Ind.

DANISH PASTRY

1⅓ cups margarine or spry	⅓ cup sugar
2 cakes yeast	2 teaspoon salt
1 cup milk	4½ cups sifted flour
3 eggs	

Dissolve yeast in milk. Beat eggs with ⅓ cup melted margarine. Add to yeast, together with sugar and salt. Stir in flour and mix well. Place in greased 10x14 pan. Chill in refrigerator for 1 to 2 hours. Roll chilled dough on lightly floured board to 13x16 inches. Spread ⅓ cup margarine on ⅔ of the dough. Fold that portion of dough having no margarine on it over ½ of the dough, then fold the other third over the first two, giving three thicknesses. Roll out dough to original size. Repeat this process twice using remaining ⅔ cup margarine. Return to refrigerator and chill overnight. When ready to bake, shape, braid or twist into any desired pastries. Place in greased pan and allow to rise again until doubled in bulk. Bake in moderate oven, 375°F until golden brown. Ice with confectioners' sugar icing, and sprinkle with nuts.

Mary Druso, Bedford, Ohio

NUT-PINEAPPLE PRESERVE CAKE

3¼ cups flour	**FILLING:**
½ pound butter, or margarine	1 - 16-ounce glass pineapple
Pinch of salt	preserves
2 tablespoons sugar	1 pound ground walnuts
1 teaspoon baking soda	
1 whole egg	
1 cake yeast	
¼ cup milk	
1 teaspoon vanilla	

Sift flour, salt, sugar and baking soda. Add butter, egg and vanilla. Dissolve yeast in lukewarm milk and add to flour mixture. Mix well. Divide dough into two parts. Line cookie sheet with wax paper. Roll out one part of dough to fit pan. Top with pineapple preserves and sprinkle walnuts over top. Roll second part of dough and place over filling. Seal edges like for pie. Place in refrigerator overnight. Next day bake at 350°F for about 25 minutes.

Agnes Thomas, Bethlehem, Pa.

- FILLED ROLLS -
(Poppy seed, Cottage Cheese or Nut)

KOLAČ

1½ cakes yeast
½ cup milk, lukewarm
1 tablespoon sugar
6 cups flour
1 teaspoon salt

½ cup sugar
1 pint milk, scalded and cooled
2 eggs, well beaten
½ pound butter, soft

Dissolve yeast and 1 tablespoon sugar in ½ cup milk. Put in mixing bowl, sifted flour, salt, sugar, milk and eggs, mixing well together. Add yeast mixture and butter. Knead until dough is smooth. Set aside for 2½ hours to rise. Turn out on lightly floured board and let rest for about ½ hour. Divide dough into six equal parts, and roll each part into a rectangle. Spread with desired filling and roll. Bake in greased baking pan about 30 minutes at 350°F Use filling such as nut, poppy seed, or prune butter.

Zuzana Kacvinsky, Youngstown, Ohio

KOLAČ

8 to 10 cups flour
1 pound butter, or margarine
1 cup crisco
2 cakes yeast

8 egg yolks
1 cup sugar
2 cans evaporated milk
1 teaspoon salt

Sift flour, work in shortening as for pie dough. Dissolve yeast in a little lukewarm milk, and add to first mixture. Add rest of the ingredients and knead until well mixed. Divide dough into small balls and allow to rise on a floured board for 3 hours. Roll dough thin and fill with nut or poppy seed filling. Brush with beaten egg and allow to rise about ½ hour. Bake at 350°F for 30 minutes.

Mary Yasso, Lansford, Pa.

KOLAČ

1 cup lukewarm water
1 cake yeast
1½ cups flour
1 egg
2 cups milk, combined with
 ½ pound melted butter
8 cups flour
1 tablespoon salt
½ cup sugar
1 teaspoon vanilla

FILLINGS:
Ground poppy seed, plus sugar
Cottage cheese, an egg, plus
 sugar
Ground walnuts, plus sugar

Dissolve yeast in lukewarm water, add flour and mix until smooth. Cover and let stand until bubbles form. Add rest of the ingredients and work this mixture together until smooth. If dough sticks to hands, add more flour until dough is firm and sticks together, or leaves the side of the bowl. Brush top and sides with melted butter, cover and let rise until doubled in bulk. Place on floured board and cut into sections. Roll each piece and spread with filling. Roll up like a jelly roll. Bake at 375°F about 40 to 50 minutes.

Julia Kristin, Chicago, Ill.

NUT ROLL

1 cake yeast	2 teaspoons salt
1 cup milk, lukewarm	2 tablespoons shortening
4 tablespoons sugar	2 cups milk, scalded and cooled,
2 cups flour, sifted	or 2 cups sweet cream
6 eggs, separated	1 teaspoon vanilla
½ pound butter, softened	7 cups flour, sifted (about)

Mix first four ingredients and set aside for about ½ hour. Add beaten egg yolks, butter, salt, shortening, milk or cream. Stir until well blended. Beat egg whites until firm, add vanilla, and add to first mixture. Mix well and gradually add about 3 cups of flour. Knead until dough is smooth and elastic. Cover with dish towel and set aside until doubled in bulk. Punch down and allow dough to rise again. Repeat this process two more times, or until dough is light. Turn out on lightly floured board and divide into six parts. Roll about ¼ inch thick and spread with nut or poppy seed filling. Bake at 350°F about 45 minutes.

Josephine Leslie, Whiting, Ind.

DELICIOUS NUT ROLLS

INGREDIENTS	1 teaspoon salt
½ pound butter	1 oz. cake yeast
½ pound margarine	Grated rind 1 lemon
½ pint sour cream	About 10 cups flour
½ cup water, warm	FILLING
1 large can evaporated milk,	1 pound ground walnuts
warm	¼ cup milk
6 egg yolks or 3 whole eggs	2 tablespoons melted butter
3 tablespoons sugar	1 cup sugar

Melt shortening, cool. Add warm liquids, blend, then add sour cream. Add yolks or eggs, one at a time, stirring after each addition. Add crumbled yeast and lemon rind. Sift dry ingredients and gradually add to first mixture, blend well. Turn out onto floured pastry cloth and knead until smooth. Form into ball and refrigerate over night. Divide dough into 8 pieces. Roll very thin, and spread with filling. Roll into long rolls, seal ends and place on greased cookie sheet. Allow to rise about 20 minutes. Bake at 375°F for 30 to 35 minutes.

Filling: Combine all ingredients and spread on rolled out dough.

Terezia Sajan. Chicago. Illinois

ECONOMY POPPY SEED OR NUT ROLL

½ pound butter, crisco, or oleo
2 cakes yeast
1 cup warm water
2 tablespoons sugar

4 cups flour
2 egg yolks
1 teaspoon salt

Dissolve yeast and sugar in warm water. Set aside to rise while preparing rest of the pastry. Sift flour and salt, cut in shortening as for pie dough. Add yolks and blend together. Add the yeast mixture. Turn out on floured board and knead for about five minutes. Divide dough into four pieces and allow to rise while preparing the filling. Roll each piece and spread with filling. Roll up and place on baking sheet. Bake at 350°F for 25 minutes. Lemon or almond extract added to poppy seed gives it an additional flavor.

Vincentian Sisters of Charity, Bedford, Oh.

FILLED COFFEE CAKE ROLLS (Slovenské Kolače-Zvinaki)

8 cups flour, sifted
½ cup powdered sugar
1 cup milk, lukewarm
1 cake yeast

8 egg yolks
1 pint cream, sweet or sour
1 tablespoon salt
1 pound butter

Sift powdered sugar, flour and salt together, and add milk with yeast dissolved in it. Work it in gradually as for pie dough. Combine cream and the well beaten eggs, and gradually add to first mixture. When well blended, knead for 20 minutes. Cover dough and let rise for about two hours. Divide dough into ten balls and let stand for another half hour. Sprinkle bread board with powdered sugar, and roll out dough balls, thin, and spread with filling you desire. Roll and place on buttered baking pan, allow to stand for ½ hour to rise. Brush with beaten egg. Bake in oven for 45 minutes, 350°F Makes five nut rolls and five poppy seed rolls.

FILLINGS:

POPPY SEED
1 pound ground poppy seed
2 cups sugar
½ teaspoon ground cinnamon
2 tablespoons melted butter or
 honey may be used

NUT
2½ pounds ground nut meats
2 cups sugar
Rind of 1 lemon
2 tablespoons melted butter

Fillings for five rolls.

Veronica Radocha, Coaldale, Pa.

TWO HOUR NUT ROLL

6 cups flour, sifted
1 teaspoon salt
3 tablespoons sugar
2 cakes yeast

½ cup warm milk
½ pound butter, or margarine
3 eggs, beaten
1 cup sour cream, or canned milk

Dissolve yeast in milk. Combine flour, butter, salt, sugar, eggs and sour cream. Add yeast and milk mixture. Blend well. Divide dough into four parts and roll out each part thin as for jelly roll. Spread with nut, or poppy seed mixture. Roll and place on greased pan and allow to rise for 1 hour, or until doubled in bulk. Bake 35 to 40 minutes at 350°F, sprinkle top with powdered sugar.

Mary Skurka, Whiting, Ind.

- FILLED ROLLS -
(Refrigerated Type)

COFFEE CRESCENTS

4 cups sifted flour
1 cup butter, or margarine
1 tablespoon sugar
1 teaspoon salt
1 ounce cake yeast
1 cup cold milk
3 egg yolks, beaten

NUT FILLING
3 egg whites, beaten stiff
1 cup brown sugar
6 tablespoons butter
½ pound walnut meats
8 large graham crackers, rolled
1 teaspoon maple flavoring
(optional)

Crumble yeast in cold milk and add beaten egg yolks. Sift flour, sugar and salt. Work in shortening as for pie dough. Add yeast mixture and blend well. Place in greased bowl, cover and place in refrigerator over night. The next day, remove dough from refrigerator and divide into three parts. Roll each part about ¼ inch thick, or less. Spread a little of beaten egg white over the dough. Then spread filling over half of dough and fold over the portion of dough having no filling on it over the filled part. Pinch edges together to keep the filling from oozing out. Next, cut approximately one-inch long strips. Take an unsharpened pencil, roll over each strip and place on greased baking sheet and let rise for about an hour. This will not raise too much. Bake at 375°F for about 15 to 20 minutes. When cool, spread with confectioners' icing on top of each crescent.

Nut Filling: Blend all ingredients, except the egg whites.

Victoria Sivulka, Whiting, Ind.

NUT HORNS

5 cups flour	**FILLING:**
½ cup sugar	1 teaspoon sugar
¼ teaspoon salt	½ pound ground nuts
½ pound butter	½ cup water
6 egg yolks	Raisins
1 cake yeast	½ cup warm milk

Sift flour and measure. Add sugar and salt. Work butter into flour mixture with fingers. Crumble yeast into warm milk. Add yolks with yeast mixture to flour. Work together until dough sticks firmly together. Divide dough in half and roll into two balls. Place in refrigerator overnight. When ready to bake, roll dough to ¼ inch thickness. Spread filling, roll up dough and shape into crescent. Bake at 350°F for 45 minutes. Filling: Bring water to a boil, add sugar and continue to cook for a few minutes. Add nuts and raisins.

Mary E. Grega, Cleveland, Oh.

NUT ROLLS

1 cup milk, lukewarm	2 teaspoons salt
2 small cakes yeast	½ pound butter
6 cups flour	½ pint sour cream
1¼ cups sugar	4 egg yolks

Crumble yeast in milk. Sift flour, sugar and salt. Work in the butter. Add sour cream, yeast mixture and egg yolks. Knead thoroughly. Cover and place in refrigerator over night. Divide dough into six parts. Form into rolls, using nut filling. Brush top with melted shortening, allow to rise for 20 minutes. Bake for 30 minutes at 350°F.

Ella D. Vlasaty, Braddock, Pa.

NUT AND POPPY SEED ROLLS

8 cups flour	1 cup sugar
1 pound butter, or margarine	1 cake yeast
1 tablespoon lard	½ cup lukewarm water
12 whole eggs	2 teaspoons salt

Dissolve yeast in lukewarm water and set aside. Sift flour, sugar and salt into a bowl, cut in shortening and gradually add well beaten eggs. Blend, then gradually add the dissolved yeast and once again blend thoroughly. Place into refrigerator over night. Next day divide dough into 7 or 8 parts, roll out each part on floured board and spread with nut or poppy seed mixture and roll. Place on greased baking sheet and let stand for about ½ hour. Bake at 350°F for 30 minutes.

Agnes Thomas, Bethlehem, Pa.

REFRIGERATOR NUT ROLLS

6 cups flour	**½ pint sweet cream**
1 pound butter, or margarine	**½ cake yeast, household**
2 tablespoons sugar	**½ teaspoon salt**
6 eggs beaten	

Sift flour into a large bowl and cut in shortening. Add sugar and cream to beaten eggs. Dissolve yeast in little milk and add salt. Add beaten egg mixture to flour, then add yeast mixture. Mix dough in the evening and store in the refrigerator. In the morning take out enough dough to make one roll. Roll out and spread with nut mixture and light raisins. Roll and place on cookie sheet. Bake for 1 hour, or until nicely browned at 350°F Yield: 6 nice sized rolls.

Mary Molson, Whiting, Ind.

NUT AND POPPY SEED ROLLS

1 large sifter of flour	**1 cake yeast**
2 tablespoons sugar	**4 egg yolks**
Pinch of salt	**½ pint sour cream**
½ pound butter	

Sift flour and resift with sugar and salt, mix with butter as for pie crust. Beat egg yolks and add together with sour cream to the flour mixture. Combine yeast with warm milk and sugar, add to flour mixture. Knead to a soft dough, adding milk if needed. Place in refrigerator over night. Divide dough into 3 pieces. Roll each piece and spread with nut or poppy seed filling. Roll up and place on greased baking sheet. Allow to rise for a while. Bake for 30 minutes at 350°F.

Mary V. Haydu, Braddock, Pa.

NUT AND POPPY SEED ROLLS

1 cup melted butter	**1 teaspoon salt**
½ cup warm milk	**4½ cups flour**
½ cup sugar	**4 eggs**
1 cake yeast	

Dissolve yeast in ½ cup warm milk. Mix ingredients in large bowl, adding one cup flour at a time, alternately with one egg at a time, until all flour and eggs are used. Mix and beat well. Let stand over night in cool place. Next morning punch down dough, place in refrigerator to chill and harden, otherwise dough would be hard to handle. Divide dough into four equal parts, put in refrigerator and work with one part. Work fast, roll thin as for pie crust. Fill with filling and roll. Place on greased baking sheet and let rise for one hour. Brush top with beaten egg to which a little milk has been added. Bake at 375°F for 40 to 45 minutes, or until brown. Yield: four 16-inch rolls.

Mary Babinchak, Cleveland, Oh.

POPPY SEED AND NUT ROLLS

2 sifters flour
½ pound butter
½ pound spry
1 cup sugar
3 teaspoons salt
1 quart milk
6 eggs yolks
1 cake yeast

FILLING
1 pound poppy seed
1 cup sugar
3 tablespoons milk
Grated rind of lemon
NUT FILLING
2 pounds walnuts, ground
2 cups sugar
4 tablespoons milk

Combine flour, butter, spry, salt, sugar and mix as for pie crust. Stir in yeast which has been blended with ½ cup cold milk. Add balance of milk and eggs. Work dough until it does not stick to hands. Shape into ball, place on floured board and let stand over night. When ready to bake, cut into eight pieces. Roll each piece and spread with walnut or poppy seed mixture. Bake 35 minutes in moderate oven.

Anna Bacho, Toledo, Ohio

SLOVAK POPPY SEED ROLLS

4 cups all-purpose flour
1 teaspoon salt
1 cup canned milk
2 cakes yeast
1 teaspoon vanilla
½ pound lard, or shortening
4 whole eggs

FILLING
1 pound ground poppy seed
2 cups sugar
1 cup seedless raisins
1 teaspoon vanilla
Milk

Sift flour and salt. Add vanilla and yeast which has been dissolved in canned milk. Cut in shortening. Add one egg at a time and beat well after each addition. Mix all ingredients well. Place dough in refrigerator over night. Next day, roll dough ¼ inch thick, spread filling and roll, like jelly roll. Brush top with egg yolk to which a little milk has been added. Bake 30 to 35 minutes, at 350°F or until brown.

Poppy seed Filling: Combine ingredients, add enough milk to make filling of right consistency.

Clara S. Matuschak, Connellsville, Pa.

- KOLAČKY - YEAST DOUGH -

KOLAČKY

½ cup sweet cream or
   evaporated milk
1 cake yeast
1 tablespoon sugar

3 cups flour
½ pound butter
3 egg yolks

Combine cream, yeast and sugar, let stand 5 minutes. Mix flour and butter, add yolks. Add yeast mixture and work with hands until dough is not sticky and hands are clean. Roll out thin, a small piece at a time. Fill and roll. Put on cookie sheet and set aside for about 20 minutes in warm place. Bake at 350°F about 20 minutes. Apricot filling is very delicious.

Elizabeth Sohovich, Gary, Ind.

KOLAČKY *(Slovak Nut Rolls)*

FIRST DOUGH
1 pound flour
1 teaspoon salt
2 tablespoons sugar
4 egg yolks, unbeaten
2 cakes yeast, dissolved in one
   cup lukewarm milk

WALNUT FILLING
1½ pounds walnuts, ground
8 egg whites
2 cups sugar
2 teaspoons vanilla

Sift flour, salt and sugar. Add yolks and dissolved yeast. Mix well.

SECOND DOUGH:
1 pound sifted flour
1 pound butter

Work butter into flour and mix well. Combine both doughs and mix well. Let rise 2 hours in covered bowl. Punch down, cover and let rise again for 2 hours. Punch dough. Roll out on powdered sugared board about ¼ inch thick. Cut in desired shapes and fill with favorite nut filling. Or: Make small balls size of walnut. Roll out on board which has been covered with powdered sugar. Fill with nut filling. Place on ungreased cookie sheet, about one inch apart. Brush with beaten egg yolk. Bake at 350°F for 30 minutes. Yield: about 120 small golden brown nut rolls.

Macko, Connellsville, Pa.

SLOVENSKE KOLAČKY

1 cup milk, scalded
½ cup sugar
1 cup shortening (half butter
   and half margarine)

1 cake yeast
4 cups flour
3 eggs

Combine scalded milk, sugar and shortening, cool to lukewarm. Add yeast. Stir well with mixing spoon. Add flour alternately with eggs as follows: One cup flour alternately with one egg, repeat three times, and ending with one cup flour. Stir well after each addition. Let rise for six hours in cool place. Roll out about ½ inch thick. Cut into squares, fill with favorite filling, such as prune, cottage cheese, apricot or walnut, sweetened to taste. Place on greased pan and let rise for one hour in warm place. Bake at 375°F until brown. To give them a nice gloss, brush with beaten egg white before baking.

Mary Schinsky, North Hollywood, Ca.

KOLAČKY

1 cake yeast	**POPPY SEED FILLING**
2½ cups potato water, lukewarm	**½ pound ground poppy seed**
½ cup shortening	**½ teaspoon salt**
2 tablespoons sugar	**½ cup sugar**
2 teaspoons salt	**½ cup milk**
5 cups flour	

Crumble yeast in half cup potato water. Cream shortening and sugar, add salt and yeast mixture. Add sifted flour gradually. Knead well. Let rise in warm place until doubled in bulk. Turn out on floured board. Pat and pull the dough. Cut in strips, then in squares. Place filling on each square. Draw the corners together and pinch edges. Place on baking sheet and let rise until light. Handle dough as little as possible. Bake at 350°F for 20 minutes.

Filling: Combine all ingredients and cook until milk is absorbed. Use prune, potato or nut filling.

Leona Chabala, Nokomis, Ill.

SUGAR ROLLED KOLAČKY

½ pound margarine	**3 egg yolks**
4 cups flour	**1 cake yeast**
2 tablespoons sugar	**¼ cup cold milk**
½ teaspoon salt	

Sift flour and cut in shortening until very fine crumbs. Add rest of ingredients and work until dough leaves sides of bowl. Divide into sections. Roll out on granulated sugar. Cut in squares and fill with prune or nut filling. Bake in moderate oven for 15 minutes, or until nice and brown.

Mary Uhely, Los Angeles, Ca.

KOLAČKY (IN WATER)

12 egg yolks	2 cups milk
2 pounds lard	Pinch of salt
1 large cake yeast	Flour
5 tablespoons water	

Combine yeast and water. Add remaining ingredients and mix well. Add enough flour to make a soft dough. Knead until dough is smooth, or until dough works clean from hands. Wrap in towel and put in cold water. Let stand five hours. Sprinkle board with powdered sugar and roll out dough. Cut into squares and fill with favorite filling.

Sophie Gometro, Nesquehoning, Pa.

PRUNE BUTTER AND COTTAGE CHEESE KOLAČKY

10 tablespoons butter or shortening	1 beaten egg with 2 tablespoons water
4 eggs	
1 ounce yeast	**COTTAGE CHEESE FILLING**
¾ cup milk, scalded and cooled	2 eggs
2½ tablespoons sugar	½ cup sugar
1½ teaspoons salt	½ teaspoon salt
Approximately 4½ cups flour	1 pound cottage cheese

Cream butter and shortening, add eggs one at a time, beating well after each addition. Dissolve yeast in lukewarm milk, add sugar and salt and set aside for 5 to 10 minutes. Add this mixture to the egg mixture alternately with flour. Beat the dough until very smooth and elastic, using flour as more is necessary. Roll dough out on a floured board to about ¼ inch thickness. Cut into 3 inch squares and fill with prune or cottage cheese filling. Gather up the four corners carefully and fold one over the other. Place on large cookie sheet and let rise 30 minutes. Brush with beaten egg and bake at 375°F about 25 minutes.

Filling: Combine ingredients and blend well.

Joliet, Illinois

ROHLIČKY

2 teaspoons sugar	**FILLING**
½ cup milk	4 egg whites, stiffly beaten
1 cake yeast	1¼ cups sugar
4 egg yolks	⅛ teaspoon salt
3½ cups flour	½ pound shelled walnuts, ground
¾ pound butter, or margarine	

Mix ingredients until well blended. Place in refrigerator for several hours. Divide dough into four pieces. Roll out each piece ⅛-inch thick. Cut in four inch squares. Spread with filling. Roll and place on greased cookie sheet. Bake at 350°F for ten minutes.

Filling: Combine sugar, salt and nuts. Fold in beaten whites.

Mary Salat, Chicago, Ill.

SLOVAK FROZEN COTTAGE CHEESE SQUARES

6 cups all-purpose flour
1 teaspoon salt
3 tablespoons sugar
2 cakes yeast
1 pound soft butter
5 egg yolks
1 whole egg
1 cup cream or milk

FILLING
2 cartons cottage cheese, partly
  drained
½ box seedless raisins
2 eggs
1 cup granulated sugar
  (Combine and blend well)

Sift dry ingredients. Crumble yeast into butter and add to first mixture. Work together until well blended. Add yolks, whole egg and cream. Mix well. Chill overnight. Roll out dough about ¼ inch thick. Cut into 3 inch squares. Place a teaspoon of filling on each square. Gather up the four corners and fold one over the other and pinch together. Place on ungreased baking sheet and allow to rise. Brush with beaten egg yolk, mixed with one tablespoon milk. Sprinkle chopped nuts combined with powdered sugar. Bake at 350°F until golden brown.

Clara S. Matuschak, Connellsville, Pa.

WALNUT FINGER ROLLS

7 cups flour
4 egg yolks
1 cake yeast
2 cups buttermilk
4 tablespoons butter

4 teaspoons vanilla
Pinch of salt
2 tablespoons sugar
1 pound crisco
4 teaspoons baking powder

Mix flour with crisco, butter, salt and sugar. Dissolve yeast in buttermilk. Add yolks and blend. Combine with flour mixture. Put in refrigerator for three hours. Roll on board which has been covered with powdered sugar. Cut in squares and fill with favorite nut filling or any other filling. Bake until nice and brown.

Anna Geroch, Kingston, PA.

-KOLAČKY - REFRIGERATED YEAST DOUGH -

KOLAČ DOUGH
(Delicious Cold Dough Recipe)

8 cups flour
12 egg yolks
1½ pounds shortening (butter
   or margarine)

1 teaspoon salt
2 cakes yeast (2 ounces)
1 pint sour cream

Sift flour. Crumble in yeast and add yolks, salt and sour cream. Knead until smooth. Put in refrigerator over night. Roll out on lightly floured and sugared board. Cut into squares, fill with any desired filling. Fold over twice, cut small slits along one side. Bake 30 minutes in 325°F oven.

Mary Nemeth, Munhall, Pa.

APRICOT AND PINEAPPLE KOLAČKY

6 cups flour
1 pound shortening
3 eggs
1 cup cream, or canned milk
1 cake yeast
1 teaspoon vanilla
Pinch of salt

FILLING
1 pound dry apricots, cooked
1 small can pineapple, drained
Sugar to taste

Sift flour and salt, cut in shortening until it looks like cornmeal. Add eggs, cream, yeast and vanilla. Beat with hand until dough forms into a ball and hands are clean. Place in refrigerator over night, or for 6 hours. Cover board with granulated sugar. Roll out small portions of dough at a time. Spread with filling, roll up pieces, or fold over. Bake at 350°F about 10 to 12 minutes.

Sue Ogurchock, New Kensington, Pa.

CRESCENTS

2 pounds sifted flour
½ pound butter
½ pound crisco
½ pound lard

3 egg yolks
½ pint sour cream
1 cake yeast

Work flour and yeast together. Add butter and shortening and cut in as for pie crust. Add beaten yolks and sour cream. Blend well. Chill in refrigerator over night. Roll out and set aside for two hours. Roll again over sugared board and fill with nut, poppy seed or prune filling. Bake at 350°F until light brown.

Ludmila Sacik, Ford City, Pa.

COTTAGE CHEESE KOLAČKY

1 pound butter	**FILLING**
4 cups flour	1 pound dry cottage cheese
6 egg yolks	¼ cup sugar
2 tablespoons sugar	1 tablespoon butter
12 tablespoons sweet cream	1 egg
(¾ cup)	
1 teaspoon salt	
1 cake yeast	

Sift flour and salt. Cut in butter with pastry blender. Heat cream, add yeast and set aside to rise. Beat yolks and sugar together. Add to flour mixture. Add softened yeast and blend well. Place in refrigerator over night. Roll out ½ inch thick, cut with small biscuit cutter. Make impression in center and fill with cheese filling. Bake at 375°F, 20 minutes or until brown. Sprinkle with powdered sugar when cool.

Filling: Mix all ingredients thoroughly.

Mary Salat, Chicago, Ill.

CREAM KOLAČKY

PART 1:

1 cup butter, or margarine
1 cup flour

Cut shortening into flour until it looks like large peas. Cover bowl and place in refrigerator.

PART 2:	**CRUMB MIXTURE**
1 cake yeast	¼ cup sugar
½ teaspoon salt	1 tablespoon flour
2 tablespoons sugar	1 teaspoon butter
1 cup light cream, scalded	
Rind of 1 lemon, grated	
4 egg yolks	
3 cups flour	

Crumble yeast into bowl. Add salt, sugar and lukewarm cream. Stir until yeast is dissolved. Add lemon rind and well beaten egg yolks. Gradually beat in flour and continue to beat until smooth. The dough will be very soft. Cover and let rise until light, about 45 minutes. Turn out on floured pastry cloth and roll out into rectangle, about ¼ inch thick. Spread ¼ of butter and flour mixture (Part 1) over ⅔ of dough. Fold unspread portion over half of spread portion and fold over envelope fashion, making three layers. Roll out again to ¼ inch thickness, spread with crumbs and fold over. Repeat two more times. Wrap dough in several thicknesses of waxed paper and put in refrigerator over night. Roll out to ¼ inch thickness and cut into 2 inch squares. Place on baking sheet and let rise until light about 45 minutes. Make a depression in center of each square and fill with filling. Sprinkle with crumb mixture. Bake in a very hot oven, 450°F, 10 to 12 minutes. Yield: about 4 dozen.

Mary Walovich, Chicago, Ill.

FROZEN KOLAČKY

½ pound shortening
3 cups flour
1 cup hot milk
Rind of 1 lemon, grated
1 cake yeast

½ teaspoon sugar
4 eggs, beaten
4 tablespoons sugar
½ teaspoon salt

Combine flour and shortening, and mix as for pie crust. Add yeast, softened in little warm milk, and ½ teaspoon sugar. Add eggs, milk, sugar, salt and lemon rind. Beat well. Cover, and place in refrigerator over night. When ready to bake, roll dough to ½ inch thickness. Cut 1½ inch rounds. Place on greased baking sheet, brush with melted butter. Cover and let rise until almost doubled. Make deep depression in center and fill with desired filling. Bake at 400°F about 20 minutes.

Mary Zibrida, Chicago, Ill..

CREAM NUT ROLLS

1 cup coffee cream
1 cake yeast
1 cup butter
1 cup almonds, or walnut
   mixture for filling

5 egg yolks
3 cups flour
⅓ cup sugar

Scald cream. Cool to lukewarm. Crumble yeast into cooled cream. Cream butter thoroughly. Add yolks one at a time, beating well after each addition. Add flour alternately with yeast mixture to creamed butter mixture. Beat thoroughly. Chill dough over night in refrigerator. Mix sugar and nutmeats and sprinkle half on bread board. Divide chilled dough in half. Roll out each portion on the sugar and nutmeat mixture to about ⅛ inch thick. Roll as for jelly roll. Cut ½ inch slices. Place on baking sheet 1½ inches apart. Let rise until light, about one hour. Bake at 350°F about 25 minutes, or until browned.

Florence Ribovich, Hammond, Ind.

SOUR CREAM KOLAČKY

4 cups flour
4 egg yolks
½ teaspoon salt
½ pint thick sour cream

1 cup butter or margarine
1 cake yeast
3 tablespoons sugar

Blend flour and butter. Mix together yolks, yeast, salt, sugar, and sour cream. Add to flour mixture and blend lightly. Cover with waxed paper and chill in refrigerator over night. Next day roll out dough and cut into small pieces and fill with filling. Roll up pieces, fold over, or bring corners to center and press together. Bake at 350°F about five minutes. Remove from oven, brush with slightly beaten egg white, return to oven and bake additional 15 to 20 minutes.

Ludmilla Cherney, Chicago, Illinois

- ROŽKY -

BUTTER ROLLS

½ cup ground walnuts
½ pound flour
½ pound sweet butter

¼ pound sugar
1 egg

Combine all ingredients and work dough until nice and smooth. Roll out, cut in squares. Fill with nut or prune filling. Roll and shape into horns. Bake in moderate oven for 20 minutes. Apricot jam is delicious for filling.

Mary Uhely, Los Angeles, Ca.

EUROPEAN CRESCENTS

1 pound butter
2 pounds flour
Pinch of salt
2 tablespoons sugar
5 egg yolks
Grated rind of lemon
1 cake yeast
½ pint sour cream, lukewarm

FILLING
1 pound nuts, ground
½ cup crushed pineapple
½ cup sugar
Grated lemon rind
5 egg whites, beaten

Sift flour, sugar and salt. Make well in center, add butter and blend with pastry blender. Add yeast to lukewarm cream, stir until dissolved. Add yolks, lemon rind and yeast to flour mixture. Knead with hands until smooth and dough does not stick to hands. Put in refrigerator for 3 hours. Roll thin, cut into squares. Place a tablespoon of filling on each square and roll. Dip top of each crescent into sugar before putting onto well greased cookie sheet. Bake at 350°F about 25 minutes, or until lightly browned.

Nut Filling: Combine nuts, pineapple, sugar and lemon rind. Beat whites and fold into mixture.

Anna Sapp, Irwin, Pa.

NUT BUTTER HORNS

½ pound flour
½ pound butter
6 egg yolks
2 tablespoons sour cream

FILLING
½ pound sugar
½ pound walnuts, ground
⅛ teaspoon salt
½ teaspoon vanilla
6 egg whites
Butter, size of walnut

Cut butter into flour, as for pie crust. Add beaten yolks and sour cream. Mix well. Chill in refrigerator for several hours before using. When ready to bake, shape into tiny balls, size of walnut. Roll thin and spread with nut filling. Bake at 350°F about 20 to 25 minutes.

Filling: Beat whites until stiff, add sugar, nuts and flavoring. Handle filling very lightly.

Anna B. Hopko, Braddock, Pa.

ROŽKY

1½ pounds flour
1 pound butter, or ½ pound
  each butter and crisco
1 tablespoon sugar

1 tablespoon baking powder
1 teaspoon salt
1 large can evaporated milk
5 egg yolks

Mix ingredients until well blended and dough does not stick to the hands. Set aside in cold place for 1 hour or longer. Roll out on floured board and cut in squares. Fill with poppy seed, prune butter or any desired filling. Roll and turn into crescents. Brush top with milk or beaten egg. Bake at 350°F for 30 minutes.

Anna Pavlik, Greensburgh, Pa.

ROŽKY

DOUGH NO.1
½ pound sifted flour
2 egg yolks

1 teaspoon powdered sugar
½ cup water, about
1 ounce glass whiskey

Add to flour, yolks, sugar, water and whiskey. Knead dough until it is smooth and elastic. Place in refrigerator.

DOUGH No.2
1 pound butter, prefer sweet
½ pound sifted flour

Sift flour, work in butter until a large ball is formed.

Method: Roll out dough No.1. Spread dough No.2 on rolled dough with knife. Fold into square. Roll out thoroughly and fold into square again. Wrap in towel and place in refrigerator for 1 hour. Remove, roll out and fold as before. Place in refrigerator for one hour. Repeat process again. After removing from refrigerator the third time, place dough on well-floured board and roll out. Cut as desired. Fill with any desired filling. Bake in hot oven 450°F for 8 to 10 minutes, or until nice and brown.

Anna Kavor, Whiting, Ind.

NUT HORNS

1 pound flour
2 egg yolks, beaten
3 tablespoons sugar
½ pound butter
3 tablespoons sour cream
1 cake yeast
½ cup milk
1 teaspoon salt
1 teaspoon vanilla

NUT FILLING:
1½ pounds nuts, ground fine
  (shelled)
1½ cups sugar, or more to
  suit taste
Milk
FIG FILLING:
1 pound dry figs
Sugar to taste

Sift flour into mixing bowl, add sugar, salt and butter. Cut with pastry blender as for pie crust. Add yeast which has been dissolved in milk. Add yolks and sour cream. Knead until smooth. Let rise for two hours. Divide dough into two parts. Keep one portion in refrigerator while working with other part. Roll out dough thin, as for pie. Make a long roll by rolling the dough as tight as you can. Cut into 24 pieces. Dust each piece lightly with flour. Roll thin to about 3x4 inches. Fill with nut filling or figs. Roll and dip top and sides in slightly beaten whites of two eggs. Then into reserved nut and sugar mixture. Shape into horns, place on greased pan and let rise 1½ hours. Bake 30 to 35 minutes at 375°F or until light brown. These nut horns will keep for a week.

Nut Filling: To the ground nuts, add sugar and enough milk to make a paste. Reserve one cup nuts and sugar mixture before adding milk to roll the horns in.

Fig Filling: Cook figs, drain well and chop fine. Add sugar to sweeten.

Mary Babinchak, Cleveland, Oh.

- ROŽKY - REFRIGERATED DOUGH -

FAST COLD DOUGH

1 pound crisco
5 eggs
1 teaspoon baking powder
3 tablespoons sugar

1 cake yeast
1 teaspoon salt
1 teaspoon vanilla
6 cups flour

Mix all ingredients for dough. Mix with hands. Knead a few minutes. Roll out on board which has been covered with flour and sugar. Shape into desired shapes and fill with favorite fillings, such as nut, apricot, prunes, etc. Bake in moderate oven for 25 minutes.

Mary Timko, Munhall, Pa.

HANDY DOUGH

1 cup sugar
½ pound butter
½ pound crisco
1 cup mashed potatoes
  (save water)

4 eggs, well beaten
1 cup warm potato water
1 teaspoon salt
5 or 6 cups flour
1 cake yeast

Combine ingredients and blend thoroughly with hands. Place in refrigerator over night. Let rise in pans 2 hours before baking. Roll out and make nut rolls or any other filling.

Mary Timko, Munhall, Pa.

RAISED DOUGH

1 pound butter
5 pounds flour
¾ cup sugar
12 eggs, separated
1 quart sour cream, or beer

2 teaspoons vanilla
1 teaspoon salt
1 cake yeast, dissolved in little
  warm water

Cream butter with flour. Add sugar to egg yolks. Beat egg whites and add to yolks. Add sour cream or beer to egg mixture. Add salt and vanilla. Mix well. Add dissolved yeast, and add to flour. Knead well. Let rise over night. Roll out and shape into nut rolls. Let rise again in pans. Bake in moderate oven until brown.

Mary Timko, Munhall, Pa.

CREAM CHEESE CRESCENTS

½ pound butter, or crisco
½ pound cream cheese
½ pound flour

Mix ingredients until smooth and creamy. Place dough in refrigerator over night. Roll out on floured board, about ⅛-inch thick. Cut in 2-inch squares. Fill with prune, walnut or apricot butter. Roll into crescents. Bake at 400°F until light brown. Sprinkle with powdered sugar when cool.

Mrs. Joseph Hritz, Phoenixville, Pa.

CREAM CHEESE ROŽKY

4 - 3-ounce packages cream cheese
1 pound butter
4 cups sifted all-purpose flour

NUT FILLING
1 pound nuts, ground
1 cup sugar

Work ingredients into a smooth dough. Place in refrigerator over night. Divide dough and roll on powdered sugar covered board or pastry cloth. Cut in squares. Fill and bring opposite corners together, bringing one corner down and roll to prevent opening when baking. Bake at 350°F for about 20 minutes or until delicately brown. Remove from pan to cooling rack.

Clara Kucka, Whiting, Ind.

CREAM CHEESE TRIANGLES

2 - 3 oz. packages cream cheese
½ pound butter, or margarine

2 cups flour
2 teaspoons sweet cream

Work cream cheese, butter and flour as for pie crust. Moisten with cream. Knead lightly until smooth. Divide dough into 4 equal parts. Wrap in waxed paper and place in refrigerator over night. Sprinkle flour and sugar on board. Roll out each part and cut in squares. Place teaspoon of filling in one corner, fold over and press corners slightly. Bake in moderate oven until light brown. When cool, dust with powdered sugar. Keep in uncovered container for crispness. Use filling such as nut, poppy seed or pineapple.

Anna Geroch, Kingston, Pa.

COTTAGE CHEESE CRESCENTS

1 pound flour
1 pound butter
1 pound cottage cheese

Work butter and flour as for biscuits. Put cottage cheese through food mill or strainer, add to first mixture. Knead until well blended. Shape dough into pieces size of egg and place on lightly floured board over night. When ready to bake, roll out each piece very thin. Fill with favorite filling and roll. Bake at 400°F until light brown.

Cecilia Kucera, Monongahela, Pa.

CREAM CHEESE PASTRY

½ pound butter
½ pound cream cheese
¾ pound flour
1 teaspoon baking powder
3 tablespoons sugar

¼ teaspoon salt
1 teaspoon vanilla
1 egg yolk
2 tablespoons water, if desired

Combine flour, butter and cream cheese in bowl and mix as for pie crust. Add sugar, baking powder, vanilla and egg yolk. Mix well. Turn out on board and knead. If dry, use the 2 tablespoons water or cream. Divide dough into 2 round balls. Wrap in waxed paper and place in refrigerator over night. When ready to roll out, remove from refrigerator and let stand in room temperature for a while. Work dough until nice and soft. Roll out, shape as desired. Spread with desired filling and roll. Make kiffles or with double crust. Cut into small pieces. Brush with egg yolk and bake at 400°F for 30 to 35 minutes. Use filling such as ground walnuts, prepared povidlo, cheese or poppy seed.

Irene Menzezoff, Long Island, NY.

CREAM CHEESE PASTRY

1 pound cream cheese
1 pound butter, or half crisco
   and half butter

2 egg yolks
4½ cups flour
2 teaspoons baking powder

Mix cheese and shortening with hands. Add yolks and continue working until well blended. Add sifted flour and baking powder. Mix well. Chill in refrigerator over night. When ready to use dough, sprinkle powdered sugar on board, roll out. Cut in squares and fill with favorite fillings. Bake in quick oven about 15 minutes. Sprinkle with powdered sugar, when cool.

Mary Timko, Munhall, Pa.

FILLED CRESCENTS

½ cup butter
1 tablespoon lard
2 cups sifted flour

¼ teaspoon salt
2 small egg yolks
½ cup sour cream

Mix butter, lard, flour and salt until consistency of cornmeal. Drop in yolks, add cream and mix well. Shape into patty. Wrap in waxed paper and chill over night. Roll on lightly floured board to ⅛-inch thickness. Cut in squares and spread with any filling. Shape into crescents. Brush with egg yolk to which 3 tablespoons of milk was added. Place on cookie sheet. Bake at 350°F until brown. Sprinkle with powdered sugar when cool.

Anna Geroch, Kingston, Pa.

FILLED HORNS

6 egg yolks
¼ pound butter, or margarine
2 cups flour

FILLING
½ pound ground nuts
½ pound powdered sugar
4 egg whites, stiffly beaten

Mix flour and butter as for pie crust. Add yolks and mix well. Shape into small balls and chill over night. Roll out each ball and fill with nut filling. Roll and shape into horns. Bake in moderate oven until light brown. Filling: combine all ingredients.

Anna Geroch, Kingston, Pa.

SPECIAL FRENCH PASTRY

6 cups flour
1 pound crisco, or lard
1 tablespoon sugar
1 teaspoon salt

1 cake yeast
3 eggs
½ pint sweet cream

Blend all ingredients as for pie dough. Handle very little. If dough sticks, add more flour. Place in refrigerator over night. Roll out and cut in squares. Fill with prunes or preserves. Place on baking sheet and set aside to rise for 1 hour. Bake in moderate oven for 25 to 30 minutes.

Mary Uhely, Los Angeles, Ca.

KIFFLES

8 to 10 cups flour
1 pound butter, or margarine
2 cups crisco
1 pint sour cream

8 eggs, separated
1 large cake yeast
Pinch of salt

Sift flour and salt, cut in the shortening with pastry blender. Add yolks, beaten egg whites and sour cream. Add yeast dissolved in little lukewarm milk. Work the dough well. Place in refrigerator over night. When ready to bake, take small portion of dough at a time, roll thin on board which has been covered with powdered sugar. Cut in squares and fill with favorite filling, such as nuts, poppy seed or povidlo. Bake in moderate oven for 30 minutes.

Mary Yasso, Lansford, Pa.

SOUR CREAM CRESCENTS

4 pounds flour
1 pound butter
1 pint sour cream

10 yolks
2 cakes yeast
Milk

Work butter and flour as for pie crust. Add cream and well beaten yolks. Add yeast dissolved in a little warm milk. Knead well. Add enough milk to make dough of right consistency for rolling. Place dough on lightly covered board and let stand over night. When ready to bake, roll out a little dough at a time, very thin. Cut in squares and fill with favorite filling, such as nut, povidlo, and jam. Roll into crescents. Brush with beaten egg and roll in a mixture of ground nuts and sugar. Place on greased cookie sheet. Bake at 425°F for 20 minutes.

Cecilia Kucera, Monongahela, Pa.

FROZEN NUT CRESCENTS

9 cups flour
9 egg yolks
Pinch of salt
3 pounds crisco, about

1 pound butter
4 yeast cakes
1 pint sour cream
9 egg whites, stiffly beaten

Combine ingredients, except egg whites, until well blended. Add egg whites. Mix thoroughly. Place in refrigerator for 4 days. To bake, take part of dough, roll on board, sprinkled with powdered sugar. Cut in squares and fill with nut filling. Bake about 20 minutes at 375°F.

Filling: Ground nuts, add sugar and enough milk to make the mixture moist.

Jollet, Ill.

ROŽKY

4½ cups flour
1 cake yeast
1 pound shortening, or crisco
4 yolks

Juice of 1 lemon
¼ teaspoon salt
½ pint sour cream

Mix ingredients until well blended. Place in refrigerator over night. Sprinkle fine sugar lightly on board. Roll out dough. Cut in squares and place a teaspoon of filling on each square. Roll and shape into half moons. Bake in 350 to 400°F oven until brown.

Filling: Use such as walnut, jam or poppy seed.

Leona Novosedlik, Windsor, Canada

ROŽKY

3 cups flour
½ teaspoon salt

Water
1 pound spry

Sift flour and salt. Add enough water to make a soft dough. Roll out thin and spread ⅓ of spry over dough. Fold in half, then in half again. Place in refrigerator for 1 hour. Remove dough from refrigerator, roll out and spread again with ⅓ of spry. Fold dough as the first time. Refrigerate for 1 hour. Repeat process, the dough now having been rolled and folded three times. Place in refrigerator over night. Roll out and cut in pieces. Fill with apricot filling. Bake at 350°F for 15 minutes.

Susan Levenda, Gary, Ind.

ROŽKY

6 cups flour	1 tablespoon sugar
1 pound salted butter	1 cake yeast
½ pound lard	4 eggs, separated
1 cup milk	1 grated lemon rind, or vanilla

Sift together flour and sugar. Rub in butter and lard as for pie crust. Dissolve yeast in milk, add beaten yolks and flavoring. Add to flour mixture and blend to a soft dough. Beat egg whites until stiff and add to dough. Let stand over night. Roll out on board sprinkled with sugar. Cut in squares and fill with any filling. Bake in moderate oven until light brown.

Mary A. Bosko, Homestead, Pa.

ROŽKY

1 pint milk	1 tablespoon salt
1½ cakes yeast	½ cup sugar
½ cup milk	½ pound butter
2 eggs, well beaten	6 cups of flour
1 tablespoon sugar	

Dissolve yeast in ½ cup milk and 1 tablespoon sugar. Combine dry ingredients and blend with dissolved yeast. Knead until smooth. Let rise for 2½ hours. Turn out on lightly floured board and let rise until light. Roll out to ⅛-inch thickness. Cut into small pieces and fill with nut, plum, or apricot butter. Roll and place on baking sheet. Bake at 350°F for 20 to 25 minutes.

J. Kacvinsky, Youngstown, Oh.

- QUICK BREADS -

APRICOT NUT BREAD

¼ teaspoon salt	1 cup chopped nut meats
2 cups all purpose flour	1 egg
2 teaspoons baking powder	¾ cup sugar
¼ teaspoon baking soda	⅔ cup orange juice
1 cup dried apricots	2 tablespoons melted fat

Sift flour, measure and resift with baking powder, baking soda and salt. Add apricots and nut meats and mix well. Beat egg slightly, add sugar, orange juice and fat and beat well. Add dry ingredients and stir only until blended. Pour into greased loaf pan and bake in preheated oven at 350°F for one hour. Yield, one 4½ by 8½ inch loaf.

Mary Vevurka, Chicago, Ill.

BANANA BREAD

1 cup sugar	3 bananas, mashed (1 cup)
½ cup butter	Pinch of salt
2 eggs	1 cup chopped nuts
1 teaspoon baking soda	1 tablespoon sour milk
2 cups flour	

Cream butter and sugar, add beaten eggs. Add flour that has been sifted with soda and salt, add sour milk and beat well. Blend in bananas and nuts. Bake in greased loaf pan for 1½ hours at 350°F.

Mary Hruskovich, Whiting, Ind.

BANANA TEA BREAD

1¾ cup, sifted all purpose flour	½ teaspoon salt
¼ teaspoon baking soda	⅔ cup granulated sugar
⅓ cup butter or shortening	1 cup mashed bananas
2 eggs, well beaten	(2 medium size)
2 teaspoons baking powder	

Sift together flour, baking powder, soda and salt. Beat shortening until creamy, add sugar gradually and continue beating until light and fluffy. Add eggs beaten well. Add flour mixture alternately with bananas, a small amount at a time, beating after each addition until smooth. Turn into greased loaf pan and bake at 350°F about one hour. If desired, ¾ cup chopped nutmeats can be included in the recipe.

Lillian Cherney, Chicago, Ill.

CHOCOLATE BREAD

3 cups sifted cake flour	1 egg, beaten
3 teaspoons baking powder	¼ cup milk
1 teaspoon salt	4 tablespoons melted shortening
1 cup brown sugar	2 squares of chocolate

Sift dry ingredients, melt shortening with chocolate. Add sugar to dry ingredients, then beaten egg, milk and melted chocolate and shortening. Bake in loaf pan, in moderate oven over 350°F for 45 minutes or until done.

Lillian Cherney, Chicago, Ill.

CORN BREAD

1 cup corn meal	2½ tablespoons melted shortening
1 cup flour	1½ tablespoons sugar
1 teaspoon baking powder	½ teaspoon soda
	1 cup sour milk

Sift dry ingredients together. Add soda and sour milk and stir into flour mixture, then add shortening. Pour into well greased pan and bake in hot oven, 415°F, about 20 minutes.

Mary Perhac, Whiting, Ind.

DATE NUT BREAD

1½ cups all purpose flour
1 teaspoon baking soda
¼ teaspoon salt
½ cup chopped nut meats
1 tablespoon melted fat

1 cup boiling water
1 cup chopped dates
1 egg
¾ cup brown sugar

Sift flour, measure and resift with baking soda and salt. Add nut meats and mix well. Add hot water to chopped dates and mix well. Beat egg slightly, add sugar and fat, beat thoroughly. Add date mixture. Add dry ingredients and stir only until blended. Pour into greased loaf pan and bake in preheated oven, 350°F for 55 minutes. Yield: one 4½ by 8½ inch loaf.

Dolores McDavid, Covington, Va.

NUT BREAD

½ cup butter
2½ cups flour
3 teaspoons baking powder
½ cup sugar

½ teaspoon salt
¾ cup chopped nuts
1 egg, beaten lightly
1 cup milk

Sift flour with baking powder, salt and sugar 3 or 4 times. Add nuts, add beaten egg to milk and melted shortening. Stir into flour mixture, only enough to moisten the flour. The batter will be somewhat lumpy. Put in a greased loaf pan and let raise 20 minutes. Bake in moderate oven, 350°F, for 45 minutes.

Mary Kowal, Whiting, Ind.

PEANUT BUTTER BREAD

2 cups sifted flour
4½ teaspoons single, or 3
  teaspoons double acting
  baking powder
1 teaspoon salt
⅓ cup firmly packed brown sugar

¼ cup shortening
½ cup peanut butter
¼ cup chopped nuts or Peanuts
1 egg, well beaten
1 cup milk

Sift flour with baking powder and salt, add sugar and mix well. Cut in shortening and peanut butter with pastry blender or 2 knives until mixture resembles coarse meal. Add nuts or peanuts, mix well. Add combined egg and milk, mixing only until all flour is dampened. Pour into greased, 9x4x3 inch loaf pan, and push batter well into corners of the pan, leaving center slightly hollowed. Bake in a preheated moderate oven, 350°F, for about 1 hour or until well done.

Justine Kasovsky, Chicago, Ill.

STEAMED BROWN BREAD

2 cups flour/white (sift once
   before measuring)
2 cups whole wheat flour
2 teaspoons baking soda
2 cups molasses or sorghum

1 cup seed raisins or chopped nuts
2 cups cornmeal, white or yellow
1 teaspoon salt
2 cups thick sour milk

Mix dry ingredients in large bowl and make a well in center. Mix molasses and sour milk and pour in. Add raisins or nuts, or both, if desired. Stir until ingredients are well blended. Beating is unnecessary. Pour into greased baking powder tins or regular steamer cans, filling not more than two thirds full. Cover cans. Steam two and one half hours, then uncover tins and dry off in a slow oven, 300°F, about a half hour.

Justine Kasovsky, Chicago, Ill.

WALNUT BREAD

Beat 1 egg. Stir in ¾ cup milk, ½ cup sugar and 3 cups bisquick. Add 1 cup chopped walnuts. Bake in greased pan 1 hour in 350°F oven.

Mary Salat, Chicago, Ill.

- QUICK COFFEE CAKES -

APPLE CAKE

1 cup all-purpose flour, sifted
1½ teaspoons baking powder
½ teaspoon salt
½ teaspoon granulated sugar
¼ cup shortening
1 egg, well beaten

¼ cup milk
3 cups apples, sliced
½ teaspoon cinnamon
½ cup sugar (additional)
2 tablespoons melted butter

Sift together: flour, salt, baking powder and ½ teaspoon sugar. Cut in shortening with pastry blender, or two knives. Stir in beaten egg and milk, mix just enough to form a soft dough, (but not until smooth). Spread in a greased baking pan. Have apples peeled, cored, and sliced; arrange in rows on top, pressing lightly into dough. Sprinkle with sugar cinnamon mixture and drizzle with melted butter over the top. Bake at 350°F for about 45 minutes. Serve with vanilla sauce.

VANILLA SAUCE

½ cup granulated sugar
2 tablespoons corn starch
¼ teaspoon salt

2 cups boiling water
4 tablespoons butter
2 tablespoon, vanilla

Combine first three ingredients in sauce pan. Slowly add boiling water, stirring until smooth. Simmer for 5 minutes. Remove from heat, add butter. Cool slightly and add vanilla. Serve warm.

APPLE CAKE

1¾ cups all-purpose flour
3 teaspoons baking powder
½ teaspoon salt
2 tablespoons shortening
½ cup milk
1 egg
½ cup sugar

TOPPING:
4 or 5 apples
½ cup sugar
1 teaspoon cinnamon

Sift the flour, measure and resift with baking powder and salt. Cut shortening into dry ingredients very lightly. Add egg, milk and sugar and mix until a soft dough. Turn out on floured board and roll out to ½ inch thickness. Place into shallow greased pan. Wash, pare and core apples, then slice evenly. Arrange in rows on top, sprinkle with sugar, dust with cinnamon. Bake in moderate oven for 30 minutes, or until apples are tender and brown. Serve warm with milk.

Anna Yokel, Piermont, NY.

CRANBERRY GLAZED COFFEE CAKE

1 can whole cranberry sauce   1 tablespoon grated orange rind

Combine sauce and rind; spread into bottom of greased 9 inch square pan.

BATTER
1 cup sugar
½ cup butter
2 eggs
½ teaspoon orange flavoring

2 cups flour
1 teaspoon baking powder
1 teaspoon baking soda
½ teaspoon salt
1 cup sour cream

Cream sugar and butter. Add an egg at a time, creaming well after each addition. Add flavoring. Combine dry ingredients and add to creamed mixture alternately with sour cream. Spread batter over cranberry topping mixture. Bake at 350°F for 45 to 50 minutes. Allow cake to cool 15 minutes; invert onto serving plate. Note: If presifted self rising flour is used, omit baking powder and salt. Yield 12 servings.

Mary Oracko, Altamonte Springs, Florida

INDIVIDUAL COFFEE CAKE

2 cups all-purpose flour	4 tablespoons shortening
¾ teaspoon salt	1 egg, beaten
4 tablespoons sugar	½ cup milk
3 teaspoons Royal baking powder	

Sift dry ingredients together. Cut in shortening with pastry blender. Add milk to beaten egg and stir into dry ingredients to make a soft dough. Divide dough into 12 pieces. Roll each piece until long and thin. Cut each strand in two and beginning in center, twist pieces together, bringing ends around to form crescent. Place on greased pan and sprinkle with chopped nuts. Bake in hot oven for 15 to 20 minutes. While still warm, brush with thin icing.

Icing: ½ cup confectioners' sugar moistened with 1 tablespoon hot water.

Anna Yokel, Piermont, N Y.

WALNUT FILLED COFFEE CAKE

2 tablespoons shortening	**FILLING:**
½ cup sugar	½ cup brown sugar
1 egg, separated	2 teaspoons cinnamon
¾ cup flour	1 cup chopped walnuts
2 teaspoons baking powder	2 tablespoons flour
¼ cup milk	2 tablespoons melted shortening
½ teaspoon vanilla	

Cream shortening and sugar until light. Add beaten egg yolk. Sift dry ingredients and add alternately with milk. Add vanilla. Fold in stiffly beaten egg white. Spread half of batter in deep greased pie tin. Spread half of filling over top. Add remaining batter and top with rest of filling. Bake at 350°F to 375°F for 45 to 60 minutes.

Maria Praskac, Coaldale, Pa.

FRUITED COFFEE CAKE *(One 8-inch round pan)*

½ cup butter, or shortening	Pinch of salt
½ cup sugar	Sugar-cinnamon
1 egg	1 tablespoon butter
¾ cup all-purpose flour	

Desired canned fruit - apricots, cherries or peaches, well drained. Cream butter, add sugar and cream until light and fluffy. Add egg and beat well. Add sifted flour and salt and blend well. Turn into greased pan. Place fruit on top, sprinkle with sugar-cinnamon and dot with butter. Bake at 325°F for about 35 minutes.

Lillian Cherney, Chicago, Ill.

NUT FILLED COFFEE CAKE

½ cup butter
2 cups sugar
4 eggs
3 cups flour
2 teaspoons baking powder
½ teaspoon salt
1 cup milk
1 teaspoon vanilla

FILLING:
1 cup brown sugar
2 tablespoons butter
2 tablespoons flour
1 teaspoon cinnamon
1 cup chopped nuts
Mix in order given

Cream butter, add sugar and beat until light. Add eggs and blend well. Sift together flour, baking powder and salt. Add alternately with milk to creamed mixture. Stir in vanilla. Grease a 9-inch tin. Pour a layer of batter, then layer of filling. Repeat until all the batter and filling is used. Bake at 350°F for 1 hour.

Mrs. Piorkowski, West Allis, Wis.

NUT BABOVKA

½ cup butter
2 cups powdered sugar
1 cup milk
4 eggs, separated

3 cups flour
2 teaspoons baking powder
Grated lemon rind
1 cup chopped nuts

Cream butter and powdered sugar together. Add beaten yolks. Add sifted flour and baking powder alternately with milk, beating until smooth. Fold in stiffly beaten egg whites. Add lemon rind and nuts. Pour into greased tube pan. Bake in moderate oven for 1 hour. When cool, sprinkle with powdered sugar.

Mary Salat, Chicago, Ill.

PLUM KUCHEN

2 cups flour
1 teaspoon baking powder
½ teaspoon salt
1 cup sugar
¼ pound butter
½ cup milk
1 egg, beaten

TOPPING
½ cup sugar
1 teaspoon cinnamon
1 egg, well beaten
Fresh Italian plums, halved
   and pitted

Sift flour, measure and resift with dry ingredients. Work in butter with pastry blender, or two knives, until it looks like coarse meal. Add milk and egg all at once and stir just enough to dampen dry ingredients. Spread dough in bottom of well buttered bread pan. Arrange halved plums, skin side down, over the dough. Sprinkle sugar and cinnamon over top. Last spread beaten egg. Bake at 350°F for about 30 minutes.

Apolonia Blahunka, Whiting, Ind.

PLUM KUCHEN

1 cup flour
1 teaspoon baking powder
1 scant teaspoon salt
2 teaspoons sugar
2 tablespoons butter
Milk
1 egg yolk

TOPPING:
Plums
Sugar

Sift flour, measure, resift with baking powder and salt. Cut in butter with pastry blender. Break yolk in cup and beat with fork, and milk to make ¾ cup full. Add to flour mixture. Spread dough evenly on buttered pie tin. Top with fruit, sprinkle with sugar. Fruits can be used-plums, peaches, pears or apricots. Sweetened whipped cream can be served on top, or make meringue with left over white of egg.

Anna B. Russell, Cleveland, Oh.

- QUICK KOLAČKY -

BAKING POWDER KOLAČKY

3 egg yolks
½ pint sweet cream
1 teaspoon vanilla
2 teaspoons baking powder

3 cups flour, more if necessary
½ pound butter
½ pound powdered sugar

Combine ingredients and blend thoroughly. Chill overnight. Roll out dough, cut in small circles. Place small amount of filling in center of each. Bake at 375°F about 12 minutes, or until done. Use filling such as nut, poppy seed, cheese, or prune.

Margaret Lissak, Berwyn, Ill.

CREAM CHEESE KOLAČKY

2 packages cream cheese,
  3 ounces each
1 cup butter, or margarine
2 cups sifted flour

2 tablespoons sugar
2 teaspoons baking powder
¼ teaspoon salt
2 eggs, well beaten

Cream butter and cream cheese together. Sift flour with salt, sugar and baking powder. Blend dry ingredients thoroughly with cheese mixture. Add beaten eggs. Stir until blended. Chill in refrigerator for ½ hour. Pat or roll out dough on floured board to about ⅓-inch thickness. Cut with floured biscuit cutter. Place ½ teaspoon of desired jam or other filling in center of each round. Bake on ungreased cookie sheet at 375°F for about 15 minutes.

POPPY SEED FILLING

1 cup moist poppy seeds
3 tablespoons milk
¼ cup corn syrup

¼ cup sugar
1 teaspoon butter
¼ teaspoon cinnamon

Place all ingredients in saucepan. Cook over low heat for 5 minutes or until mixture thickens slightly. Cool.

Sophie Marusak, Joliet, Ill.

HOLIDAY FROZEN KOLAČKY

1 pound sweet butter
6 egg yolks
¾ cup powdered sugar
1 teaspoon vanilla

½ cup sweet cream
2 teaspoons baking powder
1 teaspoon salt
1 pound flour

Measure and sift into mixing bowl half of flour, add butter, and cut in with pastry blender. Place dough in refrigerator. Sift rest of flour together with salt, sugar and baking powder. Add cream, vanilla and egg yolks. Mix until well blended. Roll out on board. Remove dough from refrigerator, roll out and place on top of second dough. Fold in half, then in half again. Cover with waxed paper, return to refrigerator for half hour. Roll out again, fold, cover and return to refrigerator. Repeat this four times in all. Refrigerate overnight. Next day roll out dough ¼-inch thick. Cut in small squares. Fill with desired filling and roll like crescents. Bake at 350°F for about 15 to 20 minutes.

Anna Kolena, Chicago, Ill.

LEAF LARD KIFFLES

2 pounds leaf lard
8 cups flour
3 tablespoons baking powder
3 tablespoons sugar
1 tablespoon salt
5 eggs
Cold milk as needed

FILLING:
2 pounds walnuts, ground
1 cup sugar to sweeten

Grind leaf lard, add flour and rub between fingers. Combine rest of ingredients with flour and blend thoroughly. Roll out dough on board. Cut small squares and fill. Bake at 350°F for half hour.

Filling: Other fillings may be used, such as, apricot, poppy seed, and prune.

Agnes Thomas, Bethlehem, Pa.

NUT ROLLS

¼ pound butter
¼ pound crisco
3 cups flour
2 teaspoons baking powder
1 teaspoon salt
3 tablespoons sugar
2 eggs or 3 yolks
1 cup canned cream, diluted
  with water

FILLING
½ pound nuts
8 graham crackers, crushed
2 tablespoons butter
1 cup sugar
Evaporated milk

Sift dry ingredients, cut in shortening until mixture has crumbly appearance. Add eggs and cream and work until dough is well mixed. Add only enough milk if needed to make a soft dough for rolling. Roll out dough. Cut in squares and fill. Place on greased cookie sheet and bake at 350°F for half hour.

Filling: Cream butter and sugar. Add graham crackers, nuts and enough canned milk to make the filling of proper consistency.

Anna Domasco, Pittsburgh, Pa.

QUICK KOLAČKY

4½ cups flour
3 teaspoons baking powder
1 pound butter, or margarine

1½ tablespoons sugar
½ pint sour cream
4 eggs

Combine all ingredients. Knead until dough is smooth. Roll out over powdered sugar. Cut into 3-inch squares and fill with nut, poppy seed or prune filling. Bake in moderate oven about 15 minutes.

Sophie Gometro, Nesquehoning, Pa.

SLOVAK BUTTERFLY KOLAČKY

¼ pound butter
2 yolks and 1 whole egg
½ teaspoon salt
Grated rind of lemon

6 tablespoons sugar
½ pound flour
2 tablespoons baking powder
½ pint sour cream

Cream butter and sugar. Add egg and yolks one at a time, beating after each addition. Add salt and lemon rind. Sift flour and baking powder six times. Add alternately with sour cream. Mix well. Put in refrigerator to harden. Roll out ½ inch thick. Cut with biscuit cutter. Place on cookie sheet. Make depression in center and fill with any jelly preserves or prune filling. Brush edges with egg whites and bake in moderate oven 375°F. Sprinkle with chopped coconut while hot. If you don't want to refrigerate dough, add more flour and dough can be used immediately.

Katherine Dymsia, Braddock, Pa.

- MUFFINS -

BRAN MUFFINS

1 cup flour
2 cups bran
1 teaspoon salt
1 egg

1 teaspoon soda
1 cup sour milk
¼ cup molasses

Sift together flour, salt and soda. Add bran, mixing thoroughly. Stir in molasses, egg and milk. Beat well, pour into greased muffin tins and bake in a moderate oven, about 30 minutes.

Anna B. Russell, Cleveland, Oh.

BUTTER MUFFINS

2 cups flour
3 teaspoons baking powder
1 teaspoon salt
1 tablespoon sugar

4 tablespoons melted butter
1 cup milk
1 egg

Sift flour, baking powder, salt and sugar together. Add melted butter, milk and egg. Stir lightly but quickly and only long enough to combine the flour. Fill buttered muffin tins and bake in a hot oven 15 to 20 minutes. Blueberries, dates, pineapple, or grated orange peel may be added to the batter. If using crushed pineapple, drain thoroughly.

Grace Margala, Los Angeles, Ca.

MUFFINS WITH EVAPORATED MILK

2 cups flour
½ teaspoon salt
3 teaspoons baking powder
2 tablespoons sugar

1 egg
½ cup water
½ cup evaporated milk

Mix and sift dry ingredients. Beat egg until light. Add water and evaporated milk, and beat again. Combine mixture and beat hard for two minutes. Pour into muffin tins and bake in a moderately hot oven, 375°F for 25 minutes. Makes 8 muffins.

Anna B. Russell, Cleveland, Oh.

OATMEAL MUFFINS

1 cup quick cooking oats
1 cup buttermilk
1 cup sifted flour
½ teaspoon salt
¼ cup sugar

1 teaspoon baking powder
½ teaspoon soda
1 egg, beaten
½ cup melted shortening

Add oatmeal to buttermilk in a bowl and let stand one hour. Sift the flour once, measure and resift with the baking powder, soda and salt. Add egg to the oatmeal-buttermilk mixture and beat well. Add sugar and melted shortening, and again beat well. Add sifted dry ingredients, and stir only until moistened. Fill greased muffin tins not more than two-thirds full, and bake in a 400°F oven for 15 to 20 minutes, or until done. Makes about 12 muffins.

Mary Osadjan, Chicago, Ill.

PRUNE MUFFINS

2 cups sifted flour	¼ teaspoon nutmeg
¼ cup sugar	¼ cup shortening
¼ cup brown sugar	1 egg
3 teaspoons baking powder	1 cup milk
½ teaspoon salt	¾ cup cooked, chopped prunes

Mix dry ingredients together, add shortening, egg and milk. Lastly add chopped prunes. Bake in 400°F oven 20 to 25 minutes. (Fill muffins tins only ⅔ full).

Mary Slifcak, Cleveland, Oh.

PRUNE MUFFINS

¼ cup shortening	1 egg
½ cup sugar	2 cups graham flour
2 teaspoons baking powder	¾ cup milk
1 scant cup stewed prunes, chopped	Pinch of salt

Beat together shortening, sugar and egg. Add flour sifted with baking powder and salt, milk and prunes. Beat well and bake in well greased muffin tins at 400°F for 20 to 25 minutes.

Anna B. Russell, Cleveland, Oh.

SOYBEAN MUFFINS

1 cup soybean flour	2 tablespoons sugar
1 cup white, or graham flour	¾ cup milk
1 teaspoon salt	1 egg, well beaten
2 teaspoons baking powder	1 tablespoon shortening

Mix and sift dry ingredients. Combine milk, beaten egg and shortening and add gradually to the dry ingredients, stirring only enough to moisten. Do not beat as batter should not be smooth. Fill greased muffin pans ⅔ full and bake in hot oven 425°F for about 15 minutes. Chopped nuts may be added, about ¼ cup.

Margaret Mihalik, Indiana Harbor, Ind.

- GRIDDLE CAKES, PANCAKES, WAFFLES -

BLUEBERRY GRIDDLE CAKES

2 eggs, slightly beaten
2 cups buttermilk
1 teaspoon baking soda
2 cups flour
2 teaspoons baking powder

1 teaspoon salt
2 teaspoons sugar
¼ cup butter, melted
1 cup fresh blueberries

Mix eggs and milk together, add sifted dry ingredients and beat until smooth. Add butter and blueberries and mix lightly. Bake on lightly greased moderately hot griddle. Serves six.

Betty Hertko, Whiting, Ind.

RAISED BUCKWHEAT CAKES

2 cups boiling water
½ cup cornmeal
½ yeast cake
¼ cup warm water
⅓ cup hot milk

1 tablespoon molasses
1 teaspoon salt
2 cups buckwheat flour
1 teaspoon soda

Pour boiling water over the cornmeal and let stand until it swells. Soften yeast in lukewarm water. After cornmeal is cool, add molasses, salt, yeast and flour. Beat thoroughly and set in a warm place to rise over night. It should rise and fall again by morning. Then add soda dissolved in hot milk, stir well and bake on a hot griddle. When the cakes are desired frequently (say, three times a week), fresh yeast will not be required after the first making, if a little more than a pint of batter is reserved each time and kept in a cool place, to be used instead of yeast. Molasses in buckwheat cakes helps to give them a good color in frying. Without it, they may be grey and unattractive.

Marie C. Radocha, Coaldale, Pa.

FRENCH PANCAKES (Palacinky)

3 eggs
½ cup sifted flour
½ teaspoon salt

½ cup milk
2 tablespoons salad oil

Beat eggs long enough to mix yolks and whites. Add flour, salt and stir again until batter is smooth. Combine milk and salad oil and stir into egg mixture until batter looks like heavy cream. Pour batter from cup or pitcher on to hot greased griddle. When little bubbles show on top, turn and brown on other side. Spread with jelly or preserves, roll up like tube and serve.

Katherine Dymsia, Braddock, Pa.

CREPE SUZETTES *(Palacinky)*

1 cup flour	1 teaspoon sugar
2 eggs	1 tablespoon butter
1 cup milk, about	½ teaspoon salt

Combine sifted flour, sugar and salt, in a mixing bowl. Add the whole eggs, one at a time, beating well after each addition. Add enough milk to make a thin batter, beat until smooth. Stir in melted butter. Pour about ½ cup batter into a heated lightly greased skillet. When brown on underside, turn and brown on other side. Spread with marmalade and roll.

Helen Butas, Bellaire, Oh.

POTATO PANCAKES *(Zemiakove Palacinky)*

2 raw potatoes, pared and grated	½ teaspoon salt
2 whole eggs, well beaten	2 tablespoons flour

Mix above ingredients thoroughly and bake in a well greased hot pan. In small frying pan bake one pancake at a time. In large one make three pancakes at one time. When brown on one side, turn over and brown on the other side. Serve hot and well buttered.

Veronica Radocha, Coaldale, Pa.

POTATO PANCAKES *(Nalesniky)*

2 pounds potatoes, Idaho	1 egg
½ cup flour	Salt to taste

Grate potatoes, mix all the ingredients. Beat well. Bake on greaseless hot griddle. Place 1½ tablespoons of batter, spread thin. Bake on both sides. When all done, brown ¼ pound butter and brush on both sides. Serve hot.

Sophie Gresko, Whiting, Ind.

POTATO PANCAKES

¾ cup mashed potatoes	1½ cup mixed evaporated milk
¾ cup flour	and potato water
¼ teaspoon salt	4 stiffly beaten egg whites
4 beaten egg yolks	

Combine potatoes, flour, salt, beaten egg yolks and liquid. Fold in egg whites and bake on greased griddle.

Margaret Kuzma, Munhall, Pa.

POTATO PANCAKES

6 potatoes, grated	½ onion, grated
2 eggs	2 tablespoons flour
Pinch of salt	¼ cup buttermilk

Grate potatoes and strain. Add grated onion, eggs, flour, salt and lastly the buttermilk. Fry in hot fat.

Mary Kukuch, East Chicago, Ind.

POTATO PANCAKES

3 or 4 potatoes, grated
1 egg
½ teaspoon baking powder

1 onion
Salt and pepper
Flour to make thin dough

Mix ingredients until well blended. Drop by spoonfuls onto hot greased frying pan and brown on both sides. If too thin, add more flour.

Barbara Bires, Pittsburgh, PA.

POTATO PANCAKES

3 slices dry bread (½ cup bread crumbs; dried)
3 potatoes
1 medium onion
1 egg

Pinch of salt
Dash of pepper
½ teaspoon baking powder

Grate bread, potatoes and onion. Add egg, salt and pepper, baking powder and flour, enough to make thin dough. Make a light batter, mix and fry on a hot skillet.

Barbara Bires, Pittsburgh, PA.

POTATO PANCAKES *(Nalesniki)*

2 medium potatoes
1 egg
Flour to make thin batter

½ cup milk
1 teaspoon salt

Peel and grate potatoes, add milk, beat into it the egg and salt. Add just enough flour to make a thin batter, beat well then pour on hot greased griddle until brown on one side, then turn on other side with spatula. Butter well and serve hot. This serves two people.

Mary Schinsky, North Hollywood, Ca.

SLOVAK PANCAKES *(Slovenske Palacinky)*

6 eggs
3 cups flour
½ cup sugar

½ teaspoon salt
1½ quarts milk

Beat the eggs well, add sugar, salt and one cup milk. Beat very well and then add flour gradually, putting in the remaining milk. Beat until very smooth. Have greased skillet hot. Put about two tablespoons of the above mixture on this skillet. Brown both sides. A filling may be used such as jelly, jam, etc., if you wish, by rolling same into a platter. This recipe will make about 30 pancakes.

Veronica Radocha, Coaldale, Pa.

SOUR MILK GRIDDLE CAKES

2 cups flour	1 tablespoon sugar
½ teaspoon salt	2 eggs
1 teaspoon soda	1½ cups sour milk
1 teaspoon baking powder	2 tablespoons melted butter

Sift flour, measure and add salt, soda, baking powder and sugar and sift together. Stir the eggs and milk (using part sour cream) gradually into sifted ingredients. Add shortening and beat until smooth. Drop from spoon on hot greased griddle; when full of bubbles, turn to brown other side. This is a small recipe for about three people.

Johanna Jurinak, Chicago, Ill.

CRISP WAFFLES

1½ cups flour, sifted	1 cup milk
3 teaspoons baking powder	2 egg yolks, beaten
¾ teaspoon salt	3 tablespoons melted butter
2 tablespoons sugar	2 egg whites

Mix and sift flour, baking powder, salt and sugar. Add gradually milk, egg yolks well beaten, and melted butter. Fold in egg whites, beaten until almost stiff. Let stand in refrigerator until very cold. Bake in preheated waffle iron until well puffed and delicately browned. Makes six waffles.

Helen Cross, Whiting, Ind.

FLUFFY WAFFLES

2 well beaten egg yolks	3 teaspoons baking powder
1½ cups milk	6 tablespoons melted butter
2 cups flour	2 stiffly beaten egg whites
¼ teaspoon salt	

Mix egg yolks, add milk, add flour, salt and baking powder which have been sifted. Add cooled shortening. Beat smooth and fold in egg whites. Bake on greased waffle iron.

Margaret Kuzma, Homestead, Pa.

CHOCOLATE NUT WAFFLES

Add to the fluffy waffles ingredients: ½ cup chopped nuts, 1 teaspoon vanilla, 2 ounces unsweetened chocolate melted.

Margaret Kuzma, Homestead, Pa.

SOUR CREAM WAFFLES

1 cup pastry flour
⅓ teaspoon salt
1 cup sour cream

¾ teaspoon soda
2 eggs, separated
2 tablespoons melted butter

Sift flour, measure and resift with salt. Combine soda and sour cream and add to flour, gradually stirring until smooth. Add beaten egg yolks and melted butter. When smooth, fold in stiffly beaten egg whites. Bake in a hot waffle iron.

Agatha Filush, St. Joseph, Mich.

PANCAKE SYRUP

1 cup honey
¼ teaspoon cinnamon

4 tablespoons melted butter
Pinch of nutmeg

Mix all ingredients well. Pour on pancakes and roll.

Margaret Kuzma, Homestead, Pa.

- PIROHY - DUMPLINGS -

BAKING POWDER DUMPLINGS

2 cups flour
4 slices white bread (cut in
   pieces)
2 teaspoons baking powder

1 cup lukewarm milk
1 egg
Pinch of salt

Mix ingredients together well until dough is quite thick. Let sand for 15 minutes on floured board, then drop dough into boiling water. Cover and boil for 20 minutes. (Do not uncover or mix dumplings while cooking.) After 20 minutes take out with large slitted spoon and put on clean towel to dry out. These dumplings are very light and tasty.

Anna Kolena, Chicago, Ill.

DUMPLINGS

2 cups flour
3 slices bread, cubed
1 teaspoon baking powder

¾ cup lukewarm water
1 egg
1 teaspoon salt

Sift flour, baking powder and salt. Add beaten egg. Add ¾ cup of lukewarm water and mix well with wooden spoon. Add bread. Mix well and roll into oblong dumplings or in 2 pieces if so desired. Place into boiling water, cover and cook about 10 minutes on one side; turn over and cook on the other side. Cut with string.

Mrs. Frank Lissak

STRUKLE (For Two)

2 cups all-purpose flour
1 teaspoon salt
2 eggs

Make noodle dough, let stand for 10 minutes. Roll dough and spread with filling. Roll jelly-roll fashion. Wrap in cheese cloth and drop in salted boiling water. Cook for 20 minutes. Drain, unwrap and slice ½ inch thick. Cover with buttered bread crumbs.

Filling: ½ lb. cottage cheese, 2 eggs, salt, pepper, chopped chives to taste. Buttered bread crumbs. Mix well.

Mrs. John Perko, Cleveland, Ohio

COTTAGE CHEESE BALLS

1 pound dry cottage cheese
4 whole eggs
1 pot of boiling water to cook
  cheese balls in

½ cup flour
1 teaspoon salt

Add all ingredients together and shape into small balls. Drop carefully into rapidly boiling water and cook about 10 minutes. Strain carefully. Sprinkle generously with the following: Brown ¼ pound butter. Add 3 tablespoons of cracker or bread crumbs. Salt to taste. Add more plain butter if desired. Serve hot.

Mary Timko, Munhall, Pa.

COTTAGE CHEESE DUMPLINGS

DOUGH
2 cups flour
2 whole eggs
Warm water

2 whole eggs, beaten
1 pint dry cottage cheese
Butter and salt
½ pint sour cream

Combine flour, 2 eggs and enough warm water to make a soft dough. Turn out on a board an knead until dough is elastic and not sticky. Cut dough into two parts and roll out half at a time on a board until the thickness of pie dough. Cut into pieces about 2 or 2½ inches square. On each put a teaspoonful of filling made by combining the cottage cheese, beaten eggs and salt. Fold over the square in half or triangle shape and pinch edges together tightly. Drop into large kettle containing 3 quarts of boiling salted water. Let simmer slowly 15 to 20 minutes, stirring occasionally with wooden spoon. It is not, necessary to keep kettle covered. Drain well. Add dabs of butter and ½ pint sour cream over dumplings and serve. Makes 40 dumplings.

Martha Weissmann

FARINA DUMPLINGS

1 cup milk or water
1 teaspoon butter
1½ teaspoons salt

½ cup farina
2 eggs
Pepper to taste

Scald milk in double boiler, or boil water, add butter. Slowly add farina, stirring until thick and smooth. Cover and cook 15 minutes. Cool and then add well beaten eggs. Mix well and add salt and pepper. Form into small balls, drop into boiling salted water or soup stock 15 minutes before serving. Serve with meat stew or gravy. Buttered crumbs, or very small croutons buttered, may be sprinkled over dumplings when served as a substitute for potatoes.

Margaret Czabala, Chicago, Ill.

POTATO DUMPLINGS

2 cups mashed potatoes
1 tablespoon butter
1 tablespoon finely chopped onion
1 egg

¾ cup flour, sifted
1¼ teaspoons salt
Dash of pepper
1 cup bread cubes, ¼ inch thick browned in butter or bacon fat

Into warm mashed potatoes add butter and allow to cool. Then add egg, onion, flour, salt and pepper and blend well. Make into 12 balls about the size of an egg, forming each ball around 4 or 5 cubes of the fried cubed bread. Place in gently boiling (salted) water and cover pan. Cook dumplings for 7 minutes. Lift dumplings with strainer, place on a large platter, sprinkle with fine bread crumbs that have been buttered. These dumplings are fine with a brown gravy.

Esther Ann Haydu, Braddock, Pa.

POTATO DUMPLINGS (Repne Halušky)

2 medium potatoes
1 egg

1 teaspoon salt
About 2 cups flour

Grate potatoes, add salt, egg and flour. Mix well. If dough is too stiff add a little water (¼ cup more or less). Drop small portions from tip of spoon into boiling water. Cook from 7 to 10 minutes. Drain. Rinse with cold water. Serve with cottage cheese or cabbage.

Cottage cheese is prepared by browning ¼ cup butter, and pouring over the dumplings. Crumble dry cottage cheese over the buttered dumplings and add salt. Mix well together and serve.

Cabbage is prepared by chopping one small onion, browned in fat or drippings, add finely chopped head cabbage with seasoning of salt and sweet paprika. Fry slowly covered until done, about 20 minutes. Add dumplings and mix well. Serve while hot.

Agnes Dvorscak, Whiting, Ind.

POTATO CAKE

5 potatoes	½ pound prunes
1 onion	3 tablespoons flour
2 eggs	Salt and pepper

Grate potatoes and onion, add eggs, chopped prunes, flour, salt, and pepper. Mix well. Put in greased pan 9x10x2. Bake in 350°F oven 15 minutes. Rub shortening on top and put back in oven to bake one hour longer. When baked, cut in squares and pour over fried browned butter. This is excellent served with bean soup.

Veronica Gluvna, Lorain, Oh.

FRUIT FILLED DUMPLINGS *(Cherries, Peaches, Prunes, etc.)*

1 pound cottage cheese or Philadelphia cream cheese
¼ pound butter (if sweet butter is used add ¼ teaspoon salt)
4 whole eggs, slightly beaten
2 tablespoons farina
Flour, enough to make a soft dough

Combine and mix cheese and butter. Add eggs, farina and flour, mix well. Cut or pinch off even sized pieces of dough, about the size of an egg, pat or roll to about ¼ inch thickness. Place fruit in the center, seal edges to keep in filling during cooking. Drop into boiling water, cover pan closely and boil about 10 minutes. Drain well. Pour over browned butter, or sprinkle with buttered bread crumbs, or nuts.

Helen Kocan, Whiting, Ind.

PIROHY

1 cup flour	About 4 tablespoons cold water
1 egg	Brown melted butter and pour
¼ teaspoon salt	over pirohy when served

Mix all ingredients with enough water to make a medium soft dough. Knead well, then roll out until thin. Cut in squares to make 50 pirohy. Place on each square 1 teaspoon filling. Fold in half to make triangles. Pinch edges well to keep filling from escaping. Drop in salted water and cook until all pirohy rise to the top of the water. Then cook for 5 minutes longer. When done, pour a small amount of cold water and strain. Place in serving dish and pour over butter that has been melted and slightly browned. Eat while hot, and if desired, add more salt. Pirohy may be spread carefully on bread board after draining, to allow them to dry a bit. Then place on serving dish and you will find them less soggy.

CHEESE FILLING FOR PIROHY

½ cup dry cottage cheese　　**1 teaspoon butter**
1 egg yolk　　**Pinch of salt**

Combine ingredients and mix thoroughly.

POTATO FILLING

One large potato cooked and mashed. Add one tablespoon melted, browned butter and salt to taste. A few dry crushed peppermint leaves may be added. However, this is optional.

CABBAGE FILLING

One pound head of cabbage chopped fine, to which add 1 teaspoon salt and set aside to stand for several minutes. Then squeeze out water from cabbage and fry in one tablespoon butter that has been allowed to brown. Add one teaspoon sugar, and stir occasionally to keep from burning. Fry until golden brown. Chopped cooked prunes or lekvar can be used.

Sophie Gresko, Whiting, Ind.

DEEP FAT FRYING

Fats and oils for deep fat frying should have high smoking temperatures. Bland lard, vegetable fats, oils, including peanut oil may be used.

Do not use butter, margarines, drippings or other lards, as they smoke at lower temperature.

Always put enough fat into a kettle to submerge the articles to be fried. Do not fill the kettle more than three quarters full of fat. This is to prevent bubbling over the fat causing a fire.

Always heat the fat gradually to the desired temperature, never allow the fat to reach a smoking point. Then add the foods to be fried in moderate amounts at one time. This will prevent boiling over.

Fat may be clarified after each use by dropping into it several pieces of raw potato. Gradually heat the fat and drop the potato into it. When browned, strain the fat through several thicknesses of cheese cloth placed over a strainer. Cool, cover and set or store in a cool place. Use over and over again.

BISMARCKS

6 cups flour	**1 cup milk, scalded and cooled**
4 eggs	**1 cake yeast, dissolved in milk**
½ cup sugar	**½ teaspoon salt**
1 cup sweet cream	

Sift flour, sugar and salt. Work eggs, cream, dissolve yeast in milk, and mix. Beat well for about 20 minutes. Place dough in a large bowl or kettle and put in a warm place, so it can rise in two hours. Then put dough on a floured board and cut into four balls or pieces. Cover the pieces and let stand for 15 minutes. One by one roll out and form thick patties into which you put either jelly or other jams and make round balls. Have about 3 pounds of heated lard or shortening and deep fat fry until bismarcks are medium brown. When drained and cooled, dust with powdered sugar.

Veronica Radocha, Coaldale, Pa.

CRULLERS *(Fanky or Božie Milosti)*

4 cups flour, sifted	**½ teaspoon salt**
4 eggs, beaten	**1 small glass of rum or**
2 tablespoons butter, melted	**1 teaspoon vanilla**
½ cup sugar	**½ cup sweet cream**
4 teaspoons baking powder	

Mix these ingredients together real well, and make a thin dough. Cut into squares or triangles and make a slit in the center and pull one end thru this slit. Deep fry these in hot shortening until delicately browned. When done and drained, sprinkle with powdered sugar.

Martina Gerek, Lorain, Oh.

CRULLERS *(Čeregi)*

3 cups flour	**8 tablespoons sugar**
½ cup crisco	**3 teaspoons baking powder**
¼ teaspoon salt	**3 eggs**
6 tablespoons orange juice	

Work all these ingredients as for pie crust. Add three eggs and six tablespoons orange juice and knead as for noodle dough. Roll out to ¼ inch thickness. Cut into squares and make a slit through the center from corner to corner and pull one end of square through the center. Fry in deep hot fat. Sprinkle with powdered sugar.

Mrs. Joseph Hritz, Phoenixville, Pa.

CRULLERS *(Čeregi)*

½ pint sour cream
1 can milk
6 beaten eggs
1 teaspoon salt
½ cup sugar

½ teaspoon baking soda
3 teaspoons baking powder
2 teaspoons vanilla
Butter, big as a walnut
Flour, enough to make soft dough

Roll out dough about ⅛ inch thick, cut dough in small squares, make a cut with knife in center and draw one end of square through this to make a bow. Fry in deep fat. Drain and dust with powdered sugar.

Mary A. Bosko, Homestead, Pa.

CRULLERS *(Čeregi)*

1½ pounds flour
3 whole eggs
6 ounces sweet butter

1 tablespoon vanilla or rum
1 teaspoon salt
¾ cup milk

Combine flour and butter and mix as for pie crust. Add eggs, vanilla or rum, salt and milk. Blend well. Roll out very thin. Cut in squares and fry in deep fat until golden color. When done, sprinkle with powdered sugar.

Sophie Kaminsky, Whiting, Ind.

SOUR CREAM CRULLERS

1 cup sugar
2 eggs
1 teaspoon baking soda
3½ cups flour

1 cup sour cream
2 tablespoons butter
Pinch of Salt

Cream butter and sugar. Add beaten eggs. Mix well. Mix soda and salt in sour cream. Add flour and cream alternately to egg mixture. Roll out on floured board. Cut with doughnut cutter and fry in deep fat. Dust with powdered sugar.

Margaret Kuzma, Homestead, Pa.

CRULLERS *(Listy or Fanky)*

6 egg yolks
6 tablespoons canned milk

1 tablespoon powdered sugar
Flour to make soft dough

Beat yolks until light then add canned milk and beat until blended, then add powdered sugar and keep adding flour until dough is soft. Cut into three pieces and roll out as for noodles, cut in triangles and fry in hot fat until light brown. When cool sprinkle with powdered sugar.

Ann Bronersky, Chicago, Ill.

APPLE FRITTERS

1 cup sifted flour
1¼ teaspoons baking powder
¼ teaspoon salt
1 egg, beaten
⅓ cup milk
2 teaspoons melted shortening

2 large apples, pared and sliced
1 tablespoon lemon juice
¼ teaspoon nutmeg
½ teaspoon cinnamon
2 tablespoons sugar

Sift flour, baking powder and salt together. Combine egg, milk and shortening. Stir liquid into dry ingredients. Sprinkle apple slices with lemon juice, spices and sugar. Dip apples in batter and fry in deep fat 360 to 370°F about five minutes or until brown. Variation: cooked prunes can also be added.

Florence Lenard, Hammond, Ind.

CORN FRITTERS

1 cup corn pulp
1 egg
¼ cup flour, little salt and sugar

Grate corn from cob, or use canned corn. Add egg, flour and seasoning. Mix till it forms a nice smooth batter. Drop by spoonfuls into hot fat and fry on one side, then turn on the other side and fry till golden brown. You can fry this batter on a hot griddle.

Mary V. Haydu, Braddock, Pa.

FRITTERS

1 cup flour
½ teaspoon salt

⅔ cup milk
2 eggs

Mix flour and salt. Add milk gradually, and well beaten eggs. This may be used as a foundation for all fritters. One tablespoon sugar should be added if fruits are used.

Anna B. Russell, Cleveland, Oh.

RASPBERRY ROSSETTES

½ teaspoon salt
¾ cup flour
1 slightly beaten egg

Powdered sugar
Jam

Add salt and flour to egg and make stiff dough. Knead well and roll very thin on floured board. Cover with towel for 20 minutes. Cut circles in three sizes. Stack circles in piles of three, with smallest on top. Pinch center. Fry delicate brown in deep fat. Drain on absorbent paper. Roll in powdered sugar and place jam in center.

Bernadette Evans, Homestead, Pa.

CRISPETTES

1 sifter full of flour
4 eggs, separated
1 pint sour cream
1 cup sugar

¾ pound of butter or shortening
½ small glass of wine
1 teaspoon baking soda

Mix flour and baking soda and sugar together. Add butter and mix like for pie crust. Add eggs, cream and wine. Roll out, cut diamond shape and fry in deep fat.

Mary Molson, Whiting, Ind.

DOUGHNUTS

4 pounds flour
2 teaspoons baking powder
¼ pound butter
1 quart milk
6 eggs

1 cup sugar
½ teaspoon salt
¾ pound lard
1 cake yeast
1 pound cooked potatoes, mashed

Sift dry ingredients into a bowl and work in the butter and lard, as for pie dough. Scald the milk and allow to cool, add well beaten eggs and when lukewarm add yeast. Then work this liquid mixture gradually into dry ingredients. Knead until elastic and place in a greased bowl. Let rise until double in bulk. Keep in a warm place while rising. Roll half inch thick and cut out rounds for doughnuts. Let stand one hour. Fry in hot fat, until browned on both sides. Drain, then roll in powdered or granulated sugar. This dough may be stored in refrigerator over night. It may be used for poppy seed rolls as well as for doughnuts.

Barbara Bires, Pittsburgh, Pa.

DOUGHNUTS

2 eggs
1 cup sugar
4 to 5 cups flour
4 teaspoons baking powder

1 teaspoon salt
1 cup milk
1 teaspoon vanilla
1 tablespoon butter

Beat eggs very light, continue beating, while adding sugar. Sift dry ingredients and add alternately with the milk. Add flavoring, melted butter, beat hard. Add more flour to make a dough as soft as can be handled. Roll, cut out and fry in deep fat, three minutes. Temperature of fat 380°F. Makes 36.

Anna B. Russell, Cleveland, Oh.

RAISED DOUGHNUTS

1 cake yeast	**1¼ cups milk**
3½ cups sifted flour	**¼ cup shortening**
½ cup sugar	**1 teaspoon salt**
1 egg	

Dissolve yeast in lukewarm milk, add 1½ cups flour, beat until smooth. Let rise in a warm place. Work your shortening into the remaining flour (2 cups) to which sugar and salt have been added. Stir into a yeast sponge, add beaten egg, knead thoroughly, let rise in a warm place until double in bulk.

Roll about ¾ inch thick, cut with doughnut cutter. Place on a floured board, leaving enough space between doughnuts and let rise until double in size. Fry in deep fat.

Sprinkle or dip into granulated sugar. Makes two dozen doughnuts.

Ella D. Vlasaty, Braddock, Pa.

SOUR CREAM DOUGHNUTS

1 cup sour cream	**½ teaspoon nutmeg or cinnamon**
1 cup buttermilk	**1½ teaspoons baking soda**
2 eggs	**4½ cups flour**
1 teaspoon salt	**2 pounds lard or crisco**
1 cup sugar	

Beat eggs, add sugar to blend well. Add sour cream and buttermilk and mix. Add sifted dry ingredients a little at a time. Dough will be thick. Put on floured bread board and roll about half inch thick. Cut with doughnut cutter and let stand till you prepare shortening. Heat about two pounds of lard or other shortening till hot. Drop doughnuts into hot fat and fry till brown, then brown on other side, take and place on paper toweling to drain excess fat.

Millie Bandor, Fort Worth, Texas

RAISED DOUGHNUTS *(Pankuški)*

1 large can evaporated milk, scald	**1 teaspoon salt**
3 tablespoons sugar	**¼ pound softened butter**
1 cake yeast	**4 cups flour**
3 egg yolks	**1 teaspoon vanilla**

Add scalded milk to salt, sugar and butter. When lukewarm add crumbled yeast, also two cups flour and mix well. Allow to stand until light and spongy, about one hour. Add yolks, vanilla and remainder of flour, mixing thoroughly. Let rise until double in bulk about 1½ or two hours. Then roll out, cut out with doughnut cutter and let rise for half hour before frying. Deep fry with raised side down first. Especially good when sprinkled with granulated sugar and cinnamon.

Mrs. Druso, Bedford, Oh.

POTATO DOUGHNUTS

6 medium size potatoes, boiled	Add pinch of salt to potatoes
2 cups sugar	⅓ cup butter
3 eggs	1 cup sweet milk
5 teaspoons baking powder	6 cups flour

To mix, mash the potatoes, add butter and sugar, mix while hot or warm. Add eggs, milk and flour, to which baking powder has been added and sifted through.

Mix all together well with as little handling as possible. Fry in deep hot fat. Few spices may be added for tasty flavor. (These are very good).

Mary Janovcik, Cleveland, Oh.

CHEESE CROQUETTES

½ cup soft cheese	2 egg yolks
2 tablespoons fat	1 egg, white
2 tablespoons flour	¼ teaspoon salt
½ cup milk	¼ teaspoon paprika
Crumbs	

Make a white sauce, using fat, flour and milk. Add slightly beaten egg yolks, the cheese (cut in small bits) and the seasoning. Stir until cheese is melted. Allow mixture to cool, then shape, roll in crumbs, then in egg white which has been diluted with 1 tablespoon water. Put in crumbs again and fry in deep fat 375°F to 390°F until lightly brown.

Veronica Radoch, Coaldale, Pa.

DOUGHNUTS *(Pirosky)*

½ cup lukewarm milk   1 small cake yeast
1 teaspoon sugar

Combine above ingredients and allow to stand for 5 minutes, or until yeast rises.

Place 6 cups sifted flour in bowl. Make a depression in center and pour raised yeast mixture, stir lightly with a spoon. Do not mix the entire amount of flour with the yeast. Set aside in a warm place to rise. Prepare following and add to first mixture:

2 cups lukewarm milk   1 teaspoon vanilla
½ cup sugar   4 egg yolks
2 teaspoons salt

Combine milk, sugar, salt, vanilla and beaten yolks. Beat well and add to yeast mixture. Mix thoroughly and knead until smooth. Then pour ¼ pound melted butter and knead well until dough leaves sides of pan and hands. Cover with clean towel and let rise. Knead dough again and let rise second time. Roll dough on a floured board about ¾ inch thick, then cut with doughnut cutter and let rise. Fry in pan of hot shortening, drain well when brown and sprinkle with powdered sugar. Yield: 36 doughnuts.

Anna Lissy, Whiting, Ind.

Cakes, Frostings
& Fillings

- CAKES FOR OCCASIONS -

ANNIVERSARY CAKE

3 cups sifted cake flour
1 teaspoon salt
3 teaspoons baking powder
½ cup shortening
1½ cups sugar

½ teaspoon lemon flavoring
½ teaspoon rose flavoring
4 egg whites
1¼ cups milk

Sift flour before measuring, then sift three times with baking powder and salt. Cream shortening, sugar and flavorings together for about three minutes. Beat egg whites for about one minute, or until moist peaks form. Add dry ingredients to shortening mixture alternately with milk while beating at low speed for 7 minutes. Add beaten whites and continue beating for one minute. Bake at 350°F for 30 to 35 minutes in greased, waxed paper lined pans. Smaller pans require slightly less baking time.

It takes three times this amount of ingredients for the entire cake. Bake the first two mixtures in two 10x14 inch pans for the foundation layer. Bake the third mixture in an 8x10 inch pan.

BUTTER CREAM ICING

4 egg whites
2 cups granulated sugar
6 tablespoons cold water
¼ teaspoon cream of tartar

1 pound butter (preferably
  unsalted)
2 teaspoons vanilla

Combine egg whites, sugar, water and cream of tartar in upper part of double boiler. Place over boiling water, remove from heat, and beat 8 minutes, until thick and light. Cover with damp cloth and allow to cool. Beat butter, which has softened to room temperature, until creamy. Add cooled egg white mixture to butter a little at a time, beating well. Stir in vanilla. Tint small portion of the icing with rose food coloring for the border and the roses.

Mary Vevurka, Chicago, Ill.

ATLANTA LANE CAKE

1 cup butter or margarine
2 cups sugar
3¼ cups sifted cake flour
2 teaspoons double acting baking
  powder
1 cup milk
1 teaspoon vanilla
8 egg whites, stiffly beaten

Filling:
½ cup butter or margarine
1 cup sugar
8 egg yolks
1 teaspoon vanilla, brandy or rum
  extract
1 cup seeded raisins
1 cup chopped pecans

Cream together the butter and sugar until light and fluffy. Sift together the dry ingredients and add alternately with milk and vanilla. Beat well. Fold in egg whites. Pour into 3 round 8-inch paper-lined cake pans (or two 9-inch pans). Bake in moderate oven (375°F) for 25 to 30 minutes.

Filling: Cream butter and sugar. Add beaten egg yolks and cook over hot water until thick, 15 to 20 minutes. Add remaining ingredients. Cool. Spread between layers of cake. If filling is not stiff enough after cooking, reheat over direct heat and stir until thick.

ICING FOR LANE CAKE

2½ cups sugar
⅛ teaspoon salt
⅓ cup dark corn syrup

⅔ cup water
2 egg whites
1 teaspoon vanilla

Dissolve sugar, salt and syrup in the water. Heat. Beat egg whites until foamy. When syrup reaches boiling point, pour 3 tablespoons into egg whites. Continue beating eggs until stiff but not dry. Boil syrup mixture to 240°F or until it spins a thread, at least 10 inches long, then pour over egg whites, beating until the frosting begins to lose its gloss and begins to hold its shape. Add vanilla. Spread over cake.

If the frosting becomes hard, add a drop or two of hot water to the mixture. This frosting does not form a crust which cracks when cutting the cake.

Courtesy of Swift & Company, Chicago, Ill.

BRIDE'S CAKE

5 cups sifted cake flour
4 teaspoons baking powder
½ teaspoon salt
1 cup butter, or margarine

4 cups sugar
¾ teaspoon vanilla
2 cups milk
10 egg whites

Cream butter until smooth, add sugar and cream until fluffy. Add vanilla. Sift flour, baking powder and salt three times; add alternately with milk to the butter mixture. Beat well until smooth. Fold in stiffly beaten egg whites. Pour batter into three graduated layer cake pans, (sizes 6, 9 and 12 inches). Fill pans about half full. Bake at 350°F for 30 to 40 minutes. Put together with frosting, pyramid fashion.

Maria Proskac, Coaldale, Pa.

WHITE WEDDING CAKE

5 pounds cake flour
2½ pounds crisco
6 pounds sugar
2 ounces salt

5 ounces baking powder
3¾ pounds egg whites
8 ounces vanilla
1¾ quarts milk

Place the first six ingredients into a large bowl and beat 7 minutes at medium speed. Add vanilla and milk in three additions, continue beating for 3 minutes at low speed. Do not over beat this cake. Complete beating time is 15 minutes, or 10 to 12 minutes in an average mixer.

Size of pans and amount of dough in each is as follows: 6-inch-½ pound; 8-inch- ¾ pound; 10-inch-1½ pounds. Make 3 pans of each size for each tier. Total amount of dough 8¼ pounds.

For a larger wedding cake, use following sizes of pans: 8-inch-¾ pound; 10-inch-1½ pounds; 12-inch-2 pounds. Total amount of dough-12¾ pounds. Bake at 370 to 375°F for 25 to 40 minutes, according to size of cake.

Trim layers to make them even on all sides. Cut edges with shears. Filling is optional. Use buttercream if desired. Fondant icing, or ½ butter and shortening and fondant will keep cake together. Place a round cake card board on bottom of each tier. Place each tier in refrigerator separately for at least six hours before putting together, so the center of the cake will hold up. While the cake is chilling in the refrigerator, make a buttercream frosting, by adding powdered sugar to fondant. Put tiers together, one on top of the other. Frost with butter cream frosting. Decorate with flowers, roses or carnations made out of icing. (Before putting the tiers together, spread second coating of butter cream frosting on each layer with a spatula.)

Martin J. Thinschmidt, Fond du Lac, Wi.

YELLOW WEDDING CAKE

5 pounds cake flour	8 ounces milk
2½ pounds Crisco	2 quarts egg yolks
6 pounds sugar	8 ounces vanilla
5 ounces baking powder	1¾ quarts milk
2 ounces salt	

Place the first 7 ingredients into a large bowl and cream for 7 minutes at medium speed. Add vanilla and milk in 3 additions and continue to beat at low speed for 3 minutes. Follow directions for the white wedding cake for baking and temperature. Use same size baking tins.

Martin J. Thinschmidt, Fond du Lac, Wi.

PARTY CAKE

½ cup butter	1 tablespoon cocoa sifted with flour
2 cups brown sugar (loosely packed)	1 cup sour milk
2 eggs	1 teaspoon soda
2 cups all purpose flour, sifted 3 times before measuring	1 teaspoon vanilla if sweet butter is used, add ¼ teaspoon salt

Cream well butter and sugar, use No. 1 speed on electric mixer. Add eggs, one at a time. Gradually add sifted dry ingredients alternately with the milk.

Add flavoring. Pour into a buttered loaf pan, or into 2 layer cake pans. Place in preheated moderate oven 350°F. Bake loaf cake for about 30 to 35 minutes, and the layers bake about 25 minutes in same moderate oven.

When cake has cooled, frost the loaf cake with a mocha or lemon frosting and decorate with walnut meats.

The filling for the layer cake is made by cooking 1 package Butterscotch Jello Pudding. When cool, spread between layers and top with mocha frosting and sprinkle with nuts.

Anna Krcha, Chicago, Ill.

- BUTTER CAKES -

APPLESAUCE CAKE

½ cup shortening
1 cup brown sugar
1 egg
1 cup thick, tart unsweetened
   applesauce
1¾ cups sifted flour

1 teaspoon baking soda
½ teaspoon cinnamon
½ teaspoon cloves
¼ teaspoon nutmeg
½ teaspoon salt

Beat shortening and sugar until fluffy; add egg, beat well; add applesauce. Mix the flour with the soda, spices and salt and add to applesauce mixture. Blend well, pour into greased loaf or 10x5x3 pan, bake in moderate oven 350°F about 60 minutes. Good served with Vanilla Sauce page 77.

Maria Proskac, Coaldale, Pa.

BANANA CAKE

2 cups cake flour
2 teaspoons baking powder
1 teaspoon baking soda
½ teaspoon salt
½ cup spry or margarine
1 cup sugar

2 eggs, well beaten
1 teaspoon vanilla
½ cup milk
3 medium sized bananas, mashed
½ cup chopped walnuts

Sift dry ingredients, cream shortening, add sugar, beat until light and fluffy. Add eggs, vanilla, beat again until fluffy. Add dry ingredients alternately with milk, blend, add bananas and nuts. Blend. Pour into 8 or 9 inch pans. Bake 350°F for 25 to 30 minutes. Put layers together with Crisco frosting, add ½ banana mashed. Frost cake with plain Crisco frosting.

Mrs. Tony Brenkus, Whiting, Ind.

BANANA CAKE

1½ cups sugar
½ cup shortening
1 egg
1 egg yolk
2 cups cake flour
1 teaspoon baking powder

1 teaspoon baking soda
½ teaspoon salt
1 cup mashed bananas
¾ cup sour milk or buttermilk
1 teaspoon vanilla

Cream shortening and sugar, add egg and egg yolk. Add sifted flour, baking powder, soda and salt. Add bananas, sour milk and vanilla. Bake at 375°F about ½ hour. Use left over egg white for frosting.

Mary Beno, Cleveland, Oh.

BANANA SPICE CAKE

2½ cups sifted cake flour
1¼ cups sugar
1 teaspoon salt
1 teaspoon cinnamon
½ teaspoon cloves
½ teaspoon nutmeg
½ teaspoon all spice
½ teaspoon baking soda

2½ teaspoons double acting
  baking powder
⅔ cup crisco
⅓ cup molasses
⅔ cup mashed bananas
3 eggs
½ cup milk

Sift together all dry ingredients into large mixing bowl. Drop in shortening, eggs and ½ cup bananas. Beat 2 minutes with electric mixer at low speed. Add remaining mashed bananas, vanilla; beat 1 minute longer. Add milk, blend. Pour into pans, bake at 375°F about 30 minutes.

Josephine Ferencik, Joliet, Ill.

BOSTON CREAM PIE

¼ teaspoon salt
2 cups sifted cake flour
3 teaspoons baking powder
1 egg, lightly beaten

⅓ cup shortening
1 cup sugar
⅔ cup milk

Sift the flour and baking powder with ¼ teaspoon salt. Cream the sugar and shortening, add egg and blend; add flour and milk alternately. Pour into 2 greased cake tins and bake in moderate oven 375°F for about 25 minutes.

FILLING

⅔ cup sugar
½ cup flour
½ cup heavy cream whipped
Pinch of salt

1 teaspoon vanilla
2 cups milk, scalded
4 egg yolks

Combine the sugar and flour and slowly add the scalded milk. Cook in top of double boiler until thick and creamy. Cover and cook 10 minutes longer. Beat the egg yolks and add a little of the hot mixture to them. Pour back into mixture. Add a pinch of salt. Cook over hot (not boiling) water about 2 minutes. Cool. Whip cream and add vanilla. Fold into custard. Chill and spread between layers. Dust with powdered sugar. To serve, cut into pie shape pieces.

Marie Proskac, Coaldale, Pa.

BUTTERMILK CAKE

1 cup shortening
2 cups sugar
4 egg yolks
3 cups flour
1 teaspoon cream of tartar
1 teaspoon baking soda
1 cup buttermilk
4 egg whites, stiffly beaten

TOPPING:
3 tablespoon butter
½ cup brown sugar
1 cup chopped nuts or coconut
3 tablespoons cream

Cream shortening, add sugar and beat until light. Add egg yolks, one at a time, and beat until fluffy. Sift the dry ingredients and add alternately with the milk. Fold in stiffly beaten egg whites. Pour into a greased pan 9x13 inches. Bake at 350°F for 50 minutes. Remove from oven and spread with topping. Put under broiler about 3 inches from unit for 1 or 2 minutes.

Topping: Melt butter, add brown sugar and nuts. Add cream and mix well. (This cake is delicious and stays moist for days.) This cake may be made in layers and spread with favorite frosting.

Leona Zientara, Whiting, Ind.

BUTTERMILK NUTMEG CAKE

½ cup butter or margarine
1½ cups sugar
3 eggs beaten
2 cups flour
¼ teaspoon salt

1 teaspoon baking powder
¼ teaspoon baking soda
2 teaspoons nutmeg
1 cup buttermilk

Cream shortening and sugar, add well beaten eggs. Sift the dry ingredients and add with buttermilk a little at a time. Mix well. Bake in two 9-inch layer or 9x9x2 pans. Sprinkle with sugar and nutmeg. Bake in a 350°F oven for 35 minutes.

Mary Chromcik, Whiting, Ind.

BUTTERMILK SPICE CAKE

⅔ cup shortening
1½ cups sugar
3 eggs
3 teaspoons baking powder
¾ teaspoon soda
¼ teaspoon salt

2¼ teaspoons cinnamon
½ teaspoon cloves
½ teaspoon nutmeg
1 cup, plus 2 tablespoons
   buttermilk
2 cups cake flour

Cream shortening, add sugar slowly, cream well with the egg yolks. Mix and sift flour, soda, salt and spices; add to the first mixture alternately with buttermilk. Fold in the stiffly beaten egg whites. Bake in 3 greased 8 inch layer cake pans at 375°F for 25 minutes. Spread with your favorite filling and frost with a good boiled icing.

Anna B. Hopko, Braddock, Pa.

CARROT CAKE

3 cups flour, sifted
2 teaspoons soda
2 teaspoons baking powder

2 teaspoons cinnamon
1 teaspoon salt

All ingredients level...sift together into a large bowl.

1¼ cups Wesson oil
1½ cups sugar
4 eggs

2 cups grated carrots
½ cup chopped walnuts or
   pecans or raisins

Into a second bowl mix thoroughly the oil and sugar. Add the grated carrots in small amounts, alternating with the addition of one egg at a time. Mix thoroughly after each egg added. When carrots and eggs have been well mixed, then add the nuts or the raisins. Or a combination of both nuts and raisins may be used. Then gradually add the dry ingredients and mix thoroughly. Pour into a lightly greased tube pan and bake in a moderate oven 350°F for one hour. At end of baking time test for doneness, if cake is firm on top, it is baked, if not, then return to oven for another five or six minutes. Usually when both nuts and raisins are used the baking time is longer.

Frosting: One Philadelphia cream cheese with 1½ cups to 2 cups of powdered sugar, and 1 teaspoon cream or enough for spreading. Flavoring or coloring is optional.

Mary Chromcik, Whiting, Ind.

CARAWAY SEED CAKE

½ cup butter or margarine
¾ cup sugar
3 eggs, well beaten
¼ cup milk
2 teaspoons baking powder

⅓ teaspoon salt
2 teaspoons caraway seeds
1½ cups cake flour
½ cup chopped citron, optional

Cream the shortening and sugar until light, gradually add the eggs. Add milk and caraway seeds, also the citron, if used and last the sifted flour, salt and baking powder. Beat thoroughly and pour into a small loaf cake pan, which has been thoroughly greased. Bake for 30 to 40 minutes at 350°F, no frosting.

Justine Kasovsky, Chicago, Ill.

CHOCOLATE CAKE

Make Custard of:
1 egg
½ cup sugar
½ cup milk
¼ cup powdered sweetened chocolate

Boil until mixture has the consistency of gravy and let cool.
½ cup butter
1 cup brown sugar
2 eggs
½ cup milk
2 cups flour
Pinch of salt
2 teaspoons baking powder
1 teaspoon vanilla

Cream butter and sugar, add eggs and mix well. Add milk. Sift dry ingredients 5 times and add to batter. Add this mixture to the custard. Add 1 teaspoon soda dissolved in small amount of water and vanilla. Pour into three 8-inch layer pans. Bake for 25 minutes at 350°F. Frost with Mocha icing.

MOCHA ICING
1 cup powdered sugar
4 tablespoons cocoa
2 tablespoons butter
3 tablespoons hot coffee

Place sugar, cocoa and butter into bowl. Add boiling coffee slowly, beat mixture until smooth and creamy.

Mrs. Bilik, Berwyn, Ill.

APRICOT CHOCOLATE CAKE

½ cup butter
1 cup sugar
½ cup egg yolks, well beaten
1⅔ cups sifted cake flour
3 teaspoons baking powder
½ teaspoon salt
¾ cup milk
½ teaspoon vanilla

Filling:
1 cup apricot jam

Cream butter and sugar until light and fluffy. Add egg yolks and beat well. Add sifted dry ingredients alternately with milk and vanilla in thirds, beating until smooth after each addition. Spread in a greased jelly roll pan 10 x 15 inches. Bake in a moderate oven 375°F for 25 minutes. Turn out on a cake cooler. Cut cake into 4 pieces, crosswise. Split each piece in two, making 8 layers in all. Spread apricot jam between layers. Frost.

FROSTING

3 ounces cream cheese

2 tablespoons milk

2 ounces unsweetened chocolate, melted and cooled

½ teaspoon salt

2 cups sifted confectioners' sugar

Mix cheese and milk together until blended. Add remaining ingredients and beat until smooth. Ice top and sides of cake. Decorate with chopped nuts. Store in refrigerator for several hours.

Ann Bronersky, Chicago, Ill.

CHOCOLATE CAKE

Mix 4 tablespoons cocoa with ½ cup boiling water. Set aside to cool.

1½ cups sugar

⅔ cup margarine

2 eggs, well beaten

1 cup sour milk

1½ teaspoons baking soda (dissolve in sour milk)

1½ teaspoons vanilla

2 cups flour

¼ teaspoon salt

Cream shortening and sugar. Add beaten eggs and vanilla. Then gradually add 1 cup flour to mixture. Next alternate cocoa and part of flour. Add sour milk with soda, then balance of flour. Bake at 375°F until done.

Mary Fedor, Streator, Ill.

CHOCOLATE CAKE

1 cup powdered sugar

2 eggs

1¼ cups flour

2 squares chocolate, melted

½ cup butter

1 cup sour milk

1 teaspoon soda

Cream the butter and sugar, add chocolate and mix till smooth. Add beaten eggs. Add sifted dry ingredients alternately with the milk. Bake about 35 minutes at 350°F.

Juliana Simek, Johnstown, NY

CHOCOLATE CAKE

½ cup butter
1 cup sour milk
1 teaspoon baking soda
1½ cups flour
1 cup sugar

1 egg, well beaten
2 tablespoons cocoa
1 teaspoon vanilla
Few grains salt

Cream butter with sugar, add egg and beat thoroughly. Sift flour, measure, and sift with cocoa, baking soda and salt. Add alternately with milk to first mixture. Add flavoring, stir until well blended. Pour into shallow well oiled pans. Bake for 30 minutes at 375°F.

Maria Radocha, Coaldale, Pa.

CHOCOLATE FUDGE CAKE

2 tablespoons butter, melted
¾ cup sugar
½ teaspoon salt
1 cup all purpose flour
4 teaspoons cocoa (5 teaspoons
  for darker cake)

2 teaspoons baking powder
½ cup milk
½ teaspoon vanilla
½ cup chopped pecans or walnuts

Mix together melted butter, sugar and salt. Sift together baking powder, flour and cocoa. Add vanilla to the milk. Add milk and sifted dry ingredients alternately to first mixture. Add chopped nuts and stir well. Spread batter in well greased square pan.

MIX
½ cup brown sugar
½ cup granulated sugar
4 tablespoons cocoa

Sprinkle over batter, then pour 1 cup cold water over mixture and bake at 350°F about 40 minutes. Serve with whipped cream or ice cream.

Elizabeth Malatin, Whiting, Ind.

CHOCOLATE YEAST CAKE

1 cup shortening
2 cups sugar
3 eggs, separated
3 squares unsweetened chocolate
combined
½ cake yeast
¼ cup lukewarm water

2¾ cups sifted cake flour
1 teaspoon salt
1 cup milk
3 tablespoons hot water

  with 1 teaspoon baking soda
1 teaspoon vanilla

Cream shortening till smooth, add sugar gradually. Cream well. Add egg yolks and melted chocolate. Dissolve yeast in lukewarm water, add to creamed mixture and beat well. Sift together three times, flour and salt. Add alternately with milk and beat well. Add baking soda mixed with hot water. Add vanilla and beat until smooth. Fold in beaten egg whites. Pour batter into two 10-inch lined cake pans. Bake for about 45 minutes at 350°F.

Eleanore Rizzo, Cleveland, Oh.

OLD FASHIONED CHOCOLATE CAKE

½ cup shortening
1 cup sugar
½ cup brown sugar
2 well beaten eggs
1 teaspoon vanilla
3 squares chocolate

½ cup hot water
2 cups cake flour
¼ teaspoon salt
1 teaspoon soda
⅔ cup buttermilk

Cream shortening, add sugars gradually. Beat 2 eggs well, add vanilla. Melt chocolate in hot water, cool slightly and add to first mixture. Sift flour, salt and soda; add alternately with buttermilk, Pour into two 9-inch greased layer cake tins or 1 square pan. Bake in a moderate oven 25-30 minutes or until cake springs back to touch of finger.

Mary Bucz, Chicago, Ill.

BLACK MIDNIGHT DEVIL'S FOOD CAKE

½ cup shortening
1¼ cups sugar
2 large eggs
1 teaspoon soda
1½ cups all purpose flour

½ teaspoon vanilla
½ cup cocoa
1 cup coffee (hot)
½ teaspoon salt
½ teaspoon baking powder

Cream shortening and sugar until light and creamy. Add eggs, one at a time, beating after each addition, until light and fluffy. Combine cocoa and hot coffee stirring until dissolved completely. Add coffee and cocoa mixture to the creamed batter alternately with the sifted dry ingredients, stirring gently until the batter is smooth, lastly add the vanilla. Bake in two 8-inch layer pans. Grease the pans well and bake in moderate oven 350°F for 30 to 35 minutes.

Anna Domasco, Pittsburgh, Pa.

DEVIL'S FOOD CAKE

½ cup shortening
1½ cups sugar
2 eggs, separated
½ cup cocoa
2 cups sifted cake flour

1½ teaspoons baking soda
¼ teaspoon salt
1 cup sour milk, or buttermilk
1 teaspoon vanilla

Cream shortening, add sugar, little at a time and cream well. Add well beaten egg yolks; mix enough hot water to cocoa to make paste, blend well. Sift together flour, salt, baking soda and add alternately with buttermilk to the creamed mixture. Add vanilla. Blend well and pour into greased square pan. Bake at 375°F about 30 minutes.

Albina Sloboda, Coaldale, Pa.

RED DEVIL'S FOOD CAKE

1½ cups sifted cake flour
1 teaspoon soda
¼ teaspoon salt
¼ cup butter or shortening
1 cup sugar

1 egg
2 squares Baker's unsweetened
  chocolate, melted
1 cup sour milk or buttermilk
1 teaspoon vanilla

Sift the flour once, measure, add soda and salt. Sift together 3 times. Cream butter, add sugar gradually, creaming well. Add egg and beat very thoroughly, then add chocolate and blend. Add flour alternately with milk, small amount at a time. Beat after each addition until smooth, add vanilla. Bake in greased pan 8x8x2 inches at 325°F for one hour or until done. Double this recipe for layer cake. Layer cake can be baked at 350°F for 30 minutes. Have all ingredients at room temperature.

Mary Demkovich, Whiting, Ind.

RED DEVIL CHOCOLATE CAKE

½ cup shortening
1½ cups sugar
2 eggs
4 tablespoons cocoa
4 tablespoons hot coffee
1 teaspoon red coloring

2 cups flour
1 teaspoon salt
1 teaspoon soda
1 cup sour milk
1 teaspoon vanilla

Cream shortening and sugar until light. Add beaten eggs. Beat well. Mix and add cocoa, hot coffee, red coloring and soda. Add sifted flour and salt alternately with sour milk, beating after each addition until smooth. Add vanilla. Pour into two greased and waxed paper-lined pans. Bake 35 minutes at 350°F.

Mary Skurka, Whiting, Ind.

RED DEVIL'S FOOD CAKE

2 cups cake flour, sifted
1½ cups sugar
1 teaspoon soda
Pinch of salt
½ cup crisco

1 teaspoon vanilla
1 cup buttermilk
2 eggs
2 tablespoons cocoa
Red coloring

Sift flour, sugar, baking soda and salt. Add crisco, vanilla, buttermilk and eggs; beat well. Make paste with cocoa and red coloring and add to batter. Bake in layers at 350°F until cake leaves sides.

Ann Sapp, Irwin, Pa.

SOUR CREAM DEVIL'S FOOD CAKE

2 cups cake flour
1 teaspoon soda
½ teaspoon salt
⅓ cup butter or shortening
1¼ cups sugar
1 egg, unbeaten

3 squares Baker's chocolate, melted
½ cup thick sour cream
¾ cup sweet milk
1 teaspoon vanilla

Sift flour once, measure, add soda and salt and sift three times. Cream butter thoroughly and add sugar gradually, cream well. Beat in egg, then chocolate. Add ¼ of flour and beat well, then sour cream. Add remaining flour alternately with milk in small amounts, beating after each addition. Add vanilla. Bake in two greased 9-inch layer pans in moderate oven 350°F 30 minutes. Frost with peppermint icing.

Anna K. Hruskovich, Whiting, Ind.

COCOA DEVIL'S FOOD CAKE

½ cup butter
1 cup brown sugar
1 cup granulated sugar
2 eggs, separated
½ cup cocoa

½ cup water
2½ cups cake flour, sifted
1 teaspoon soda
½ teaspoon salt
1 cup buttermilk, or sour milk

Cream shortening, add sugars gradually and cream well. Add egg yolks one at a time, beating until light and fluffy after each addition. Combine cocoa and water, add to the creamed mixture. Sift flour, salt and soda, add alternately with the milk, stirring till the batter is smooth. Fold in egg whites that were beaten stiff, but not dry. Bake in two 10 inch pans for 35 minutes at 350°F. Frost as desired.

Mary V. Haydu, Braddock, Pa.

CRUMB CAKE

1 cup butter
1 cup sugar
4 eggs, unbeaten
2 cups flour, sifted

2 teaspoons baking powder
Grated rind of lemon or vanilla
  for flavor

Cream butter, add sugar, lemon rind or vanilla. Add eggs one at a time, beating well. Add flour and baking powder. Stir well. Pour batter into buttered oblong shallow pan. Bake for ½ hour at 350°F. Remove from oven, spread a little unbeaten white of egg over the top and cover with crumb mixture.

CRUMB MIXTURE

2 tablespoons flour
2 tablespoons butter

4 tablespoons sugar
½ teaspoon cinnamon

Mix together by rubbing well with the finger tips until small crumbs are formed. Sprinkle over cake and return to oven for a few minutes.

Elizabeth Lipovsky, Bethlehem, Pa.

CREAM CAKE

½ cup butter
1 cup sugar
3 eggs
2 cups flour

2 teaspoons baking powder
⅛ teaspoon salt
1 teaspoon vanilla
½ cup milk

Cream butter and sugar well, add eggs beaten until lemon color and mix well. Then add milk and vanilla. Lastly add sifted flour, baking powder and salt. Bake in a greased and floured loaf pan in a 350°F oven for one hour.

Susan Galgan, Chicago, Ill.

DATE CAKE

1 cup sugar
Butter, size of egg
1 egg, well beaten
1½ cups flour
1 teaspoon baking powder

¼ teaspoon salt
½ cup chopped nuts
1 package pitted dates
1 cup boiling water
1 teaspoon baking soda

Mix dates, boiling water and baking soda and let stand a while. Cream butter and sugar, and well beaten egg. Mix together and stir in date mixture. Add sifted flour, baking powder and salt and mix well. Add chopped nuts, and bake at 350°F about 25 minutes. Bake in 2 nine-inch layer pans.

Helen Cross, Whiting, Ind.

DATE LOAF CAKE

1 cup dates, washed and pitted
Dissolve 1 tablespoon soda in a cup of hot water and pour over dates
  and let stand for several hours
Pinch of salt
1 cup granulated sugar
1 tablespoon butter
1 egg
1½ cups sifted flour
1 cup nut meals broken, not chopped

Mix all ingredients together, add dates last and mix thoroughly. Bake in moderate oven for 45 minutes.

Emily Bobot, Mich.

DATE NUT CAKE

1 cup sliced dates
1 cup boiling water
2 cups flour
1 teaspoon baking powder
2 eggs
1 teaspoon soda
½ teaspoon salt
½ cup shortening
1 cup brown sugar
½ cup chopped nuts
1 teaspoon vanilla

Pour boiling water over dates and let stand until cool. Cream butter and sugar, add eggs and beat well. Sift flour, baking powder and soda three times and add to mixture with dates and mix well. Add nuts and vanilla. Bake in a 8 x 9 pan in 300°F oven for 30 to 35 minutes.

Anna Kollada, Hammond, Ind.

DATE NUT LOAF

1 package dates
1 teaspoon baking soda
½ cup boiling water

Cut up dates in small pieces, mix the soda with the water, then pour over the dates. Let this cool.

1 tablespoon butter
1 cup sugar
2 eggs
1½ cups flour
1½ teaspoons baking powder
1 teaspoon vanilla extract
½ cup chopped nuts

Cream butter and sugar, and beaten eggs, sifted flour and baking powder. Then add vanilla, chopped nuts and date mixture. Bake in loaf pan for one hour at 350°F oven.

Rose Leslie, Whiting, Ind.

EASY METHOD CAKE AND FROSTING

1 cup sugar
½ cup butter or oleo
3 eggs, hold white out from 1
   for frosting
2 cups flour

2½ teaspoons baking powder
½ cup milk, combined with 1
   teaspoon vanilla
¼ teaspoon salt

Put butter and sugar into mixer, mix until blended, add remaining ingredients' in order given. Bake about 30 minutes at 350°F. If Electric roaster is used, bake at 375°F.

FROSTING

1 egg white, previously held out
1 cup sugar
¼ teaspoon cream of tartar

Put all into mixer but do not beat. Boil ½ cup of water, when water boils, start mixer and pour this water into it. Mix about 7 minutes until proper consistency for spreading. If colored frosting is desired, add 2 teaspoons of liquid coloring.

Anita Jambor, McKees Rocks, Pa.

FUNNY CAKE (PIE EFFECT)

Line a 9 to 10 inch glass pie plate with Pastry, making a high fluted rim. Then make a sauce, and let it cool while mixing the cake.

INGREDIENTS

2 cups sifted cake flour
2 teaspoons baking powder
½ teaspoon salt
1 cup sugar

½ cup crisco
1 cup milk
1 teaspoon vanilla
2 eggs, unbeaten

Sift dry ingredients. Cream crisco and sugar, add eggs and beat well. Add dry ingredients alternately with milk. Add vanilla. Beat until smooth. Pour batter into pastry-lined pie plate. Pour sauce gently over the batter. Bake in 350°F oven for 1 hour.

SAUCE

1 cup sugar
½ cup cocoa

¾ cup hot water
½ teaspoon vanilla

Combine and mix until blended.

Mrs. Hritz, Phoenixville, Pa.

GERMAN CRUMB CAKE

2 cups flour
1 cup sour milk
2 cups sugar
1 teaspoon baking soda
1 cup shortening

1 teaspoon cinnamon
1 teaspoon cloves
1 teaspoon salt
1 teaspoon nutmeg
2 whole eggs

Mix salt, sugar, shortening and flour, until mixture resembles coarse meal. Save ½ cup of this mixture for the topping, also ½ cup nuts. Add spices, well beaten eggs and sour milk with soda to the mixture. Bake in 350°F oven.

Mary Fedor, Streator, Ill.

GRAHAM CRACKER CAKE

½ cup shortening
1 cup sugar
3 egg yolks
2¼ cups sifted graham cracker
  crumbs
¼ cup sifted cake flour

3 teaspoons baking powder
½ teaspoon salt
1 cup milk
1 teaspoon vanilla
½ cup nutmeats, chopped
3 egg whites beaten

Cream shortening and sugar until mixture is light and fluffy. Add yolks, one at a time and beat thoroughly after each addition. Roll graham crackers to crumbs, sift and measure. Sift flour once, measure and resift twice with baking powder, salt and graham crackers crumbs added. Add to the batter alternating with milk, beating until smooth after each addition. Add nuts, vanilla, and blend. Beat the egg whites until stiff but not dry. Fold into cake batter, gently but thoroughly. Pour batter into two greased 9-inch layer cake pans and bake in a moderate oven 350°F for 30 minutes or until done. When cool, fill with Pineapple Filling and Sea Foam Frosting.

Kate Pempek

GRAHAM CRACKER CAKE

1 cup sugar
½ cup butter
3 eggs separated
1 cup milk

½ cup flour
23 graham crackers
2 teaspoons baking powder
1 cup chopped nuts

Cream sugar and butter, add egg yolks, milk and flour sifted with the baking powder, then graham crackers ground very fine, then walnuts and lastly egg whites beaten stiffly. Fold in slowly. Pour batter into greased two 9-inch layer pans. Bake 35 minutes in 350°F oven. You may use any frosting you wish.

Anna Bacho, Toledo, Oh.

GRAHAM CAKE

3 tablespoons butter
1 cup sugar
4 eggs separated
2 teaspoons baking powder

1 cup shredded coconut
1 cup milk (slightly warmed)
1 teaspoon vanilla
20 graham crackers

Cream butter with the sugar, add the beaten egg yolks. Crush graham crackers, add baking powder and coconut Then add warm milk and vanilla, mixing well. Beat egg whites until stiff, then fold into batter. Bake in two 9-inch layer pans. Place in a hot oven, 400°F and bake ½ hour, reducing heat gradually every 6 minutes, until temperature is 325°F.

Agnes Sorota, Whiting, Ind.

LADY BALTIMORE CAKE

2¼ cups cake flour
1½ teaspoons baking powder
½ teaspoon salt
½ cup butter

1⅓ cups sugar
1 teaspoon vanilla
⅔ cup milk
4 egg whites

Sift the flour, measure and resift 3 times with baking powder and salt. Cream butter thoroughly; add the sugar gradually and continue creaming until fluffy. Stir in the vanilla. Add sifted dry ingredients alternately with milk and beating after each addition. Fold in stiffly beaten whites. Pour into two 8-inch layer pans, lined with waxed paper. Bake at 375°F about 25 minutes. Cool in pan 5 minutes, turn onto cake racks. Make double recipe of seven-minute frosting. Take out ⅓ of the icing to another bowl and stir in the following ingredients:

12 maraschino cherries, well drained and chopped
½ cup finely chopped moist dried figs
½ cup chopped pecans.

Spread between layers of cake. Spread top and sides with rest of plain frosting.

Justine Uhlarik, Chicago, Ill.

LAMB CAKE

½ cup butter
¾ cup sugar
¼ cup milk
1¼ cups cake flour
¼ cup raisins

3 eggs
¼ teaspoon lemon extract
¼ teaspoon salt
1½ teaspoons baking powder

Directions continued on page 121.

Cream butter, add sugar and yolks and mix well, add milk and raisins. Sift flour, salt and baking powder, add to first mixture. Lastly fold in beaten egg whites and lemon extract. Pour in greased lamb form. Bake in a 350°F oven for 45 minutes. Put butter frosting on lamb and sprinkle with coconut. Use large raisins for eyes.

Mary Walovich, Chicago, Ill.

LAZY DAISY CAKE

2 eggs
1 cup sugar
1 teaspoon vanilla
1 cup sifted cake flour

1 teaspoon baking powder
⅛ teaspoon salt
2 tablespoons butter or margarine
½ cup milk

Beat eggs until light. Gradually add sugar and vanilla. Sift together flour, baking powder and salt; add gradually to the egg mixture, stirring after each addition until all flour is moistened and there are no lumps. Melt butter in saucepan and add milk, heating to lukewarm. Add this to flour mixture, stirring until smooth. Spread in square pan, 9 x 9 x 2. Bake at 350°F for 25 minutes. Spread with Lazy Daisy Frosting and place under broiler until lightly browned.

FROSTING:
8 tablespoons brown sugar
4½ tablespoons butter

3 tablespoons cream
1½ cups moist coconut

Combine all ingredients, but coconut and place over low flame to melt the soft ingredients. Stir well and add the coconut. Spread on cake as soon as it comes out of oven and place under broiler until lightly browned.

Anna K. Hruskovich, Whiting, Ind.

LEMON NUT CRUNCH CAKE

¾ cup butter
1½ cups sugar
3 eggs, well beaten
3 cups flour
3 teaspoons baking powder

½ teaspoon salt
1 cup milk
Juice and grated rind of 1 lemon
1 cup chopped nuts

Cream butter until light; gradually beat in sugar, beating until light and fluffy. Add eggs; blend well. Sift dry ingredients together and add alternately with milk to creamed mixture. Stir in lemon juice and rind. Bake in greased 10 inch tube pan. Cover bottom with nuts. Pour in batter. Bake at 375°F for 1 hour. Turn out on rack to cool.

Theresa Krasula, Chicago, Ill.

LIGHTNING CAKE

½ cup butter
½ cup sugar
4 eggs, separated
½ teaspoon salt
2 teaspoons baking powder
1 cup sifted cake flour
5 tablespoons milk
1 teaspoon vanilla

MERINGUE:
4 egg whites
½ teaspoon salt
8 tablespoons sugar
¼ teaspoon baking powder

Cream shortening with sugar. Add egg yolks and beat until well mixed. Add sifted dry ingredients alternately with milk to which the vanilla has been added. Pour into two 8-inch cake pans, which have been greased. Put meringue on top and bake at 350°F for 25 to 30 minutes.

Beat the above Meringue ingredients together until it forms stiff peaks. Spread on top of cake batter.

WHEN CAKE IS COOL, FILL WITH A CUSTARD MADE OF:

2 tablespoons flour
3 tablespoons sugar
⅛ teaspoons salt

1 cup scalded milk
2 egg yolks, beaten
1 teaspoon vanilla extract

Combine flour, sugar, and salt in top of double boiler. Add milk gradually. Continue beating until smooth and thick, about 10 minutes. Pour slowly over the beaten egg yolks, return to double boiler and cook for 2 minutes. Cool and add flavoring. Spread between the layers of cake. Two bananas may be sliced and placed on custard between the layers.

Clara Kucka, Whiting, Ind.

LOAF CAKE

2 cups sifted cake flour
¼ teaspoon salt
1 cup shortening or butter
1 cup sugar

5 eggs
1 teaspoon vanilla
¼ teaspoon orange extract

Cream shortening and sugar until fluffy. Add eggs one at a time and beat thoroughly. Then beat for 3 minutes. Add flavorings. Add sifted dry ingredients in small amounts, beating well after each addition. Bake in greased and floured loaf pan, 9x5x3, in 325°F oven, about 1½ hours.

Mary Salat, Chicago, Ill.

MARBLE CAKE

¼ pound butter
1 cup sugar
4 eggs, separated
1¾ cups sifted cake flour

3 teaspoons baking powder
3 tablespoons chocolate or cocoa
1 teaspoon vanilla
¾ cup milk

Cream butter, sugar and yolks until fluffy. Add half of flour and half of milk alternately. Add baking powder and blend well. Add remaining flour and milk gradually. Add vanilla. Fold in stiffly beaten egg whites. Pour ¾ of batter in well greased 10 x 14 pan. To the remaining ¼ of batter, mix in cocoa or chocolate. Blend well. Drop by tablespoons into the white batter. Sprinkle 1 tablespoon sugar and 2 tablespoons ground walnuts over the top. Bake 35 to 40 minutes in a 375°F oven. Cool on cake rack.

Irene Menzezoff, Long Island, N. Y.

MOLASSES CAKE

1 cup molasses
½ cup shortening
½ cup sour milk
1 teaspoon baking soda

½ teaspoon ginger
2½ cups flour
Pinch of salt

Mix in order given and bake in square baking pan or loaf pan. Bake about 35 minutes in 350°F oven.

Julianna Simek, Johnstown, NY.

FAMILY SIZE NUT CAKE

⅔ cup shortening (half butter
   for flavor)
1⅔ cups sugar
3 eggs
2⅔ cups sifted flour

2 teaspoons baking powder
1 teaspoon salt
1 cup milk
1 teaspoon vanilla
1 cup walnuts (ground fine)

Cream together until fluffy-shortening, sugar and eggs. Add sifted flour, baking powder and salt with milk and vanilla alternately. Beat well, then add ground walnuts. Pour into greased oblong pan, 13 x 9 x 2 inches. Bake 40 minutes in moderate oven, 350°F. When cool, frost with caramel icing or white icing made with:

1 egg white, vanilla and powdered sugar, add 1 teaspoon milk if necessary. Top with walnut halves.

Barbara Bires, Pittsburgh, Pa.

NUT CAKE

½ pound butter or ¼ pound butter and ¼ pound oleo margarine
½ pound flour
1½ teaspoons baking powder
½ pound sugar
2 eggs
1 teaspoon vanilla (or lemon rind)

Mix flour, butter and baking powder together like for a pie crust, add sugar, eggs and vanilla. Make a smooth dough from this and spread in a square pan.

TOP NUT FILLING

8 egg yolks	**½ pound ground walnuts**
½ pound sugar	**1 teaspoon vanilla**
8 egg whites	

Mix together well, the yolks and sugar, then add nuts. Beat egg whites and add to the above, stirring lightly. Then add vanilla, stir again lightly and spread over dough. Bake 1 hour in 350°F oven.

Eleanor G. Lissy, Whiting, Ind.

FRESH ORANGE LAYER CAKE

SIFT
2¼ cups sifted cake flour
1½ cups sugar
2 teaspoons double acting baking powder
¼ teaspoon soda
1 teaspoon salt

ADD
½ cup high grade shortening
Grated rind of one orange (about 1 teaspoon)

MEASURE
¼ cup unstrained orange juice into ¾ cup water

Add ⅔ of this liquid to dry ingredients. Beat vigorously with spoon for 2 minutes by clock (about 150 strokes per minute). Or mix with electric mixer of medium speed for 2 minutes.

ADD
Remaining liquid
⅓ to ½ cup unbeaten eggs (2 medium)

Beat 2 more minutes. Pour batter into 2 well greased and floured round layer pans 9x1½ inches deep. Bake about 30 minutes in moderate oven, 350°F.

Helen Cross, Whiting, Ind.

POPPY SEED CAKE

2 cups flour
3 teaspoons baking powder
¾ cup butter or oleo
1 teaspoon vanilla
1¼ cups sugar

Pinch of salt
4 eggs, separated
1 cup poppy seed
1 cup milk

Step 1 - Add milk to poppy seed, let stand over night or until moist. Sift flour, baking powder and salt, add with the poppy seed mixture.

Step 2 - Cream together butter, sugar, and vanilla, gradually add the beaten egg yolks.

Gradually add the step 1 mixture to step 2 mixture and beat until smooth. Fold in the stiffly beaten egg whites. Pour in two 8-inch greased cake tins or square pans. Bake for 45 minutes in 350°F oven. Top with plain or fancy frosting, according to taste.

Florence Ribovich, Hammond, Ind.

GROUND POPPY SEED BATTER CAKE

3 tablespoons crisco
1½ cups sugar
1½ cups milk
2 teaspoons vanilla
2 teaspoons baking powder

2 cups flour
¼ teaspoon salt
4 egg whites beaten
¼ pound poppy seeds

Soak poppy seed in milk over night. Cream crisco and sugar, add vanilla. Gradually add sifted flour, salt and baking powder with poppy seed and milk mixture and beat well. Fold in stiffly beaten egg whites. Use 2 nine-inch cake pans, or loaf pan. Bake at 350°F for 30 minutes. Test with toothpick or cake tester.

Agnes Thomas, Bethlehem, Pa.

POPPY SEED CAKE

1 cup shortening
1½ cups sugar
¼ pound ground poppy seed
4 egg yolks
1 teaspoon baking soda

2 cups flour
½ pint sour cream
4 egg whites
1 teaspoon vanilla

Cream shortening and sugar, add beaten yolks, sour cream, vanilla, flour, baking soda, poppy seed and lastly fold in stiffly beaten egg whites. Bake from 50 to 55 minutes in a 350°F oven.

Mary Zibrida, Chicago, Ill.

POSTUM CAKE

4 egg yolks
2 tablespoons cold water
1 cup sifted cake flour
1 cup sugar

1 teaspoon baking powder
2 tablespoons postum
4 egg whites

Beat egg yolks until light, slowly add ½ cup sugar and cold water. Then add sifted cake flour, baking powder and postum. Last, beat egg whites and ½ cup sugar until stiff and fold into mixture. Bake in two 8-inch cake pans, for 25 minutes in 350°F oven.

Mary E. Grega, Cleveland, Oh.

OLD FASHIONED POUND CAKE

1 pound butter
4 cups sifted cake flour
2 cups sugar

10 eggs separated
1 teaspoon vanilla
1 teaspoon baking powder

Cream butter, gradually work in flour until mixture is meally. Beat egg yolks, add sugar and vanilla and beat until thick and fluffy. Add first mixture gradually, beating thoroughly. Fold in stiffly beaten egg whites. Beat vigorously 5 minutes. Bake in 2 loaf pans, lined with waxed paper, in a moderately slow oven, 325°F, for 1¼ hours. Makes two loaves 8 x 4 inches.

Maria Proskach, Coaldale, Pa.

ORANGE CAKE

3 cups powdered sugar
½ cup sweet butter
6 eggs, separated
2 cups flour

1 cup orange juice from 2 large
  oranges
3 teaspoons baking powder

Cream butter and sugar, add yolks gradually, and beat until creamy, gradually add flour and orange juice alternately, stir well. Then add baking powder. Fold in beaten egg whites. Bake in two 9-inch layer cake pans, about 30 minutes in 375°F oven. When cool, frost and fill with orange frosting.

Anna Vizza, Chicago, Ill.

POUND CAKE

1 pound butter (no substitute)
2 cups sugar
9 eggs
1 teaspoon vanilla

½ teaspoon mace
4 cups sifted all purpose flour
½ teaspoon cream of tartar
½ teaspoon salt

Cream thoroughly butter and sugar, add eggs, one at a time, beat after each addition. Add vanilla and mace. Sift together flour, cream of tartar and salt, then dribble, at lower speed, the sifted ingredients, mixing until thoroughly blended. Pour batter into two greased loaf pans, lined with heavy waxed paper. Bake in slow oven, 325°F, for about 1 hour, or until toothpick is clear when inserted. Yields two loaf cakes.

SOMETIMES I ADD TO ½ OF MIXTURE:

½ **cup candied pineapple**
½ **cup citron**
½ **cup seedless raisins**

½ **cup walnuts**
½ **cup candied cherries or**
  maraschino cherries

This makes a delicious pound fruit cake.

Clara S. Matuschak, Connellsville, Pa.

POUND CAKE (OLD FASHIONED CAKE)

1 pound butter
1 pound sugar
1 pound flour
½ teaspoon mace

10 large eggs, separated
½ teaspoon baking powder
2 tablespoons whiskey
2 tablespoons water

Cream butter, then add sugar and cream well. Beat egg yolks, add to the sugar and butter. Add flour, baking powder, and mix well, then add whiskey, water and mace and mix for 10 or 15 minutes. Then add beaten egg whites and fold in slowly. Put in loaf pan lined with waxed paper and bake in 200 or 250°F oven for 1½ hours.

Frosting for Pound Cake: ¼ pound butter creamed well. Add about ⅔ box powdered sugar, mix well, add unbeaten egg white, mix. Add ½ of lemon, juice and rind, beat well. Then spread on cake.

Lydia Valencik, Chicago, Ill.

POUND CAKE

2 cups sifted cake flour
1 teaspoon baking powder
½ teaspoon salt
1 cup butter or margarine

1 cup granulated sugar
4 eggs, unbeaten
1 teaspoon vanilla
¼ cup milk

Sift together flour, salt and baking powder. Cream shortening, add sugar, add eggs, one at a time, beating after each addition, add vanilla. Add flour alternately with milk, blend well. Turn into greased loaf pan 5 x 9¼ inches and bake at 325°F for 1 hour to 1¼ hours or till done.

Icing: Cream together ½ package Philadelphia Cream Cheese, 2 tablespoons butter, and ⅛ teaspoon salt until light and fluffy. Beat in 2 to 2½ cups sifted confectioners' sugar and ½ teaspoon vanilla. Spread on cool cake.

Lillian Cherney, Chicago, Ill.

POUND CAKE

1 cup butter	¼ teaspoon mace
1 cup sugar	1 tablespoon brandy or
5 eggs, well beaten	1 teaspoon lemon extract
2 cups sifted cake flour	½ teaspoon baking powder

Cream butter thoroughly, add sugar gradually and continue beating until light and fluffy. Add well beaten eggs, then beat about 10 minutes with electric mixer at moderate speed. Blend in dry ingredients and brandy, using low speed. Pour into greased loaf pan 9½ x 5½ x 2¾ inches. Bake in preheated moderate oven, 325°F, for 1¼ hours.

Helen Kalata

PRUNE CAKE

1½ cups flour	1 teaspoon vanilla
½ cup butter	½ teaspoon cloves
1 cup sugar	1 teaspoon cinnamon
2 eggs, beaten separately	½ teaspoon nutmeg
½ cup sour cream	1 teaspoon baking soda
1 cup cooked prunes	

Cream butter with sugar, add eggs. Sift flour with soda and spices. Add to the batter; add chopped prunes, then sour cream and vanilla. If too thick, add milk, but batter will be heavy because of the prunes. Put into tube pan or square greased pan, bake at 350°F for 30 minutes or until done.

Mary Ceykovsky, Allentown, Pa.

PRUNE CAKE

1½ cups prunes, cooked	2 cups sugar
3 cups sifted cake flour	4 eggs, beaten
3 teaspoons baking powder	2 teaspoons vanilla
1 teaspoon salt	1 cup buttermilk
1 cup shortening	1 teaspoon soda
½ cup butter	

Cut cooked prunes into small pieces. Sift flour, add baking powder, salt and sift 3 times. Cream shortening and butter. Add sugar and cream until light and fluffy. Add eggs and vanilla and beat well. Dissolve soda in buttermilk and add to creamed mixture, alternately with sifted dry ingredients. Stir until smooth after each addition. Fold in prunes. Pour batter into three large layer cake pans. Bake at 350°F, 25 minutes. Frost top and sides.

Anna Sabol, Whiting, Ind.

CALIFORNIA PRUNE CAKE

1 cup chopped, cooked prunes
1 cup chopped walnuts
2 cups sifted flour
3 teaspoons baking powder
1 teaspoon salt
¼ teaspoon soda
½ cup shortening

1 cup sugar
1 teaspoon cinnamon
½ teaspoon nutmeg
¼ teaspoon cloves
2 eggs, beaten
¾ cup prune juice and milk mixed

Combine prunes and walnuts and set aside. Sift flour with next 3 ingredients. Cream together shortening, sugar and spices until fluffy. Add eggs, and continue to beat until creamy. Add flour mixture alternately with prune juice mixture, beating smooth after each addition. Stir in prunes and nuts. Pour into 8 x 8 x 2 cake pan, greased and floured. Bake at 350°F about 50 minutes. Let stand 5 to 10 minutes. Turn cake out on rack, and cool. Serve plain, or frost with 7 minute frosting which has been made with prune juice instead of water.

Florence J. Ribovich, Hammond, Ind.

PRUNE SPICE CAKE

2½ cups sifted cake flour
1 teaspoon baking powder
1 teaspoon soda
¾ teaspoon salt
¾ teaspoon cinnamon
¾ teaspoon cloves

1 cup granulated sugar
½ cup shortening
1¼ cups sour milk or buttermilk
⅔ cup brown sugar
2 eggs, unbeaten

Stir shortening just to soften. Measure dry ingredients and sift into shortening. Add brown sugar and 1 cup of the milk and mix until all flour is dampened. Then beat 2 minutes. Add eggs and remaining milk and beat 1 minute longer. Turn batter into two 9-inch layer pans. Bake in moderate oven, 375°F, 25 minutes or until done. When cool, frost with your favorite seven-minute frosting to which has been added 1 cup cooked prunes, cut in ½-inch pieces and drained. Spread between layers and on top and sides of cake.

Beatrice Pihulic, Hammond, Ind.

PRUNE AND APRICOT UPSIDE-DOWN CAKE

¼ cup butter
½ cup brown sugar
½ teaspoon lemon rind
Stewed apricot halves
Stewed prune halves
5 tablespoons shortening

⅔ cup sugar
1 egg, beaten
1 cup milk
2¼ cups flour
4 teaspoons baking powder
½ teaspoon salt

Cream butter and brown sugar, add lemon rind, spread on bottom of 8 x 8 x 2-inch pan. Arrange apricot and prune halves to form design on top of sugar mixture. Cream shortening, add sugar slowly, then egg; beat well. Add milk alternately with flour, baking powder and salt sifted together. Mix thoroughly. Pour batter carefully over fruit in pan, bake 50 minutes at 350°F. Turn onto serving platter, upside down.

Veronica Radocha, Coaldale, Pa.

SALAD DRESSING CAKE

2 cups sifted cake flour	4 tablespoons cocoa
2 teaspoons baking soda	1 cup salad dressing
Pinch of salt	1 cup cold water
1 cup sugar	1 teaspoon vanilla

Sift the dry ingredients, add salad dressing, mix well, add water and vanilla, mix well. Pour into greased floured 8 x 12 cake pan. Bake in moderate oven 350°F 45 minutes. Cool, cover with any desired icing.

Mary C. Lucas, Lakewood, Oh.

SPANISH CAKE

1½ cups sugar	2 cups flour
2 tablespoons butter	1 teaspoon baking soda
2 eggs, separated	2 teaspoons cinnamon
1 cup sour milk	1 cup chopped walnuts

Beat whites of eggs until stiff. Mix all the ingredients together and bake one hour, in loaf pan, in a moderate oven.

Mrs. A. Grapenthin, Chicago, Ill.

SPANISH CAKE

2 cups brown sugar	¾ cup butter
4 eggs (save 2 whites for icing)	2 teaspoons baking powder
1 cup sour milk	1 teaspoon baking soda
2½ cups flour	1 teaspoon vanilla

Cream butter, add sugar and well beaten eggs. Beat well and add sour milk in which soda has been dissolved. Add remaining ingredients and beat again. Pour cake batter into sheet cake pan and spread icing on cake batter before baking. Bake in 375°F oven 40 or 45 minutes. Do not fill pan too full.

Icing: To 2 egg whites beaten stiff, add 1 cup brown sugar, beat till smooth.

Katherine Dymsia, Braddock, Pa.

SPICE CAKE

½ cup butter
1½ cups sugar
3 eggs, unbeaten
1⅛ cups milk
3 tablespoons molasses
3 cups sifted flour
3 teaspoons baking powder

⅜ teaspoon ginger
⅜ teaspoon mace
⅜ teaspoon allspice
¾ teaspoon nutmeg
1 teaspoon cloves
1 teaspoon cinnamon

Sift flour once, measure, add baking powder and spices. Sift 3 times. Cream butter, add sugar gradually and cream together until fluffy, add eggs one at a time, beating well after each addition, add molasses. Add flour and milk in small amounts, beating well. Bake in 350°F oven for 25 minutes.

Anges Sabol, Whiting, Ind.

SPICE CAKE

½ cup shortening
1 cup sugar (brown or white)
2 eggs
1 cup sour milk
2 cups flour
1 teaspoon soda

½ teaspoon baking powder
1 teaspoon cinnamon
½ teaspoon allspice
1 teaspoon vanilla
1 cup each, raisins and nuts

Mix in order given by creaming butter and sugar. Add beaten eggs and rest of ingredients. When batter is ready, add the chopped raisins and nuts. (Before adding raisins and nuts, they can be mixed with a little flour.) Bake in two 8-inch greased pans at 350°F oven for 25 minutes.

Julianna Simek, Johnstown, NY.

STRAWBERRY SHORTCAKE

2 cups flour
4 teaspoons baking powder
½ teaspoon salt

2 teaspoons sugar
¼ cup butter
¾ cup milk

Sift dry ingredients, cut in butter and add milk gradually. Toss on floured board and divide into two parts. Pat, roll out, and bake in a 400°F oven for 12 minutes. Spread with butter and place sweetened berries between layers and on top.

Anna B. Russell, Cleveland, Oh.

TOMATO SOUP CAKE

½ cup melted shortening
1 cup sugar
2 cups cake flour
2 teaspoon baking powder
1 teaspoon cinnamon
1 teaspoon cloves

1 teaspoon nutmeg
1 teaspoon soda
⅛ teaspoon salt
1 cup chopped nuts
1 cup chopped dates
1 can tomato soup

Sift dry ingredients. Add to melted shortening and sugar mix and add tomato soup. nuts and chopped dates. Turn into a well greased loaf pan. Bake 350°F, 45 minutes.

Mary Osadjan, Chicago, Ill.

VIENNA SPECKLED CAKE

¾ cup cake flour
¾ cup grated baking chocolate
  (2½ squares)
6 egg yolks, beaten
1 cup sugar

¾ teaspoon vanilla
¼ teaspoon almond flavoring
¼ teaspoon salt
7 egg whites stiffly beaten

Sift flour three times after it has been measured, then mix with grated chocolate and divide into two parts. Beat egg yolks until thick and lemon colored, add sugar and beat until thick and fluffy. Add flavorings and ½ of flour mixture and beat until thoroughly mixed. Add salt to egg whites and beat until stiff. Fold in remaining half of flour mixture. Fold egg white mixture into egg yolk mixture. Place in ungreased spring tube pan and bake at 350°F for 45 minutes. When done, invert pan until cool. Remove cake from pan and slice in half crosswise, using wet, sharp knife.

Fill with following filling:

CREAM FILLING
½ cup chopped pecans
10 drained and chopped maraschino cherries
1 cup heavy cream, whipped
4½ tablespoons confectioners' sugar

Fold the pecans and cherries into the cream and spread one-half the filling on the lower half of cake. Replace the top half of cake, pile on roughly the remaining half of the filling and sprinkle with the confectioners' sugar.

Florence Hovanec, Whiting, Ind.

FLUFFY WHITE CAKE

½ cup shortening
1⅓ cups sugar
3 egg whites
2¼ cups sifted all purpose flour

½ teaspoon baking powder
½ teaspoon baking soda
1 cup sour milk or buttermilk
1 teaspoon lemon extract

Cream shortening and sugar until fluffy, sift flour, measure and resift with baking powder and soda. Add flavoring to creamed mixture, then alternately add flour mixture and sour milk, stirring gently until smooth. Fold in egg whites beaten until stiff, but not dry. Bake in two 9-inch layer pans. Bake at 350°F for 35 to 45 minutes.

Sue Ogurchock, New Kensington, Pa.

WHITE CAKE

¾ cup shortening
2½ cups sugar
3¾ cups flour
4½ teaspoons baking powder

½ teaspoon salt
2 teaspoons vanilla
1½ cups milk
6 beaten egg whites

Cream shortening and sugar, add flour, baking powder and salt, alternately with the milk. Add vanilla. Fold in the beaten egg whites. Bake in 350°F oven for 45 to 60 minutes.

Ann Bronersky, Chicago, Ill.

FLUFFY LAYER CAKE

1 cup butter or margarine
2 cups sugar
4 eggs
1½ teaspoons vanilla

3 cups cake flour
3 teaspoons baking powder
½ teaspoon salt
1 cup milk

Cream butter, add sugar gradually, creaming continually until very light and fluffy. Add unbeaten eggs, one at a time and beat well. Add flavoring. Sift flour, baking powder and salt three times. Add flour alternately with small amounts of milk, mixing after each addition. Bake in three greased 9-inch layer pans in moderate oven 350°F for 25 to 30 minutes. Frost with favorite frosting.

Dorothy Hanchar, Valparaiso, Ind.

SOUR CREAM RAISIN CAKE

1½ cups seedless raisins
2 cups sifted all-purpose flour
1½ cups sugar
½ cup cocoa
1 teaspoon cinnamon
1 teaspoon cloves
½ teaspoon nutmeg
1 teaspoon salt

1 teaspoon baking soda
1 cup chopped walnuts
1 cup sour cream
2 eggs
3 tablespoons melted shortening,
   or oil
1 teaspoon vanilla

Rinse and drain raisins. Snip with scissors. Sift together the 8 dry ingredients. Mix in raisins and nuts. Add cream, eggs, shortening and vanilla all at once and beat well. Pour into tube pan. Bake at 325°F for 75 minutes or until done. Invert on wire rack for about 15 minutes. Loosen and remove from pan.

Mary Ceykovsky, Allentown, Pa.

RAISIN CAKE

1 box raisins
2 cups brown sugar
2 cups water
2 teaspoons cinnamon
1 teaspoon clove
½ teaspoon nutmeg

½ cup shortening
4 cups all-purpose flour
1 teaspoon baking powder
2 teaspoons baking soda,
   dissolved in warm water

Combine the first seven ingredients and place in sauce pan, bring to a boil and boil 3 minutes. Cool. Add flour, baking powder and baking soda mixture. Bake at 350°F for about 40 to 45 minutes. (This recipe makes a good foundation for fruit cake, add nuts and candied fruit.)

Sue Ogurchock, New Kensingston, Pa.

FRUIT CAKE

½ pound butter
2 cups sugar
4 eggs, separated
1 cup white raisins
1 cup dark raisins
1 cup chopped nuts
½ pound mixed candied fruit
3½ cups flour

1 teaspoon cinnamon
1 teaspoon allspice
3 teaspoons baking powder
4 tablespoons cocoa dissolved In
   ½ cup hot water
1½ cups milk
1 teaspoon salt
1 tablespoon vanilla

Directions continued on page 135.

Cream butter and sugar. Add egg yolks and mix thoroughly. Mix in nuts, raisins and candied fruit. Sift flour, cinnamon, allspice, salt and baking powder. Mix sifted ingredients alternately with milk, vanilla and beaten egg whites. If mixture is too stiff, add more milk. Pour into large tube pan or two smaller ones. Grease pan and dust with cracker crumbs. Bake about 2 hours at 325°F. Yield: 8 pounds of fruit cake.

Mary Salat, Chicago, Ill.

FRUIT CAKE

1 cup sugar
½ pound butter
3 eggs
1 cup chopped dates
1 small bottle maraschino cherries(soaked in rum for a couple of days (use rum mixture)
1 teaspoon baking powder
1 teaspoon baking soda

1 cup chopped nuts
1 cup white raisins
1 cup black coffee warm

1 cup or more flour
1 teaspoon vanilla

Cream butter and sugar until fluffy. Sift dry ingredients and combine with the fruit. Add eggs to creamed mixture. Add dry ingredients and fruit, alternately with coffee and vanilla. Bake slowly for 1 hour or more.

Mrs. Bilik, Berwyn, Ill.

CHRISTMAS FRUIT CAKE

1 pound butter
1½ pounds brown sugar
1½ pounds flour
2 teaspoons nutmeg
1 teaspoon mace
1 teaspoon cloves
2 teaspoons cinnamon
1 teaspoon baking soda
3 teaspoons baking powder
3 pounds raisins

2 pounds currants
1 pound citron, sliced
1 pound dates, sliced
10 eggs, well beaten
1 cup molasses
1 cup strong cold coffee
Juice and grated rind of 2 oranges
Juice and grated rind of 1 lemon
1 cup tart jelly
¼ pound almonds, sliced

Cream butter and sugar until fluffy. Sift dry ingredients together 3 times and mix with the fruit. Add eggs to creamed mixture. Add flour-fruit mixture alternately with next 5 ingredients and beat thoroughly. Pour into pans lined with greased paper. Sprinkle almonds on top. Cover cakes with greased paper. Steam for 2 hours, then bake in slow oven 300°F, 1½ to 2 hours, removing paper last ½ hour to dry surface.

Veronica Radocha, Coaldale, Pa.

CARAMEL FRUIT CAKE

1 pound dates	1 cup chopped pecans
¾ cup candied cherries	¼ cup candied lemon
1 slice green candied pineapple	¼ cup candied citron
1 slice red candied pineapple	1 can moist coconut
¼ cup candied orange peel	1 can sweetened condensed milk

Cut dates and cherries into thirds, cut remaining fruits about the same size. Mix all ingredients together thoroughly and press in a small greased loaf pan lined with greased brown paper or an 8 inch tube pan greased and lined with brown paper. Bake in a slow oven 300°F for 2 hours. Turn out on a cake cooler. Decorate with candied cherries and blanched almonds. Cover with waxed paper and store in refrigerator. Will keep for several months.

Helen Kalata, Chicago, Ill.

ORANGE BREAKFAST CAKE

2 or 3 large oranges	2 cups sifted flour
¾ cup butter or margarine	1 teaspoon baking soda
1 cup sugar	½ teaspoon salt
1 cup finely chopped dates	1 teaspoon vanilla flavoring
2 eggs	

Ream juice from oranges to make 1 cup. Grind rind to make one cup. Cream butter; gradually add sugar and cream until light and fluffy. Blend in eggs. Stir in dates and orange rind. Sift flour, soda and salt; add alternately to creamed mixture with orange juice. Add vanilla. Turn into a greased 13x9 inch baking pan. Bake at 350 degrees for 40 minutes. Cool; cut into squares. Yield 12 servings.

Loretta J. Tylka, North Riverside, Ill.

ORANGE FRUIT CAKE

1½ cups brown sugar	½ teaspoon each of cinnamon
2 tablespoons shortening	and cloves
1 egg	½ cup raisins
1 cup sour milk	½ cup nuts
½ teaspoon salt	2 cups flour
1 teaspoon soda	½ teaspoon vanilla
1 whole orange	

Put the orange, nuts and raisins through food chopper, using finest knife. Mix and sift flour, soda, salt, cinnamon and cloves. Cream shortening, gradually add sugar. Beat in vanilla and eggs, then fruit-nut mixture. Add the flour alternately with the sour milk, beating well after each addition. Pour into greased loaf pan and bake at 300°F about 1¼ hours. Cool in pan and allow to stand several hours or over night before cutting.

Julianna Simek, Johnstown, NY.

DARK FRUIT CAKE

½ pound seedless raisins
½ pound dates, finely cut
½ pound candied citron
½ pound lemon peel
½ pound orange peel
½ pound pineapple
½ pound cherries
1 pound nutmeats
2½ cups flour
1 teaspoon baking powder

1 teaspoon salt
1 teaspoon cinnamon
½ teaspoon allspice
½ teaspoon cloves
½ teaspoon nutmeg
1 cup shortening
1 cup brown sugar
1 cup Karo syrup, red or blue label
4 eggs
1 cup orange juice

First prepare fruit and nuts. Slice finely citron, orange and lemon peel. Cut candied cherries, pineapple, dates, in larger pieces. Wash and plump raisins, if too dry. Sift dry ingredients, flour, baking powder, salt, cinnamon, allspice, cloves and nutmeg. Dredge fruit with ½ cup of sifted dry ingredients. Cream shortening, add brown sugar and cream until light. Add syrup, mix all ingredients well. Add 1 cup dry ingredients, beat until smooth. Add well beaten eggs and beat batter well. Add orange juice and mix well, add fruit mixture, fold remaining dry ingredients. Bake in well greased loaf pans, lined with waxed paper, 250°F for 4 to 5 hours, depending on size of pans. Place shallow pan of water on bottom oven rack during baking. Remove pan of water during last hour of baking. Wrap and store. Makes about 5 pounds. Cake improves with age.

H. Macko, Connellsville, Pa.

DARK FRUIT CAKE

2 cups brown sugar
2 cups butter
4 cups flour
12 eggs, beaten separately
1 teaspoon soda
1 teaspoon grated nutmeg
¼ pound each candied orange
  lemon rind and citron, cut fine
½ cup molasses
2 teaspoons cinnamon

1 teaspoon ground cloves
½ pound walnut meats
½ pound pecans
2 pounds seeded raisins
1 pound currants
1 pound dates
1 pound figs
1 pound candied cherries
1 pound pineapple rings
½ cup fruit juice, wine or brandy

Cut pineapple rings in slices, cut figs and dates. Mix with 1 cup of flour. Mix the rest of the flour with soda and spices. Cream butter and sugar, then add the well beaten egg yolks. Add the flour mixture alternately with the liquids. Gently fold in the beaten egg whites, then the dates and gradually the raisins. Line 4 bread pans with waxed paper, add a layer of fruit and nuts and another layer of the batter. Have pans ⅔ full. Set pans in a pan filled with one inch of hot water. Place in a 300°F oven. Bake ½ hour, cover with paper.

Bake 2 hours longer, remove from water and bake ½ hour more in slow oven. Remove from pans. Remove paper. Wrap in fresh waxed paper. Store in tightly covered tin box. (May also be baked in a slower oven 4 to 5 hours from 200°F to 250°F.)

Elizabeth Lipovsky, Bethlehem, Pa.

EUROPEAN FRUIT CAKE

1 cup butter
2 cups sugar
3 whole eggs
2 cups sour milk
3 cups flour
1 teaspoon baking soda

1 teaspoon salt
1 cup chopped raisins
1 cup ground walnuts
1 cup chopped dates
2 tablespoons molasses

Cream butter and sugar and add the rest of the ingredients in the order they are given and mix well. Bake in loaf or tube pan at 300°F until done.

Anna Sapp, Irwin, Pa.

GOLD FRUIT CAKE

1 cup currants
1 cup bleached raisins
1 cup dates, cut up
1 cup candied cherries
½ cup orange Juice

3 cups mixed candied fruit
    (Citron, orange, pineapple and
    lemon peel)
1 cup honey
½ cup brandy or sherry wine

Combine all above fruit, honey, juice and brandy. Cover in bowl and let stand over night.

NEXT DAY PREPARE THE FOLLOWING:

1½ cups butter
1½ cups sugar
6 eggs
4 cups flour, sifted
1 teaspoon baking soda
1 teaspoon salt (scant)

2 teaspoons ginger
2 teaspoons mace or nutmeg
2 teaspoons vanilla
3 cups coarsely chopped walnut
    meats

Cream butter and sugar. Add eggs, well beaten and mix. Add flour, sifted with soda and spices. Add flavoring, nuts and fruit mixture. Blend well. Pour into loaf or tube pans, lined with heavy brown paper. Grease pans before lining with paper. Bake in slow oven, 275°F to 300°F, about 3 hours, if large pan is used. If smaller loaf pans are used, bake about 2½ hours. Makes about 8 pounds of fruit cake.

Susan Matuscak, Cleveland, Oh.

UNBAKED FRUIT CAKE

9 cups bran flakes
1½ cups cooked, chopped prunes
¾ cup chopped dates
¾ cup chopped raisins
¾ cup chopped walnuts
1½ teaspoons grated orange rind

1½ teaspoons grated lemon rind
¾ cup brown sugar, firmly packed
1 teaspoon salt
½ teaspoon nutmeg and cinnamon
½ teaspoon ginger
½ cup orange juice

Roll bran flakes to make 3 cups fine crumbs. Combine all ingredients and mix thoroughly. Line an 8-inch square pan or 9 x 5 x 3 inch loaf pan with waxed paper, press fruit mixture into pan and smooth top. Cover with several thicknesses of waxed paper and place in refrigerator for 3 days before serving. Storage improves flavor of the cake. To serve, cut in small cubes or slices and serve with whipped cream if desired.

Mary Skurka, Whiting, Ind.

WHITE COCONUT FRUIT CAKE

3½ cups sifted flour
3 tablespoons baking powder
1 pound coconut
½ pound candied pineapple
½ pound citron
½ pound lemon and orange peel
½ pound cherries, red and green

½ pound almonds, cut in pieces
½ pound walnuts, chopped
1 cup butter or other shortening
2 cups white sugar
1 teaspoon almond extract
1 cup milk
5 egg whites, beaten stiff

Sift flour, measure and resift with baking powder, into large mixing bowl. Add coconut, pineapple, citron, peel, cherries and nuts. Mix well. Cream butter in large bowl, add sugar gradually, beating until light and fluffy. Add almond extract. Beat until well blended. Add flour, fruit mixture alternately with milk, beginning and ending with flour mixture. Mix well after each addition. Fold in stiffly beaten egg whites. Turn out into 1 large, greased and floured, 10 inch tube pan, or two smaller tube pans, or loaf pans. Bake at 250°F for about 2 hours, or until cake shrinks from sides of pan.

For a yellow cake, use 3 whole eggs, beaten well, in place of 5 egg whites.

Decorate top with walnut halves and whole almonds.

Carmine V. Molinaro, Connellsville, Pa.

- SPONGECAKES -

ALMOND CAKE

14 eggs, separated	½ cup bread crumbs
1 pound powdered sugar	1 pound almonds, ground

Beat yolks with sugar until smooth and thick. Add bread crumbs and almonds. Fold in gently stiffly beaten egg whites. Bake for 1 hour in 275°F oven.

BUTTER ICING

3 eggs yolks	½ pound butter
½ box powdered sugar	Juice of 1 orange

Cream until light and fluffy.

Mary Salat, Chicago, Ill.

COFFEE CUSTARD CAKE

1½ cups cake flour	2 tablespoons extra strong coffee
1 teaspoon baking powder	1 cup sugar
½ teaspoon salt	½ teaspoon vanilla
3 eggs	

Mix together and sift the flour, baking powder and salt. Beat the eggs slightly, then add, little by little, the coffee, beating briskly after each addition till light and fluffy. Gradually beat in the sugar. Beat in the flour mixture, small amount at a time. Add the vanilla. Bake in 2 buttered and floured 8-inch pans, in a moderate oven 350°F for 20 minutes. Turn out and cool on cake racks. When cold, split each layer and spread with custard coffee filling.

FILLING

2 eggs	1 cup milk
¾ cup sugar	½ teaspoon salt
2 tablespoons flour	½ teaspoon vanilla
1 cup strong coffee	3 tablespoons butter

Beat the eggs slightly in the top of a double boiler, add the sugar sifted with flour and mixed smoothly with the coffee, milk and salt. Cook over hot water until mixture begins to thicken, stirring constantly, then add vanilla and butter. Blend well. Cool and spread between layers. Let stand about two hours before serving; dust the top with powdered sugar.

Justine Uhlarik, Chicago, Ill.

DREAM CAKE

10 eggs, separated	1 tablespoon water or lemon juice
½ teaspoon cream of tartar	1 cup sugar
Dash of salt	¾ cup sifted cake flour

Beat egg whites until frothy, add cream of tartar and beat until stiff. Beat egg yolks and salt until very thick and lemon colored, add water, beat in and add sugar gradually, beating until thick enough to hold a soft peak. Fold egg whites and flour into egg yolk mixture. Pour into ungreased tube pan and bake in moderate oven 350°F about 40 minutes. Invert pan and let cake hang in pan until cool.

Anna Kolena, Chicago, Ill.

GOLDEN CAKE

1½ cups flour (measured and
  sifted 5 times)
1⅞ cups sugar (sifted)
10 egg whites

6 egg yolks
Pinch of salt
1½ teaspoons cream of tartar
1 teaspoon vanilla

Beat egg whites with salt until foamy. Add cream of tartar and beat until stiff but not dry. Add sugar, one tablespoon at a time. Beat egg yolks until light and lemon colored, add to egg whites and sugar. Fold in flour, one tablespoon at a time, add flavoring. Pour into ungreased tube cake pan. Bake 1½ hours starting with slow oven 275°F, increasing every 15 minutes to 350°F. When done turn upside down until cool.

WHIPPED CREAM FILLING:

4 egg yolks
1 cup sugar
1 tablespoon flour
1 teaspoon vanilla
1 cup milk

Pinch of salt
½ pint whipped cream
1 envelope gelatin combined with
  1 tablespoon cold water

Put egg yolks to which salt has been added in double boiler, beat well. Add sugar, flour, milk. Cook until creamy. While still hot add gelatin. Cool. Add the cream which has been whipped and beat well. Add flavoring. Cut cake in two when cold and spread filling between layers and top of cake.

Eleanor Marko, Whiting, Ind.

GRAHAM CRACKER SPONGE CAKE

6 egg yolks beaten until thick
1 cup sugar
1 teaspoon vanilla
1 cup sifted graham cracker
  crumbs

1 teaspoon baking powder
6 egg whites beaten stiff
½ teaspoon salt
1 cup ground nuts

Beat egg yolks until they are thick and lemon colored. Add sugar gradually, continue to beat until thoroughly dissolved and mixture is very light. Add vanilla. Combine sifted crumbs and baking powder and fold into the egg mixture. Add nuts. Beat egg whites until stiff with salt and fold into the batter. Bake in ungreased tube pan at 325°F for about 1 hour.

Millie Krull, Whiting, Ind.

OLD FASHIONED JELLY ROLL

1 cup sifted cake flour
1 teaspoon baking powder
¼ teaspoon salt
4 eggs

¾ cup sugar, sifted
1 teaspoon vanilla
1 cups jelly (any flavor)

Sift flour once, measure, combine baking powder, salt and eggs in bowl over hot water and beat with rotary egg beater, adding sugar gradually until mixture becomes thick and light colored. Remove bowl from hot water. Fold in flour and add vanilla. Turn into 15 x 10-inch pan, which has been greased, lined with paper, to within ½ inch of edge and again greased. Bake in hot oven 400°F for 13 minutes. Quickly cut off crisp edges of cake. Turn out on cloth covered with powdered sugar, remove paper. Spread with jelly and roll. Wrap in cloth and cool on rack.

Anna B. Russell, Cleveland, Oh.

OLD FASHIONED JELLY ROLL

Sift together:
1 cup sifted cake flour

1¼ teaspoons baking powder
¼ teaspoon salt

Beat 4 egg yolks with ½ cup granulated sugar, 3 tablespoons cold water and 1 teaspoon vanilla, till lemon colored and thick. In second large bowl beat the 4 egg whites with ½ cup granulated sugar. Fold yolk mixture into whites with egg whisk (wire beater), then fold in the sifted dry ingredients. Pour into greased shallow long pan lined with greased wax paper. Bake in a 375°F oven for 15 to 18 minutes. Quickly turn from pan onto damp tea towel and let rest a minute. Unroll, cut off crisp edges, spread with beaten red raspberry jelly and roll up at once, cover with the towel for a minute. To serve, sprinkle with confectioners' sugar if desired.

Lillian Cherney, Chicago, Ill.

PINEAPPLE FEATHER CAKE

1½ cups sifted cake flour
1 teaspoon baking powder
6 eggs, separated
¼ teaspoon salt

1½ cups sugar
½ cup pineapple juice
1 tablespoon lemon juice

Sift the flour and baking powder together four times. Beat egg whites and salt until stiff, but not dry. Add ¾ cup sugar, about two tablespoons at a time, beating well after each addition. Beat egg yolks, add remaining sugar and fruit juice and beat until thick enough to hold a soft peak. Fold flour, about ¼ of it at a time, into yolk mixture, folding just enough to moisten flour. Fold in egg white mixture. Pour into an ungreased tube pan. Cut through batter with spatula to remove large air bubbles. Bake in a slow oven 325°F 50 to 60 minutes. Invert in pan and let cake hang in pan until cool. Makes one 9-inch cake.

Anna Kolena, Chicago, Ill.

THREE EGG WATER SPONGE CAKE

1 cup sugar
¾ cup water
1¾ cups flour
3 teaspoons baking powder

Juice and rind of one lemon
3 egg whites
3 egg yolks

Put water and sugar in saucepan and cook 5 minutes. Beat egg whites stiff in large bowl, then slowly pour syrup over whites, beating constantly. Sift flour and baking powder and fold gently into egg whites, add lemon juice and rind. Last the egg yolks which have been slightly beaten. Pour into well greased pan, 10 x 14 or in 2 layer pans. Bake 25 to 30 minutes at 375°F. Makes excellent strawberry shortcake or banana cake.

Irene Menzezoff, Long Island, NY.

PINEAPPLE BUTTERSCOTCH CAKE (Upside Down Cake)

¼ cup butter
1 cup sugar
2 eggs, separated
2 cups sifted flour

3 teaspoons baking powder
½ teaspoon salt
¾ cup cold water
1 teaspoon vanilla

Cream butter, add sugar gradually and beat well. Add beaten yolks. Sift flour, salt, baking powder and add alternately with cold water to creamed mixture. Add vanilla and beat well. Fold in beaten egg whites. Butter 8 x 12 pan and line with 1 cup brown sugar. Dot with 3 tablespoons butter. Place pineapple slices with maraschino cherry in center of each. Pour cake batter over mixture. Bake at 350°F for 50 minutes. Let cool. Turn upside down.

Mary E. Grega, Cleveland, Oh.

PINEAPPLE SKILLET CAKE

½ cup butter
1 cup brown sugar
1 cup Pecan meats
1 cup canned pineapple pieces

Melt butter in 9 inch iron skillet. Add brown sugar. Stir until melted. On this, place nuts and pineapple.

1 cup sifted cake flour	1 tablespoon melted butter
1½ teaspoons baking powder	1 teaspoon vanilla
4 egg yolks, beaten until thick and lemon colored	4 egg whites, stiffly beaten
	1 cup sifted sugar

Sift flour once, measure, add baking powder and sift flour four more times. Combine egg yolks, butter and vanilla. Beat egg whites with flat wire whisk until stiff enough to hold in peaks, fold in sugar a small amount at a time, then egg yolks and finally flour. Pour batter over contents of skillet and bake in moderate oven, 325°F, for 60 minutes. Let stand several minutes. Loosen cake from sides of skillet with spatula. Serve upside down on dish, with pineapple on top. Garnish with whipped cream, if desired. Serves 8.

Anna K. Hruskovich, Whiting, Ind.

PINEAPPLE UPSIDE-DOWN CAKE

½ cup brown sugar
¼ cup butter
1 can sliced drained pineapple

Melt butter in large 10-inch cast aluminum skillet, add sugar and arrange pineapple in it and let stand while batter is being prepared.

3 eggs	1 cup sifted cake flour
1 cup granulated sugar	1 tablespoon fruit juice
1 teaspoon baking powder	Pinch of salt

Beat eggs, add sugar and pineapple juice. Blend in flour, salt and baking powder. Pour over prepared fruit in skillet, bake at 350°F for about 30 minutes. Turn out on cake plate immediately after removing cake from oven.

Lillian Cherney, Chicago, Ill.

PINEAPPLE UPSIDE-DOWN CAKE

⅓ cup vegetable shortening	1¼ cups flour
¼ teaspoon salt	1½ teaspoons baking powder
1 teaspoon vanilla	½ cup pineapple juice
½ cup sugar	½ cup brown sugar
1 egg	5 slices pineapple

Cream the first five ingredients. Sift the flour and baking powder. Add alternately with the pineapple juice. Arrange the brown sugar and pineapple in the bottom of the pan, liberally greased with the shortening and pour over the batter. Bake at 350°F about 50 minutes. Turn upside down at once, so that the syrup may run into the cake.

Mary E. Grega, Cleveland, Oh.

POSTUM CAKE

Sponge Layer	Postum Layer
3 eggs	3 eggs
¾ cup sugar	¾ cup sugar
¾ cup flour	¾ cup flour
¾ teaspoon baking powder	¾ teaspoon baking powder
3 tablespoons cold water	1⅓ tablespoons cold water
¾ teaspoon vanilla	3 tablespoons instant postum

Make and bake each layer separately.

Beat egg whites until stiff but not dry, add ½ the sugar slowly. Set to one side. Beat egg yolks, add rest of the sugar and beat. Add cold water. Sift dry ingredients and fold into yolk mixture. Fold in egg whites and add vanilla. Bake in 9-inch layer pan in 350°F oven for 25 to 30 minutes.

ICING AND FILLING FOR THE POSTUM CAKE

1 package vanilla pudding	½ cup butter
1 cup milk	½ cup sifted powdered sugar

Make pudding with one cup of milk only and follow the directions on the package of pudding. When pudding is cold, cream the butter and add to pudding a tablespoonful at a time. Cream thoroughly and add the powdered sugar. Spread in between both layers and cover top and sides of cake.

Marie Mizenko, Cleveland, Oh.

SPONGE CAKE

1 cup sifted cake flour	1½ tablespoons lemon juice
1 cup sifted sugar	5 eggs, separated
4 tablespoons water	½ teaspoon cream of tartar
¼ teaspoon salt	1 teaspoon baking powder
1½ teaspoons grated lemon rind	

Sift flour once, measure, sift four times. Add ½ cup sugar, lemon rind and water to egg yolks. Beat with rotary beater until very thick and light. Add lemon juice gradually, beating well. Add flour, stir until just blended. Beat egg whites and salt until foamy, add cream of tartar and beat until stiff enough to hold in peaks, but not dry. Add remaining sugar, about 2 tablespoons at a time, beating well. Fold in egg yolk mixture. Turn into ungreased 9-inch pan. Cut gently through batter to remove bubbles. Bake in slow oven 325°F, one hour or until done. Cool in inverted pan.

Albina Sloboda, Coaldale, Pa.

STRAWBERRY WHIPPED CREAM CAKE

3 eggs	**1½ cups sifted cake flour**
1 cup sugar	**1½ teaspoons baking powder**
6 tablespoons water	**1 teaspoon vanilla or lemon extract**

Separate eggs. Beat yolks until thick, gradually adding the sugar, flavoring and then the water. When thoroughly mixed, add the sifted dry ingredients and blend. Fold in the stiffly beaten egg whites and bake in two 9-inch waxed paper lined cake pans at 350°F for 20 minutes or until cake tests done. Remove from pans, cool.

FILLING
1 pint whipping cream
**1 package frozen strawberries, well drained or 1 pint fresh
   berries, sweetened and drained**

Fold into 2 pint stiffly beaten or whipped cream. Frost top and sides of cake with remaining whipped cream and decorate with berries.

Clara Kucka, Whiting, Ind.

SELF-FROSTED CAKE

½ cup shortening, Crisco or Spry	**TOPPING**
1¼ cups sugar	**¼ pound marshmallows**
2 eggs	**½ cup brown sugar**
2½ cups sifted flour	**½ cup nuts**
3 teaspoons baking powder	
1 cup milk	
1 teaspoon vanilla	

Cream shortening and add other ingredients. When blended place in 8 x 12 inch pan. Cover with marshmallows cut in halves, then spread ½ cup brown sugar and ½ cup chopped nuts. Bake in 350°F for 30 minutes.

LITTLE MISS SPONGE CAKE

4 eggs	**1 teaspoon baking powder**
1 cup sugar	**Pinch of salt**
4 tablespoons cold water	**1 teaspoon vanilla**
1 cup sifted cake flour	

Beat eggs until thick and lemon colored. Add sugar and beat well again. Add water and beat, then fold in the flour very lightly in small amounts. Bake in ungreased tube pan in slow oven, 325°F, for 45 minutes. Remove from oven, invert pan one hour.

Helen Beres, Toledo, Oh.

SPONGE WALNUT CAKE

9 eggs
9 tablespoons sugar
5 tablespoons flour
1 teaspoon baking powder

¼ teaspoon salt
1 teaspoon vanilla
1 cup ground walnuts

Separate eggs. Beat egg whites until stiff. Add sugar gradually to the egg yolks, beating until light and fluffy. Add vanilla. Fold in the beaten egg whites and the flour lightly. Add ground nuts. Pour into three 9-inch layer cake pans which have been greased and floured lightly. Bake 25 to 30 minutes in a 350°F oven.

Mary E. Grega, Cleveland, Oh.

SUNSHINE CAKE

12 eggs, separated
1 cup flour
1 cup powdered sugar

1 teaspoon vanilla
½ teaspoon salt
1 teaspoon cream of tartar

Beat yolks. Add flour, sugar, vanilla, salt and cream of tartar and mix until smooth and thick. Fold in gently well beaten egg whites. Bake at 300 to 325°F for one hour. When done, invert to cool. Cover with butter icing and sprinkle with ground nuts or toasted coconut.

Mary Salat, Chicago, Ill.

HOT MILK SPONGE CAKE

2 teaspoons baking powder
4 eggs
2 cups sugar
2 cups cake flour

1 cup hot milk
1 teaspoon lemon extract
2 tablespoons butter

Beat eggs until lemon colored, slowly add sugar. Beat after each addition. Heat milk to boiling point, add butter. Then add flour and milk folding in very carefully. Add lemon extract. Bake 25 minutes in 350°F oven.

Mary Skriba, Riverside, Ill.

HOT MILK JELLY CAKE OR BANANA CAKE

¼ cup butter	1 cup flour
½ cup milk	1 teaspoon baking powder
2 eggs	½ teaspoon salt
1 cup sugar	1 teaspoon vanilla

Scald milk together with butter. Let cool until slightly warm. Beat eggs with sugar until light and thick. Stir in the flour, sifted with the salt and baking powder. Stir only until blended. Add scalded milk and vanilla. Stir quickly and pour into greased cake pan. Bake at 325°F until done. Cool, cut in half, spread with preserves and frost top with a thin confectioners' icing. This is a good cake to serve as Boston Cream Pie or shortcake. For Banana Cake, fill with sliced, sweetened bananas mixed with 1 tablespoon lemon juice.

Vincentian Sisters of Charity, Bedford, Oh.

WALNUT SPONGE CAKE

9 egg yolks	2 teaspoons baking powder
2 cups powdered sugar	1 teaspoon cinnamon
½ cup chopped walnuts	1 teaspoon nutmeg
2 teaspoons lemon juice	9 egg whites
1 cup cake flour	

Beat egg yolks until thick and lemon colored. Add powdered sugar and beat until creamy. Add the nuts and lemon juice. Blend well. Sift flour, baking powder, cinnamon and nutmeg. Add to the egg mixture. Blend well. Fold in stiffly beaten egg whites. Bake one hour in 350°F oven in an ungreased tube pan. Remove cake from oven and invert pan until cake is cold. Frost with a simple frosting or sprinkle with powdered sugar.

Leona Zientara, Whiting, Ind.

WARM WATER CAKE

1½ cups sugar	4 eggs yolks
1½ cups sifted cake flour	½ cup warm water
1 teaspoon baking powder	¼ teaspoon salt
3 tablespoons orange juice	4 egg whites

Beat egg yolks until thick, add sugar gradually, beat well. Add water and orange juice, fold in flour which has been sifted with salt and baking powder. Mix gently. Fold in stiffly beaten egg whites. Bake in tube pan at 325°F for one hour.

Mary Uhely, Los Angeles, Ca.

ANGEL FOOD CAKE

12 egg whites
1½ cups sifted sugar
1 cup sifted pastry flour
¼ teaspoon salt

1¼ teaspoons cream of tartar
1 teaspoon vanilla
¼ teaspoon almond extract

Add salt to egg whites. Beat with wire whisk until frothy, add cream of tartar and beat till stiff, but not too dry. Sift 1 cup of sugar into dish. Sift ½ cup of sugar with one cup of flour four times. After egg whites are beaten add the sugar, 3 tablespoons at a time. Beat until just blended after each addition. Add flavorings and beat just a few strokes. Add flour and sugar about 4 tablespoons at a time, folding in gently. Pour in ungreased angel food pan. Bake at 375°F for 30 to 35 minutes. Remove from oven and invert pan, cool for hour or longer. Remove from pan, loosen sides and center with spatula or knife. Frost with either whipping cream or any other desired frosting.

Mary Canner, Whiting, Ind.

ANGEL FOOD CAKE

1⅓ cups egg whites
1¼ cups granulated sugar, sifted
1 cup cake flour, sifted

1 teaspoon cream of tartar
¼ teaspoon salt
1 teaspoon vanilla

Use cold eggs, as they will separate more easily. Separate, and allow whites to stand in a warm room for about one hour or longer. Add half the sugar to flour and sift together several times. Add salt to egg whites and beat until foamy. Add cream of tartar and continue to beat until mixture clings to bowl. Do not overbeat. Fold in half the sugar about ¼ cup at a time, mixing only until smooth. Gradually fold in flour and sugar mixture, add flavoring, blending gently. Pour into ungreased 9-inch angel food pan. Cut through batter especially on sides a few times and strike pan on table. Bake 40 minutes at 325°F and 10 minutes more at 375°F. Remove from oven. Invert pan and let stand 2 hours or until cake is cold. With a knife or spatula loosen sides, bottom and around tube. Turn out on cake platter. Ice as desired.

Mary Skurka, Whiting, Ind.

CHOCOLATE ANGEL FOOD CAKE

1½ cups sifted cake flour
½ cup sifted cocoa
2 cups egg whites
⅓ teaspoon salt

1 teaspoon cream of tartar
2¼ cups sugar
2 teaspoons vanilla extract

Sift flour, and cocoa together 2 or 3 times. Separate eggs and to the whites add the salt. With dover or electric mixer, beat until foamy, then add cream of tartar and continue to beat until whites cling to bottom and sides of bowl. Fold sugar in a little at a time, add vanilla and lastly the flour and cocoa. Pour batter into an ungreased angel food pan and cut through batter with a knife or spatula a few times. Bake at 300°F about one hour and 10 minutes. Increase oven to 375°F the last 10 minutes. When done, remove from oven, invert pan and let stand only until cake is cold.

Vivian Stopka

YELLOW ANGEL FOOD CAKE

6 or 7 eggs
1½ cups sugar
½ cup cold water
½ teaspoon salt

½ or ¾ teaspoon baking powder
¾ teaspoon cream of tartar
1½ cups flour
1 teaspoon vanilla

Beat egg yolks well, beat ½ cup cold water into egg yolks. Add the sugar and beat mixture well again. Add baking powder, flour and salt sifted together three times, then add vanilla. Beat the egg whites until foamy and add cream of tartar, beat until stiff. Fold whites into batter and pour into ungreased angel food pan. Bake in slow oven 325°F for 15 minutes, then increase heat to 350°F for one hour.

Note: Do not preheat your oven. Light your oven just before putting your cake in.

Sophie Marusak, Joliet, Ill.

- CHIFFON CAKES -

BANANA CHIFFON CAKE

2 cups cake flour
1½ cups sugar
3 teaspoons baking powder
1 teaspoon salt
½ cup salad oil
7 unbeaten egg yolks

¾ cup cold water
1 sieved ripe banana
1 teaspoon vanilla
1 cup egg whites (7 or 8 eggs)
½ teaspoon cream of tartar

Sift flour, sugar, baking powder and salt into mixing bowl. Make a well in the center and add oil, egg yolks, water, banana and flavoring. Beat with a spoon until smooth. Whip egg whites and cream of tartar until whites form very stiff peaks. Pour egg yolk mixture gradually over whipped whites, gently folding until just blended. Do not stir. Pour into ungreased 10-inch tube pan, 4 inches deep. Bake in 325°F oven for 55 minutes, then at 350°F for 10 or 15 minutes. Immediately turn pan upside down, placing tube part over neck of funnel or bottle. Let hang until cold. Loosen from sides and tube with spatula.

Mary Kolena, Chicago, Ill.

CHIFFON CAKE

2¼ cups sifted cake flour
1½ cups sugar
3 teaspoons double acting baking
   powder
1 teaspoon salt
½ cup salad oil

¾ cup water
4 egg yolks
1 teaspoon lemon extract
½ teaspoon cream of tartar
1 cup egg whites (about 8)
1 teaspoon vanilla

Sift flour, sugar, baking powder and salt into mixing bowl. Make a well in the center and add oil, egg yolks, water and flavoring. Beat with a spoon until smooth. Whip egg whites and cream of tartar until whites form very stiff peaks. Pour egg yolk mixture gradually over whipped whites, gently folding until just blended. Do not stir. Pour into ungreased 10-inch tube pan, 4 inches deep. Bake in moderately slow oven 325°F for one hour. Immediately turn pan upside down, placing tube part over neck of funnel or bottle. Let hang until cold.

Apolonia Blahunka, Whiting, Ind.

ORANGE CHIFFON CAKE

8 eggs, separated
¼ cup lemon juice
¼ cup orange juice
1½ cups sugar
1½ cups flour

1½ teaspoons cream of tartar
1½ teaspoons baking powder
½ teaspoon salt
1 teaspoon grated orange rind
1 teaspoon grated lemon rind

Beat egg yolks until thick and lemon colored. Add the juices and rinds. Beat well. Add sugar gradually. Sift flour, baking powder and salt. Add to egg mixture. Beat the egg whites until stiff. Add cream of tartar and blend. Fold into the first mixture. Pour into ungreased tube pan. Bake 50 minutes at 325°F. Cool upside down on cake rack.

Leona Zientara, Whiting, Ind.

PINEAPPLE CHIFFON CAKE

2¼ cups sifted cake flour	5 unbeaten egg yolks
1½ cups sugar	¾ cup unsweetened pineapple
1 teaspoon salt	juice
3 teaspoons baking powder	1 cup egg whites
½ cup salad oil	½ teaspoon cream of tartar

Sift dry ingredients into mixing bowl. Make a well and add oil, egg yolks and pineapple juice. Beat until smooth. Beat egg whites until frothy, add cream of tartar and beat until stiff peaks are formed. Gradually add egg yolk batter into egg whites. Bake in 10-inch tube pan in 325°F oven for 55 minutes, then for 10 minutes at 350°F. Frost cooled cake with Pineapple-Butter Cream Icing.

PINEAPPLE-BUTTER-CREAM ICING

½ cup butter
4 cups sifted powdered sugar
6 tablespoons crushed pineapple
1 to 2 tablespoons pineapple juice

Cream butter, add sugar. Stir in well-drained crushed pineapple. Add pineapple juice. Beat thoroughly. Spread on top and sides of cake. Decorate with half pineapple slices and maraschino cherries.

Sophie Vavrinec, Chicago, Illinois,

- CUPCAKES -

Practically any butter or sponge layer cake mixture may be baked as cupcakes. The flour may be slightly decreased. Bake in small greased muffin pans or cupcake pans at 375°F for 13 to 20 minutes, depending on size. Frost when cold, using any desired frosting.

APPLE, BANANA CUPCAKES

⅔ cup shortening	4 tablespoons sour milk
1¼ cups sugar	2 cups flour
2 eggs	1 teaspoon soda
1 cup mashed, bananas	½ teaspoon nutmeg
2 small apples, grated	½ cup chopped nuts
½ teaspoon cinnamon	

Cream shortening, add sugar gradually, cream again. Add unbeaten eggs, one at a time, beating thoroughly after each addition. Then add mashed bananas, grated apples, and sour milk. Stir well. Fold in flour and spices. Bake 15 minutes at 375°F. Makes 2 dozen cupcakes.

Ann Kuva

BANANA SPICE CUPCAKES

2¾ cups sifted flour
2 teaspoons baking powder
1 teaspoon soda
1 teaspoon salt
¼ teaspoon cloves
1½ teaspoon cinnamon

1 teaspoon nutmeg
⅔ cup shortening
1½ cups sugar
2 eggs, well beaten
1⅔ cups mashed bananas
2 teaspoons vanilla

Sift flour once, measure and resift 3 or 4 times with the rest of the dry ingredients, except sugar. Cream together shortening and sugar until very light. Add eggs and beat well. Alternately add sifted dry ingredients and mashed bananas in small amounts and beat until batter is smooth after each addition. Add vanilla and spoon the batter into medium size cupcake pans which have been greased. Bake in moderate oven 350°F for about 35 minutes.

Florence Hovanec, Whiting, Ind.

CHOCOLATE CUPCAKES

½ cup shortening
1 cup sugar
1 egg
1⅓ cups flour
¼ teaspoon salt
1 teaspoon baking powder

½ teaspoon baking soda
½ cup cocoa
½ cup milk
1 teaspoon vanilla
½ cup hot coffee

Cream shortening and sugar, add egg and beat well. Add flour sifted with salt, baking powder, soda and cocoa, alternately with milk and vanilla. Add coffee. Fill cupcake tins ⅔ full. Bake in moderate oven 350°F 20 minutes. Frost cakes.

Anna Sabol, Whiting, Ind.

SOUR MILK CUPCAKES

1½ cups flour
1 cup sugar
2 tablespoons cocoa
1 teaspoon soda
Pinch of salt

1 cup sour milk
1 egg
2 tablespoons melted butter
1 teaspoon vanilla

Sift dry ingredients. Beat egg, add melted butter, vanilla and sour milk. Add to dry ingredients. Beat well. Fill muffin tins ⅔ full. Bake at 350°F for 20 minutes.

Anna B. Russell, Cleveland, Oh.

FEATHERY CUPCAKES

2 cups sifted flour	2 eggs, unbeaten
2½ teaspoons baking powder	⅔ cup milk
¼ teaspoon salt	½ teaspoon vanilla
½ cup butter or shortening	¼ teaspoon almond extract
1 cup sugar	

Sift flour, baking powder and salt three times. Cream butter and sugar and add 2 eggs, beat until fluffy. Add sifted dry ingredients alternately with milk. Add flavorings. Fill well greased cupcake pans ⅔ full of the batter. Bake in 375°F oven for about 20 minutes or until done. Remove from pans when cool, frost with any desired icing. Makes about 18 cupcakes.

Lillian Cherney, Chicago, Ill.

GINGER TEA CAKES

¼ cup butter	1 egg, beaten
¼ cup brown sugar, packed	1½ cups sifted cake flour
½ teaspoon salt	1½ teaspoons baking powder
¼ teaspoon cloves	¼ teaspoon soda
1½ teaspoons ginger	½ cup molasses
½ teaspoon cinnamon	½ cup boiling water

Cream butter thoroughly and add the brown sugar. Mix until light and fluffy. Add salt and spices, stirring them in well. Add egg and mix. Sift flour, baking powder and soda together and add alternately with molasses. Add hot water last. Mix quickly until smooth and fill greased cupcake pans half full. Bake at 375°F for 20 minutes or until done. Cool.

Dorothy Hanchar, Valparaiso, Ind.

MAPLE SYRUP CUPCAKES

½ cup butter	4 teaspoons baking powder
¼ cup light corn syrup	½ cup water
¼ cup maple corn syrup	½ teaspoon salt
2 eggs	2 cups sifted cake flour

Cream butter. Add syrups gradually, beating constantly while adding. Beat in one egg at a time. Add 1 cup flour alternately with ¼ cup water. Beat well. Add remaining flour, sifted with baking powder and salt. Add remaining water. Mix well. Fill muffin tins about half full. Bake at 375°F for 15 to 20 minutes. Makes about 1 to 1½ dozen cupcakes, depending on size of muffin tins.

Catherine Otrembiak, Chicago, Ill.

ORANGE CUPCAKES

4 tablespoons butter
2 cups sugar
4 eggs, separated
1 cup milk

3 cups flour
2½ teaspoons baking powder
1 teaspoon vanilla
Grated rind of one orange

Cream butter and sugar. Add egg yolks and mix. Add milk. Sift flour, baking powder together and add. Add grated rind and vanilla. Mix, fold in well beaten egg whites. Bake at 375°F for 25 minutes. Makes 24 cupcakes.

Anna Stanek, Whiting, Ind.

PEANUT BUTTER CUPCAKES

⅓ cup shortening
1 cup brown sugar
½ cup peanut butter
2 eggs, beaten
½ cup brown sugar

2 cups flour
½ teaspoon salt
2½ teaspoons baking powder
¾ cup milk
1 teaspoon vanilla

Thoroughly cream shortening and 1 cup sugar. Add peanut butter, mix well. Add eggs beaten with remaining ½ cup sugar. Add sifted ingredients alternately with milk and vanilla extract. Fill greased cupcake pans ½ full. Bake in 350°F oven for 25 minutes. Makes 24 cupcakes.

Mary Salat, Chicago, Ill.

- FROSTINGS AND FILLINGS -

BUTTER FROSTING

4 tablespoons butter
2 cups sifted confectioners'
   sugar

3 tablespoons milk
1 teaspoon vanilla
Dash of salt

Cream butter, add part of sugar gradually, blending after each addition, add remaining sugar, alternating with milk, until of right consistency to spread. Beat after each addition until smooth. Add vanilla and salt. Makes enough frosting to cover top of two 9-inch layers.

Anna B. Russell, Cleveland, Oh.

BOILED CHOCOLATE BUTTERMILK FILLING

6 tablespoons flour
½ cup cocoa
¾ cup sugar
1½ teaspoons vanilla

⅛ teaspoon salt
2 cups buttermilk
1 egg

Mix flour, cocoa, sugar, salt in double boiler. Add buttermilk slowly and cook, stirring constantly for about 5 minutes or until thickened. Cook about 10 minutes longer, stirring constantly. Add small amount of this mixture to the slightly beaten egg and mix well. Beat into first mixture, cook for a minute longer, stirring constantly. Add vanilla, cool slightly.

Ella D. Vlasaty, Braddock, Pa.

CHIFFON FILLING

1½ cups milk
1 cup sugar
2 tablespoons flour
3 egg yolks
Dash of salt

2 tablespoons gelatin
¼ cup cold water
1 cup whipped cream
1 teaspoon flavoring

Scald milk and set aside. Add sugar, salt and flour to beaten egg yolks. Add to scalded milk, gradually, and cook over hot water until eggs are done. Remove from heat, add gelatin, which has been soaked in cold water. Chill. Fold the whipped cream and chill again. Pile between layers of sponge cake. Top with whipped cream.

Mary Vevurka, Chicago, Illinois

COFFEE FROSTING

½ cup sweet butter
½ pound powdered sugar
1 whole egg
2 teaspoons instant powdered coffee

Mix well the above ingredients.

Anna Kolena, Chicago, Ill.

CREAMY CHOCOLATE FROSTING

¼ cup strong coffee
2 squares chocolate
2 cups powdered sugar

1 teaspoon vanilla
2 tablespoons butter

Combine coffee, butter and chocolate. Heat until melted. Remove from fire and add sugar gradually. Beat to desired consistency. Add vanilla.

Marcella Halloran, Streator, Ill.

CREAMY FILLING AND FROSTING

2½ tablespoons cake flour
½ cup milk
¼ teaspoon salt

Mix and strain before cooking. Put in saucepan over fire and cook until thick paste, then cool to lukewarm. Put in mixing bowl: ½ cup sugar and ½ cup shortening (spry). Mix well with electric beater. Add paste a little at a time. Add flavoring. Add about one cup powdered sugar. Beat until nice and creamy. Nuts may be added. Makes enough for two layer 9-inch cake.

Helen Cross, Whiting, Ind.

FLUFFY WHITE FROSTING

2 cups sifted powdered sugar
10 tablespoons water
¼ teaspoon salt

½ teaspoon cream of tartar
1 teaspoon vanilla
2 egg whites, beaten stiff

Combine sugar, water, salt and cream of tartar in saucepan. Heat to boiling point one minute only. Remove from heat immediately and pour over egg whites to which vanilla has been added. Beat with electric mixer until stiff enough to spread. Flavoring may be changed to suit taste.

Helen Cross, Whiting, Ind.

FLUFFY WHITE ICING

1½ cups granulated sugar
½ cup water
⅛ teaspoon cream of tartar

2 egg whites
½ teaspoon vanilla

Boil water, sugar and cream of tartar together until it threads, or 238°F. Pour hot syrup over stiffly beaten egg whites, beat until cool. Add vanilla. Spread on cake at once.

Anna B. Russell, Cleveland, Oh.

DOUBLE BOILER FROSTING

2 egg whites
1½ teaspoons vanilla or
**   peppermint**
¼ teaspoon cream of tartar

⅓ cup water
Few drops of pink or green
**   coloring**
1½ cups sugar

Place over boiling water, and beat with rotary beater until mixture holds its shape.

Anna K. Hruskovich, Whiting, Ind.

MOCHA FROSTING

6 tablespoons butter
3 cups confectioners' sugar

6 tablespoons cocoa
6 tablespoons boiling coffee

Mix butter into the sugar, add cocoa and the boiling coffee. Stir and beat well, then spread on cake.

Anna B. Russell, Cleveland, Oh.

ORANGE FROSTING

1 pound powdered sugar
3 egg whites

Lump of butter, size of an egg
Rind of 2 small oranges

Cream altogether and spread between and on top of orange cake.

Anna Vizza, Chicago, Ill.

ORANGE FROSTING

2 tablespoons orange juice
1 tablespoon melted butter
About 1¼ cups sifted confectioners' sugar (more or less depending on consistency of icing).

Add sifted sugar (little by little) to the orange juice and melted butter, and beat thoroughly until smooth. Spread on top of cake, let stand until icing is slightly set, then cut cake.

Theresa A. Krasula, Chicago, Ill.

PINEAPPLE FILLING

2 tablespoons cornstarch
¼ cup sugar
2½ cups drained crushed pineapple

4 tablespoons orange juice
1 teaspoon lemon juice

Mix cornstarch and sugar. Add pineapple and cook until smooth and thickened. Add juices. Cool and spread between layers of cake.

Catherine Otrembiak, Chicago, Ill.

PRUNE FILLING

2 tablespoons sugar
3½ tablespoons cornstarch
1 cup prune juice
2 teaspoons lemon juice

1 teaspoon orange juice
1 teaspoon grated orange rind
¾ teaspoon grated lemon rind
1 cup chopped, cooked prunes

Combine sugar and cornstarch in top of double boiler, add prune juice, lemon juice and orange juice with the grated rinds and mix thoroughly. Add prunes and mix well. Place over rapidly boiling water and cook 10 minutes, stirring occasionally. Cool. This recipe makes enough filling to spread between two 9-inch layers.

Justine Kasovsky, Chicago, Ill.

SEA FOAM ICING

1 cup light brown sugar
2 egg whites

3 tablespoons cold water
¼ teaspoon vanilla

Place in top of double boiler, stir well. Place over vigorously boiling water. Water in lower part of double boiler should touch upper part. Beat constantly until mixture holds a peak, about 4 to 5 minutes. Remove, add flavoring and spread on cake.

Mary Vevurka, Chicago, Ill.

SOUR CREAM FILLING

½ cup sugar
2 beaten eggs
2 tablespoons butter

2 tablespoons flour
½ cup sour cream
½ cup chopped nut meats

Mix sugar and flour, add eggs, cream, flour and butter. Cook until thickened. Cool and fold in nuts. Filling enough for two layers.

Anna Hook, Munhall, Pa.

WHIPPED CREAM FROSTING

4 tablespoons flour
1 cup milk
½ cup butter

½ cup shortening
1 cup sugar
2 teaspoons vanilla

Mix flour and milk in saucepan. Cook over low flame until thick. Put in bowl and cool. Cream butter and shortening 4 minutes with electric mixer. Add sugar gradually and beat 4 minutes. Add flour paste and beat 4 minutes. Add vanilla and blend. Makes enough frosting for large cake, sides and top.

Clara Kucka, Whiting, Ind.

WHIPPED FROSTING

3 heaping tablespoons flour
¾ cup milk
6 tablespoons butter

6 tablespoons crisco
¾ cup powdered sugar
1 teaspoon vanilla

Use a double boiler in making this frosting for success. Place in top of double boiler the flour and gradually add the milk, and mix into a smooth paste. Cook over a low flame, (the bottom pan should have boiling water to start) until consistency is like mashed potatoes, stir constantly. Set aside and cool.

In a bowl, cream butter and Crisco for 5 minutes, add powdered sugar gradually and beat 5 minutes, add flour mixture and vanilla and beat another 5 minutes.

Margaret Czabala, Chicago, Ill.

MOCHA BUTTER FROSTING

2 tablespoons butter
1 cup confectioners' sugar
2 tablespoons strong hot coffee

1 teaspoon cocoa, dry
½ teaspoon vanilla

Cream the butter and sugar well, adding liquid and flavoring in any desired proportion, until thin enough to spread.

Try sometimes melting the butter and slowly adding to the other ingredients. You may find it a smoother frosting. This is excellent for a party cake.

Anna Krcha, Chicago, Ill.

LEMON FROSTING

2 tablespoons soft butter
1 cup confectioners' sugar

2 tablespoons lemon juice
Rind of 1 lemon

Cream the butter and sugar, add liquid flavoring and rind.

Anna Krcha, Chicago, Ill.

Candies

CANDY MAKING TESTS

SOFT BALL: 234 to 240 degrees on candy thermometer; syrup forms a soft ball in cold water when this degree is reached and is the test used when no thermometer is to be had. On rainy or damp days boil to a higher temperature; boil to a higher temperature when using brown sugar, and test for the soft ball stage. This temperature is usually used for fudges, penuche, fondant, frosting and some pop corn balls.

FIRM BALL: 244 to 248 degrees form a firm ball in cold water which will hold its shape on removal. This stage is used for caramels and taffy apples.

HARD BALL: 250 to 265 degrees forms a hard ball in cold water but is plastic and chewy on removal (use a little higher temperature on rainy or damp days); this stage is used for divinity, nougat and popcorn balls.

CRACK: 270 to 290 degrees; separates into heavy threads in cold water and will make crackling sound when rapped against side of cup; used for butterscotch and taffy.

HARD CRACK: 295 to 310 degrees; threads in cold water and is hard and brittle on removal. Care must be taken to avoid scorching, carmelizing and melting at this temperature. Used for brittles and glaces.

APRICOT MARBLES

1 cup dried apricots	**4 teaspoons lemon juice**
1 cup shredded coconut	**2 teaspoons grated orange rind**
½ cup nut meats	**⅛ teaspoon salt**
1 teaspoon grated lemon rind	

These require no cooking. Put through a food chopper the washed apricots, coconut, and nut meats and mix with the remaining ingredients. Knead, add confectioners' powdered sugar, if too soft to mold, use just enough to handle well for molding into balls. If too stiff, add a little orange juice to allow molding consistency. Form into balls measuring from ¾ to 1 inches in diameter and roll in granulated sugar.

Joan Oberta, Los Angeles, Ca.

STUFFED APRICOTS

1 pound dried apricots
10 ounces marshmallows
1 cup granulated sugar

½ cup water
Confectioners' sugar, powdered

Wash the apricots. Steam them over hot water in a colander for 20 minutes. Boil sugar and water together until it spins a thread. Place apricots in the syrup and stir them gently with a fork. Drain the apricots for a few minutes and place a piece of marshmallow in the center of each. Roll in powdered sugar before serving.

Helen Kubasak, Burbank, Ca.

CANDIED PEEL

Cut orange, lemon or grapefruit peel into narrow strips. Cook in boiling water until tender, or until the white is partly clear. Drain the peel.

Make a syrup of sugar and water. Quantity depending on the amount of peel. Use two parts of sugar to one part of water. Measure the peel and double the amount to get the correct measure of sugar. Equal the quantity of peel for correct measure of water. Boil sugar and water ten minutes or until the thread stage is reached. Add peel and simmer for 20 or 25 minutes, stirring occasionally with a fork. (During the boiling, a few drops of either red or green coloring may be added to the grapefruit or lemon peel, if desired to give it a delicate tint). Drain the pieces and roll in granulated sugar. Spread out on a paper and dry over night. The pieces may be shaped before they harden.

Justine Kasovsky, Chicago, Ill.

BUTTERSCOTCH

1 pound sugar
3 tablespoons water
3 tablespoons butter

Mix sugar and water in a porcelain saucepan. Add butter and simmer without stirring until a spoonful tested in cold water becomes brittle. Turn into well buttered pans and set aside to cool. Cut into squares with a buttered knife before the candy hardens.

Anna B. Russell, Cleveland, Oh.

CARAMELS

1 cup molasses
1 cup brown sugar
2 tablespoons butter

1 cup chocolate
Nuts

Mix molasses, brown sugar and butter. Boil until a spoonful dropped into cold water will form a soft ball between the fingers. Add chocolate, cook three minutes and turn into well buttered pans. Add nut meats if desired. Cut into squares with a buttered knife, when nearly cold.

Anna B. Russell, Cleveland, Oh.

CARAMEL CORN *(1½ quarts)*

6 cups popped corn, ½ cup
  unpopped
1 cup granulated sugar
¼ cup light corn syrup

½ cup hot water
2 tablespoons butter or margarine
½ teaspoon salt
2½ tablespoons molasses

Cook sugar, corn syrup and hot water rapidly in a heavy two quart saucepan to 260 degrees on candy thermometer. Then reduce heat to medium, add butter, salt and molasses. Continue cooking until golden brown, 260-270 degrees. Stir occasionally across bottom of pan to prevent scorcing. When done, pour this syrup at once over the popped corn in a very large bowl and mix quickly with two forks to distribute syrup. Spread caramel corn on table top. When cool enough to handle, break apart in good size pieces.

Clara Kucka, Whiting, Ind.

CARAMEL TAFFY APPLES

1 cup sugar
½ cup white corn syrup
1 can sweetened condensed milk
1 teaspoon vanilla

6 to 8 medium apples
Shredded coconut, if desired
Chopped nuts, if desired

Place sugar, corn syrup, sweetened condensed milk, and vanilla in a heavy saucepan. Cook slowly, stir gently and constantly until the mixture registers 244 degrees on the candy thermometer, or until it forms a firm ball when tried in cold water. Cool mixture slightly. Wash, dry, remove stems, and place a skewer in each apple. Dip apples into syrup one at a time; twirl gently to coat evenly, then roll in chopped nuts or shredded coconut or leave plain. Place on waxed paper and let stand until caramel is set.

Rose Fedorko, Whiting, Ind.

CINNAMON TAFFY APPLES

2 cups sugar
1 cup water
½ cup corn syrup
½ teaspoon cinnamon flavoring

1 teaspoon red coloring
1 dozen small firm apples
1 dozen wooden skewers

Boil water, syrup and sugar together until a brown caramel color is reached (at about 250°F) . Remove from the heat and add cinnamon and red coloring. Cool slightly. Meanwhile force a skewer firmly into the core of each apple. Dip the apples one at a time into the heavy red syrup, drain well, and then place on a buttered baking sheet to cool.

Emily Jurinak, Chicago, Ill.

CHOCOLATE BALL CONFECTION

½ **pound walnut meats**
½ **pound sweet chocolate**
9 pieces zwieback

½ **teaspoon cinnamon**
1½ **teaspoons sugar**
2 tablespoons rose water

Grind walnuts, chocolate and zwieback together using fine knife. Mix with cinnamon, sugar and rosewater, using fingertips to blend. Form into balls about 1 inch in diameter. Press firmly in palm of hand. Roll in sugar. Ready to serve.

Lillian Renfro, Whiting, Ind.

MAPLE FUDGE

1 cup granulated sugar
1 cup maple sugar
1 tablespoon corn syrup

Few grains salt
½ **cup rich milk or light cream**
2 tablespoons butter

Boil all ingredients to soft ball stage (235 degrees on candy thermometer). Cool by placing the pan in cold water until it is possible to hold the hand on the bottom of pan with comfort. Beat vigorously. When beating is started, the cooled candy mixture is quite stiff and has a shiny appearance. With continued beating the candy grows clear, then a light color and finally it suddenly softens. At this point, turn out quickly into a buttered pan. If turned out at the right instant it spreads easily over the pan, stiffens quickly and has a glossy finish. Mark in squares.

Loretta Kasovsky, Chicago, Ill

VASSAR FUDGE

2 cups sugar
1 cup milk
1 tablespoon butter
¼ **teaspoon salt**

2 teaspoons vanilla
1½ **cups figs and dates chopped**
1 cup walnuts

Cook first four ingredients until it forms a soft ball in water, or spins a thread. Remove from fire and add vanilla, chopped figs and dates and walnut meats. Beat to a cream in sauce pan.

Anna B. Russell, Cleveland, Oh.

NEW ORLEANS PRALINES

3 cups granulated sugar
1¼ cups water
¼ teaspoon cream of tartar

1½ cups pecan meats
1 tablespoon maple extract

Cook all the above ingredients together to themometer reading of 238° (soft ball stage), remove from fire and mix with spoon about four minutes until mixture appears granular. Drop tablespoon of mix onto waxed paper (double your waxed paper) forming individual pralines. Be sure to lift waxed paper from table slightly as heat of candy will cause paper to stick to table.

Justine Uhlarik, Chicago, Ill.

OCEAN FOAM CANDY

3 cups brown sugar
1 cup boiling water
2 egg whites

Stir sugar in boiling water until dissolved and cook until it forms a soft ball in cold water. Take off from fire. When the mixture stops bubbling pour the beaten eggs gradually and beat well. Add nuts. When candy stiffens drop from spoon the same as sea foam.

Anna Domasco, Pittsburgh, Pa.

PEANUT BRITTLE

2 cups sugar
1 cup syrup, light
½ cup water
2 cups raw peanuts

2 teaspoons soda
1 teaspoon vanilla
1 teaspoon butter

Boil sugar, syrup and water to crack stage, (a sample dropped into cold water will clink against the cup) add peanuts, cook about three minutes or until golden brown. Add soda to syrup and remove from heat at once. This causes the syrup to bubble furiously and produce a spongy texture. Add vanilla and butter, as soon as foaming has subsided. Pour candy without stirring onto large shallow greased platter or pan. When cold, break up and it is ready to eat.

Lillian Renfro, Whiting, Ind.

UNCOOKED PEANUT BUTTER CANDY

½ cup peanut butter
⅔ cup eagle brand condensed milk

¼ cup chopped nuts
2 squares melted baking chocolate
1¾ cups powdered sugar

Mix well peanut butter, milk and chocolate. Add sugar and nuts. Knead well with hand. Shape into roll two inches in diameter. Wrap in waxed paper and set in refrigerator for four or five hours before cutting. Yields 18 slices.

Bernadette Evans, Homestead, Pa.

PINEAPPLE CREAM CANDY

1 cup white sugar
½ cup light brown sugar
½ cup grated pineapple and juice

Boil together until mixture forms a soft ball in cold water. Add one teaspoon butter. Remove from fire and add: 12 marshmallows, ½ teaspoon lemon extract, one cup nuts. Beat until creamy, and spread on buttered platter to cool. Cut in squares.

Van Offelen Juniors, Chicago, Ill.

POPCORN BALLS

1½ pounds shelled popcorn
1 cup white sugar
½ cup brown sugar

⅜ cup karo syrup
½ cup water

Pop the popcorn, sift out any unpopped kernels and put in a slow oven to keep warm until you have finished cooking the syrup. Cook and stir white sugar, brown sugar, syrup and water until sugar is dissolved. Then cook to 240 degrees, or until it makes a soft ball when dropped from a teaspoon into a little cold water. Mix syrup with popcorn and let cool. When cool enough to handle, butter hands and shape into balls.

Joanne Stoffel, Chicago, Ill.

POPCORN PATTIES

1 cup brown sugar
⅓ cup cream
½ teaspoon vinegar

Few grains salt
2 cups freshly popped, coarsely chopped corn

Bring cream and sugar to boiling point. Add vinegar and boil to soft ball form, or about 238°F. Add salt and corn. Stir thoroughly until all of the corn is coated with this creamy mixture. Drop from a spoon in patty shapes on oiled paper. Use double thickness of waxed paper, if desired, and lift paper occasionally to prevent sticking.

Joanne Stoffel, Chicago, Ill.

PUFFED RICE FAVORS (Easter Baskets)

3 tablespoons dark syrup
1 tablespoon butter
½ cup sugar

⅓ cup water
¼ teaspoon salt
2 tablespoons vinegar

Boil until it threads. Remove from stove and add ¼ teaspoon soda. Pour over 1 box of puffed rice. Mold while hot in cereal bowls forming a nest in the center. Color 1 package coconut with green vegetable coloring. Use coconut in nest for green grass. Add candy chicks or bunnies and Easter eggs. Makes nice favors for children because all can be eaten.

Mary Fedor, Streator, Ill.

RICE FLAKE CANDY

½ cup butter
1 box rice flakes

30 marshmallows
1 cup chopped nuts

Melt butter in large kettle. Add marshmallows and melt. Add rice flakes and chopped nuts. Pour into shallow pan and press with spoon occasionally until cold. When partly cooled, cut in squares.

Bernadette Evans, Homestead, Pa.

POTATO CANDY

One medium sized baked potato mashed while hot. Add one pound powdered sugar and beat well. Add one tablespoon butter, one can of moist coconut. Cream all together well and spread in a buttered pan. Melt two squares of chocolate and pour on top.

Mary Rengh, Johnstown, Pa.

ENGLISH TOFFEE

1 cup granulated sugar
½ pound butter
3 tablespoons water

1 teaspoon vanilla
3 plain Hersheys
¾ cup chopped pecans

Place first four ingredients in a saucepan and cook until brown, (about ten minutes after boiling point is reached) stirring all the time to prevent burning. Pour into a buttered fudge pan. Lay Hersheys across the hot mass and spread. Sprinkle pecans over top. Cool and break into pieces.

Margaret Rengh, Johnstown, Pa.

FRUIT ROLL OR BAKELESS FRUIT BALLS *(a confection)*

½ **pound dates**	1½ **pound seedless raisins**
½ **pound figs, dried**	1 **cup nuts, pecans preferred**

Grind all together, fine, then work in one cup pulverized or powdered sugar. Form into rolls or small balls. Roll in crushed nuts when ready to serve. Keep in a cool place.

Margaret Rengh, Johnstown, Pa.

FRUIT JELLY CANDY

2 cans undiluted frozen fruit juice (lemon, orange, grape)
4 tablespoons unflavored gelatin
⅔ cup sugar
1 cup light corn syrup
¼ cup cold water
½ cup sifted confectioners' sugar or powdered coconut

Mix the water and gelatin and let stand five minutes. In the meantime place undiluted frozen juice in heavy pan and melt over low heat, when melted remove from heat, stir in gelatin. Return to a low fire to dissolve the gelatin and then add the sugar and stir until dissolved. Then blend in well the corn syrup. Remove from heat and pour into 8 x 8 inch pan that had been rinsed in cold water. Cool, then chill until firm. Cut in 1 inch squares and roll each square in sifted confectioners' sugar, or coconut. Makes 64 pieces.

Canning

- JELLIES - MARMALADES - PRESERVES -

APPLE ORANGE MARMALADE

10½ cups apple juice
6 cups sugar
1 cup orange pulp, rind and juice (ground in food chopper)

Combine all ingredients and cook together until it jells. Pour into jelly glasses and seal.

Margaret DeSilva, Chicago, Ill.

APRICOT MARMALADE

1 pound dried apricots
1 pint water
2 cups sugar

Wash fruit and soak 8 hours. Cook in same water and simmer until very soft. Rub through coarse sieve, return to fire, when it reaches boiling point, add sugar and simmer gently for 40 to 45 minutes, stirring almost constantly, as it scorches very easily. Pour into hot glasses and seal while hot.

Helen Cross, Whiting, Ind.

BLACK RASPBERRY JELLY

2 pints raspberry juice
2 apples
2 pints sugar

Cook berries and apples, strain. Add sugar. Cook until a jelly consistency. Pour into sterilized glasses and seal with paraffin.

Margaret Mihalik, Indiana Harbor, Ind.

CURRANT JELLY

2 quarts currants
1 cup water
3 cups granulated sugar to each 4 cups of juice

Wash, pick over currants, but do not remove stems. Mash in bottom of preserving kettle. Add cup of water, cover and simmer about 15 minutes. Put into jelly bag and drain off juice. Measure 4 cups juice into kettle. Bring to boiling point and boil 5 minutes. Add 3 cups granulated sugar, again bring to boil and boil 5 to 8 minutes or until thermometer registers 218 to 220°F. Pour into sterilized jelly glasses, cover with melted paraffin; when paraffin is set, place cover on jelly glass. Store in dry place. Continue cooking 4 cups juice at a time, as above, until all juice is cooked.

Daughters of St. Francis, Lacon, Ill.

GRAPE JAM

4 cups washed and stemmed grapes
3 cups sugar

Mix together and mash well. Put on to boil for 15 to 20 minutes. Put through strainer and put in jars immediately and seal.

Rose Fedorko, Whiting, Ind.

PEACH JAM

18 peaches
5 whole oranges
Sugar

1 cup chopped maraschino
cherries

Peel peaches, cut in halves and remove seeds. Put peaches and oranges through food chopper, using coarse blade. Measure fruit; add 1½ times as much sugar as fruit. Cook until mixture sheets from spoon as for jelly. Add 1 cup chopped cherries. Pour into sterilized glasses, cover with paraffin. Makes about 5 pints.

Vern Jadrnak, Gary, Ind.

STRAWBERRY AND PINEAPPLE JAM

3⅓ cups (1¾ pounds) prepared fruit
6½ cups (2¾ pounds) sugar
½ bottle certo

To prepare fruit, crush completely or grind about 1 quart fully ripe berries. Each berry must be reduced to a pulp. Cut fine or grind 1 medium fully ripe pineapple or use a No. 2 can crushed pineapple. Combine fruits. Measure sugar and prepared fruit into large kettle, mix well. Bring to a full rolling boil over hottest fire. Stir constantly, before and while boiling. Boil hard 3 minutes. Remove from fire and stir in Certo. Then stir and skim by turns for just 5 minutes to cool slightly, to prevent floating fruit. Pour quickly. Paraffin at once. Makes about 9 glasses (6 fluid ounces each).

Rosemary Van Arkle, St. Joseph, Mich.

STRAWBERRY PRESERVES

8 cups berries
4 cups sugar
½ teaspoon red food coloring

Wash strawberries then stem, pour sugar over berries, place over low flame until sugar dissolves, allowing to boil 15 to 20 minutes, or use thermometer to temperature 218°F. Pour into glasses and top each with melted paraffin wax.

Helen Cross, Whiting, Ind.

SPICED PLUMS

5 pounds plums, pitted
5 pounds sugar

1 tablespoon cloves
2 tablespoons cinnamon

Mix plums and sugar, let stand until enough juice, to prevent scorching, is extracted. Put the spices in a cheesecloth bag and boil with the fruit and sugar until thick, stirring frequently. Remove spices and seal in hot sterilized glasses. Yield: Ten 6-ounce glasses.

Theresa Krasula, Chicago, Ill.

- RELISHES -

CHILI SAUCE

50 tomatoes
25 onions
1 bunch celery
1 quart vinegar
10 green peppers
3 cups sugar
3 tablespoons salt

1 tablespoon whole allspice
1 tablespoon whole cloves
(remove heads)
1 tablespoon whole cinnamon,
broken
1 teaspoon grated nutmeg

Put tomatoes, peppers, onions, celery through food chopper or cut in small pieces. Add all other ingredients and boil 2½ hours or until thick, stirring frequently to prevent burning. As soon as sauce is of desired consistency, pour into sterilized jars and seal at once. (Tie spices in cheese cloth).

Mary Osadjan, Chicago, Ill.

CHILI SAUCE

20 pounds tomatoes
12 hot peppers
2 stalks celery
3 pounds onions
½ teaspoon nutmeg

1 teaspoon cinnamon
2 teaspoons black pepper
2 tablespoons mixed-spices
1½ cups vinegar

Peel tomatoes, add ground peppers, onions and celery. Add rest of the ingredients. Add salt and sugar to taste. Tie mixed spices in cheesecloth. Cook for 3 hours. Mix occasionally to prevent scorching. Remove mixed-spices. Put in sterilized pint jars and seal.

Anna Stanek, Whiting, Ind.

CHILI SAUCE

5 cups stewed tomatoes
2 onions, chopped
2 red peppers, chopped
3 green peppers, chopped
⅓ cup honey
½ cup lemon juice
1 teaspoon dry mustard

3 whole cloves
½ teaspoon allspice
½ teaspoon celery seed
½ teaspoon cinnamon
¼ teaspoon salt
3 bay leaves

Strain tomatoes and add rest of the ingredients. Heat gradually to a boiling point and allow to simmer slowly for about two hours. Pour, while boiling hot into hot jars and seal at once. Will keep for sometime.

Grace Margala, Los Angeles, Ca.

CHILI SAUCE

12 large ripe tomatoes
2 large onions
4 green peppers
2 tablespoons salt

2 tablespoons sugar
1 tablespoon cinnamon
2½ cups vinegar

Peel the tomatoes and onions and chop them fine. Chop the peppers very fine. Stir all together, add salt, sugar, cinnamon and vinegar. Boil for one hour stirring well. Pour into clean, hot jars and seal.

Veronica Radocha, Coaldale, Pa.

CHILI SAUCE

½ bushel tomatoes (red)
3 stalks celery
9 medium green peppers, chopped
9 medium hot peppers, chopped

3 cups onions, chopped
3 cups sugar
1⅛ cups vinegar
9 rounded tablespoons salt

Peel tomatoes and put on to boil. Drain off about one quart of juice. Add chopped peppers, onions and celery to the tomatoes. Boil for three hours. If sauce is too thick add the juice that was taken out. Add sugar, vinegar and salt in the last 15 minutes of boiling. Preserve in mason jars.

Benedictine Slovak Sisters, Chicago, Ill.

HOT DOG RELISH

5 cups ground cucumber
3 cups ground onion
3 cups chopped celery
2 hot red peppers, ground
2 sweet red or green peppers, ground

¾ cup salt
1½ quarts water
1 quart white vinegar
3 cups sugar
2 teaspoons mustard seed
2 tablespoons celery seed

Combine vegetables, add salt and water; let stand overnight; drain. Heat vinegar, sugar, mustard and celery seed to boiling point. Add vegetables, bring to a boil. Cook slowly 10 minutes. Seal in hot sterilized jars. Makes 5 pints.

Anna K. Hruskovich, Whiting, Ind.

GREEN TOMATO RELISH

1 peck green tomatoes	3 hot red peppers
1 cup salt	2 cups sugar
8 sweet green peppers	¼ cup salt
1 small head cabbage	2 tablespoons allspice
2 bunches celery	2 tablespoons mustard seed
6 medium size onions	3½ cups vinegar

Wash tomatoes, cut out the stem end. Cut in pieces, sprinkle with salt, and let stand over night. In the morning, drain and rinse well with water. Wash other vegetables and prepare. Remove stems, seeds and white membrane from peppers, chop fine. Chop cabbage, celery and onion, or run through food chopper. Put sugar, vinegar and spices, into large saucepan and bring to boiling point. Stir until sugar is dissolved. Add the vegetables to vinegar, putting the hot red peppers in whole. Cook slowly until the vegetables are just tender, about 30 minutes. Pack into hot sterilized jars and seal at once.

Anna B. Russell, Cleveland, Oh.

CABBAGE TOMATO RELISH

1 peck green tomatoes	6 onions
1 cabbage	1 stalk celery
6 red peppers	½ cup salt
3 cups sugar	1 tablespoon cloves
3 quarts vinegar	2 tablespoons celery seed

Put through grinder tomatoes, cabbage, peppers, onions and celery. Add salt, let stand over night. Drain in the morning, add the sugar, cloves, celery seed and vinegar. Cook ½ hour. Pour into hot, sterilized jars and seal.

Veronica Radocha, Coaldale, Pa.

- CANNED VEGETABLES -

MINCE MEAT

1 peck green tomatoes
1 peck cooking apples
3 pounds dark raisins

3 pounds brown sugar
1 pound suet

Grind all ingredients together and cook, add ½ pint vinegar, cook for 45 minutes. Keep mixing. Pour into warm jars and seal, store in cool place.

Mary Slifcak, Cleveland, Oh

MUSHROOMS

Wash mushrooms, cover with 1 quart of water, add 1 tablespoon vinegar and let stand 10 minutes. Drain. Cover mushrooms with 1 quart hot water, 1 teaspoon salt and 1 tablespoon vinegar and cook for 5 minutes, drain. Put mushrooms ¾ full in pint jars. In each jar put 1 teaspoon salt and pour boiling water to fill jar, put on cap and boil 2½ hours in boiling water bath, then tighten caps.

Veronica Gluvna, Lorain, Oh.

CANNED MUSHROOMS

Wash and clean fresh mushrooms, boil for 15 minutes. Rinse off and pack in quart size fruit jars. Fill jars with clear water and add 1 teaspoon salt to each quart. Tighten lids, then loosen slightly. Process in steam pressure cooker 60 minutes, at 10 lbs. pressure. They may be used any way.

Mary Fedor, Streator, Ill.

- PICKLING -

PICKLED SLICED CARROTS

4 bunches carrots
1 teaspoon salt
½ cup granulated sugar

1 large clove of garlic
2½ cups cider vinegar
1 small hot red pepper, sliced

Wash and clean carrots. Steam in small amount of water until tender, about 10 minutes. Drain and slice. Bring vinegar and sugar to the boiling point. Fill sterilized jars with sliced carrots, add garlic, salt and sliced red hot pepper. Pour boiling vinegar syrup over the carrots within 1 inch of top of jar. Seal. This does not need processing.

Helen Kubasak, Burbank, Ca.

PICKLED BEETS

2 cups sugar
2 cups water
2 cups strong vinegar
1 teaspoon whole cloves

1 teaspoon whole allspice
1 teaspoon cinnamon stick
1 thinly sliced lemon

Select young beets, cook until tender, dip into cold water. Peel off skins, slice and drop into hot syrup made of sugar, water, vinegar and spices, which have been put in a bag. Add the sliced lemon and bring to boiling point. Simmer gently for a few minutes. Pack into sterilized jar and seal.

Dorothy Sabol, Whiting, Ind.

PICKLED ONIONS

4 quarts small pearl onions
2 quarts vinegar
1 cup salt

2 cups sugar
½ cup mixed pickle spices

Pour boiling water over onions. Let stand two minutes. Drain, cover with cold water and peel. Cover onions with cold water and sprinkle with 1 cup salt. Let stand over night. Rinse with fresh cold water. Tie spices in thin bag and boil with sugar and vinegar. Add onions and bring to a boil. Remove spices. Pack while hot into hot sterilized jars and seal.

Mary Vevurka, Chicago, Ill.

PICKLED ONIONS

Peel small onions until the white is reached. Scald in strong salted water, (4 tablespoons salt to 1 quart water), then drain. Pack in jars and sprinkle white mustard and pepper over the onions. Cover them with a boiling hot solution of vinegar. When cold, put in clean, cold jars and seal. One tablespoon salad oil may be added to the top of the mixture.

Veronica Radocha, Coaldale, Pa.

PICKLED PEARS

1 peck of pears
½ gallon cider vinegar
1 quart water

2 pounds brown sugar (light)
Cinnamon sticks

Boil vinegar, sugar and spices. Put pears into vinegar and boil until tender. Stick a clove into each pear. Pack in hot sterilized jars, adding syrup to within ½ inch of top. Seal.

Anna B. Russell, Cleveland, Oh.

CRISP PICKLE SLICES

4 quarts sliced cucumbers
  (medium size)
6 white onions, sliced
3 cloves garlic
1 green pepper
1 red pepper

⅓ cup salt
3 cups white vinegar
5 cups sugar
1½ teaspoons turmeric
1½ teaspoons celery seed
2 tablespoons mustard seed

Slice cucumbers thin. Add sliced onions, garlic, and peppers cut in narrow strips. Add salt, cover with cracked ice, mix thoroughly. Let stand 3 hours. Drain. Combine remaining ingredients, pour over cucumber mixture. Heat to boiling, seal in sterilized jars. Makes 8 pints.

Florence Hovanec, Whiting, Ind.

CRYSTAL PICKLES

25 cucumbers (dill size)

Wash, put into brine strong enough to float an egg, plenty of salt. Put pickles into brine, let stand 2 weeks. Make sure the pickles are all covered. The 15th day remove pickles and wash them, slice ½ inch thick. Put pickles back into clean water, add piece of alum size of walnut. Let stand overnight. Drain and wash again. Make syrup.

1 quart cider vinegar
2 quarts sugar

1 teaspoon whole clove
2 sticks cinnamon

Boil together, then pour over sliced pickles. Repeat this for 3 mornings. Fourth morning put pickles in jars and pour boiling vinegar over and seal. Best time to put up these pickles is latter part of August or early September.

Mary Skriba, Riverside, Ill.

BREAD AND BUTTER PICKLES

12 onions
25 medium cucumbers
½ cup salt

SYRUP
4 teaspoons mustard seed
4 teaspoons celery seed
4 teaspoons turmeric
2 quarts vinegar
4 cups sugar

Slice cucumbers and onions. Add salt and ice water to cover. Let stand 3 hours, in order to make pickles very crisp. Drain, and heat in syrup which has been made during the soaking. Heat 2 minutes in syrup. Do not boil. Place in hot, scalded jars and seal.

Helen Cross, Whiting, Ind.

BREAD AND BUTTER PICKLES

1 gallon medium sized cucumbers	5 cups sugar
6 small white onions	1½ teaspoons turmeric
1 green pepper	½ teaspoon ground cloves
1 sweet red pepper	2 tablespoons mustard seed
½ cup salt	4 cups vinegar
Cracked ice	2 teaspoons celery seed

Thin-slice cucumbers. Add sliced onions and peppers cut in narrow strips. Add salt, cover with cracked ice, mix thoroughly. Let stand 3 hours, drain. Combine remaining ingredients, pour over cucumber mixture. Bring to boiling. Seal in sterilized jars. Makes 8 pints.

Anna K. Hruskovich, Whiting, Ind.

CUCUMBER PICKLES

1 gallon vinegar	1 cup salt
1 large cup sugar	1 tablespoon mustard seed

Put a layer of large grape leaves in the bottom of a 3 gallon jar and fill the jar with cucumbers. On top of the cucumbers put sugar, salt and mustard seed. Pour over this the vinegar, and cover with grape leaves. Keep the cucumbers covered, they must be in the vinegar. Ready for use in 2 or 3 weeks.

Leona Chabala, Nokomis, Ill.

CUCUMBER PICKLES

100 cucumbers	1 cups sugar
1 ounce mustard seed	2 red peppers, cut in rings
1 ounce cloves	Vinegar
2 teaspoons salt	

Use the smallest cucumbers you can get, making 2½ inches the limit in length. Put the spices in thin muslin bags, using at least two bags. Place the cucumbers in a kettle with enough good vinegar of medium strength to cover them. Place bags of spices in the vinegar, together with the salt, sugar and peppers. Heat the vinegar as slowly as possible; when it is scalding hot, but not boiling, the pickles are ready to set away. If this recipe is carefully followed, satisfactory results will be obtained. If the vinegar boils, the pickles will soften.

Veronica Radocha, Coaldale, Pa.

DILL PICKLES

1 bushel pickles, 3 inches long
1 gallon vinegar
8 quarts water
2 cups sugar

2 tablespoons mixed spices
Garlic
Dill

Wash pickles, in bottom of jar put dill, clove garlic and 1 tablespoon salt, pack pickles in jars, boil vinegar, water, sugar and spices 5 minutes, pour over pickles. Put caps on jars and boil 15 minutes in boiling water bath.

Veronica Gluvna, Lorain, Oh.

DILL PICKLES

1 peck pickles

Wash pickles, soak in salty water for 4 hours. Pack into clean jars, put into each jar a little dill, teaspoon salt and 1 teaspoon sugar.

Prepare: Cook 1 cup vinegar, and 2 cups water for each quart of pickles, let cool, then pour over pickles, and put on covers. Put in steam bath for 15 minutes.

Theresa Sajan, Chicago, Ill.

DILL PICKLES

Pickles
8 quarts water
1 quart vinegar

1 cup salt
Dill

Let water, vinegar and salt boil hard and pour over pickles and dill that have been packed in jars. Seal hot.

Sue Ogurchock, New Kensington, Pa.

DILL PICKLES

Boil 1 quart vinegar, 2 quarts water. To each quart jar add: 1 teaspoon salt, 1 teaspoon sugar, 1 or 2 cloves of garlic and some dill.

Put washed and scrubbed pickles in jars, add hot brine, cover and cold pack until pickles start to turn yellow. Remove from canner. Cool and store away.

Helen Cross, Whiting, Ind.

KOSHER DILL PICKLES

1 bushel cucumbers, 4 inch	1 dozen sweet peppers
2 gallons white vinegar	Garlic
1 bag of salt	Dill

Wash peppers and dill. Wash cucumbers well with a cloth. Place in sterilized jar sprig of dill, ¼ piece of pepper, ½ clove of garlic and cucumbers.

Make a solution of: 2 quarts white vinegar, 6 quarts water, 2 cups salt. Bring to boiling point. Pour over cucumbers slowly so jar won't crack. Fill about 6 or 8 jars at a time. Allow to stand until pickles turn color, about 5 or 10 minutes, then pour off the vinegar from all the jars back into the kettle and use again for rest of the cucumbers. Always heat to boiling point.

Have another kettle ready of the same solution as above, allow to come to a boil, pour over the 6 to 8 jars, having liquid cover the cucumbers to overflowing and seal while hot. Put away in dark place. Will stay clear, crisp and delicious for a long time.

Mary Pataky, Whiting, Ind.

KOSHER DILL PICKLES

20 to 23 dill sized cucumbers	1 quart vinegar
¼ teaspoon powdered alum	1 cup salt
1 piece of garlic	2 quarts water
1 hot red pepper	Grape leaves and dill

Wash and dry cucumbers. Put layer of dill and grape leaves and red pepper in stone jar. Add the cucumbers. Put more dill, red pepper and grape leaves on top. Boil salt, water and vinegar, pour over the cucumbers, add garlic and alum. Cover and keep cucumbers weighted down under the brine.

LUNCHEON PICKLES

3 quarts water	2 pounds sugar
1 quart vinegar	1 tablespoon celery seed

Slice pickles, let stand overnight in salt water. Mix ingredients and boil. Put sliced cucumbers in jar and let stand 20 minutes and seal.

Sue Ogurchock, New Kensington, Pa.

MUSTARD PICKLES

1 pint cucumbers, about 2 inches long
1 pint large cucumbers, sliced
1 pint pickling onions
1 cup string beans, cut in 1 inch diagonal pieces
1 pint small green tomatoes
1 pint cauliflower, cut in small pieces
3 red peppers, chopped
3 green peppers, chopped
1 cup carrots, sliced or quartered
1¼ cups white sugar
4 tablespoons flour
½ teaspoon turmeric
1 teaspoon celery salt
4 tablespoons dry mustard
Vinegar
1 cup salt to one gallon water for soaking vegetables

All vegetables should be tender. Soak vegetables in salt water brine overnight. Drain and soak in clear water for 3 hours. Drain and rinse vegetables. Cover with equal parts vinegar and water. Allow to stand 1 hour, then scald the vegetables in this liquid. Make a dressing by mixing the sugar, flour, mustard, turmeric and celery salt, then add 3 pints of hot vinegar slowly, stirring to make a smooth paste. Cook the mixture over a pan of hot water until the sauce thickens. Drain vegetables thoroughly. Pour mustard dressing over them while they are hot and simmer for five minutes. Pack into hot, clean jars and seal.

Veronica Radocha, Coaldale, Pa.

SLICED SWEET PICKLES

1 gallon small cucumbers, sliced very thin
8 small onions, sliced thin
2 green peppers
½ cup salt

BRINE
5 cups sugar
1½ teaspoon ground cloves
2 tablespoons mustard seed
5 cups vinegar
1 teaspoon celery seed

Put in crock cucumbers, onions, peppers and salt. Place weight on top and let stand for 3 hours, then drain. Combine vinegar, sugar and spices. Bring to a good boil, add cucumbers, onions and peppers. Heat through, then pack in jars at once. Seal while hot.

Mary Fedor, Streator, Ill.

SAUERKRAUT

Select good firm cabbage. Shred very fine. Mix every 5 pounds of cabbage with 4 tablespoons salt. Press down into a crock with a potato masher. Cover with a cloth, weigh cabbage down with a plate and let stand. Fermentation will require 8 to 10 days. Pack cabbage into clean jars, add enough of the brine to come to within ½ inch of the top of the jar, seal and process in water bath 15 minutes. During the time the kraut is ripening the brine should be skimmed as often as necessary and the cloth scalded after each skimming.

Sophie Kaminsky, Whiting, Ind.

DILL GREEN TOMATO PICKLES

Small sturdy green tomatoes	2 quarts water
Stalk of celery	1 quart vinegar
Sweet green peppers	1 cup salt
Garlic	Dill to taste

Fill the sterilized jar with small firm green tomatoes and add to each quart one piece of garlic, one piece of celery, about half a green pepper sliced and a piece of dill. Make a brine of the water, vinegar and salt and boil for about five minutes. (You may add a little sugar into the brine if you wish). Pour over the pickles and seal. Ready for use in 4 to 6 weeks.

PICKLED TOMATOES

1 peck green tomatoes, cut in quarters, salt overnight
20 green peppers, cut in quarters, salt over night
In the morning rinse and drain, both tomatoes and peppers

Combine vinegar and water: 2 parts water to 1 part vinegar, enough to cover, add 1½ cups sugar, 2 tablespoons mustard seed, 2 tablespoons celery seed, bring to a boil. Have jars sterilized. Put tomatoes and peppers into solution while boiling. Pack immediately and seal.

Gizella Tapajna, Whiting, Ind.

WATERMELON PICKLES

9 pounds prepared rind	1 tablespoon whole cloves
3¼ quarts water	2 sticks cinnamon
½ cup salt	1 teaspoon cassia buds
3 quarts sugar	¼ teaspoon (few) broken pieces
3½ cups cider vinegar	nutmeg
1½ lemons, thinly sliced	

Prepare the rind by cutting away all green and pink portions, and cutting the white part into 2 inch lengths. Cover with water and salt, and let soak over night. Next morning, rinse thoroughly with several changes of fresh water, barely cover with fresh water and cook until tender. It will take a little more than one hour. Drain, and drop rind into syrup made by heating sugar and vinegar to boiling point; add lemon slices, and spices in a cheesecloth bag. Cook until rind is transparent, which will take about 1½ hours, perhaps a little longer. During this time the syrup should be simmering gently. Pack in clean, hot sterile jars, cover with syrup and seal. Makes about 3½ quarts. These are excellent if chilled well before serving. The cassia buds may be purchased in the drug store.

Irene Pekarcik, Los Angeles, Ca.

CANNED GRAPE JUICE

Grapes should be picked over, washed, and stems removed before putting into preserving kettle. Mash, heat to boiling point, cover and simmer 30 minutes. Strain through heavy jelly bag, do not squeeze. Measure juice, and add 1 cup sugar for each 4 cups of juice. Bring to boiling point and boil 5 minutes. Fill hot sterilized jars and seal at once.

Anna Lissy, Whiting, Ind.

TOMATO JUICE

10 pounds tomatoes   **1 cup chopped celery**
½ cup chopped onion   **2 teaspoons salt**
⅔ cup chopped green pepper **1 tablespoon sugar**

Cook until boiled apart, strain, pour into hot sterilized pint jars, and seal. Makes about 6 pints.

Susan Galgan, Chicago, Ill.

HOME CANNED LEMON SYRUP

Juice of 12 lemons   **6 cups water**
6 cups sugar   **Rind of 3 lemons**

Put sugar, water and rind in kettle, boil hard for five minutes. Add juice and boil one minute longer. Pour into clean hot sterilized jars and seal. Use one cup syrup for each one quart water. Best to make this recipe when lemons are reasonable.

Mary Pilat, Chicago, Ill.

Cookies

ALMOND COOKIES

1 cup butter or half butter and
   half lard
1 cup sugar
½ teaspoon almond extract
½ teaspoon vanilla

2 eggs, separated
2⅔ cups sifted flour
½ teaspoon salt
50 blanched almonds

Cream butter and sugar. Add flavoring and egg yolks, one at a time. Beat until light; add flour, salt and mix well. Roll into balls about 1-inch in diameter, dip into unbeaten egg whites and place 2 inches apart on greased cookie sheet, pressed down with half an almond. Bake in moderate oven, 350°F, about 10 minutes, until light brown. Makes 4 dozen.

Joliet, Ill.

ALMOND COOKIES

1 cup sweet butter
1 cup sugar
Pinch of salt
1 egg
5 hard boiled egg yolks

3 cups pastry flour
1 teaspoon baking powder
1 teaspoon almond extract
½ pound blanched almonds,
   chopped fine

Cream butter and sugar, add salt and well beaten egg. Mix thoroughly. Put the hard boiled egg yolks through a coarse sieve and blend into the first mixture. Gradually add the sifted flour and baking powder, add the almond extract. Lastly add the chopped almonds, reserving about ¼ cup for topping. When thoroughly mixed, turn out on floured board and roll out thin. If more flour is needed, add gradually. Cut out forms with cookie cutter and place on buttered baking sheet. Spread each cookie with whipped egg white and sprinkle with chopped almonds that have been mixed with sugar. Bake at 350°F about 12 minutes or until light brown.

Loretta Kasovsky, Chicago, Ill.

ALMOND BUTTER COOKIES

1 pound sugar
1 pound butter
1 pound flour

6 egg yolks
Few grains of salt
½ pound almonds, ground fine

Mix well, the sugar, butter, flour, egg yolks and salt, then lastly add ground almonds. Shape into little round cookies or any other shape you desire. Bake in moderate oven, 350°F.

Marie Hornick, Chicago, Ill.

ALMOND CRESCENTS

½ pound butter
¼ pound ground almonds, with skins
¼ cup powdered sugar
2 cups flour

Cream butter, add powdered sugar, almonds and flour. Form into crescents. Bake 15 to 20 minutes in moderate oven. When cool, sprinkle with powdered sugar.

Mary Bucz, Chicago, Ill.

ALMOND CRESCENTS

½ pound butter   2 cups flour
½ cup sugar   ½ pound almonds, cut coarse
2 teaspoons milk

Cream butter, sugar, add milk. Add sifted flour and almonds, mix just enough to hold together, then form little half moons. Bake in 325 or 350°F oven for 12 to 15 minutes.

Lydia Valencik, Chicago, Ill.

ALMOND HORNS

½ pound butter   Juice of 1 lemon
½ pound powdered sugar   ½ pound flour
2 egg yolks   ½ pound almonds, cut coarse
¼ teaspoon cinnamon

Cream butter, powdered sugar, yolks, cinnamon and lemon juice until creamy, then add flour and almonds. Form horns and bake 15 minutes at 350°F. Sprinkle with powdered sugar before serving.

Lydia Valencik, Chicago, Ill.

ANISE SEED COOKIES

1 cup butter   4 teaspoons baking powder
4 cups sugar   2 tablespoons Anise seed
4 eggs   8 cups flour
1 cup milk

Cream butter until light, gradually add sugar, creaming until light and fluffy. Beat eggs and stir them into creamed mixture. Add milk and enough flour to make a soft dough. Sift remaining flour with baking powder, add Anise seed, which has been rolled fine with the rolling pin. Chill dough, roll out to one-eighth inch thickness. Cut with animal cookie cutters. Bake at 425°F for about 8 to 10 minutes.

Anna B. Russell, Cleveland, Oh.

BANANA COOKIES

1½ cups flour
1 cup sugar
½ teaspoon soda

¾ teaspoon cinnamon
¼ teaspoon nutmeg
½ cup shortening

Mix all of the above ingredients together. Add:

1 cup mashed bananas
1¾ cups oatmeal

½ cup nuts

Mix all together and drop on greased cookie sheet. Bake at 350°F for 12 to 15 minutes.

Mary Skurka, Whiting, Ind.

BANANA NUT BARS

⅔ cup shortening
1½ cups sugar
2 egg yolks
1 cup mashed banana pulp
1½ cups sifted all purpose flour
1 teaspoon baking soda

¼ teaspoon salt
4 tablespoons sour cream
½ teaspoon vanilla
2 egg whites
¼ cup chopped nut meats

Cream shortening and sugar together. Stir in egg yolk. Add mashed banana pulp. Sift flour, soda and salt, add to creamed mixture alternately with sour cream. Mix well, add vanilla and stiffly beaten egg whites. Stir in nuts. Pour into buttered pan 8 x 13 inches. Bake at 325°F for 45 minutes. When cool, cut into strips and roll in powdered sugar.

Mary Lucas, Lakewood, Oh.

BLACK WALNUT COOKIES

½ cup shortening (part butter)
½ cup white sugar
½ cup brown sugar
1 egg
½ teaspoon vanilla

½ teaspoon salt
1½ tablespoons water
1½ cups cake flour
½ teaspoon soda
½ cup chopped black walnuts

Cream shortening and sugars, add egg, beat until mixture is fluffy. Add vanilla, salt and water. Gently stir in flour that has been sifted with soda. Stir just enough to make a smooth batter. Stir in nutmeats. Drop by small spoonfuls onto a baking sheet, well apart. Bake at 370°F for 8 to 10 minutes, or until done. Remove from pan immediately. Makes about 6 dozen cookies.

Carmine V. Molinaro, Connellsville, Pa.

BRAN COOKIES

2 cups All Bran
2 cups powdered sugar
2 cups flour
1 cup chopped raisins
1 teaspoon baking soda

½ teaspoon salt
3 well beaten eggs
6 tablespoons milk
1 cup melted butter
Juice from ½ lemon

Sift the dry ingredients, add eggs, milk, lemon juice and butter. Mix until well blended. Add raisins. Drop from a teaspoon onto a greased cookie sheet. Bake in moderate oven till done.

Mary Yasso, Lansford, Pa.

BROWN SUGAR COOKIES

1 cup brown sugar
½ pound butter
1 egg yolk
2 cups flour
1 teaspoon vanilla

Cream butter and sugar, add egg yolk, flour and vanilla. Mix well. Take pieces of dough and roll into small balls, size of a marble. Press down with prongs of fork which has been dipped into flour. Brush top with unbeaten egg white. Place in center candied bit of cherry or walnut. Bake in moderate oven for 20 minutes.

Mary Bucz, Chicago, Ill.

BUTTER COOKIES

1 pound sweet butter
2 tablespoons powdered sugar
6 egg yolks

Salt
1 pound flour

Cream butter and sugar until light and creamy, add egg yolks, salt and blend well, then add flour. The dough should be fluffy. Roll out on floured board about ¼ inch thick. Cut in small round forms, from half of the rounds cut small holes as for doughnuts. Bake at 350°F oven until they are a light brown color, from 10 to 12 minutes. When cool, place in center of each bottom cookie a little jelly and cover with cookie with the hole on top.

Lydia Valencik, Chicago, Ill.

BUTTER THIN COOKIES

1 pound butter
1 cup sugar
4½ cups flour

3½ tablespoons or more sweet cream
2 egg yolks

Cream butter, sugar and flour together until it forms little beads. Add cream and yolks, mix very well. Roll out on floured board as thin as desired. Cut with cookie cutter. Dip in unbeaten egg whites, sprinkle with mixture of cinnamon and sugar. Place a few chopped nuts on top. Bake at 350°F about 10 minutes, or until light brown.

CHEWY BROWNIES

1 cup flour
1 teaspoon baking powder
¼ teaspoon salt
¾ cup butter
1¼ cups sugar

½ cup brown sugar
3 eggs, separated
4 squares unsweetened chocolate
¾ cup chopped walnuts
2 teaspoons vanilla

Mix and sift flour, baking powder and salt. Cream butter, add sugars and cream well. Add beaten egg yolks, chocolate, which has been melted and cooled, nuts and vanilla. Add flour and beat until smooth. Fold in stiffly beaten egg whites. Turn into large shallow pan and bake in moderate oven 350°F for 40 minutes. Cut in squares while warm and remove from pan when cold. Makes 24 brownies.

Rose Sabol, Whiting, Ind.

FUDGE FROSTED BROWNIES

½ cup butter
1 cup sugar
2 eggs
2 - 1-ounce squares unsweetened chocolate

1 teaspoon vanilla
½ cup flour
½ cup chopped walnuts

Thoroughly cream butter and sugar. Add eggs and beat well. Blend in the melted chocolate and vanilla. Stir in the flour, then the walnuts. Pour batter into greased 8 x 8 x 2 inch pan. Bake in 325°F oven for 35 minutes. When the brownies are done, lightly press around the edges of the pan with the bottom of the glass to make the top level. Cool. Spread with fudge frosting.

Fudge Frosting: Combine 1 cup sifted confectioners' sugar, 1 tablespoon cocoa, 2 tablespoons cream, 1 tablespoon butter. Cook till mixture boils around side of pan. Remove from heat, beat till frosting is of spreading consistency.

Dominican Sisters, Oxford, Mich.

BUTTERSCOTCH COOKIES

½ cup butter
2 cups brown sugar
2 eggs
1 teaspoon vanilla

2 cups flour
¼ teaspoon salt
2 teaspoons baking powder
1 cup dry shredded coconut

Cook butter and sugar over low heat until bubbly. Cool. Add eggs, one at a time, beating thoroughly after each addition. Add vanilla, then sifted dry ingredients and coconut. Mix thoroughly. One cup nutmeats may also be added. Spread in shallow 10½ x15 inch pan and bake in 350°F oven about 25 minutes. While warm, cut in squares. Makes about 3 dozen cookies.

Mary Salat, Chicago, Ill.

BUTTERSCOTCH SOUR CREAM COOKIES

1 cup butter or other shortening
2 cups brown sugar
1 egg
1 cup heavy sour cream
4 cups fine whole wheat flour

2 teaspoons double acting
    baking powder
½ teaspoon salt
¼ teaspoon soda
Pecan halves for top

Cream butter, add sugar slowly, mixing well. Add unbeaten egg, mix well. Add sour cream. Add flour sifted with baking powder, salt and soda. Drop by small spoonfuls on greased baking sheets. Place pecan on top. Bake in oven 400°F about 15 minutes. Makes 4 dozen 3 inch cookies.

Carmine V. Molinaro, Connellsville, Pa.

CHOCOLATE CHIP COOKIES

1 cup brown sugar
1 cup shortening (part butter)
2 eggs
1 teaspoon baking soda
1 teaspoon vanilla

1 teaspoon salt
2½ cups flour
½ cup chopped nuts
2 packages chocolate chips

Mix sugar and shortening till smooth, beat in eggs and add baking soda which has been dissolved in 1 tablespoon hot water. Sift flour and salt together and add to creamed mixture. Add vanilla and fold in nuts and chocolate chips. Bake 10 minutes at 375°F oven.

Grace Chomlstek, Whiting, Ind.

CHOCOLATE CHIP DROP COOKIES

½ cup butter or other shortening
⅔ cup brown sugar
1 egg
2 cups flour
½ teaspoon soda
Dash of salt

½ cup milk
1 teaspoon vanilla
3 squares chocolate, melted
½ cup walnuts, chopped
1 package chocolate chips

Cream shortening and sugar, add egg. Beat well. Sift flour once, add soda and salt and sift together, add to creamed mixture alternately with milk. Beat till smooth. Add chocolate and blend. Add vanilla and mix, fold in nuts and chocolate chips. Bake at 350°F for 10 minutes. Frost with chocolate butter icing.

Elizabeth Dedinsky, Whiting, Ind.

CHOCOLATE CRUNCH COOKIES

1⅛ cups sifted flour
½ teaspoon baking soda
½ cup butter or other shortening
6 tablespoons granulated sugar
6 tablespoons brown sugar

1 egg, beaten
½ cup chopped nuts
1 package semi-sweet chocolate
½ teaspoon vanilla

Sift flour with soda and salt, set aside. Blend shortening with sugars until light. Add egg, beat well. Add flour to mixture and mix then add a few drops of hot water and mix together until well blended. Add chopped nuts, semisweet chocolate and vanilla. Drop from teaspoon onto a greased cookie sheet. Bake in moderate oven 350°F for 10 to 12 minutes. Yield: 50 cookies.

Mary Osadjan, Chicago, Ill.

CHOCOLATE MACAROONS

Butter, size of an egg
2 squares chocolate
1 cup sugar
2 unbeaten eggs

1 teaspoon vanilla
1 cup flour, scant
1 teaspoon baking powder

Melt the butter and chocolate into a smooth paste. Add sugar, eggs and vanilla, blend well. Add flour with the baking powder and mix. Sprinkle powdered sugar on pastry cloth. Make small balls, rolling them in the sugar. Place on buttered tins and bake in hot oven 2 to 3 minutes. Makes about 50.

Anna B. Russell, Cleveland, Oh.

CHOCOLATE NUT DROP COOKIES

2 cups brown sugar
1 cup melted butter
1 cup sweet milk
3 cups flour
2 teaspoons baking powder

1 cup chopped nut meats
2 eggs
½ teaspoon baking soda
4 squares melted chocolate

Sift flour, measure and sift together with baking soda, baking powder and salt. Combine butter and sugar and blend well. Add melted chocolate, then the eggs, one at a time, beating well after each addition. Add sifted dry ingredients alternately with milk. Fold in nut meats. Drop by spoonfuls on a greased baking sheet. Bake at 400°F for 10 to 12 minutes.

Julianna Simek, Johnstown, NY.

CHOCOLATE PINWHEEL COOKIES

½ cup shortening
½ cup sugar
1 egg yolk
1½ teaspoons vanilla
1½ cups flour

¼ teaspoon salt
½ teaspoon baking powder
3 tablespoons milk
1 - 1-ounce square unsweetened
  chocolate (melted)

Thoroughly cream shortening and sugar, add egg yolk and vanilla. Add sifted dry ingredients alternately with milk. Divide dough in half, to one half add chocolate, mix thoroughly. Roll each half ⅛ inch thick on heavy waxed paper. Turn white part on chocolate with dough extending ½ inch beyond white part on edge toward which you roll. Remove paper and roll as for jelly roll. Wrap in waxed paper, chill thoroughly. Slice thin. Bake on ungreased cookie sheet in 375°F oven, about 10 minutes. Makes 4 dozen cookies.

Mary Salat, Chicago, Ill.

CHOCOLATE PINWHEELS

6 tablespoons Crisco
½ cup sugar
1 egg yolk
4 tablespoons milk
1¾ cups flour

1 teaspoon baking powder
½ teaspoon salt
1 square chocolate, melted
1 teaspoon vanilla

Blend crisco with sugar and egg yolk in one quick operation. Add milk, then sifted dry ingredients and vanilla. Divide mixture in half and add chocolate to one half. Roll white dough into thin sheet, then place chocolate over, roll like jelly roll. Chill in refrigerator 1 hour. Cut thin slices, place on greased cookie sheet. Bake in moderate oven, 375°F, for 15 minutes.

Mary E. Grega, Cleveland, Oh.

CHOP SUEY COOKIES

1 cup sugar
¾ cup shortening
2 eggs
⅛ teaspoon salt
2 cups flour, sifted
1 teaspoon cinnamon
6 tablespoons milk

1 cup coconut
2 cups oatmeal
1 cup raisins
1 cup green and red cherries
1 cup nutmeats
½ teaspoon soda, dissolved in
   2 teaspoons milk

Cream sugar and shortening, add eggs. Add flour and salt alternately with milk and mix well. Add all other ingredients. Drop on greased pan and bake at 350°F for 15 minutes.

Mary Skurka, Whiting, Ind.

COCONUT BARS

½ cup butter
1 cup flour, sifted
¼ cup brown sugar
2 eggs, beaten
1½ cups brown sugar, firmly
  packed

2 tablespoons flour
½ teaspoon baking powder
½ teaspoon salt
½ cup coconut
1 teaspoon vanilla
1 cup walnuts

Mix flour, butter and ¼ cup brown sugar together. Pat mixture into pan, 8 x 10 inches. Bake at 350°F for 12 to 15 minutes. Combine eggs, 1½ cups brown sugar, 2 tablespoons flour, baking powder, salt, coconut, nuts and vanilla. Spread this mixture over baked pastry. Return to oven and bake 20 to 25 minutes. When cold, ice with powdered sugar icing. Sprinkle some chopped nuts before icing sets. When cold, cut into bars.

Mrs. Frank Lissak, Berwyn, Ill.

COCONUT COOKIES

1 cup butter
2 cups sugar
2 cups coconut, finely cut
2 eggs

5 tablespoons milk
2 teaspoons baking powder
1 teaspoon vanilla
Flour

Cream the butter and sugar, add the rest of the ingredients and enough flour to make a stiff dough. Roll out and cut with cookie cutters and bake in moderate oven, 350°F, till done.

Mary Yasso, Lansford, Pa.

CREAM CHEESE COOKIES

2 packages cream cheese
2 eggs well beaten
½ pint sour cream
3 cups flour

½ cake yeast
¼ pound butter
1 teaspoon salt

Dissolve yeast in the cream. Cream butter and cream cheese, add well beaten eggs. Then add the dissolved yeast, salt and the flour. Mix well, then roll thin small portions of dough. Cut with cookie cutters. Bake on greased cookie sheet in moderate oven for 30 minutes.

DAMEN CAPRIZEN

2 egg yolks
¼ cup sugar
½ cup butter
⅛ teaspoon salt
½ teaspoon vanilla
½ cup warm milk
¼ teaspoon cinnamon (optional)

1 cake yeast
2 cups sifted flour
1 cup apricot jam
2 egg whites
½ cup sugar
1 cup finely chopped filberts

Mix beaten egg yolks, sugar and butter and add salt and vanilla. Add warm milk in which yeast has been dissolved. Work in flour gradually. Turn onto floured board and knead well. Roll out to fit a 9 x 10 inch or square greased pan. Spread with jam. Set in warm place to double in bulk. Beat egg whites until frothy. Add sugar, a small amount at a time, beating well after each addition. Continue to beat until meringue is formed. Fold in filberts and cinnamon. Spread evenly over jam. Bake at 350°F for 25 minutes or until meringue is done. Then cool and cut into squares. Serves 9. Note: Use prepared apricot filling in place of jam.

Maria Walovich, Chicago, Ill.

DATE BARS

1 package (7½-oz) dates, chopped
½ cup dark brown sugar
¾ cup water
1¼ cups sifted flour
1¼ cups quick cooking oatmeal

1 teaspoon soda
½ teaspoon salt
1 cup dark brown sugar
½ cup butter or margarine

Combine dates, ½ cup brown sugar and water in saucepan. Cook over moderate heat, stirring occasionally until mixture comes to a boil and is thickened. Mix remaining dry ingredients. Cut in shortening until well blended. Press half of mixture in greased 8 x 8 x 2 inch pan. Spread with date mixture, cover with remaining oatmeal mixture. Bake in moderate oven 350°F for 30 minutes or until lightly browned. Cool. Sprinkle with confectioners' sugar and cut into squares.

Vern Jadrnak, Gary, Ind.

DATE COOKIES

DOUGH
2 cups brown sugar
1 cup shortening
3 whole eggs beaten
1 teaspoon soda
½ teaspoon salt
1 teaspoon vanilla
4 cups all purpose flour

FILLING
2 cups dates
1 cup sugar
1 cup boiling water

Cream the shortening and sugar, add the beaten eggs and mix well. Add vanilla and rest of the ingredients and blend well. Chill dough and then roll thin and spread with date mixture. Roll it like a jelly roll and chill overnight. Slice and bake in moderate oven 8 to 10 minutes.

Mary Fedor, Streator, Ill.

DATE DROP COOKIES

1 cup butter
1 cup crisco
2 cups sugar
2 cups ground nuts
6 eggs

1 cup raisins
1 pound chopped dates
5 cups flour
1 teaspoon baking soda
1 teaspoon cinnamon

Cream the shortening and gradually add rest of the ingredients until well mixed. Drop as large as a walnut on a greased cookie sheet and bake in a moderate oven 350°F for 20 minutes.

Mary Yasso, Lansford, Pa.

DATE AND NUT COOKIES

1 cup butter
1½ cups sugar
3 eggs, separated
2½ cups flour

1 teaspoon baking soda
½ cup warm water
1 cup walnuts
½ pound pitted dates

Cream butter, add sugar and beat until light. Add yolks of eggs and beat well. Add the flour and soda which has been dissolved in warm water. Then fold in the stiffly beaten egg whites. Last, add the nuts and dates cut into small pieces. Drop from end of teaspoon on a greased cookie sheet. Bake in slow oven 300°F about 15 minutes.

Susan Galga, Chicago, Ill.

DATE NUT SQUARES

1½ cups flour
½ teaspoon baking powder
¼ teaspoon salt
½ cup butter or shortening
½ cup granulated sugar

1 egg beaten
1 cup chopped, pitted dates
¼ cup chopped walnuts
Confectioners' sugar

Sift flour, measure, resift three times with baking powder and salt. Cream butter and sugar. Add egg, beat well. Add flour mixture in three portions. Mix well after each addition. Stir in dates and walnuts. Turn into 8 x 8 x 1 inch greased pan. Bake 30 minutes in a 325°F oven. Cool, cut into 1 inch squares and roll in confectioners' sugar.

Mary C. Lucas, Lakewood, Oh.

DATE OATMEAL COOKIES

1½ cups quick cooking oatmeal
1 cup brown sugar
1 cup butter
1½ cups sifted all purpose flour
1 teaspoon baking powder

FILLING
1 - 10-oz. package dates
1¼ cups water
⅚ cup white sugar

Combine the above ingredients and pat half of dough into two 9-inch cake tins, covering only the bottom. Combine the dates, water and sugar and boil together until thick. Cool. Spread over the dough in pans, cover with remaining dough and bake in oven 350°F for 40 to 50 minutes, until quite brown. Makes about 40 pieces. Cut when cool.

Clara Kucka, Whiting, Ind.

DREAM BARS

½ cup butter
2 tablespoons powdered sugar
1 cup cake flour

Thoroughly blend butter, confectioners' sugar and flour; spread evenly in waxed paper lined 8 inch square pan. Bake in moderate oven, 350°F, for 30 minutes.

2 eggs
1¼ cups brown sugar
2 tablespoons flour
¼ teaspoon salt

1½ teaspoons baking powder
1 cup broken nutmeats
1 cup moist, shredded coconut

Beat eggs and brown sugar until thick; add sifted dry ingredients, nut meats and coconut. Spread over first mixture. Continue baking 30 minutes. Cut in squares and cool in pan. Makes 2 dozen squares.

Teresa J. Hroma, Chesterton, Ind.

DATE SQUARES

1 package dates
2 eggs, well beaten
1 cup sugar
¼ cup butter
1⅔ cups cake flour

1 teaspoon baking soda
½ teaspoon salt
1 teaspoon vanilla
½ cup nuts
1 cup boiling hot water

Cut dates fine, pour the hot water over the dates, let stand till cool. Cream butter, sugar and beaten eggs. Add the date mixture, then all the flour and nuts. Put into well greased tin. Bake at 350°F for 45 minutes.

Mary Skriba, Riverside, Ill.

FILLED DATE SQUARES

⅔ cup soft butter or other
  shortening
⅔ cup brown sugar, firmly packed
1¼ cups sifted flour, combined with
  ½ teaspoon salt and cinnamon
¾ teaspoon baking soda
1 cup Quick Quaker Oats

FILLING:
½ pound pitted dates
1 cup hot water
2 tablespoons pecans or walnuts
  chopped coarsely

Cook pitted dates with hot water for about 15 minutes, until like a paste, stirring occasionally. Add chopped nuts. Let cool. Cream together butter and brown sugar, add sifted flour with salt and baking soda. Then add gradually the Quaker Oats and blend well with fingers. Pat half of the mixture into a well greased 9 x 9 square pan. Spread the date filling over the dough. Spread this filling within ¼ inch of sides of pan. Then with a covered rolling pin, roll rest of dough over sheet of wax paper to 8½ x 8½ inches, and invert onto top of filling, pressing edges down with fingers; remove wax paper. Bake in 400°F oven for 35 minutes or until brown.

When baked, remove from oven, loosen sides of pan, place on cake rack until cool, then loosen again on sides and turn onto a flat board. When cold, with a sharp knife cut into about 1 inch squares. Sprinkle with sifted confectioners' sugar. Makes about 3 dozen squares.

Justine Kasovsky, Chicago, Ill.

DAY AND NIGHT SQUARES

1 pound flour
½ pound powdered sugar
½ pound butter
½ pound butter with 1 tablespoon lard

5 whole eggs
1 egg, separated
1 teaspoon vanilla
2 teaspoons baking powder

Sift together the dry ingredients. Cream in the butter. Add the five whole eggs and 1 yolk. Add vanilla. Divide the dough into two equal parts. Spread or pat one half of the dough into a shallow pan, then spread dough with plum jam or povidlo. To the remaining dough, add one square finely grated chocolate and mix well together. Place this dough on top of filling. Spread beaten egg white over the top, and sprinkle with chopped nuts. Bake in moderate oven for 30 minutes. Allow to cool, then cut into small squares.

Stefania Letrich, Chicago, Ill.

DUTCH CHEESE WAFERS

1 - 3-oz. package cream cheese
½ cup butter
½ cup sugar

1 cup flour
Dried peaches or apricots

Blend cheese, butter, sugar and flour. Shape in roll, one inch in diameter, wrap in wax paper, chill. Slice thin with a sharp knife. Place piece of dry fruit on each slice, cover with other slice. Brush with milk. Place on cookie sheet and bake for 7 minutes at 350°F.

Bernadette Evans, Homestead, Pa.

ENGLISH TOFFEE COOKIES

½ pound butter
1 cup sugar
1 teaspoon cinnamon
1 egg yolk
2 cups flour

TOPPING:
Spread with unbeaten egg white and sprinkle with ground walnuts or pecans.

Pat dough into a shallow pan size 10 x 15, then smooth out with floured rolling pin. Spread unbeaten egg white, sprinkle nuts and pat down with hand. Have oven warm and bake immediately. (If allowed to stand, egg white will not adhere and as a result will separate from dough when baked.) Bake in moderate oven for 20 minutes. Remove and while warm mark off into squares. When cooled cut through and remove.

Mazy Bucz, Chicago, Ill.

FIG HONEY COOKIES

1 cup dried figs, cut in small
  pieces
½ cup shortening
2 eggs, well beaten
3 teaspoons baking powder
3 tablespoons chopped orange rind

½ cup coconut
½ cup honey
2¾ cups flour
1 tablespoon milk
1 teaspoon lemon flavoring

Wash figs, cover with cold water, simmer 10 minutes, drain. Cut figs in pieces. Cream shortening and sugar, add honey, eggs and milk. Mix well. Measure and sift with flour, the baking powder and salt. Add to sugar and shortening mixture. Add fruit, coconut and flavoring. Mix thoroughly. Drop by teaspoonfuls onto well greased cookie sheet. Bake in hot oven 435°F for 12 to 15 minutes.

Carmine V. Molinaro, Connellsville, Pa.

FILBERT COOKIES

1 pound filberts, ground	Cinnamon
3 egg whites	Juice of 1 lemon
1 pound powdered sugar	

Combine all together at once and work out dough until it is like texture of noodle dough. Then roll out very thin, cut in little oblongs. Bake about 10 to 15 minutes in 350 or 375°F oven. When cool, decorate.

Lydia Valencik, Chicago, Ill.

FILLED COOKIES

DOUGH:	FILLING:
½ cup shortening	1 cup ground raisins or dates
1½ cups brown sugar	1 cup sugar
1 egg	2 tablespoons flour
½ cup sour milk	1 cup water
3½ cups sifted flour	Cook 10 minutes, add:
¾ teaspoon salt	1 cup crushed pineapple
½ teaspoon soda	½ cup nuts
1 teaspoon baking powder	

Cream shortening, sugar, eggs and milk. Add sifted flour mixture to the batter. Set in refrigerator for 2 hours. Roll out thin, cut with cookie cutter. Put 1 teaspoon of filling in center and cover with another cookie. Press edges together. Bake in 300°F oven for 10 minutes.

Mary Fedor, Streator, Ill.

FRUIT SQUARES FROM EUROPE

½ pound butter	4 egg yolks
3 cups flour	½ teaspoon salt
1 cup sugar	½ pint sour cream
1 teaspoon baking powder	Grated rind of 1 lemon
1 teaspoon baking soda	1 teaspoon lemon juice

Work the butter and flour like for pie crust, add the rest of the ingredients and mix well. Spread on ungreased cookie sheet with spatula. Retain a little batter and add enough flour to make it thick enough to roll between the palms of the hands to make criss cross strips. Spread Raspberry preserve over the batter and sprinkle the top with nuts, then place the strips in criss cross fashion. Bake in 325°F oven for ½ hour. Sprinkle with powdered sugar and cut into squares.

Anna Sapp, Irwin, Pa.

GINGER COOKIES

12 egg yolks	**1 tablespoon ground ginger**
1 pound powdered sugar	**Flour**

Beat yolks until light and creamy, then gradually add the powdered sugar, beat well, and add the ground ginger. This mixture should be beaten with an electric mixer. Then with hands add enough flour so that the dough should be spongy. Then roll out about ½ inch thick, cut in leaf forms, place on cookie sheet and let stand over night, then bake about 10 minutes in a 400°F oven.

Lydia Valencik, Chicago, Ill.

GRANDMA'S FANCY COOKIES

2 hard cooked eggs	**Juice and grated rind of lemon**
1 cup butter or margarine	**3½ cups sifted flour**
¾ cup sugar	**¼ teaspoon salt**
2 raw egg yolks	**Colored sugar, nuts, etc. to decorate**

Rub hard cooked egg yolks thru sieve; add to creamed shortening. Cream, then add sugar and cream again. Beat in raw egg yolks. Add juice and rind of lemon. Fold in sifted flour and salt. Chill thoroughly. Roll out to ⅛-inch thickness. Cut with fancy cutters and decorate. Bake at 375°F from 10 to 15 minutes. Yield 60 cookies.

Leona Novosedlik, Windsor, Canada

HALF MOON CRESCENTS

¼ cup pet milk	**½ cup powdered sugar**
½ teaspoon vanilla	**½ teaspoon salt**
½ cup soft butter	**½ cup chopped nuts**
1½ cups sifted flour	

Add vanilla to the milk, then beat into the butter. Sift dry ingredients together and add to the butter mixture. Cream well. Add nuts, pinch off teaspoonful of dough, roll 2½ inches long, then shape into half moon. Place on ungreased pan one inch apart. Bake on top shelf of oven at 375°F for 12 minutes, or until light brown. Roll at once in 6 tablespoons powdered sugar. Makes 3 dozen.

Agnes Sorota, Whiting, Ind.

HAWAIIAN OATMEAL COOKIES

1 cup sifted flour	**½ cup brown sugar (firmly packed)**
1 teaspoon baking powder	
1 teaspoon baking soda	**1 egg**
¾ teaspoon salt	**½ teaspoon vanilla**
½ cup shortening	**1 cup rolled oats**
½ cup granulated sugar	**1 cup shredded coconut**

Sift the flour once, measure, add baking powder, soda and salt and sift together twice. Cream the shortening, add the sugar, cream until light and fluffy. Add the eggs and beat well. Add vanilla and sifted dry ingredients to the creamed mixture and mix well. Then add the rolled oats and coconut and mix until well blended. Shape into small balls, place on an ungreased baking sheet and bake in 350°F oven for 12 to 15 minutes, or until done. Makes 3 dozen cookies.

Agnes Sorota, Whiting, Ind.

HONEY HORNS

1¼ cups flour
½ teaspoon soda
½ teaspoon salt
⅓ cup shortening
½ cup honey

1 egg
1 package chocolate chips
½ cup chopped nuts
1 teaspoon vanilla

Mix all ingredients together and bake at 375°F for 12 minutes.

Mary Uhely, Los Angeles, Ca.

ICE BOX COOKIES

4 cups flour
1 teaspoon baking soda
1 teaspoon cream of tartar
1 cup butter

2 eggs
2 cups brown sugar
1 teaspoon vanilla
1 cup nuts

Sift first three ingredients. Cream butter, eggs and brown sugar till creamy. Add flour mixture, vanilla and nuts, mix well. Shape into two rolls, wrap in waxed paper and let stand in cool place. Slice dough thin, place on cookie sheet. Bake in moderate oven about 10 minutes.

Mary Fedor, Streator, Ill.

IRENE'S COOKIES

½ cup butter
1 egg, separated
¼ cup brown sugar

1 cup flour
1 teaspoon vanilla

Cream butter and sugar, add beaten egg yolk and beat until light. Add sifted flour and vanilla. Roll in your hand little balls the size of a marble, roll in egg white, then in rolled nuts, place on cookie sheet, make a hole in each cookie with a thimble, put in oven for 5 minutes, then press hole in center again and bake 15 minutes more in 350°F oven. When cool, fill center with jelly.

Irene Galos, Warrenville, Ill.

JELLY AND NUT COOKIES

5 cups flour
1 cup sugar
1 tablespoon baking powder
½ teaspoon salt
½ pound butter
2 tablespoons lard

FILLING:
1 pound ground walnuts
1 pint peach jam

Mix the above ingredients as for pie. Then beat together:

4 egg yolks
½ pint sour cream
1 teaspoon vanilla

Mix the two dough mixtures together and cut them into 3 parts. Roll out one piece and place in a slightly greased pan. Place on dough and spread 1 pound of ground walnuts, which you mix with little water to keep it moist. Put other dough on top and spread 1 pint of peach jam. With the remaining dough make a lattice on top. Bake at 350°F for 1 hour and 15 minutes.

Mary Kukuch, East Chicago, Ind.

HAZEL NUT COOKIES

½ pound filberts
½ pound sweet butter
½ pound granulated sugar
½ pound flour

2 egg whites, unbeaten
7 whole cloves
Prune butter

Grind finely nuts and cloves. Cream butter, add sugar gradually, add the ground nuts and egg whites. Blend in the flour. Spread half of dough on greased cookie sheet or pan 10 x 10 inches. Spread with prune butter (povidla) and roll rest of dough in long strips and make a lattice top. Bake in oven 350°F about 15 minutes. Cool slightly and cut in squares.

Ludmilla Cherney, Chicago, Ill.

HELLO DOLLY COOKIES *(2 dozen 1½ inch by 3 inch bars)*

½ cup (1 stick) butter or margarine, melted
1½ cups graham cracker crumbs
1 cup chopped nutmeats
1 cup (6 oz. pkg.) semi-sweet chocolate pieces
1⅓ cups (3½ oz. can) flaked coconut
1⅓ cups (15 oz. can) Borden's Eagle Brand sweetened condensed milk

Into bottom of 9x13 inch pan, pour melted butter or margarine. Now add rest of ingredients one by one on top of each other. Sprinkle crumbs evenly over melted butter or margarine, chopped nuts carefully over crumbs. Then distribute chocolate pieces over nuts, flaked coconut over chocolate. Pour condensed milk over all. Bake in 350°F (moderate) oven 25 minutes or until lighly browned on top. Allow to cool 15 minutes before cutting. Cut into finger length bars.

Susan Pihulic, Munster, Ind.

HERMITS

2 cups sugar	3 tablespoons milk
1 cup nuts	1 cup butter or oleo
2 cups raisins	1 teaspoon nutmeg
3 eggs	1 teaspoon cloves
1 teaspoon baking soda, dissolved in	1 teaspoon cinnamon
	3½ cups flour

Chop nuts and raisins. Mix in order given. Drop on cookie sheet and bake at 350°F about 20 minutes.

Cecilia Shurina, Union, NJ.

HOLIDAY COOKIES

3 cups sifted flour	½ cup sugar
½ teaspoon baking powder	1 egg unbeaten
⅛ teaspoon salt	2 teaspoons vanilla
1 cup margarine	

Sift flour, baking powder and salt together. Cream margarine and sugar thoroughly. Add egg and vanilla. Beat until fluffy. Gradually stir in sifted dry ingredients until well blended. Roll small amounts of dough ⅛ inch thick on a lightly floured board. Shape with cookie cutters as desired. Bake on ungreased baking sheet at 350°F until delicately brown, 10 to 12 minutes.

Mary Salat, Chicago, Ill.

JAM STRIP COOKIES

½ pound shortening	2½ cups flour
1 cup sugar	2 teaspoons baking powder
2 whole eggs	¼ cup milk
1 cup ground walnuts	

Mix the above ingredients together and take about ⅘ of the dough to make two separate pieces. Take the larger of the two and roll out the dough, then place it on a 18 x 12 inch pan. Spread over the dough a little jam. Take the remainder of the dough and roll into long strips over the jam in a check pattern. Bake in 350°F oven for about 45 minutes.

Eleanor Marko, Whiting, Ind.

JAM SQUARES

¼ pound butter
½ cup sugar
1 tablespoon vanilla
2 egg yolks
1½ cups flour

½ teaspoon baking powder
½ cup nutmeats
⅛ teaspoon baking soda
Plum butter or jam

Cream butter and sugar, add vanilla and egg yolks and cream together, add sifted flour, baking powder and soda. Knead dough. Put in pan and pat out. Spread dough with plum butter or jam, over this spread egg whites stiffly beaten with 2 tablespoons sugar, sprinkle with nuts. Bake in 350°F oven for 30 minutes. Cut in squares.

Eleanor Kochis, Whiting, Ind.

LANDONE STRANGLE

1½ cups flour
½ teaspoon baking powder
¼ pound, plus 1 tablespoon
  butter
½ cup sugar
Juice and rind of ½ lemon
4 egg yolks (if not enough, add
  little water)

TOPPING
¾ pound prune butter
4 egg whites
Almonds, thinly sliced

Mix the ingredients as for pie dough. Spread on board and roll to about ½ inch thickness to fit a pan 14 x 10 inches. Bake until light brown. Cool, then spread ¾ pound prune butter, then stiffly beaten whites of eggs; sprinkle split, thinly sliced almonds over the meringue. Brown in the oven for a few minutes.

SOFT MOLASSES COOKIES

1¼ cups sugar
2¼ cups molasses
2¼ cups shortening
1⅛ cups buttermilk
3⅓ teaspoons baking soda

2¼ teaspoons salt
4 teaspoons ginger
2 teaspoons cinnamon
6 cups flour

Heat molasses, melt shortening in it, cool and add sugar. Mix again. Add buttermilk and then the flour which has been sifted with the dry ingredients. Let stand in refrigerator overnight. Roll about ⅓ inch thick. Sprinkle with sugar before cutting. Bake in moderate oven, 350°F.

Ella D. Vlasaty, Braddock, Pa.

NIGHT AND DAY COOKIES

1 cup flour
¼ pound butter
½ cup sugar
1 whole egg
1 teaspoon baking powder
Pinch of salt
1 teaspoon vanilla

TOPPING
7 eggs, separated
½ pound walnuts, ground fine
1 cup sugar
1 teaspoon vanilla

Sift flour and baking powder, combine with butter as for pie crust. Add beaten egg with sugar and vanilla. Add salt and mix well. Spread dough on 18 x 10 pan, spread with any desired filling, such as strawberry or raspberry jam, or plum butter. Beat egg whites until foamy, add sugar gradually and beat until stiff. Add beaten egg yolks and vanilla. Add walnuts and mix. Spread on top over filling and bake 325°F for 45 minutes. Let cool in pan, then cut in slices.

Anna Stanek, Whiting, Ind.

NUT DELIGHTS

1 cup powdered sugar
1 cup broken nuts

3 egg whites
Pinch of salt

Beat egg whites stiff. Add sugar, salt and nuts. Drop by teaspoonfuls on greased and floured cookie sheet. Bake in moderate oven.

Bernadette Evans, Homestead, Pa.

NUT PILLOWS

½ pound butter
½ pound flour
6 egg yolks

FILLING
½ pound ground nuts
6 egg whites, beaten stiffly
½ pound powdered sugar

Cream butter and gradually add yolks and flour. Mix well. Form into balls about size of walnuts. Place in refrigerator over night or at least four hours. Beat egg whites stiffly, add powdered sugar and the ground walnuts and mix thoroughly. Take the refrigerated balls of dough and roll out, add filling and make small pillows. Bake in moderate oven until light brown, approximately 15 minutes.

Paula Wondrasek, Chicago, Ill.

NUT SQUARES

1 pound flour, sifted	2 eggs
1 pound butter	1 tablespoon rum
1 pound sugar	1 teaspoon vanilla
1 pound ground nuts	

Work ingredients together, cut dough in two. Roll out one half to fill large baking pan and spread strawberry preserves, then roll out other half and cover first half. Sprinkle top with a few ground nuts. Bake in 400°F oven for 45 minutes.

Ludmilla Sacik, Ford City, Pa.

OATMEAL COOKIES

1 cup shortening, or chicken fat	1 teaspoon vanilla
1½ cups flour	1 teaspoon baking soda
1 cup brown sugar	3 cups Quick Quaker Oats
1 cup granulated sugar	Scant teaspoon salt
2 eggs	½ cup nuts

Cream shortening, sugar, eggs, add vanilla. Sift flour with salt, soda and add to mixture alternately with the oatmeal. Add nuts. Roll in waxed paper in long rolls. Place in refrigerator overnight. Slice thin and bake about 8 minutes in 350°F oven.

Mary Fedor, Streator, Ill.

SLOVAK MEDOVNIKY (Honey Cookies)

2 oz. salt butter or ½ bar	½ teaspoon cinnamon
1 cup sugar	¼ teaspoon allspice
3 whole eggs	5½ cups sifted all-purpose flour
3 tablespoons honey	1 teaspoon baking soda

Mix butter and sugar; add eggs and honey and mix thoroughly. Sift dry ingredients and mix together with other batter. Knead dough, roll out to ¼ inch thickness, and cut with desired dough cutter. Bake on buttered cookie sheet twelve minutes at 325°F. If desired, cookies may be decorated with sugar icing.

Susan Alexovic, Whiting, Ind.

PLUM BUTTER CRISS-CROSS COOKIES

3 tablespoons cream, or top of milk	½ pound sugar
	2 eggs
2 cups flour	1 teaspoon vanilla
½ pound butter	1½ teaspoons baking powder

Mix all the ingredients by hand. Take ¾ of the dough and roll out on a floured board to fit a 15 x 10 inch pan. Place in unbuttered pan. Put the remaining dough in the refrigerator until ready to use. Spread one pound of plum butter on dough in pan. Take remaining dough which has been kept in refrigerator, roll on floured board into long strips and place in a criss cross pattern on the plum butter. Bake in 350°F oven for 25 to 35 minutes.

Anna Stanek, Whiting, Ind.

ORANGE-PEANUT BUTTER COOKIES

½ cup butter
½ cup peanut butter
½ cup brown sugar
½ cup granulated sugar
1 egg
2 tablespoons orange juice

1 tablespoon grated orange rind
2¼ cups sifted flour
½ teaspoon baking soda
¼ teaspoon salt
1 cup chopped nuts

Combine butter, peanut butter, sugars, egg, orange juice and rind into a bowl, beat vigorously until mixture is smooth, light and fluffy. Combine sifted flour with the soda and salt, sift again and add to the first mixture, a small portion at a time, until all flour has been added. Add the chopped nuts. Knead dough with hands until smooth. Pack firmly in two bars. Wrap in waxed paper, place in refrigerator. Chill until firm. Cut in ⅛ inch thick slices, place on greased baking sheet. Bake in hot oven 400°F for 8 to 10 minutes, or until baked. Makes 6 dozen cookies.

Florence Hovanec, Whiting, Ind.

PEANUT BUTTER COOKIES

½ cup brown sugar
½ cup cane sugar
½ cup butter
1 egg
1 cup peanut butter

1 teaspoon salt
½ teaspoon soda
1½ cups flour
½ teaspoon vanilla

Sift brown and white sugars. Cream butter until soft, add sugars gradually. Add egg, peanut butter, salt and soda. Beat until creamy. Sift flour before measuring, resift and add to batter, mix well. Add vanilla. Roll dough into small balls. Place on greased tins. Press with fork both ways. Bake at 375°F for about 15 minutes. Makes 60 medium size cookies.

Clara S. Matuschak, Connellsville, Pa.

PEANUT BUTTER DROP COOKIES

2 cups sifted flour
¾ teaspoon salt
2 teaspoons baking powder
¾ cup shortening
½ cup peanut butter

1 cup brown sugar (firmly packed)
2 eggs, beaten
¼ cup milk
¾ cup raisins (chopped)
1 teaspoon vanilla

Sift flour once, measure, add salt and baking powder, and sift again. Cream shortening, peanut butter and sugar together until the mixture is light and fluffy. Add the eggs one at a time. Beating well after each addition. Add dry ingredients alternately with the milk, beating until smooth. Fold in raisins and vanilla and blend. Drop from a teaspoon onto a lightly greased baking sheet and flatten with a fork. Bake in a 375°F oven for 10 minutes or until done. Makes 4 dozen.

Mary Salat, Chicago, Ill.

PECAN ICE BOX COOKIES

⅓ cup butter
½ cup sugar
1 egg yolk
3 tablespoons milk
½ teaspoon vanilla

1½ cup flour, more or less
½ teaspoon salt
½ teaspoon baking powder
1 cup ground pecans

Cream butter and sugar. Add yolk and beat well. Add milk and vanilla. Sift flour, salt and baking powder, add pecans to dry ingredients, then combine with creamed mixture and blend well. Chill at least one hour after rolling dough into rolls. Wrap in waxed paper. To bake slice ⅛ inch thick and bake at 375°F for 8 to 10 minutes, or until light brown.

Mrs. Macko, Connellsville, Pa.

PECAN SQUARES

1 cup condensed milk, (not evaporated)
6 tablespoons flour

1 tablespoon molasses
⅛ teaspoon salt
½ cup finely chopped pecans

Blend milk with flour, add molasses and salt. Fold in pecans. Spread about ¼ inch thick on well greased pan. Bake in moderate oven for 25 minutes. Cut in squares.

Anna B. Russell, Cleveland, Oh.

PECAN TASSIES *(26 1¾ inch tarts)*

DOUGH
1 cup sifted flour
⅓ cup (1 stick) butter
1 package (3 ounces) cream
   cheese

FILLING
1 egg, slightly beaten
¾ cup light brown sugar firmly
   packed
Dash of salt
1 tablespoon melted butter
1 teaspoon vanilla
½ to 1 cup chopped pecans

Sift flour once and measure. Cream butter and cheese together until blended. Add flour and mix well. Press dough into 1¾ inch muffin cups. Mix ingredients for filling. Fill muffin cups a little more than half full of this mixture and bake in a 350°F oven for 15 minutes, then reduce the heat to 250°F and bake for 10 minutes. While tarts are still warm remove from the pans and sprinkle with confectioners' sugar.

Phyllis Spencer, Valparaiso, Ind.

PHILADELPHIA CREAM CHEESE CRESCENTS

1 pound shortening
2 packages Cream Cheese
1 cup sugar

1 teaspoon vanilla
4 or 5 cups flour
½ pound ground nuts

Mix above, adding flour until dough is suitable for forming crescents. Bake until light brown at 350°F.

Margaret Lissak, Berwyn, Ill.

PINEAPPLE BARS

1 cup flour
1 teaspoon salt
1 cup brown sugar
2½ cups Quick Oatmeal
1 cup shortening

FILLING:
½ cup sugar
1 tablespoon cornstarch
1 No. 1 can crushed pineapple
   with juice
1 teaspoon lemon juice

Combine above ingredients, spread half on 9 x 13 inch pan. Spread filling and cover with remaining half. (Combine sugar and cornstarch, add the pineapple and lemon juice and cook slowly until thick and clear. Cool.) Bake 45 minutes at 350°F oven.

Margaret Lissak, Berwyn, Ill.

POPPY SEED COOKIES

2½ cups sifted flour
½ teaspoon soda
½ teaspoon salt
¾ cup sugar
1 egg, well beaten

½ cup sour cream
½ cup cooking or salad oil
1 teaspoon vanilla
4 tablespoons poppy seed

Mix and sift dry ingredients into a mixing bowl. Make a well in the center and add beaten egg, sour cream, oil, vanilla and poppy seeds. Stir well. Roll dough to ¼ inch thickness on lightly floured board. Cut into desired shapes with cookie cutter. Place on greased baking sheet. Bake in 375°F for 15 minutes or until delicately browned. Makes 4 dozen 3 inch cookies.

Dorota Sabol, Whiting, Ind.

POWDERED SUGAR COOKIES

½ cup butter
½ cup powdered sugar
2 cups flour

¼ cup milk
1 cup chopped nuts

Cream butter and sugar. Add flour and milk alternately, blending well. Lastly add chopped nuts. Shape into crescents and sticks. Bake in a moderate oven 350°F for about 30 minutes, or until delicately browned. Cool. Coat some with powdered sugar, dip others in melted sweet chocolate and chopped nuts. Makes 4 dozen.

Mary Salat, Chicago, Ill.

PRUNE NUT SQUARES

1 pound ground walnut meats
1 pound butter
1 pound powdered sugar
4 cups flour

4 eggs
2 teaspoons baking powder
1 teaspoon vanilla
Grated lemon rind

Combine the butter, sugar and eggs, add vanilla and baking powder which has been sifted with the flour. Roll ¾ of the dough to one-half inch thickness and put on greased pan. Cover with prune butter. Make strips of remaining dough and arrange in lattice fashion over the top. Bake in moderate oven until done about 20 minutes. Cut in squares.

Sophie Gometro, Nesquohoning, Pa.

QUICK DROP COOKIES

⅓ cup butter
½ cup sugar
1 egg

1 cup flour
⅓ teaspoon salt
1 teaspoon baking powder

Cream butter and sugar, add egg, then add dry ingredients. Drop from spoon onto greased cookie sheet and bake in moderately hot oven 375°F about 10 minutes. Yields about 1½ dozen cookies. Can use nuts, chocolate bits, or just grated lemon rind of ½ lemon.

Barbara Bires, Pittsburgh, Pa.

SALTED PEANUT COOKIES

1½ cups light brown sugar
¾ cup melted butter
1 egg beaten
1 teaspoon vanilla
¼ teaspoon salt
1¼ cups flour

1 teaspoon baking powder
⅓ teaspoon baking soda
1 cup salted-peanuts (with skins)
1 cup oatmeal
1 cup cornflake

Mix sugar, melted butter, beaten egg and vanilla in large bowl, beat thoroughly. Sift flour twice, then resift with salt, baking powder and soda. Add peanuts to flour mixture, then oatmeal. Fold in flour mixture to the batter and finally fold in cornflakes. Drop from teaspoon onto greased cookie sheet. Space about 2½ inches apart. Bake at 400°F for 10 to 12 minutes. Remove from cookie sheet immediately.

Kate Pempek

SANDWICH NUT COOKIES

1 pound butter or margarine
1 cup sugar
4 cups of sifted all purpose flour
4 eggs, save 2 egg whites for trimming

Mix butter and sugar together on a floured board. Add the sifted flour and eggs. Mix well. Roll cookie dough on board. Cut out with round cookie cutter. Place half of the rounds on lightly greased baking sheet. The other half of rounds, cut out center with thimble. Dip into egg whites and then ground nuts. Place on baking sheet, bake 12 minutes. Put together with strawberry jam or preserves. Makes about 48 cookies. Very delicious and attractive.

Mary Nemeth, Munhall, Pa.

SNOW BALLS

1 cup butter
½ cup powdered sugar
2¼ cups flour

¼ teaspoon salt
1 teaspoon vanilla
¾ cup chopped nuts, or coconut

Cream butter and sugar together, sift flour, add salt and resift, add to creamed mixture, working it thoroughly with fingers. Work in vanilla and nuts (or coconut). Chill about one hour, then roll about one inch in diameter. Cut one inch lengths and roll into balls. Place on lightly greased pan. Bake in moderate oven for about 14 to 17 minutes, or until lightly brown. Roll in confectioners' sugar.

Louise Krockmally, Woodbridge, N.J.

CHOCOLATE SNOWBALLS

1¼ cups butter
⅔ cup sugar
2 teaspoons vanilla
2 cups sifted flour

⅛ teaspoon salt
½ cup cocoa
2 cups finely chopped pecans
Confectioners' sugar

Cream butter thoroughly, add sugar gradually and keep beating until mixture is light and fluffy. Add vanilla, combine flour with salt and cocoa. Add gradually to the creamed mixture, blend thoroughly. Add pecans and mix well. Form dough into balls about the size of a marble between the palms of the hand. Bake in moderate oven, 350°F, for 20 to 25 minutes. Cool. Roll in confectioners' sugar. Yield 6 dozen cookies.

If dough is too soft for rolling, chill in refrigerator for an hour or two. Avoid over baking, chocolate cookies of this type must not be browned because of an already dark color.

Rose Sabol, Whiting, Ind.

SONIA COOKIES

1 cup butter
1 cup brown sugar
2 eggs, separated

2 cups sifted flour
Chopped nuts, or shredded coconut
Jelly

Cream butter until soft. Blend in brown sugar. Add egg yolks beaten until light. Blend in the sifted flour. Using your palms, roll the dough into small balls about 1 inch in diameter. Dip them in the egg white, then roll in chopped nuts or shredded coconut. Put on a greased cookie sheet and make an indentation in the center of each cookie with your thumb. Bake at 300°F for 5 minutes. Remove from the oven and make the impression again with your thumb. Bake 15 minutes longer. When cookies are cool fill the center depression with assorted jellies.

Rose Scolaro, Oak Park, Ill.

SOUR CREAM DROP COOKIES

1 cup shortening
2 cups sugar
1 egg well beaten
3 cups flour

1 teaspoon baking soda
1 cup sour cream
½ teaspoon lemon or orange
flavoring

Cream shortening and sugar, beat well, add beaten egg. Mix and sift flour and soda together and add alternately with sour cream. Add lemon or orange flavoring. Drop from spoon on greased cookie sheet. Bake in 375°F oven 12 minutes.

Sue Ogurchock, New Kensington, Pa.

SQUARE COOKIES

½ pound butter
2 tablespoons sugar
2½ cups flour
4 egg yolks
2 teaspoons baking powder
½ cup cream or milk

TOPPING:
4 egg whites, beaten stiffly
1½ cups ground walnuts
1 cup powdered sugar
Mix these ingredients together

Mix the above ingredients and roll out flat, then place the dough on an 18 x 12 inch pan. Spread with any desired jam or preserves, then take the filling and spread it over the jam. Bake in 350°F oven for 45 minutes. Cut in squares when cool.

Leona Novosedlik, Windsor, Canada

STRAWBERRY PRESERVE SQUARES

2 cups flour
1 cup sugar
1 egg
5 hard boiled egg yolks, grated

½ pound butter
1 grated lemon rind
½ teaspoon lemon juice

Sift together flour and sugar. Add egg, egg yolks and butter. Mix together. Add grated lemon rind and lemon juice, and mix well. Knead dough on bread board until it is smooth (about 5 minutes) sprinkling lightly with flour. Cut dough in two pieces. One piece should be ¾ the size and the other ¼. Roll larger piece of dough to ¼ inch in thickness and place in pan 10 x 12 inches. Top with strawberry preserves. Take the other dough and roll into thin narrow pieces to fit in a criss-cross fashion on top of the preserves. Bake at 350°F for about 30 minutes. Remove from oven and cool. Cut into squares. Yield 25 pieces.

Johanna Kapitan, Whiting, Ind.

SUGAR COOKIES *(Cukrove Zakusky)*

2 pounds flour
1 pound sweet butter
1 pound powdered sugar
10 hard-boiled egg yolks

2 whole eggs (raw)
2 teaspoons baking powder
Juice and rind of 1 lemon
Dash of salt

Sift dry ingredients together, work in butter as for pie crust. Add the whole eggs, lemon juice and rind. Put egg yolks through sieve and add to the mixture. Work out very well. Place dough on a floured board and roll out to medium thickness. Use any forms to cut out designs. Brush egg whites on the cookies and sprinkle with crushed walnuts. Bake at 375°F oven until lightly browned.

Stefania Letrich, Chicago, Illinois

VIRGINIA ROCKS

½ cup light brown sugar
1 cup powdered sugar
3 eggs
1 teaspoon baking soda
1½ cups sour milk

3 cups flour
1 teaspoon ground mixed spices
1 cup walnuts, chopped
1 pound dates, chopped
1 teaspoon vanilla

Beat eggs and add gradually the sugars and mix well. Mix the baking soda into the sour milk, and add to the sugar and egg mixture. Into this sift the flour and mixed spices, add nuts and dates. When thoroughly mixed, add the vanilla. Drop on a greased cookie sheet and bake at 400°F for about 8 minutes. (Drop at least 2 inches apart.)

Veronica Radocha, Coaldale, Pa.

WALNUT CRESCENTS

½ pound soft butter
1 cup sifted confectioners' sugar
1 teaspoon vanilla

½ pound chopped walnut
2¼ cups sifted flour (about)

Cream butter thoroughly, add sifted sugar a little at a time and then vanilla. Add flour alternately with nuts, beating well after each addition. Mold at once with fingers into desired shapes, such as crescents, etc. Bake on lightly greased inverted side of tin about 25 minutes at 350°F until brown. Bake on upper rack last 5 minutes. When cold, dip into powdered sugar. Makes about 60 cookies.

Maria Walovich, Chicago, Ill.

WALNUT COOKIES

1 pound butter
½ pound ground walnuts
4 tablespoons powdered sugar

3 egg yolks
4 tablespoons milk
Flour

Mix butter, powdered sugar and yolks. Add milk, nuts and mix well. Add enough flour until the dough is thick enough to roll. Roll dough about ¼ inch thick, then cut with cookie cutter. Bake in 350°F to 400°F oven for about 20 minutes.

Leona Novosedlik, Windsor, Canada

WALNUT ROLL COOKIES

2 cups flour
½ pound sweet butter
6 egg yolks
Juice from ½ lemon

FILLING:
6 egg whites, stiffly beaten
½ pound ground walnuts
½ pound powdered sugar

Work butter into flour, add egg yolks and lemon juice. Mix well. Make 45 little balls and let this dough stand for two hours. Beat egg whites until they stand in peaks, fold in sugar and the ground nuts. Take each ball and roll until the dough is very thin, then spread on some filling and roll in the shape of half moon. Bake in 350°F oven until lightly brown.

Leona Novosedlik, Windsor, Canada

WALNUT SQUARES

2 cups flour	**TOPPING:**
⅓ cup sugar	**1 cup sugar**
5 oz. butter	**½ pound chopped walnuts**
5 egg yolks	**5 egg whites**
Pinch of salt	**1 teaspoon vanilla**

Sift together flour and sugar. Add butter, egg yolks, and salt. Mix together. Knead dough on bread board until it is smooth, sprinkling lightly with flour. Roll dough to ¼ inch in thickness. Place in pan 10 x 12 inches and bake at 350°F for about 15 minutes. While dough is baking, mix together sugar, walnuts, egg whites and vanilla and cook, stirring continuously until brown. Cover dough with topping and put back in oven for about 15 minutes. Let cool and cut into squares. Yield: 25 pieces.

Johanna Kapitan, Whiting, Ind.

APRICOT SQUARES

4 cups of sifted flour	**4 egg yolks**
¾ pound butter	**1 large cake of yeast**
¼ teaspoon of salt	**½ pint sour cream**
2 tablespoons of sugar	**2 pound jar of apricot preserves**

Mix all above ingredients as for pie dough. Four egg yolks only, beat lightly. One large cake of yeast, dissolve in one tablespoon of warm water, add ½ pint sour cream, add this mixture to the dough mixture, mix well together, makes soft pliable dough, do not knead too much.

Divide dough in half. Use one half dough for your cooking or baking pans, roll out thin, will make two large sheets, about 10 x 16 or 18 inch. Use other half of dough to make cross strip like a lattice on top of filling.

Apricot preserves two pound jar, or better yet, use one pound jar on each pan.

Make at night, let stand until morning, bake about 20 to 25 minutes in 350°F oven. Keeps well, nice crisp dough.

Louise M. Yash, Cleveland, Ohio

LEMON BARS

½ cup butter
1 cup sifted flour
¼ cup sugar
2 eggs, well beaten
1 cup sugar

Grated rind and juice of 1 lemon
¼ teaspoon salt
2 tablespoons flour
½ teaspoon baking powder

Sift flour once, measure, add sugar and butter and cut butter into the mixture to make coarse crumbs. Pat or press into bottom of an 8 inch square pan and bake in a 350°F oven for 20 minutes, then remove and cool. Beat eggs thoroughly. Add sugar, a tablespoon at a time and continue to beat until thick and light. Beat in lemon juice and rind, salt, 2 tablespoons flour, and baking powder and pour over the baked crust. Return to the oven and bake at 350°F for 30 minutes. Remove from the oven and sprinkle while warm with confectioners' sugar. Cool completely and cut into 1 by 2 inch bars. Or, cut into squares 2 by 2 inches and serve as dessert with a topping of slightly sweetened whipped cream. Yields 32 1x2" bars.

Sally Pihulic, Munster, Ind.

Desserts

DESSERTS

The dessert course gives the finishing touch to a good meal, so make it interesting and attractive, colorful and flavorful. Choose the last course to suit the menu-a light dessert if the meal has been heavy; a richer one if the meal has been light. A dessert should not repeat a food or flavor served elsewhere in the meal. If a fruit cup or fruit cocktail has been served, a fruit dessert should be avoided.

Serve a light dessert, such as fruit, with a heavy meat dinner and usual accompaniments. Serve a starchy dessert with a meal that has not included potatoes, spaghetti, or a similar starchy food. Serve a protein dessert with a custard foundation, such as baked custard, or custard pie, with a vegetable luncheon or dinner.

CUSTARDS

CUSTARD-HINTS: Custard may be sweetened or not. As a dessert, it can be prepared with fruits or nuts and may be served plain or with a sauce. It can be served hot or chilled as desired. A curdled custard is a failure; a thin custard a disappointment; at a point between the two is a perfect custard.

Common causes of custard failure are cooking too long or cooking at too high temperature. The custard should be set in a pan of hot water and baked in a moderate oven (325-350°F) only until it is set or until a silver knife inserted in it comes out clean.

If boiled custard shows signs of curdling, remove from heat at once and cool quickly by placing the pan in ice water to stop further cooking. To improve the texture, pour custard into a jar, close securely and shake well.

Baked custards are used for desserts and many variations can be made. A spoonful of jelly or a little maple, caramel, or other sugar syrup in the bottom of the custard cup before the custard preparation is poured in, makes a pretty dish when unmolded after baking.

BAKED CUSTARD

2 or 3 slightly beaten eggs	**2 cups milk**
¼ cup sugar	**1 teaspoon vanilla**
¼ teaspoon salt	**Nutmeg**

Combine eggs, sugar and salt. Bring milk to scalding and stir into egg mixture; add vanilla, pour into custard cups, sprinkle with nutmeg. Place cups in pan of hot water. Bake in slow oven (325°F) until mixture does not adhere to a knife about 30 minutes.

Helen Valacak, Benton Harbor, Mi.

PERFECT BAKED CUSTARD

3 cups milk, scalded	**3 eggs**
¼ teaspoon salt	**1 teaspoon vanilla**
6 tablespoons sugar	

Add sugar and salt to the scalded milk, stirring until the sugar is completely dissolved. Add well beaten eggs and vanilla. Turn into slightly buttered custard cups. Place in a pan of warm water and bake at 325°F for 30 minutes. Test by running a knife blade into the custard, if it comes out perfectly clean, the custard is done. Be careful not to overbake. Cool and serve in custard cups with raspberry or caramel sauce. Makes 5 servings.

Mary V. Haydu, Braddock, Pa.

SOFT CUSTARD

2 cups rich milk	**½ teaspoon vanilla**
4 slightly beaten eggs	**Dash of salt**
2 tablespoons sugar	

Scald milk. Combine eggs with sugar and salt, and stir into the milk. Cook over gently simmering water, stirring constantly with a metal spoon, until custard begins to thicken. Remove from heat. stir in the vanilla and turn into a bowl to cool, stirring occasionally during the cooling.

VARIATIONS OF PLAIN SOFT CUSTARD

Caramel-Caramelize ¼ cup of sugar and add to one cup scalded milk. Follow recipe for soft custard, using this milk with caramel as part of the milk, and using in addition the full amount of sugar called for in the recipe.

Chocolate-Melt one ounce of chocolate and add to it two tablespoons of sugar dissolved in two tablespoons of boiling water. Mix thoroughly. Add this chocolate mixture to two cups of scalded milk and use as the milk in a plain soft custard.

Mary Vevurka, Chicago, Ill.

CORNSTARCH MOLD

1 quart milk	4 tablespoons cornstarch
2 tablespoons sugar	1 teaspoon vanilla
2 eggs	Pinch of salt

Scald milk. Blend cornstarch, sugar and salt. Pour over scalded milk, stirring constantly. Add beaten eggs, then return to the saucepan and cook over hot water until thick and smooth. Cool slightly, add vanilla and pour into a mold which has been dipped into cold water. Chill and unmold for serving. Serve with canned peaches, raspberries, or strawberries.

To make a lighter cornstarch mold, fold in beaten egg whites to the cooled cornstarch, then chill.

Mary Ethel Haydu, Braddock, Pa.

EGG NOODLE CUSTARD

6 ounces egg noodles	1 teaspoon salt
2 cups milk	4 eggs, separated
1 cup sugar	1¼ teaspoons lemon extract

Cook noodles until tender, drain. Add milk and let stand 45 minutes. Add half of sugar, salt, lemon extract and lightly beaten yolks. Beat egg whites until very stiff, beat in remaining sugar. Fold into first mixture. Pour into buttered mold and bake in moderate oven (325°F) for 1 hour. Serve with Yankee Doodle Sauce.

Yankee Doodle Sauce-Chop candied ginger fine, add an equal quantity of finely ground orange rind. Sprinkle over each individual dish as desired.

Agnes Bayus, Cleveland, Oh.

- FROZEN AND GELATIN DESSERTS -

BAKED ALASKA

4 individual shortcakes	½ cup sugar
1 package frozen strawberries	Pinch of salt
1 pint ice cream	1 teaspoon vanilla
6 egg whites	

Cut fruit and ice cream in small pieces. Place in freezer to refreeze. Prepare meringue as follows: Beat whites slightly, add salt and vanilla, and continue beating until very stiff. Add sugar, a tablespoon at a time, and beat only until sugar is well blended. Place shortcakes on cookie sheet. Place frozen fruit in center of each shortcake. Put ice cream on top of fruit. Cover generously with meringue. Bake at 450°F for 4 or 5 minutes. Watch carefully.

Mary Schinsky, North Hollywood, Calif.

LEMON ICE CREAM

3 tablespoons lemon juice
1 cup sugar

1 pint cream
2 drops yellow food coloring

Blend lemon juice and sugar and slowly stir in the cream. Add coloring and blend well. Pour into freezing tray and quick freeze for 3 hours. Do not stir. Other flavors, fruits or nuts and coloring may be substituted.

Mrs. Macko, Connellsville, Pa.

ORANGE SHERBET

2 cups orange juice
3 tablespoons lemon juice
1½ cups sugar
1 cup water

1 tablespoon plain gelatin, softened
   in 2 tablespoons cold water
2 egg whites

Combine sugar and water. Bring to boiling point and boil for 5 minutes. Dissolve the softened gelatin in the hot syrup. Beat egg whites until stiff. Pour the syrup gradually over the beaten whites, beating constantly. Add fruit juices. Pour into freezing tray and freeze at coldest temperature. When almost frozen, remove to chilled bowl and beat well. Return to tray and freeze until firm.

Mrs. Martha Weismann

REFRIGERATOR ICE CREAM

2 eggs
2 cans evaporated milk
¾ cup sugar

1 small can crushed pineapple
2 teaspoons vanilla

Beat the eggs, add sugar and continue beating. Add vanilla and mix well. Keep canned milk in refrigerator until well chilled, if possible overnight. Whip milk until thick, then fold in beaten eggs and beat some more. Stir in pineapple and pour in trays in refrigerator. When it begins to freeze remove from refrigerator and stir well. Return to refrigerator and freeze until ready to serve. This makes 8 servings. Any other fruit can be substituted or it can be plain vanilla.

Beatrice Pihulic, Hammond, Ind.

JELLO DELIGHT

1 package Jello
1 cup whipping cream
1 tablespoon sugar

Make jello according to directions and allow to congeal. When at the shimmering stage, fold in the sweetened whipped cream with a fork. Return to refrigerator to set. Rainbow effect can be obtained by making lime and cherry or raspberry separately, then spooning portions of each into sherbets. Canned fruit or marshmallows may also be added. Substitute fruit juice for part of the water when making the jello base.

Mary Bucz, Chicago, Ill.

MAPLE NUT SPONGE

1½ cups hot milk
2 egg yolks, slightly beaten
1 tablespoon plain gelatin
¼ cup cold water
1 cup maple syrup

¼ teaspoon salt
2 egg whites, stiffly beaten
¼ cup chopped nuts
½ teaspoon vanilla

Add hot milk to slightly beaten egg yolks and cook over boiling water until the mixture thickens slightly. Remove from heat. Soften gelatin in cold water for five minutes. Add to first mixture and stir until dissolved; then add maple syrup and salt. Cool and when mixture begins to congeal, fold in stiffly beaten egg whites, vanilla and nuts. Turn into serving glasses and chill.

Anna Sabol, Whiting, Ind.

MACAROON TORTE

1 tablespoon unflavored gelatin
¼ cup cold water
½ cup hot water
½ cup drained crushed pineapple
cookies

½ cup sugar
2 egg whites, stiffly beaten
1 cup heavy cream, whipped
1 - 8-oz. package Macaroon

Soften gelatin in cold water, dissolve in hot water and chill until partially set. Line side of 8-inch square pan with macaroons; roll remaining macaroons to cover bottom of pan; reserve ¼ cup crumbs to sprinkle on top. Add pineapple to gelatin in whipped cream. Pour into pan. Top with remaining crumbs. Chill thoroughly. Serves 9.

Mary Skurka, Whiting, Ind.

MACAROON GELATIN TORTE

1 teaspoon gelatin
1 teaspoon cold water
¾ cup crushed macaroons
1 teaspoon vanilla
½ cup chopped walnuts
¾ cup blanched almonds

1 cup sugar
½ cup water
¼ teaspoon salt
6 egg yolks
2 cups heavy cream, whipped

Soften gelatin with 1 teaspoon water, 5 minutes. Boil sugar, water, salt. together till syrup spins a thread. Pour slowly over beaten egg yolks, stirring constantly. Add softened gelatin and stir until completely dissolved. Cool. Then fold in macaroons, nut meats, vanilla and whipped cream. Pour into mold or paper cups and freeze in refrigerator.

Mary Ethel Haydu, Braddock, Pa.

PINEAPPLE DESSERT

¾ cup crushed pineapple,
　drained
2 tablespoons lemon juice
⅓ cup sugar

⅛ teaspoon salt
½ pint whipped cream
2 cups rice, cooked
½ cup shredded coconut

To the pineapple, add lemon juice, sugar, salt and mix. Whip cream and fold into mixture. Fold in chilled rice and coconut. Chill. Serve topped with whipped cream.

Mary Pataky, Whiting, Ind.

PINEAPPLE AND COCONUT DESSERT

3 egg yolks
⅓ cup sugar
⅓ teaspoon salt
3 cups milk
1½ cups or 9-ounce can crushed
　pineapple

1½ cups whipping cream
3 tablespoons unflavored gelatin
¾ cups cold water
1½ cups fresh grated or canned
　coconut

Beat together egg yolks, sugar and salt. Add to milk that has been scalded and cooled. Cook over hot water in double boiler until custard coats spoon. Meanwhile, soften the unflavored gelatin by soaking in cold water for 5 minutes. Add to the hot custard and stir until dissolved. Cook until partly thickened, then fold in coconut, pineapple and whipped cream. Pile into lightly buttered mold, chill until firm. Unmold and decorate. Recipe fills a 2 quart mold.

Irene Galos, Warrenville, Ill.

BANANA ICE BOX CAKE

6 bananas
1 pint whipping cream
1 pound vanilla wafers

Line a layer of vanilla wafers on a flat cake plate. Then spread on whipping cream, sliced bananas and repeat until all ingredients have been used. You may trim the top with cherries, or with colored jelly drops. Chill until firm.

Ann Bronersky, Chicago, Ill.

BANANA-NUT ICE BOX CAKE

½ pound vanilla wafers
1 cup powdered sugar
1 cup chopped nutmeats
3 bananas

½ cup butter
4 eggs, beaten separately
1 teaspoon lemon extract

Cream butter and sugar. Add beaten egg yolks, lemon extract and beat several minutes. Beat egg whites stiff, fold into mixture and add nuts. Crush vanilla wafers. Put into pan a layer of crumbs, a layer of custard, then bananas sliced thin, then custard, etc. Finish up with crumbs. Set overnight to chill. Serve with whipped cream.

Anna Kolena, Chicago, Ill.

CHOCOLATE CHIFFON DESSERT

½ cup chopped Brazil nuts
½ cup chocolate cookie crumbs
1 envelope unflavored gelatin
¼ cup cold water
1 package semi-sweet chocolate

½ cup sugar
¼ teaspoon salt
½ cup milk
3 eggs, separated
1 cup cream, whipped

Mix chopped Brazil nuts and cookie crumbs. Rinse an 8 inch spring-form pan with cold water; line with waxed paper cut to fit bottom and sides (the water makes the waxed paper adhere to the pan). Cover the bottom of the pan with half the mixture. Soften gelatin in cold water. In top of double boiler put semi-sweet chocolate, ¼ cup sugar, salt and milk. Cook over hot water until blended. Beat egg yolks, add hot mixture slowly, stirring rapidly. Return to double boiler, cook over hot water stirring constantly until thickened. Remove from heat, add gelatin, stir until dissolved. Chill until thickened. Beat egg whites until stiff. Fold in chocolate mixture and whipped cream. Turn into prepared pan, top with remaining crumb mixture. Chill until firm, to unmold, remove sides of mold carefully, take off paper. Place serving platter on top; remove bottom of pan and paper. Yield: 8 to 10 servings.

Rosemarie Baumann, Seattle, Wa.

CHOCOLATE REFRIGERATOR CAKE

3 bars German sweet chocolate
5 tablespoons water
5 tablespoons powdered sugar

6 egg yolks and whites
18 lady fingers

Melt chocolate, add water and sugar and cook in double boiler until a smooth paste. When cool, add egg yolks one at a time, beating each time. When thoroughly cool, add stiffly beaten egg whites. Line pan with Lady Fingers and pour in mixture. Place in refrigerator for 4 to 5 hours. Top with whipped cream.

Mary Schlee, Chicago, Ill.

FROZEN CHEESE DESSERT

2 tablespoons gelatin
½ cup cold water
2 egg yolks
½ teaspoon salt
½ cup milk

1 cup sugar
1 pound cottage cheese
½ teaspoon vanilla
2 egg whites
1 pint heavy cream

Pour cold water in bowl and dissolve gelatin. Beat egg yolks slightly, add sugar, salt and milk. Cook over boiling water until custard thickens (stir while cooking). Add gelatin to hot mixture and stir until dissolved. Cool mixture. When it thickens, add cheese. Mix cottage cheese and vanilla with egg beater until light and fluffy. Whip cream, beat egg whites until stiff and dry. Fold into cheese mixture. Line pan with cracker crumbs made from 18 graham crackers, ⅓ cup sugar, ⅓ cup melted butter and 1 teaspoon cinnamon. Freeze 12 hours.

Joan Bobek, Riverside, Ill.

FROZEN COTTAGE CHEESE CAKE

GRAHAM CRACKER CRUST:
2 cups Graham cracker crumbs
⅓ cup powdered sugar
½ cup butter

Crush graham crackers, mix with butter and sugar. Pat mixture firmly into loaf pan. Place in refrigerator, allow to stand for 1 hour.

FILLING:
½ cup warm water
2 packages plain gelatin
½ cup milk
1 cup sugar
½ pint whipped cream

2 egg yolks
2 egg whites, stiffly beaten
1½ pounds creamed cottage cheese

Dissolve the gelatin in ½ cup warm water. Add milk and sugar to the gelatin and boil for 15 minutes. Let cool at room temperature. Then add the cheese and egg yolks and beaten egg whites. Add whipped cream and mix it well; beat with electric beater or with rotary beater. Put in loaf pan lined with graham cracker crust. Place in refrigerator and freeze.

Anna M. Bacik, Cleveland, Oh.

FROZEN PINEAPPLE TORTE

3 egg yolks
Pinch of salt
½ cup sugar
1-9 oz. can crushed pineapples drained

2 tablespoons lemon juice
3 egg whites
2 tablespoons sugar
1 cup heavy cream, whipped
2 cups vanilla wafer crumbs

Directions continued on page 230.

Beat egg yolks, salt and sugar; add pineapple syrup and lemon juice. Cook over hot (not boiling) water until mixture coats spoon, stirring constantly. Add pineapple. Cool. Make meringue of egg whites and sugar. Fold in whipped cream and custard. Coat sides of oiled refrigerator tray with wafer crumbs. Spread half of remaining crumbs over bottom of tray. Pour in custard mixture, cover with remaining crumbs. Freeze firm, about 4 hours. Serves 6 to 8. (This may be made the day before it is to be used.)

Emma Bertha, Gary, Ind.

GELATIN ICE BOX CAKE

1 package gelatin	1 cup sugar
3 cups milk	1 teaspoon vanilla
4 eggs, separated	18 lady fingers

Mix the gelatin in the milk and let stand for 2 hours. Then put in double boiler. Mix the yolks with the sugar and the gelatin until cooked. Remove from stove, add the vanilla and the whites of the eggs, which have been beaten stiffly. Let stand until cold. Pour into a spring-form pan lined with lady fingers and place in refrigerator over night. Before serving add whipped cream.

Apolonia Blahunka, Whiting, Ind.

GRAHAM CRACKER CAKE

⅓ cup sugar	½ teaspoon vanilla
¼ cup cocoa	Dash of salt
1 cup heavy cream, whipped	16 single graham crackers

Combine the sugar and cocoa. Whip the cream until it is stiff, but still shiny, then fold in the cocoa and sugar and add the salt and vanilla. Spread crackers with cream, standing them upright on a cookie sheet or platter, press together gently, then spread the remaining cream over the top and sides. Chill at least 4 hours. When ready to serve, slice diagonally and serve with additional whipped cream if desired. This makes 6 servings.

Eleanor Marko, Whiting, Ind.

GRAHAM CRACKER REFRIGERATOR CAKE

½ cup butter	1 cup crushed pineapple
1 cup sugar	2¼ cups Graham cracker crumbs
1 egg	1 cup chopped nuts
3 teaspoons cream	

Directions continued on page 231.

Cream butter and sugar together, add beaten egg and cream until light; then add drained pineapple. Have oblong pan lined with waxed paper. Place a layer of fine cracker crumbs about ½ inch deep on the bottom. Over this pour 3 or 4 tablespoons of pineapple and chopped nuts. Complete by adding third layer. Cover with waxed paper. Let stand in refrigerator 24 hours. Cut in thick slices and serve with whipped cream. Cottage cheese may be used between pineapple.

Maria Talla, Binghampton, NY

ICE BOX CREAM CAKE

2 cans Eagle Brand Sweetened Condensed Milk
1 sponge cake
1 pint whipping cream, whipped and seasoned with vanilla and
  sweetened with powdered sugar. This amount of whipped cream
  should be enough for a 9-inch cake.
Chopped pecans to suit your own taste

Place two cans of unopened Eagle Brand SC milk into a kettle of water. Keep the water boiling for 3 hours, adding water to kettle if necessary. This boiling can be done the day before so the caramel filling (which the milk has now become) can be cold when ready to use. (Chill in refrigerator.) You can either open the cans of caramel immediately after boiling or keep them unopened in the refrigerator until ready to use. You use the caramel directly from the can, no whipping or mixing, or seasoning. It is ready to use as it is. If you are using a sponge cake that has the hole in the center, cut the cake so that you have two layers. Cover the bottom layer with a nice thick layer of caramel filling, right out of the can, then sprinkle with chopped pecans, then cover with a generous layer of whipped cream. Lay the second layer on top of this and cover the entire cake, top and sides with a layer of caramel filling, chopped nuts and finally the whipped cream. Place into refrigerator until ready to use or freeze in the freezer compartment and have a dessert for any emergency.

Second Method-If you do not want the separate fillings, you can fold the whipped cream in the caramel filling and spread between and over the cake. This is good, but many prefer the first method.

Anna B. Hopko, Braddock, Pa.

ICE BOX FRUIT CAKE

1 pound Graham Crackers, rolled   **1 cup nuts, cut small**
1 pound marshmallows, cut fine   **½ cup thin cream**
1 pound dates

Mix well. Freeze over night, slice as you use.

Anna B. Russell, Cleveland, Oh.

JELLO CAKE

1 package Jello
2 cups water
½ cup sugar

Juice of 1 lemon
1 pound vanilla wafers
1 can chilled evaporated milk

Dissolve jello in water, add sugar and lemon juice. Set in a cool place until syrupy. 1. Beat until foamy. 2. Beat milk until it stands in a peak. 3. Beat jello and milk together. Crush enough vanilla wafers to make a layer in bottom of pan (it helps if you mix a little melted butter with wafer crumbs). Then pour jello mixture into pan. Then sprinkle some of the wafers over jello. Set in refrigerator until firm. If you wish you can cover with whipped cream. Use a spring form pan. This can be made day before using. Chilling evaporated milk for a few days makes it beat better.

Mary Skriba, Riverside, Ill.

PINEAPPLE-CHEESE ICE BOX PIE

CRUMB CRUST
4 cups corn flakes
2 tablespoons sugar
4 tablespoons melted butter

Crush corn flakes very fine, add sugar and shortening. Mix well. Press in 9-inch pie pan, reserving 3 tablespoons crumbs for topping. Chill in refrigerator or bake 8 minutes at 375°F.

FILLING
1 tablespoon gelatin, softened in
  ½ cup cold water
3 eggs separated
1 cup crushed pineapple, not
  drained

1 cup soft cottage cheese
¼ teaspoon salt
¾ cup sugar
1 teaspoon grated lemon rind
2 tablespoons lemon juice

In cold double boiler beat egg yolks slightly, add crushed pineapple, lemon rind, lemon juice, ¼ cup sugar and cook over hot water, stirring until thick. Add gelatin, stir until melted. Remove from heat. Press cottage cheese through sieve, add to hot mixture. Cool until it begins to thicken. Beat whites, add salt, when stiff gradually beat in ½ cup sugar, then fold in pineapple-cheese mixture. Pour onto crust, sprinkle with reserved crumbs and chill 3 hours or longer.

Florence Ribovich, Hammond, Ind.

STRAWBERRY-SOUR CREAM JELLO MOLD

2 packages of strawberry jello
1½ cups of hot water
1 small can of crushed pineapple (drained thoroughly)
2 bananas, mashed
1 small can of sour cream
2 small packages of frozen strawberries

Dissolve the jello in boiling water, and add the frozen strawberries. After they have thawed, add the bananas and pineapple. Spread half this mixture on the bottom of the mold, and let chill until firm. Cover this half with the sour cream, then spread the other half on top. Chill until firm.

Anne Fusillo, Gary, Ind.

PINEAPPLE REFRIGERATOR CAKE

1 cup butter or oleo
2¾ cups confectioners' sugar
4 eggs
1 teaspoon lemon extract
2 packages lady fingers
1 cup candied cherries, chopped
2 No. 2 cans crushed pineapple, drained
2 cups cream, whipped

Cream butter until soft. Add sugar and cream until fluffy. Beat eggs well and beat into butter mixture. Add flavoring. Line deep spring-form pan with split lady fingers. Cover with ⅓ of sugar mixture, spread with half mixed fruit, over this spread half whipped cream, then layer of lady fingers. Repeat this procedure, topping with sugar mixture. Chill in refrigerator at least 12 hours. Before serving top with reserved half of whipped cream.

Alice Hruskovich, Whiting, Ind.

REFRIGERATOR CHEESE CAKE

½ cup melted butter
¾ cup sugar
2 cups fine zwieback crumbs
2 teaspoons cinnamon
2 tablespoons gelatin
1 cup cold water
3 eggs, separated
2 cups cream cheese
3 tablespoons lemon juice
1 tablespoon grated lemon rind
¼ teaspoon salt
½ cup whipping cream

Blend together butter, ¼ cup sugar, crumbs and cinnamon. Press ¾ of this mixture on the bottom of a 9-inch spring form pan. Soak gelatin in ½ cup cold water for 5 minutes. Cook egg yolks, ½ cup sugar and ½ cup water in a double boiler, stirring constantly until mixture coats a metal spoon. Add gelatin and stir until dissolved. Add gradually to cream cheese, add lemon juice, rind and salt. Beat thoroughly. Cool, when beginning to congeal, beat several minutes with egg beater. Whip cream and fold in with stiffly beaten egg whites, blending thoroughly. Pour onto crumbs. Sprinkle remaining crumbs over top. Chill until firm. For variety, use crumbs made from graham crackers, vanilla wafers, ginger snaps, chocolate cookies, crushed cornflakes, browned dried bread crumbs or other suitable prepared breakfast foods.

Maria Proskac, Coalsdale, Pa.

GRAPE NUT TORTONI

¼ cup grape nuts
6 tablespoons powdered sugar
Dash of ground cinnamon
2 egg yolks

½ pint heavy whipping cream
2 tablespoons grape nuts
   (additional)

Combine grape nuts, sugar, cinnamon and well beaten yolks. Whip cream until thick, not solid. Add grapenut mixture. Put into baking paper cups or refrigerator tray and sprinkle with additional grape nuts, finely chopped. Freeze. Yield: 6 servings.

You may place vanilla, chocolate or crushed macaroon cookies on bottom of tray or paper cup.

Agnes Bayus, Cleveland, Oh.

GRAHAM CRACKER ICE BOX CAKE

½ pound graham crackers
⅓ cup chopped nuts
½ pound marshmallows
½ cup coffee cream

1 tablespoon orange juice
10 maraschino cherries
½ pound dates

Roll crackers fine. Cut marshmallows and dates in small pieces. Combine in order given. Line loaf pan with waxed paper and butter the paper. Pack mixture firmly into pan, cover with waxed paper and place in refrigerator overnight. Turn out on platter and slice. Serve with whipped cream.

Agnes Bayus, Cleveland, Oh.

LEMON ICE BOX CAKE

2 tablespoons gelatin
¾ cup cold water
1½ cups milk
6 eggs, separated
Grated rind and juice of 2 lemons
1 cup sugar

Pinch of salt
1 tablespoon butter
½ teaspoon soda
Lady fingers
Whipped cream

Soak gelatin in water. Scald milk in top of double boiler. Beat yolks until thick. Add lemon rind. Add sugar and beat until thick. Beat scalded milk into egg mixture. Place in double boiler and cook until thick. Add salt. (This mixture does not get too thick.) Stir in butter, add soda and lemon juice. Remove from fire and stir in gelatin at once, beating well. Cool. Add stiffly beaten egg whites and blend well. Line bottom of pan with lady fingers, pour half of mixture over lady fingers. Cover again with lady fingers, then pour remaining mixture. Cover with lady fingers. Chill for 24 hours. Serve with whipped cream.

Agnes Bayus, Cleveland, Oh.

LEMON WONDER CAKE

1 package lemon flavored
  gelatin
1 cup boiling water
1 package lemon flavored cake
  mix
¾ cup cooking oil
4 eggs

GLAZE
1 cup confectioners' sugar
Juice of 1 lemon (about 3
  tablespoons)

Dissolve the gelatin in boiling water and set aside to cool. Mix cake mix with oil and add eggs, one at a time, beating well after each addition. Add cooled gelatin mixture and beat to blend. Pour into a well greased and lightly floured pan and bake in a 350°F oven for about 40 minutes, or until a cake tester inserted in the center comes out clean. Remove from the oven and puncture the top thoroughly with the tines of a fork. While still warm spread cake with glaze made with the lemon juice and confectioners' sugar. Yeilds one 9x3x2" cake.

Geraldine Cross, Crown Point, Ind.

- CAKE AND PUDDING DESSERTS -

APPLE PUDDING

8 apples, sliced
6 tablespoons sugar
4 tablespoons butter
6 beaten eggs
1 pint sour cream

½ cup sugar
1 teaspoon vanilla
Dash nutmeg
Graham crackers, rolled

Combine apples, 6 tablespoons sugar and butter. Place in pan and cook until apples are soft. Place in top of double boiler the beaten eggs, sour cream and sugar. Cook to a custard, remove from fire and add vanilla and nutmeg. Combine custard and apples. Butter bottom and sides of frying pan, press graham cracker crumbs on sides and bottom. Pour mixture into pan and sprinkle additional cracker crumbs on top. Bake one hour in slow oven, 325 to 350°F. It takes about 2 cups of graham cracker crumbs.

Betty Hertko, Whiting, Ind.

CRUMB PUDDING

1 ounce unsweetened chocolate	½ cup sugar
½ cup milk	2 cups soft bread crumbs
½ cup butter	1 cup blanched shredded almonds
4 egg yolks, well beaten	4 egg whites, beaten stiff

Heat chocolate, milk and butter together in top of double boiler until chocolate is melted. Mix egg yolks and sugar together and add a small amount of hot mixture, return to double boiler and cook for 3 minutes, add crumbs and almonds. Fold in egg whites, cover double boiler, steam for 30 minutes. Serve hot with lemon sauce or whipped cream.

Betty Hertko, Whiting, Ind.

BAVARIAN CREAM PUDDING

1 tablespoon gelatin	½ cup hot milk
¼ cup cold water	1 tablespoon vanilla
5 egg yolks	1 cup cream, whipped
½ cup powdered sugar	12 lady fingers

Soften the gelatin in water a few minutes. Beat yolks and sugar until very light, add milk and the softened gelatin. Cook in double boiler until the mixture coats the spoon, stirring constantly. Let cool. Add vanilla and fold in the whipped cream. Turn into a mold lined with lady fingers, let stand several hours to chill. Serve with fresh fruit, caramel or chocolate sauce.

Florence Leonard, Hammond, Ind.

GRAHAM CRACKER PUDDING

1 pound graham crackers	1 cup raisins
1½ cups brown sugar	1 teaspoon vanilla
3 teaspoons baking powder	3 eggs, well beaten
½ teaspoon salt	1½ cups milk

Combine rolled graham crackers, sugar, baking powder, salt and raisins. Add vanilla and milk with beaten eggs. Blend into dry ingredients. Dates and nuts may be substituted for raisins. Pour batter into 7 x 11 inch pan and bake in 350°F oven for 35 minutes.

CARAMEL SAUCE FOR PUDDING

¼ cup butter	1 cup cold water
1 cup brown sugar	2 teaspoons vanilla
1 tablespoon cornstarch	

Melt butter, add sugar, then cornstarch which has been dissolved in the water. Bring slowly to the boiling point, stirring to blend. Remove from heat, add vanilla. Brandy or Rum may be substituted. Serve warm sauce on pudding.

Marcella Halloran, Streator, Ill.

FRUIT BREAD PUDDING

1 loaf of second day bread or equivalent amount of second day pastry
1½ cups fruit preserves, such as apples, peaches, cooked raisins or
  prunes or combination of each
2 tablespoons sugar
1 tablespoon shortening

Dice the bread or pastry. Combine all ingredients. Bake in oven 250°F for half hour. Serve hot. Fresh fruits may be substituted for preserves and nuts, may be added.

Benedictine Slovak Sisters, Chicago, Ill.

POPPY SEED PUDDING

1 loaf of day old bread
½ cup ground poppy seed
3 tablespoons sugar

1 tablespoon shortening
1 cup milk

Dice the bread. Mix the sugar and poppy seed well. Combine all ingredients and mix. Place in pan and bake at 350°F for half an hour. Serve hot.

Benedictine Slovak Sisters, Chicago, Ill.

GLORIFIED RICE

½ cup uncooked rice
2 cups water
½ teaspoon salt

1 cup grated or diced pineapple
20 marshmallows, diced
½ pint whipping cream

Cook rice until tender and water is absorbed, chill. Combine rice, pineapple, diced marshmallows and the cream which has been whipped until stiff. Serve in sherbet glasses.

Anna Sabol, Whiting, Ind.

PINEAPPLE RICE PUDDING

2 cups cooked rice
3 eggs separated
½ cup sugar

½ cup milk
½ can grated pineapple

Beat yolks of eggs well, then mix with rice, add sugar, milk and pineapple. Fold in the stiffly beaten egg whites, pour into a buttered pan or glass ovenware. Bake ½ hour, serve with whipped cream.

Leona Chabala, Nokomis, Ill.

MOLASSES BREAD PUDDING

10 slices stale bread, cubed
2 eggs
3 tablespoons molasses
2 tablespoons sugar

¼ teaspoon salt
2 cups milk, scalded
2 tablespoons butter melted

Arrange bread cubes in a well greased baking dish. Beat eggs, molasses, sugar and salt together. Add milk and butter. Pour over bread cubes. Bake in moderate oven, 350°F for 1 hour or until firm. Serve cold with milk or cream.

Ella D. Vlasaty, Braddock, Pa.

RICE PUDDING

1½ cups rice
1 quart water
Pinch of salt
1 pint milk, scalded
3 eggs, separated

3 teaspoons heavy cream
½ cup sugar
1 cup raisins
2 teaspoons powdered sugar

Boil rice in water, add little salt. When tender and thick, add scalded milk. Add beaten yolks, cream, sugar and raisins. Turn into a buttered baking dish and bake in moderate oven for 30 minutes. Top with a meringue made by beating the egg whites until stiff, then fold in the powdered sugar. Brown in a slow oven for about 12 minutes.

Helen Butas, Bellaire, Oh.

RICE AND MARSHMALLOW DESSERT

¼ cup rice
1 small package marshmallows

1 small can crushed pineapple
1 pint whipping cream

Boil rice until well done. Wash through with cold water and let drain dry. Cut up marshmallows into crushed pineapple. Add rice. Put in refrigerator over night. When ready to serve, add whipped cream.

Susan Chizmark, Joliet, Ill.

RICE COOKED IN MILK

½ cup rice, well washed and
    drained
3½ cups milk
½ teaspoon salt

2 tablespoons butter
½ cup sugar
Cinnamon to taste

Bring milk to a boil, add rice and cook over a low flame or in top of a double boiler, stirring occasionally until rice is tender but not soft. When rice is done, remove from heat, add butter and sugar and blend well. If served hot, then rice dish is served with a lump of butter and cinnamon sprinkled over it. Serves 8.

Florence Gresko, Whiting, Ind.

ORANGE BREAKFAST CAKE

2 or 3 large oranges
¾ cup butter or margarine
1 cup sugar
1 cup finely chopped dates
2 eggs

2 cups sifted flour
1 teaspoon baking soda
¼ teaspoon salt
1 teaspoon vanilla flavoring

Ream juice from oranges to make 1 cup. Grind rind to make one cup. Cream butter; gradually add sugar and cream until light and fluffy. Blend in eggs. Stir in dates and orange rind. Sift flour, soda and salt; add alternately to creamed mixture with orange juice. Add vanilla. Turn into a greased 13x9 inch baking pan. Bake at 350°F for 40 minutes. Cool; cut into squares. Yield 12 servings.

Loretta J. Tylka, North Riverside, Ill.

FRESH RHUBARB BETTY

⅓ cup margarine
2 cups soft bread crumbs
6 cups cut up rhubarb
1 cup sugar

¾ cup brown sugar, firmly packed
¼ teaspoon cinnamon

Melt butter. Toss with crumbs. Arrange ⅓ of crumbs in greased 1½ quart casserole. Cover with half of rhubarb and half of combined sugars and cinnamon. Nutmeg or cloves may be used. Cover with another ⅓ crumbs, remaining rhubarb and rest or sugar mixture. Cover with remaining crumbs and cover casserole to bake. Bake in a 375°F oven for ½ hour. Uncover, bake ½ hour longer or till rhubarb is done. Makes six servings. Serve warm, topped with cream cheese softened with a little milk or cream. Add a little sugar and a dash of cinnamon if cheese is desired sweetened.

BLACKBERRY OR BLUEBERRY COBBLER

FRUIT:
3 cups fruit, drained
2 tablespoons butter
½ cup brown sugar
1 tablespoon lemon juice

RICH BISCUIT DOUGH
1 cup all-purpose flour, not sifted
1½ teaspoons baking powder
½ teaspoon salt
1 tablespoon sugar
4 tablespoons butter, or 3
    tablespoons lard
Milk

Melt 2 tablespoons butter in pyrex baking dish (10 x 6 x 1½-inches). Add brown sugar and drained berries. Sprinkle with lemon juice. (Quick frozen berries may be used to which add 2 or 3 tablespoons of water.) Put in hot oven, 450°F, to heat through. In the meantime make the biscuit dough. Combine dry ingredients. Blend in butter or lard and add just enough milk to moisten. Roll out and brush top with melted butter. Roll like jelly roll. Cut into ½-inch slices. Place over hot berries. Bake at 350°F for 15 minutes, or until biscuits are nicely browned. Serve with whipped cream or with sweetened and thickened berry juice.

Berry Juice: ¾ cup berry juice, ¼ cup sugar, 1 tablespoon cornstarch and 1 teaspoon lemon juice. Combine ingredients and bring to boiling point. Simmer until thick, stirring constantly. Cool and serve.

Agnes Bayus, Cleveland, Oh.

HOLLAND RUSK PUDDING

1 package Holland rusk　　　　**½ cup melted butter**
½ cup sugar

Crumble rusk, add sugar and butter.

1½ cups milk　　　　　　　**3 egg whites**
½ cup sugar　　　　　　　　**Powdered sugar**
1 tablespoon cornstrach　　**Nut meats, ground**
3 egg yolks

In top of double boiler, combine milk, sugar, cornstarch and egg yolks. Cook as custard. Line baking dish with ⅔ crumb mixture. Pour custard over mixture. Whip egg whites, sweeten with powdered sugar and spread over custard. Sprinkle with nut meats and remaining crumb mixture. Bake in moderate oven for 30 minutes. Cool and serve.

Agnes Bayus, Cleveland, Oh.

SUNSHINE PUDDING

6 egg yolks　　　　　　　**½ cup farina**
6 egg whites　　　　　　　**Pinch of salt**
1 tablespoon sugar

Beat egg yolks until thick and lemon colored. Beat egg whites until stiff. Fold the beaten eggs together lightly. Add sugar and salt. Add the farina very gradually and mix slowly. Grease pan. Place mixture into pan and bake at 350°F until top turns into golden brown. Cut into two inch squares and pour hot milk over the pudding and bake 10 more minutes to complete the cooking of eggs and farina. Serve hot.

Benedictine Slovak Sisters, Chicago, Ill.

APPLE SLICES

2 cups flour　　　　　　　**2 egg yolks**
½ teaspoon salt　　　　　**1 tablespoon lemon juice**
½ cup shortening　　　　　**8 tablespoons cold water**

Sift flour and salt, cut in shortening. Mix well the egg yolks, lemon juice and cold water. Add gradually to dry ingredients. Stir until flour is moistened, divide into two parts. Roll dough as thin as for pie crust and line 7x12 inch pan. Fill with apple mixture made by sprinkling:

8 apples, sliced	**1 tablespoon flour**
½ cup sugar	**½ teaspoon cinnamon**
¼ teaspoon salt	**½ teaspoon nutmeg**
½ cup raisins	

Roll second portion of dough to fit top of the pan and layover the apples. Press edges of dough firmly together. Bake in moderate oven 350°F for about 45 minutes or until apples are tender and crust is nicely browned. When cool drizzle a thin confectioners' frosting over the top and cut into slices.

Agnes Sabol, Whiting, Ind.

APPLE SLICES

CRUST	**FILLING**
2 cups flour	**3 pounds cooking apples, tart**
½ teaspoon salt	**1 cup water**
¾ cup lard	**1¼ cups sugar**
1 teaspoon lemon juice	**1 teaspoon cinnamon**
2 egg yolks, beaten	**¼ teaspoon salt**
½ teaspoon baking powder	**2 tablespoons cornstarch**
½ cup water	**¼ cup cold water**

Cut apples into eighths. Bring water, sugar, cinnamon and salt to boiling point, add apples and cook slowly for 10 minutes. Blend cornstarch and cold water and add to hot mixture. Cook 5 minutes longer stirring gently. Cut lard into sifted flour, baking powder and salt as for pie crust. Mix lemon juice, egg yolks and water together and sprinkle over flour mixture. Blend it in lightly, divide into two parts. Roll first piece to fit bottom and sides of shallow pan about 9x13 inches, fill with apple mixture. Roll remaining dough to fit top and seal edges. Cut a design for steam vents. Bake in hot oven 450°F for 20 minutes and then reduce heat to 350°F and bake 30 minutes longer. Ice with a thin confectioners' sugar icing. (12 servings).

Mary Kovacik, Whiting, Ind.

APPLE SQUARES

CRUST

1½ cups sifted flour	**¼ cup lard**
½ teaspoon baking powder	**¼ cup butter**
¾ teaspoon salt	**¼ cup cold milk**

Work the above ingredients together and knead for 1 minute.

Directions continued on page 242.

FILLING

1½ pounds apples	¼ teaspoon salt
2 tablespoons lemon juice	½ cup hot water
¼ cup raisins (optional)	1 tablespoon butter
½ cup sugar	2 tablespoons bread crumbs
¼ teaspoon cinnamon	¼ teaspoon nutmeg

Cook apples, lemon juice, sugar, raisins, salt and water until tender about 7 minutes, then add 1 tablespoon cornstarch mixed with 2 tablespoons water. Cook until clear. Use ⅔ of dough for bottom and sides of pan as for pie. Sprinkle with crumbs, pour in apple filling and add butter cut in small pieces, cinnamon and nutmeg. Roll out balance of dough and cover top. Bake at 425°F about 40 minutes. Use 8-inch square pan. Ice with following icing: 1 tablespoon hot milk, ¾ cup powdered sugar, ¼ teaspoon vanilla. Mix well and pour on baked apple squares. Cut in squares as desired.

Helen Cross, Whiting, Ind.

PINEAPPLE SLICES

⅔ cup milk, scalded and cooled	3 cups flour
1 tablespoon sugar	1 teaspoon salt
1 cake yeast	3 yolks, beaten
1 cup butter or oleo (½ pound)	1 teaspoon vanilla or lemon extract

Dissolve sugar and yeast in warm milk, set aside. Sift flour, then measure. Add butter and mix as for pie crust. Add yeast and milk mixture and eggs, mix well. Divide dough into two parts. Roll one part to fit 12x18 inch cookie sheet, then spread cooled filling over the dough. Roll remaining dough to fit over the top. Let rise until light, about one hour. Bake at 350°F for 45 minutes or until brown. Frost with thin frosting and sprinkle with chopped nuts or coconut.

FILLING

1 No. 2 can crushed pineapple	½ cup sugar
¾ cup water	1 egg yolk, beaten
3 tablespoons cornstarch	

Combine cornstarch and sugar, add pineapple and water, cook until thick and clear. Add beaten yolk and mix well. Let cool before spreading on dough.

Louise Zaremba, Joliet, Ill.

PINEAPPLE SLICES

1 cup sifted flour	½ pint sour cream
1½ teaspoons baking powder	1 can crushed pineapple and
5 tablespoons sugar	1 cup sugar, (boil together until
½ pound butter	it jells, cool)
3 eggs, separated	

Sift dry ingredients, cut in butter as for pie dough. Beat egg yolks, add sour cream and beat together, gradually add to the flour. Work the dough and then roll about one inch thick. Divide dough into two parts. Line pan, spread cooled pineapple mixture. Cut the remaining dough in strips and criss-cross over the pineapple. Sprinkle chopped nuts and slightly beaten whites of 2 eggs, over entire top. Bake in moderate oven for about 45 minutes. Sprinkle with powdered sugar when ready to serve.

Mary E. Grega, Cleveland, Oh.

RASPBERRY SLICES

¼ pound sweet butter
½ cup sugar
4 egg yolks, beaten
1½ cups flour

1 teaspoon baking powder
1 teaspoon baking soda
Raspberry preserves

Cream butter, add sugar and beat until well creamed. Add yolks and beat together until light. Add sifted dry ingredients. Mix well. Pat dough into a 9x14 ungreased pan, spread raspberry preserves. Beat egg whites until stiff, add 4 tablespoons powdered sugar. Spread on top of jelly and top with chopped nuts. Bake at 350°F for about 25 minutes. Cover the dough with paper until done and whites are browned.

Mary E. Grega, Cleveland, Oh.

CREAM PUFFS

1 cup water
½ cup butter

1 cup flour
4 eggs, whole

Place butter and water in saucepan and bring to a quick boil. As soon as the mixture comes to a boil, add the sifted bread flour all at once, lower flame and with spoon stir vigorously for 2 or 3 minutes, until mixture leaves sides of pan. Remove the pan from the heat and then add eggs, one at a time, beating after each addition, until the dough is smooth and glossy. Drop mixture by tablespoons, 3 inches apart, on a greased cookie sheet. Bake in hot oven 450°F for 10 minutes, then at 400°F for 25 minutes. Cream Puffs should be puffed high and golden-brown. Remove to wire cake rack. Cool, cut in halves and fill.

CREAM FILLING

2 cups milk
¾ cup sugar
3 tablespoons flour

1 teaspoon vanilla
3 egg yolks

Warm milk, add sugar which has been mixed with the flour, beat egg yolks and add to the milk and cook until it coats the spoon. Cool and beat occasionally to prevent crust. Add vanilla.

Mary Koval, Whiting, Ind.

FRUIT COCKTAIL CAKE

2¼ cups flour	½ teaspoon salt
2 teaspoons baking soda	2 eggs well beaten
2 cups sugar	1 large can fruit cocktail (drained)

Mix all ingredients for 3 minutes by hand. Pour into a 9x13x2 greased and floured pan. Take ½ cup brown sugar and sprinkle on top of batter, also ½ cup of chopped nuts on top of sugar. Bake in 375°F oven for 40 minutes.

Mary Markovich, Whiting, Ind.

HONEYMOON PIE

1 box vanilla wafers (70) crushed
½ stick butter, melted
2 cups powdered sugar
½ cup softened butter
3 eggs
½ cup coarsely chopped nuts
1 cup crushed pineapple, drained
½ pint whipping cream, whipped until stiff

Mix all but 4 tablespoons of the wafer crumbs with the melted butter. Oblong glass baking pan (9x13") or a 9" square pan may be used. Spread buttered crumbs into bottom of pan. Add the sugar gradually to the soft butter and cream thoroughly. Add eggs one at a time to this mixture. Then spread this mixture over the crumb crust. Sprinkle on the nuts, top with the pineapple, and then spread on the whipped cream in swirls. Sprinkle the remaining wafer crumbs on top. Refrigerate overnight.

Deloros Geffert, Highland, Ind.

FUDGE RIBBON CAKE *(One 13 x 9" loaf pan)*

2 tablespoons butter	1½ teaspoons vanilla
2¼ cups sugar	2 cups sifted flour
1 tablespoon cornstarch	1 teaspoon salt
1 package (8 oz.) cream cheese	1 teaspoon baking powder
3 eggs	½ teaspoon soda
2 tablespoons, plus 1½ cups milk	½ cup shortening
4 oz. unsweetened chocolate or	

   4 - 1-oz. envelopes of no-melt chocolate flavored ingredient

Cream butter with ¼ cup of sugar and cornstarch and cream cheese. Beat until light and fluffy; add 1 egg, 2 tablespoons of milk and ½ teaspoon of vanilla. Beat at high speed of mixer until smooth and creamy. Grease and flour the bottom of the pan. Combine flour with 2 cups of sugar, salt, baking powder and soda in a large mixing bowl. Add shortening, and 1½ cups of milk and blend well at lowest speed of mixer. Beat 1½ minutes at low speed or

225 strokes by hand. Add two eggs, chocolate or no-melt chocolate flavored ingredient and 1 teaspoon of vanilla. Continue to beat 1½ minutes at low speed. Spread 3 cups of batter in the pan. Spoon cheese mixture over the batter, spreading it carefully to cover. Top with remaining batter and spread to cover. Bake in a 350°F oven for about 50 minutes, or until a cake tester inserted in the center comes out clean.

Cool and frost.

FROSTING

⅓ cup milk
¼ cup butter
1 teaspoon vanilla

1 package (6 oz.) or
1 cup semi-sweet chocolate pieces
2¼ cups sifted confectioners' sugar

Bring milk and butter to a boil and remove from the heat. Blend in chocolate pieces, stir in vanilla and sugar. If necessary, thin with a few drops of milk.

Virginia Dancik, Chicago, Ill.

RASPBERRY DESSERT

16 graham crackers, crushed
¼ cup melted butter or margarine
½ lb. marshmallows
½ cup milk
1 cup heavy cream, whipped or 1 package dessert topping mix
1½ cups frozen or fresh red raspberries with juice
2 tablespoons cornstarch
¼ cup sugar
⅛ teaspoon salt
2 tablespoons lemon juice

Mix graham crumbs with melted butter, reserving ¼ cup of mixture for topping. Press mixture into bottom of an 8x11 inch pan.

Melt marshmallows in milk. Cool. Add whipped cream or whipped topping. Cook raspberries, cornstarch, sugar, and salt until thick; add lemon juice; cool.

Pour one-half of cream mixture over graham crackers; add berry mixture and spread evenly over cream mixture. Spread remaining cream mixture over cool berries. Sprinkle reserved crumbs on top. Yield 12 servings.

Anne Fusillo, Gary, Ind.

CHOCOLATE REFRESHERS

1¼ cups sifted flour
¾ teaspoon soda
½ teaspoon salt
1¼ cups (8 oz. pkg.) cut dates
¾ cup firmly packed brown
  sugar
½ cup water

½ cup butter
1 cup Nestle semi-sweet
  chocolate morsels (6 oz.)
2 eggs
½ cup orange juice
½ cup milk
1 cup chopped nuts

Sift together flour, soda and salt; combine in large saucepan the dates, brown sugar, water and butter; cook over low heat, stirring constantly, until dates soften. Remove from heat. Stir in semi-sweet chocolate; add the unbeaten eggs and mix well. Add dry ingredients alternately with orange juice and milk. Blend thoroughly. Stir in chopped nuts. Spread batter in well greased 15x10x1 jelly roll pan. Bake at 350°F for 25 to 30 minutes. Cool. Use your own butter cream icing.

Theresa Krasula, Chicago, Ill.

- TORTES -

ALMOND TORTE

6 egg yolks
6 tablespoons sugar
2 tablespoons rum or good
  whiskey
2 squares shredded chocolate

6 egg whites
6 tablespoons almonds, finely
  ground
3 tablespoons cake flour

Beat the egg yolks, sugar, rum and chocolate until the sugar has dissolved. (This will take about 15 minutes with an electric beater.) Beat egg whites until they are stiff. Mix the egg whites into the above mixture gradually. Add to the mixture the almonds and flour. This must be added gradually. Pour into 2 greased pans and bake in 400°F oven for 45 minutes.

FILLING FOR ALMOND TORTE

3 whole eggs
1 cup sugar
½ pound sweet butter

1 cup confectioners' sugar
1 square unsweetened chocolate

Put the eggs and sugar into the top of the double boiler and beat for 15 minutes continually until thick. Let this mixture stand until it is cool, in a cool place. When cool, add the butter, confectioners' sugar and square of shredded bitter chocolate and beat with egg beater. This will make a filling and topping for the 2 layer torte.

Margaret Marko, Whiting, Ind.

CHEESE TORTE CAKE

COATING FOR PAN
2 packages zweiback
¼ pound butter
1 teaspoon cinnamon
4 tablespoons sugar

FILLING FOR CAKE
2 pounds dry cottage cheese
6 eggs
2 cups sugar
½ pint sweet cream
½ teaspoon salt
½ cup flour
1 teaspoon vanilla

Melt butter in skillet and add crushed zweiback with sugar and cinnamon. Press into 9 inch spring-form torte pan. Reserve some crumbs for the top of cake. Mash cottage cheese very well, add eggs one at a time, beating well after each addition. Then add sugar gradually. Mix well. Add ½ pint sweet cream, sifted flour and salt. Beat well. Fold in vanilla and pour into pan and bake ½ hour at 325°F and ½ hour at 350°F.

Important: Let stand in pan until cake is thoroughly cold.

Helen Chapek, Whiting, Ind.

CHEESE CAKE

COATING FOR PAN
½ pound Graham crackers
½ cup sugar
1 teaspoon cinnamon
4 tablespoons melted butter
2 tablespoons flour
2 tablespoons milk

FILLING FOR CAKE
2 pounds cottage cheese
1 cup milk
4 tablespoons flour
1 cup sugar
1 teaspoon vanilla
4 eggs, beaten

Roll graham crackers until fine, add all the ingredients and mix well. Line the well greased baking pans and press down well. Fill with cheese filling and cover with more graham cracker crumbs. Bake in moderate oven for one hour.

Catherine Otrembiak, Chicago, Ill.

CHEESE CAKE

COATING FOR PAN
1 pound Graham crackers
½ cup sugar
½ teaspoon vanilla
¾ cup melted butter

FILLING FOR CAKE
2 pounds dry cottage cheese
1 cup sugar
4 eggs
1¼ cups sweet cream
1 teaspoon vanilla

Rub cheese very fine, mix sugar, beat eggs and mix, add cream and vanilla. Beat very creamy. Roll crackers fine, take couple spoonfuls of cracker crumbs and melted butter until well mixed. Add sugar and cinnamon. Put into deep buttered tin and pat down until very firm, for lower crust. Pour cheese mixture onto crumb layer and sprinkle couple tablespoons of cracker mixture over top. Bake in slow oven for 1 hour.

Anna B. Russell, Cleveland, Oh.

CHEESE CAKE

1 pound cottage cheese
1 cup sugar
4 egg yolks
Pinch of salt
4 tablespoons flour

1 cup milk or cream
4 egg whites, stiffly beaten
Vanilla or orange flavoring
3 tablespoons butter
Bread crumbs

Mix the cheese, sugar, egg yolks, salt, flour and cream and beat well. Add the egg whites and flavoring. Melt the butter in saucepan and mix with the bread crumbs. Sprinkle side and bottom of pan with the bread crumbs. Pour the mixture in and bake in slow oven, 325°F, about one hour.

Veronica Radocha, Coaldale, Pa.

CHEESELESS CHEESE CAKE

4 eggs, separated
1⅓ cups Eagle Brand milk
1 teaspoon grated lemon rind
⅓ cup lemon juice

1 teaspoon vanilla
½ teaspoon nutmeg
2 tablespoons melted butter
⅔ cup (12) Zweiback crumbs

Beat egg yolks and combine with Eagle Brand Milk, add lemon rind, juice, vanilla and nutmeg; blend well. Fold in stiffly beaten egg whites. Combine melted butter and crumbs. Sprinkle buttered 8x8x2 inches square pan or 9x2 inch layer cake pan with half the crumbs. Pour in mixture and sprinkle with remaining crumbs. Bake in slow oven, 325°F, 30 minutes. Turn off heat, cool for 1 hour in oven with door closed.

Albina Sloboda, Coaldale, Pa.

COTTAGE CHEESE CAKE

DOUGH
2 cups flour
1 teaspoon baking soda
2 tablespoons sugar
1 egg yolk
¼ cup milk
¼ cup butter

FILLING
1½ cups sugar
2 pounds cottage cheese
6 eggs separated
1 cup sweet cream
3 tablespoons flour
1 teaspoon grated lemon rind
¼ cup butter

Dough: Cut butter, flour, and baking powder together, like for a pie, then mix milk, sugar, and egg yolk in a cup and add to the dry mixture. Spread on a 8x12 inch pan.

Filling: Put cheese through a fine sieve and add butter, egg yolks and rest of ingredients, mixing well. Then beat egg whites stiff and add to the cheese mixture. Pour onto the dough. Bake one hour at 300°F oven.

Anna Lissy, Whiting, Ind.

CREAM CHEESE CAKE

¾ package zweiback
2 tablespoons butter
2 tablespoons sugar

FILLING
½ cup sugar
2 tablespoons flour
½ teaspoon salt
1 pound cream cheese
1 teaspoon vanilla
4 eggs, separated
1 cup cream

Roll zweiback into crumbs, and blend with butter and sugar. Press onto bottom and sides of 9-inch spring pan.

Blend the ½ cup sugar with flour, salt and cream cheese. Add vanilla, and egg yolks one at a time, blending well after each yolk is added. Add the cream, mix again. Fold in stiffly beaten egg whites. Pour mixture on top of the crumbs. Bake in moderate oven 325°F for one hour, or until "set" in the center. Cool cheese cake before removing the rim of the pan. Do not invert. Serves 8 to 10.

Beatrice Pihulic, Hammond, Ind.

PINEAPPLE CHEESE CAKE

DOUGH
1 cup flour
¼ cup butter
1 tablespoon Spry
1 whole egg
2 tablespoons sour cream
2 tablespoons sugar
1 teaspoon baking powder
Pinch of salt

FILLING
2 cups cottage cheese, sieved
1 No. 2 can crushed pineapple,
  strained
4 egg yolks, beaten
½ cup sugar
Dash of cinnamon

Work flour, butter and Spry together, add the whole egg, sour cream and rest of the ingredients. When well mixed spread in ungreased oblong pan. Mix cottage cheese, crushed pineapple, egg yolks, sugar and cinnamon and blend well together. Spread on batter. Bake 15 minutes in 400°F oven. While the cake is baking, beat the 4 egg whites with pinch of cream of tartar, gradually add two tablespoons sugar. Remove cake from oven and spread meringue on top. Return to oven and bake till golden brown, about 15 minutes.

Anna Crowe, Bridgeport, Conn.

CHEESE CAKE

Crust: ¼ pound butter, 22 to 24 graham crackers, 1 cup chopped nuts, and dash of cinnamon; reserve ¼ cup of crumbs for topping. Roll graham crackers into crumbs, blend with butter and sugar. Press onto bottom and sides of spring pan.

Filling: Two large Philadelphia cream cheese-mashed with 1 tablespoon cream. Beat 4 eggs and 1 cup sugar, 1 teaspoon lemon juice and rind of 1 lemon. Combine all on medium speed in electric mixer. Bake 30 minutes at 350°F. Combine 1 pint sour cream, 1 teaspoon vanilla, scant ½ cup sugar and pour over top of cake. Sprinkle graham crackers over top and bake 20 minutes more.

Rose Michuda, Chicago, Ill.

CHERRY TORTE

1¼ cups sugar	1 teaspoon cinnamon
1 cup flour	¼ teaspoon salt
1 teaspoon baking soda	½ cup chopped nutmeats

Mix dry ingredients. Add cup, well drained, sour cherries. Add 1 egg well beaten and 1 tablespoon melted butter. Bake 45 minutes at 350°F oven.

SAUCE

1 cup cherry juice	½ cup sugar
1 tablespoon cornstarch	1 tablespoon melted butter
½ teaspoon salt	

Cook until thick and chill. Pour over tarts and serve with whipped cream.

Mary Demkovich, Whiting, Ind.

CHOCOLATE TORTE

Filling: Cream well 1 cup sweet butter, beat in 2 cups confectioners' sugar, creaming until light and fluffy. Add 1 teaspoon vanilla and 2 squares unsweetened chocolate, melted. Mix well, then spread between layers of cake. Bake or buy deep angel food or sponge cake. Using long, thin, sharp bladed knife, slice through cake, cutting it into layers. Frost with cream. Make icing by sifting together ½ cup confectioners' sugar, 6 tablespoons cocoa and ⅛ teaspoon salt. Add to 2 cups whipping cream. Chill 2 hours or more, then add 1 teaspoon vanilla and whip until stiff. Spread on cake. Garnish with nuts.

Sprinkle ½ cup chopped salted pistachio nuts around sides of cake. Chill several hours before serving. Cake may be filled the day before serving, but ice it the day it is to be served. 12 to 16 servings.

Clara Kucka, Whiting, Ind.

CUSTARD TORTE

1 package Zweiback, rolled fine	½ cup butter, melted
½ cup sugar	1 teaspoon cinnamon

Mix well together and line torte pan, leaving 1 cup of crumbs for top.

Filling

4 egg yolks	2 cups sweet milk
1 tablespoon cornstarch	Pinch of salt
½ cup sugar	1 teaspoon vanilla

Cook in double boiler until thick. Pour into torte pan. Beat 4 egg whites stiffly and add 3 tablespoons sugar gradually. Spread on top of custard; sprinkle with remaining crumbs over meringue and bake in moderate oven, 350°F, for ½ hour. Serve with whipped cream.

Anna K. Hruskovich, Whiting, Ind.

HELENA TORTE

7 eggs, separated	2 cups ground pecans
1 cup sugar	3 teaspoons brandy
Pinch of salt	1 teaspoon lemon juice

Beat egg yolks with sugar until creamy and lemon-colored. Beat egg whites with salt until stiff. Add ground nuts alternately with stiffly beaten egg whites to the beaten egg yolk and sugar mixture. Add brandy and lemon juice. Bake in 2 well buttered 9-inch cake pans 20 to 30 minutes in 350°F oven. When cool, fill and cover with raspberry whipped cream frosting.

RASPBERRY WHIPPED CREAM FROSTING
5 tablespoons confectioners' sugar
1 teaspoon vanilla
1 pint whipping cream
2 cups fresh raspberries (1 pint)

Stir sugar and vanilla into whipping cream. Then whip until stiff. Select ½ cup choice berries for decorating top of cake. To ⅓ of whipped cream add the rest of the berries and fill layers. Cover top and sides of cake with rest of the whipped cream. Then arrange the ½ cup choice berries decoratively on top.

Anna K. Hruskovich, Whiting, Ind.

INSTANT POSTUM TORTE

6 eggs, separated
1½ cups sugar
1½ cups cake flour
1½ teaspoons baking powder

3 tablespoons water
3 tablespoon instant postum
(buy in glass jar)

Beat egg yolks and ¾ cup sugar and water. Beat egg whites stiff with ¾ cup sugar. Add to yolk mixture, flour, baking powder and postum (sifted together) and mix, then fold in the egg whites. Bake in long pan or 3 round pans. Bake at 375°F oven for 25 minutes. Let cool in pan and invert.

Vincentian Sisters of Charity, Bedford, Oh.

COTTAGE CHEESE CAKE

5 eggs, well beaten
1 cup sugar
4 tablespoons melted butter
2 pounds cottage cheese, sieved
Grated rind of lemon

1 pint heavy sour cream
1 teaspoon vanilla
Pinch of salt
3 tablespoons flour

Combine all ingredients and pour into buttered baking pan. Bake at 450°F for 5 minutes, then reduce temperature to 350°F and bake for 1 hour. Turn off heat, open oven door and leave cake in oven to cool for one hour.

Julianna Simek, Johnstown, NY

DATE AND NUT TORTE

3 tablespoons butter
1 cup sugar
2 eggs
1½ cups flour
1 teaspoon baking powder

1 teaspoon baking soda
1 cup boiling water
1 teaspoon vanilla
1 cup ground nuts
1 cup chopped dates

Cream butter, add sugar and beaten eggs. Add flour sifted with baking powder. Add soda to boiling water and pour over dates, set aside to cool for 5 minutes. Add to creamed mixture and mix well. Add vanilla and nuts. Pour into oblong baking pan and bake at 375°F, from 30 to 45 minutes. When cool, cut in squares and top with whipped cream and serve.

Mary V. Haydu, Braddock, Pa.

GRAHAM TORTE

1 cup sugar
½ cup butter
2 eggs, separated
17 graham crackers, rolled fine
1 cup milk
1 cup flour
2 teaspoons baking powder
Pinch of salt
Pinch of soda

FILLING
1 cup sugar
⅓ cup flour
⅛ teaspoon salt
2 eggs, slightly beaten
1 teaspoon vanilla
½ teaspoon lemon extract
2 cups scalded milk

Blend sugar and butter, add well beaten yolks. Add rolled crackers and milk, alternately with flour sifted together with baking powder, salt and soda. Add stiffly beaten egg whites. Bake in two layers.

Filling: Add slightly beaten eggs gradually to scalded milk. Mix dry ingredients and add to egg and milk mixture. Cook 15 minutes in top of double boiler. Add vanilla and lemon extract. Put between layers and on top of cake. Cover with finely chopped nuts.

Agnes Bayus, Cleveland, Oh.

NUT TORTE

10 eggs, separated
1 box powdered sugar, sifted
5 tablespoons bread crumbs
Pinch of cloves
½ pound ground walnuts
1 teaspoon vanilla
⅛ teaspoon cinnamon
⅛ teaspoon nutmeg

FILLING & TOPPING
½ pound butter
1 egg
6 tablespoons cocoa
½ pound powdered sugar
1 teaspoon vanilla

In a large mixing bowl, beat yolks until creamy and lemon-colored. Gradually beat in powdered sugar. Mix until mixture is thick and creamy. Add bread crumbs, nut and seasonings. Mix well. Fold in stiffly beaten egg whites. Pour into greased and floured cake tins. Bake at 375°F for 30 minutes.

Filling: Cream butter. Add egg, vanilla, cocoa and powdered sugar. Mix until sugar and cocoa is well blended. Fill between layers and over the top.

Margaret Kuzma, Munhall, Pa.

POPPY SEED TORTE

1 cup ground poppy seed, soak
  overnight in 1 cup milk
½ cup butter
1½ cups sugar
2 cups pastry flour

2 teaspoons double acting
  baking powder
4 egg whites
1 teaspoon vanilla

Cream shortening and sugar until fluffy. Sift flour and baking powder. Add alternately with poppy seed mixture. Beat whites until stiff. Fold into batter. Add vanilla. Pour into a 10x6x3 loaf pan. Bake at 350°F for one hour. Top with butter frosting, adding a little lemon juice for flavor. Or use following frosting:

Frosting: Beat 1 egg, add ½ cup sugar, 1 cup milk and 2 tablespoons flour. Cook to custard consistency, when thick, add 1 teaspoon vanilla. Whip ¼ pound sweet butter, add 4 tablespoons powdered sugar then add custard very slowly. Spread on top and sides.

Agnes Bayus, Cleveland, Oh.

BLITZ TORTE

½ cup butter
½ cup sugar
4 eggs yolks, well beaten
1 cup sifted cake flour

1 teaspoon baking powder
⅛ teaspoon salt
3 tablespoons milk
1 teaspoon vanilla

MERINGUE

4 egg whites
¾ cup sugar
½ cup slivered unblanched almonds

½ teaspoon cinnamon
1 tablespoon sugar

Cream butter and ½ cup sugar thoroughly, beat in egg yolks. Sift dry ingredients together, and add alternately with combined milk and vanilla, blending until smooth. Spread batter evenly in 2 greased 9 inch loose bottom pans, lined with greased waxed paper. Cover with meringue made by beating egg whites until stiff and gradually folding in ¾ cup sugar. Spread meringue smoothly over unbaked batter, sprinkle almonds over meringue, then sprinkle cinnamon and remaining sugar. Bake 40 minutes in moderate oven, 350°F. Cool in pans. Spread cooled custard filling between layers.

CUSTARD FILLING

½ cup sugar
4 tablespoons cornstarch
2 cups scalded milk

1 egg slightly beaten
1 teaspoon almond extract

Combine sugar, cornstarch, and milk in top of double boiler. Cook until slightly thickened, about 10 minutes. Add small amount hot mixture to egg, return to double boiler and cook 3 minutes longer. Add flavoring. Cool before using. Sometimes fresh or canned fruit sauce is spooned over servings.

Dorothy Hanchar, Valparaiso, Ind.

DOBOS CAKE

6 eggs, separated
1¼ cups sugar
2 tablespoons lemon juice

¾ cup sifted pastry flour
¼ cup cornstarch
½ teaspoon salt

Beat yolks until creamy and light, gradually add sugar, beating well after each addition and adding with the last portion 1 tablespoon lemon juice. Mix and sift flour, cornstarch and salt, add half of it to the egg yolk mixture, stirring gently till blended and adding while blending another tablespoon of lemon juice. Fold in stiffly beaten egg whites alternately with remaining flour mixture, a little at a time, stirring gently. Butter and line an 8-inch spring mold with waxed paper. Turn in a few tablespoons of batter at a time, spreading evenly over bottom of mold, bake in a hot oven (450°F) 5 to 6 minutes or until very lightly browned. Remove cake to cake rack and repeat process until batter is entirely used. You get 8 layers. When cool put 1 layer aside, spread the following filling between and on top of remaining seven layers, pressing the layers firmly, but gently together, then chill.

CHOCOLATE FILLING FOR DOBOS CAKE

4 squares unsweetened chocolate
4 egg yolks
½ cup heavy cream

⅔ cup granulated sugar
1¼ cups sweet butter
2 or 3 drops coffee extract

Melt chocolate over hot water, then add little at a time slightly beaten yolks combined with cream and sugar, stirring briskly after each addition. Cook over hot water 5 to 6 minutes, stirring constantly until thick and smooth. Cream butter with coffee extract until light, then add to chocolate mixture a tablespoon at a time, beating and stirring at the same time after each addition until blended. Remove from hot water and cool until of spreading consistency.

Icing for Dobos Cake: Melt ¾ cup of powdered sugar over very low heat until of a light caramel color, stirring constantly; then pour quickly onto remaining cake layer, spreading evenly and working rapidly. Place this layer on top of the cake, pressing firmly. Spread remaining chocolate filling on sides of cake and if desired, dust very lightly with chopped nuts. Cool, and keep in a cool place for at least 24 hours before slicing. This cake will keep a week in a refrigerator.

Mary Vevurka, Chicago, Ill.

PECAN CREAM CAKE

3 cups pecans, ground to meat
1½ cups sugar
2 teaspoons baking powder

2 tablespoons flour
6 eggs, separated
1½ cups whipping cream

Measure pecans after grinding. Beat egg yolks, add sugar and beat well. Sift flour, baking powder and ground nuts. Fold nut and flour mixture into stiffly beaten egg whites. Then fold into egg yolks and sugar. Blend and pour into two cake pans lined with greased paper. Bake in hot oven 20 minutes. Let cool in pans, remove and serve with the whipped cream.

Mary Galos, Warrenville, Ill.

PRESIDENT'S TORTE

5 egg whites, stiffly beaten
¾ cup sugar
1 cup walnut meats or almonds,
    ground
1½ cups bread crumbs, fine

Juice and rind of one lemon
4 tablespoons chopped candied
    fruit
1 teaspoon baking powder
½ cup raspberry jelly

Mix ½ cup of the sugar with the well beaten egg whites. Fold in gently the remaining sugar, add ground nuts and bread crumbs. Add the candied fruit and mix altogether and place into well greased and floured cake tin. Bake in oven 350°F. After cake is cool, cover with jelly and top with chocolate frosting.

PINEAPPLE TORTE

PART 1:
½ cup butter
1¼ cups flour
2 tablespoons sugar

Combine the three ingredients and pack the mixture in a 9 x 12 cake pan. Bake in a moderate oven, 350°F, for 20 minutes.

PART 2:
1 medium can crushed pineapple
1 tablespoon cornstarch
1 cup sugar
4 egg whites

Combine the pineapple, sugar and cornstarch. Cook till thick. When cold, add the stiffly beaten egg whites. Pour over baked layer. Return to oven and bake 20 minutes longer. Serve with whipped cream.

Theresa Sabol, Whiting, Ind.

SEVEN EGG NUT TORTE

7 egg yolks	7 egg whites
1 cup sugar	1 teaspoon baking powder
1 cup walnuts	1 teaspoon vanilla
1 cup Zweiback	

Cream sugar and egg yolks until lemon colored. Grind zweiback and walnuts in food chopper; add baking powder and pour into sugar mixture. Mix until well blended (not too long). Add vanilla. Whip egg whites and fold in slowly. Pour in well greased pan, bake 30-35 minutes at 375°F. Cool on cake rack. This can be baked in 2 layers or in 10x14 inch pan. This makes an excellent dessert with whipped cream, or if baked in layers it can be filled with mocha or chocolate icing.

Irene Menzezoff, Long Island, NY

SLOVAK WALNUT TORTE

5 egg yolks	1 cup flour, sifted with 1 heaping
1 cup sugar	tablespoon baking powder
4 tablespoons warm water	10 drops almond extract
½ teaspoon vanilla	1 cup chopped walnuts

Beat yolks until lemon colored, then add sugar, beating at the same time. Add water and continue beating. Add flour, combined with baking powder and walnuts, slowly and beating continually. Then cut and fold in the beaten egg whites. Pour into pans and bake in moderate oven.

Sophie Gometro, Nesquohoning, Pa.

STRAWBERRY SCHAUM TORTE

6 egg whites	½ teaspoon cream of tartar
2 cups granulated sugar	1 teaspoon vanilla

Combine egg whites and sugar, beat until very stiff and sugar is dissolved (about 15 minutes) . Add cream of tartar and beat 10 minutes longer. Add vanilla and beat 5 minutes longer. Bake in well greased and floured spring form pan. Bake in very slow oven 275°F about one hour. After it is cooled, remove sides of pan. Gently take off top of torte. The lower part can be used as one torte or cut in pieces and serve individually. Place whipping cream and sliced strawberries on bottom torte. Then place top piece back on top.

Mary Canner, Whiting, Ind.

WALNUT TORTE

1 cup graham cracker crumbs	4 egg yolks
1 teaspoon baking powder	½ cup sugar
1 cup chopped nuts	½ pint whipped cream

To mix, take graham cracker crumbs, add baking powder, nuts and stir, then add the egg yolks, which have been beaten until lemon colored. Stir gradually into crumb and nut mixture. Beat sugar into egg yolks. Turn into 2 greased layer cake pans and bake about 15 minutes in a 375°F oven. Cool thoroughly, put layers together with whipped cream and on top cover with nuts.

Mary Janovcik, Cleveland, Oh.

WALNUT TORTE

10 eggs, separated	7 ounces finely ground walnuts
7 ounces powdered sugar	

Beat egg yolks with powdered sugar well. Beat egg whites until stiff but not dry. Fold egg yolks and powdered sugar into beaten egg whites. Then fold in walnuts gradually. Bake in 3 greased layer pans at 300°F for one hour. Remove cakes from oven. Cool completely before removing from pan.

FILLING
½ pound butter
½ pound powdered sugar
2 egg yolks and 1 small whole egg
1 teaspoon vanilla

Cream butter and powdered sugar together, add eggs one at a time, beat until smooth and fluffy. Add vanilla. Spread between layers and remaining frosting on top and sides of cake. Keep in cool place. (For chocolate filling use Hershey syrup).

Gustie Pohl Ballon, Whiting, Ind.

WALNUT TORTE

12 eggs, separated	Pinch of salt
2 cups sugar	2 cups ground walnuts
1 cup fine bread crumbs	1 teaspoon vanilla or other
1 teaspoon baking powder	flavoring

Beat yolks and sugar until smooth, add bread crumbs, baking powder, salt, ground walnuts and vanilla. Mix well. Whip egg whites until very stiff peaks form. Do not under whip. Pour yolk mixture gradually over whipped egg whites, gently folding until blended. Pour into greased and floured 3 layer pans, bake at 350°F for one hour.

FILLING

¼ pound sweet butter
¾ pound powdered sugar
1 egg

2 teaspoons of instant coffee
Add vanilla or rum extract
Cream well with Mixmaster

Anna Kolena, Chicago, Ill.

WALNUT TORTE

8 egg whites
8 egg yolks, put these in separate
   bowls
½ cup sugar

½ teaspoon vanilla
½ cup walnuts, ground
¼ cup bread crumbs

Beat whites until they stand in stiff peaks. To the egg yolks add sugar and vanilla. Beat until sugar is dissolved. Add walnuts gradually, mixing while adding. Add breadcrumbs gradually while mixing. Pour into two greased baking pans. Bake at 350 to 400°F for 45 minutes.

Eleanore Marko, Whiting, Ind.

WHIPPED CREAM TORTE

½ cup butter
1¼ cups sugar
4 eggs, separated
1 teaspoon vanilla
2 cups flour

2 teaspoons baking powder
Pinch of salt
½ cup milk
¼ cup water
Whipping cream

Soften butter and mix with sugar. Add beaten yolks and vanilla. Add sifted flour with salt and baking powder alternately with milk and water. Beat egg whites until stiff, add sugar gradually and beat until very stiff. Fold into cake mixture. Bake in two layers, at 350°F for 30 minutes. Whip whipping cream and frost cake.

Anna Koseal

WARNER'S DELIGHT

1 cup grated pineapple (canned)
Juice of 2 oranges
Juice of 1 lemon
1 cup sugar

1½ tablespoons gelatin
3 cups cold milk
½ pint cream

Combine first 4 ingredients and put in refrigerator to chill. Dissolve gelatin in half a cup milk, place over boiling water. Add remaining milk to gelatin mixture and put in refrigerator until it begins to congeal. Whip cream. Combine all ingredients and mix thoroughly. Put in refrigerator trays and freeze quickly, stirring 3 times at 20 minute intervals. Add 12 maraschino cherries, chopped fine to make it exceptionally good. Fruit content may be varied.

Agnes Bayus, Cleveland, Oh.

- STRUDELS AND STRUDEL FILLINGS -

STRUDEL DOUGH

¾ pound all purpose flour   1 teaspoon sugar
1 whole egg   1 teaspoon melted pure lard
1 cup lukewarm water   Pinch of salt

Sift flour in bowl, add egg, sugar, salt, lard and water. Knead well until the dough is very smooth (dough is very soft). Roll into ball and brush with butter and little flour and place it on floured towel in deep bowl and cover. Let it stand for 1 hour, meanwhile prepare your filling.

APPLE FILLING

1 cup walnuts (ground)
1 cup bread crumbs, toasted to light brown in 3 tablespoons
    melted butter
3½ pounds apples (cooking apples), peeled, cored and sliced thin
¼ pound raisins (if desired)
1 teaspoon cinnamon
¾ pound sugar
Approx. ¾ pound of butter is needed for the toasting, sprinkling and
    buttering of dough

Stretching dough: Spread table cloth on the table, sprinkle with flour. Remove dough, place down gently in the center of tablecloth. Butter the top with warm melted butter (butter tips of fingers to prevent sticking). Place hands under dough and work slowly and gently stretching the dough from the center until it completely covers the table. When dough is stretched large enough it will be as thin as tissue paper. Cut away the heavy edges. Sprinkle the dough with melted butter, then sprinkle buttered bread crumbs, apples, raisins, cinnamon and sugar. Sprinkle filling with melted butter. Leave a two inch border free. Lap side edges over about two inches and fold end of dough nearest you over the filling. Then with both hands raise the cloth and the strudel will roll itself. Cut roll to the size of baking pan, brush with melted butter and bake until brown. Bake 375°F for one hour in pan well brushed with melted butter.

Helen Kocan, Whiting, Ind.

STRUDEL

3 cups flour   ½ teaspoon salt
3 tablespoons crisco   1¼ cups lukewarm water
3 whole eggs

Mix ingredients together and knead, then put on well floured cloth and cover with a warm bowl, letting it stand about half-hour or longer. Stretch on a floured cloth and sprinkle with melted butter.

NUT FILLING:

1 pound nuts, ground	**2 cups sugar**
10 eggs, separated	**1 teaspoon cream of tartar**

Beat yolks until lemon colored. Add one cup of sugar and beat until well blended. Add cream of tartar to egg whites and beat until stiff, then gradually beat in one cup sugar. Fold the yolk mixture into the whites of eggs, then fold in the nuts.

Note: Dry cottage cheese may be used in place of the ground nuts for a delicious variation of the above recipe.

Louise Zaremba, Joliet, Ill.

BRATISLAVA APPLE STRUDEL

Strudel dough: 1½ cups flour, ¼ teaspoon salt, 1 egg, 1 heaping tablespoon lard. Put in bowl, add enough lukewarm water (⅓ to ½ cup) to make soft dough. Beat with hand until dough blisters. Cover with warm bowl and set in warm place for one-half hour, or until apples are peeled. Peel and slice about 4 pounds apples as for pie. Melt about ¼ cup butter and lightly brown about 1 cup bread crumbs. Have a little grated lemon rind and a few raisins ready.

Spread a tablecloth on the table and sprinkle lightly with flour. Take the dough and roll lightly with rolling pin, on tablecloth, until dough is about ½ inch thick. Now starting in the center, put your hands under the dough, pull and stretch gently, with back of hand, being careful not to tear the dough with fingers. Keep working round and round the table, until dough is of paper thinness. The thinner the dough the better the strudel.

Strudel filling: First take the buttered and browned crumbs and spread on dough. Then use apples, just a thin layer. Sprinkle sugar to taste, dot with butter, add raisins and lemon rind. Sprinkle with cinnamon. Take one end of the tablecloth, hold it up, and dough will start rolling till the end. With tablecloth form into horseshoe, put hand underneath and flip into greased pan, 8x12. Bake in moderate oven, 350°F, forty-five to sixty minutes. Serve in slices sprinkled with powdered sugar.

Mary Walovich, Chicago, Ill.

QUICK APPLE STRUDEL

Prepare crust for strudel by first dissolving two tablespoons butter in ¼ cup boiling water. Cool. Blend in one slightly beaten egg yolk and ⅞ cup flour (one cup minus two tablespoons), sifted with ¼ teaspoon salt. Beat until very smooth. Now let pastry stand while preparing the filling.

Filling: Chop pared, cored apples (about two pounds) to make five cups. Mix with ½ cup white raisins, one cup fine dry bread crumbs, one cup sugar, ½ teaspoon salt, one tablespoon cinnamon and ½ cup butter melted with

½ cup lard. Blend thoroughly. Set aside; now knead pastry gently for one minute. Roll pastry on well floured cloth with floured rolling pin that has been covered, to rectangle 19 by 16 inches. Spoon filling on pastry, spread to with in one inch of sides. Roll up gently from wide end as for jelly roll by lifting cloth and allowing pastry to roll itself. Press ends together securely. Place on baking sheet with side rims. Brush with diluted egg white; bake in pre-heated oven 350°F for one hour and fifteen minutes. Drippings which flow from strudel in baking will be absorbed by strudel on cooling. Serve warm, plain or with whipped cream. Eight servings.

Clara Kucka, Whiting, Ind.

CABBAGE STRUDEL *(Kapustna Štrudia)*

1½ pounds all purpose flour　　　**½ teaspoon salt**
1 egg yolk　　　　　　　　　　　**Lukewarm water**
1 tablespoon butter

Mix ingredients gradually, add the sifted flour with salt, egg yolk and butter. Knead dough, until it is smooth and elastic. Then allow to stand for 20 minutes in a warm place.

CABBAGE FILLING
3 pound head of cabbage　　　　**2 cups fine bread crumbs or**
1 cup nut meats, crushed　　　　　**crushed graham crackers**
¾ cup shortening　　　　　　　　**1 teaspoon cinnamon**
1 cup raisins, washed and dried

Select a solid white head of cabbage, chop fine or grate coarsely, into one-half cup shortening. Allow to simmer until light brown, stirring frequently to prevent burning. Allow to cool. Prepare strudel dough and stretch. Cut off the thick portions all around the stretched dough. Then spread on the cabbage filling that has been cooled, sprinkle over the crushed walnuts, raisins and crumbs. Fold over two sides and roll strudel with aid of table cloth. Place in well greased pan, brush top with shortening and bake in quick oven to golden brown. Serve hot.

Mary Ruzicka, Muskegon, Mich.

CHERRY AND CHEESE FILLING FOR STRUDEL

2 pounds cottage cheese
2 quarts cherries, canned or fresh
2 yolks
½ teaspoon salt
2 cups buttered crumbs
1 cup yellow raisins

Sugar to taste, depending on kind of cherries used Mix yolks into cottage cheese, add salt when mixed. Spread on strudel dough, over which spread the cherries, sprinkle with sugar and buttered bread crumbs. Roll and bake until golden brown.

Mary Ruzicka, Muskegon, Mich.

COTTAGE CHEESE STRUDEL FILLING

2 pounds cottage cheese,
  pressed through sieve
6 egg yolks
1 teaspoon vanilla

½ teaspoon salt
Rind of one lemon, grated
3 apples pared and grated
Sugar to taste

Mix into the sieved cottage cheese the egg yolks, vanilla, salt and lemon rind. Then grate into the mixture the apples and add sugar. The amount of sugar will depend on the sweetness of the apples, or sweetness of the filling. Mix well and set aside until strudel dough is ready and stretched. When strudel dough has been stretched to paper thinness, then melt one half pound sweet butter, and sprinkle well over the dough. On one half of dough spread cottage cheese filling, sprinkle some well washed and drained raisins over cheese filling (desired amount). Then scatter six stiffly beaten egg whites over the filling. Roll and place on a buttered pan for baking. Brush well with melted butter and bake in moderate oven until nicely browned.

Veronica Radoch, Coaldale, Pa.

STRAWBERRY DESSERT

CRUST
36 Graham Crackers
1 tablespoon sugar
½ pound melted butter

Roll out graham crackers, add sugar and melted butter and mix well. Line an oblong pan with half of this mixture, then pour in filling. Put other half of mixture on top. Put in refrigerator and let set overnight.

FILLING
1 cup scalded milk
1 pound cut marshmallows

1 package frozen strawberries
1 pint cream, whipped

Scald milk, add marshmallows and let cool. Then add frozen strawberries, less ½ cup juice. Add whipped cream and mix everything together.

Josephine Ferencik, Joliet, Ill.

SNOW BALLS

1 pound vanilla wafers
1 pint whipped cream
No. 2 can crushed pineapple

18 marshmallows
Shredded coconut

Drain juice from pineapple. Put pineapple in bowl. Cut marshmallows and combine with pineapple and let stand for 2 hours. Then build-up vanilla wafers and put filling between, (4 wafers make a nice size). Cover with whipped cream and coconut. Let stand for 5 or 6 hours in refrigerator. Garnish with maraschino cherry.

Eleanor Kochis, Whiting, Ind.

- SAUCES FOR PUDDING DESSERTS -

SAUCE FOR PUDDING

¼ cup butter
1 cup brown sugar
1 tablespoon cornstarch

1 cup cold water
2 teaspoons vanilla

Melt butter. Add sugar, then cornstarch dissolved in the water. Bring slowly to boiling point, stirring to blend. Remove from heat, add vanilla, (brandy or rum may be substituted). Serve warm sauce on pudding.

Marcella Halloran, Streator, Ill.

CHOCOLATE SAUCE

1½ cups confectioners' sugar
½ cup cocoa
¼ teaspoon salt

½ cup water
½ cup milk
2 teaspoons vanilla

Sift together sugar, cocoa and salt. Gradually add water and milk mixing until smooth. Cook over boiling water for 25 minutes, stirring frequently until thickened. Cool, add vanilla. Sauce will keep for several months in covered container in refrigerator. Will not harden on ice cream. Makes 1¼ cups.

Mary Kinsock, Whiting, Ind.

ORANGE SAUCE *(Excellent for Gingerbread)*

½ cup orange juice
½ cup sugar
2 tablespoons light corn syrup

1 tablespoon grated orange rind
2 oranges, sectioned

Combine juice, sugar, corn syrup and orange rind in sauce pan. Stir over low heat until it comes to a boil. Boil 5 minutes, slowly, add orange sections and cook 1 minute longer. Serve over hot gingerbread or other plain cakes or cup cakes.

HOT BUTTERSCOTCH SAUCE

1½ cups brown sugar
1 tablespoon butter
⅔ cup light corn syrup

Few grains salt
¾ cup evaporated milk

Cook together butter, sugar, syrup and salt until a teaspoonful will form a soft ball in cold water or 236°F. Remove from fire and briskly stir in evaporated milk. Keep hot in covered double boiler.

Rita Barenia, Griffith, Ind.

MARSHMALLOW MINT SAUCE

½ cup sugar
¼ cup water
8 marshmallows

1 egg-white, beaten stiff
1 drop oil of peppermint
Green coloring

Make a thin syrup of the sugar and water (220°F to 230°F). Cut the marshmallows in quarters and add to the syrup. Pour mixture over the beaten egg white gradually. Beating vigorously. Add the flavoring and tint a delicate green. This sauce is excellent with chocolate ice cream.

Rita Barenie, Griffith, Ind.

HONEY SAUCE

1 egg
½ cup honey
1 cup hot water

1½ tablespoons butter
½ of lemon juice and grated rind

Beat the egg, and add the other ingredients in the order given. Cook over hot water for about 15 minutes, stirring constantly.

Geraldine Jadrnak, Gary, Ind.

FLUFFY TOPPING FOR FANCY DESSERTS

A simple but fluffy topping can be made of whipped evaporated milk. Gelatin in the recipe helps to make the whipped evaporated milk stand up longer.

1 cup evaporated milk
½ teaspoon gelatin
2 teaspoons cold water

½ teaspoon vanilla or other
flavoring
2 tablespoons sugar

Heat milk to scalding. Dissolve gelatin in cold water. Add to milk and chill thoroughly, either by pouring into the freezing tray of the refrigerator, for quick use, or letting it stand until cold. Place in a cold bowl and quickly whip until stiff. Add sugar and vanilla. This may be used instead of whipped cream on fancy desserts.

Eggs, Cheese & Casseroles

- EGGS -

EGG CASSEROLE

¼ pound potato chips
3 tablespoons melted butter
2 tablespoons finely chopped
  green pepper
2 tablespoons flour

10 ounce can mushroom soup
10 hard cooked eggs
1 cup milk
1 teaspoon salt
Few grains garlic salt

Crumble potato chips until like corn flakes. Cook green pepper in butter for three minutes and add garlic salt. Add flour, mixing well. Add milk and salt, cook until thickened. Stir in gradually the mushroom soup, when thoroughly blended set aside and prepare casserole. Sprinkle ⅓ of the chips in the bottom of a large greased casserole. Cut eggs in length wise halves and place cut side on potato chips. Cover with another ⅓ of the chips. Pour cooked mixture over this and sprinkle with remaining potato chips. Bake for 20 minutes in moderately hot oven, 375°F.

Theresa Klausner, Chicago, Ill.

EGG FOO YONG

2 teaspoons soy sauce
1 teaspoon corn starch
1 teaspoon sugar
1 teaspoon salt
½ cup cold water
½ cup thinly sliced onion
1 cup drained, washed bean sprouts

6 eggs, well beaten
2 tablespoons salad oil, or
  margarine
Use meat if you wish: 1 cup
  cooked sliced thinly pork

Mix everything together. Place on large heavy frying pan, the salad oil or margarine, pour half cup of the mixture on hot frying pan and cook quickly until set and browned on each side; stack on hot plate until all cooked. Serve while hot with cooked rice. For fast days, use without meat.

Mary Kollar, Scranton, Pa.

SCRAMBLED EGGS AND MUSHROOMS

5 eggs, slightly beaten
¼ cup milk or cream
½ cup mushrooms, either
  canned or fresh
½ teaspoon salt

Pepper to taste
2 tablespoons butter
½ teaspoon finely chopped chives
  or grated onion

Add seasonings to beaten eggs, stir in the milk. Heat pan, put in butter and when melted, sauté mushrooms and chives or onions, when slightly browned add egg mixture. Cook until creamy consistency, constantly stirring and scraping from bottom and sides of pan. Sliced onions may be sautéed according to taste in larger quantity.

Mary Dano, Chicago, Ill.

EGG IN TOMATO SAUCE

1 tablespoon shortening	1 teaspoon sugar
1 tablespoon flour	½ teaspoon salt
1 cup water	2 eggs
1 cup tomato juice	

Place shortening in small pan, add flour, when brown take off fire and let cool one minute, stir slowly adding water and tomato juice, sugar and salt, put back on fire and cook slowly until thickened. Then break two raw eggs and cook three minutes more. Take out eggs, and put them on a plate and pour sauce over them.

Veronica Gluvna, Lorain, Oh.

EGG-CHEESE BAKE

⅓ cup butter	2 cups milk
⅓ cup flour	2 cups grated American cheese
¾ teaspoon salt	6 eggs
Pepper to taste	Dash of nutmeg

Make white sauce of butter, flour, milk and seasoning. Blend in one cup cheese. Pour into greased casserole. Slip eggs onto sauce. Sprinkle with remaining cheese. Cover and bake twenty minutes at 325°F. Uncover and bake another five minutes. Serves six. (Serve on toast).

Mary Vevurka, Chicago, Ill.

OMELET *(Made in Omelet Pan)*

4 large eggs, separated	½ teaspoon salt
4 tablespoons milk, room temp.	Pepper to taste
About ¼ teaspoon cream of tartar	

Preheat oven at 350°F. Melt 1½ teaspoons shortening in each side of omelet pan and brush the sides with part of it. Separate eggs, and beat egg whites until foamy, sprinkle cream of tartar over them and continue beating until egg whites are very stiff. It is important that the whites are very stiffly beaten. Then beat the egg yolks with the same beater, for about ½ minute, add seasonings and milk and blend well. Then gradually add this yolk mixture to the whites, blend carefully but do not overwork. Pour one half mixture in each side of heated omelet pan and place over two burners, with low flame and cook for about ten minutes, leaving pan opened. When lightly brown underneath and on the sides then place in preheated oven, 350°F, and bake for about seven minutes, or until eggs do not cling to finger when tested. When done fold over, and turn out onto platter carefully. Serve at once, as all fluffy omelets will drop if they stand more than a few minutes. Serves two large portions, or three smaller. Above recipe may be made in a seven inch skillet (round). Proceed to make same as above, do not fold when serving.

Irene Pekarcik, Los Angeles, Ca.

OMELET

4 eggs, separated	**½ cup milk**
1 teaspoon flour	**Salt and pepper to taste**

Beat egg yolks until thick. Stir in flour and milk. Fold in stiffly beaten egg whites and add seasonings. Pour into a well greased round skillet. Cook over low flame until well puffed and slightly brown on bottom. Omelet should be firm when touched at this stage. Complete cooking process in a moderate oven 350°F. Serve at once.

Emily Jurinak, Chicago, Ill.

EGG AND SPINACH CASSEROLE

1 package of frozen spinach or 1½ pounds fresh spinach
2 eggs or 3 eggs if desired to serve three people
½ teaspoon salt
½ of small can evaporated milk
4 tablespoons freshly grated cheese (American cheese if possible)
1½ tablespoons melted butter
1 cup well rounded freshly pulled bread crumbs

Pull crumbs from inside of bread and measure, packing lightly. Place in bowl the crumbs, the melted butter and mix thoroughly with two forks. If fresh spinach is used make sure it is thoroughly washed several times in lukewarm water. Drain well and cook in a small amount of water, in covered saucepan, until tender. When done drain very thoroughly, and chop fine. Season with half teaspoon salt and pepper to taste. Place spinach in a well buttered casserole, or shallow baking dish, not too large because this is a small recipe. Make two depressions in spinach with a spoon, and drop the raw eggs into the depressions. Sprinkle eggs slightly with salt and pepper. Heat milk and cheese until cheese is melted, season and pour this cheese sauce slowly over the eggs and spinach. Cover with the buttered bread crumbs and bake in a 375°F oven for about 20-25 minutes. If not brown at this stage then place under slow broiler to brown, and serve. Serves two or three portions.

Justine Zubo, Chicago, Ill.

CIHAK *(Easter Cheese)* EGG ROLL

12 eggs	**Variation of spices**
1 quart milk	
Pinch of salt	

Directions continued on page 271.

Pour milk into saucepan and bring to a boil. Beat eggs slightly and add gradually to the milk. Cook over low heat for about seven minutes. Add pepper and salt. Stir constantly so mixture will not scorch. Pour mixture into a linen towel, squeeze and tie tightly. Hang and let drain for two hours. Cover with wet napkin and place in refrigerator.

Helen Kocan, Whiting, Ind.

- CHEESE -

CHEESE CUTLETS

⅔ cup grated cheese
2 cups mashed potatoes
4 tablespoons minced pimiento

1 cup cooked lima or navy
  beans, ground
1 teaspoon salt

Combine ingredients and shape the mixture into cutlets about 2 inch thick. Sauté them in a small amount of hot fat and serve with horseradish sauce.

Anna Yanega, Lansford, Pa.

CORN MEAL CHEESE SOUFFLE

1½ cups milk
⅓ cup yellow corn meal
3 tablespoons butter
1 teaspoon salt
5 eggs

1 cup medium-sharp cheese,
  grated
⅛ teaspoon nutmeg or celery salt
Dash of pepper

Cook in double boiler the milk, cornmeal, butter and seasonings. When thick, set aside. Be sure this mixture is smooth, in order to accomplish this, gradually add the milk to the cornmeal, stirring to keep free of lumps. Beat the egg yolks and gradually beat them into the hot cornmeal mixture. Then add the grated cheese and mix well. Last of all fold in the stiffly beaten egg whites, and pour the mixture into a buttered casserole. Place casserole in a pan of hot water, and bake for 45 to 50 minutes in a moderate oven about 325°F. Serve immediately while still high and fluffy.

Daughters of St. Francis, Lacon, Ill.

ELBOW MACARONI AND COTTAGE CHEESE CASSEROLE

1 box elbow macaroni, cooked
  and drained
¼ pound melted butter
1 package cream cheese

1 pound cottage cheese
1 egg, beaten
½ pint sour cream

Mix all the above together and place in a buttered casserole, or greased pan and bake in oven until brown.

Joliet, Ill.

NOODLES WITH DRY CHEESE (Rezanky s tvarohom)

Cook noodles in salted water until well done. Drain well. Brown some butter until all moisture is out of it, pour over hot noodles, salt to taste. Crumble some dry cottage cheese over it. Mix well and serve quite hot. A little fresh dill sprinkled over all is tastier. For ½ pound package of noodles use ¼ pound butter.

Mary Schinsky, Los Angeles, Ca.

- MISCELLANEOUS CASSEROLES -

ASPARAGUS CASSEROLE

15 to 20 asparagus tips, frozen asparagus may be used	2 cups whole milk
	½ teaspoon salt
5 hard cooked eggs	⅛ teaspoon pepper
4 tablespoons margarine	¼ cup grated cheese
4 tablespoons flour	1 cup buttered bread crumbs

Cut asparagus into one inch lengths if fresh asparagus is used. Cook in boiling water, which has been salted. Cook until barely tender, then drain. Make a cream sauce of margarine, flour, milk and seasonings. Arrange alternate layers of asparagus, sliced cooked eggs, cream sauce and cheese in greased 1½ quart casserole. Sprinkle with buttered crumbs. Bake in a moderate oven, 350°F for 30 minutes. Serves six.

Helen Kubasak, Burbank, Ca.

SCALLOPED CORN

1 can corn	1 teaspoon salt
1 green pepper	1 cup milk
½ cup onion	¼ cup soft bread crumbs
2 tablespoons butter	

Put corn, finely chopped green pepper and onion in alternate layers in baking dish. Add salt, butter and milk. Sprinkle with bread crumbs and bake in slow oven about 325°F for about 45 minutes or until set and browned.

Julia Kristin, Chicago, Ill.

BEEF-RICE CASSEROLE

1 pound ground beef	1 tablespoon butter
1 medium onion, minced	½ cup cooked rice
Dash of pepper	Pinch of salt

Brown meat in butter; add water and let simmer for one hour. Add rice, put in casserole and bake in oven.

Barbara Bires, Pittsburgh, Pa.

HAM AND NOODLES *(Šunka a haluški)*

2 pounds cooked ham, ground
1 pound torn noodles, cooked and strained

Mix ham and noodles together, season to taste. Bake in oven in casserole about 45 minutes. Serve piping hot.

Mary Timko, Munhall, Pa.

HAM AND RICE CASSEROLE

Place one slice of pre-cooked ham (about one inch thick) in a baking dish, spread with orange marmalade, top with ¼ cup cooked rice. Dot with butter and more marmalade. Bake at 350°F for 45 minutes, basting frequently. Add cooked sweet potatoes and brown.

Anna Crowe, Bridgeport, Conn.

HAMBURGER CASSEROLE WITH CORN

8 or 10 potatoes
1 pound round steak, ground
1 cup hot milk
1 teaspoon salt
1 chicken bouillon cube

1 No. 2 can whole kernel corn
1 tablespoon butter
1 tablespoon fat
⅛ teaspoon pepper

Boil potatoes in salted water, drain. Reserve water for gravy. Mash potatoes, using butter and milk. Put fat into frying pan and brown meat, seasoning with salt and pepper. Empty can of corn into meat. Cover with mashed potatoes. Broil until potatoes are slightly browned. Make gravy using potato water and bouillon cube.

Mary Skurka, Whiting, Ind.

HAMBURGER VEGETABLE CASSEROLE

6 or 8 large potatoes
1 pound hamburger
2 large onions, sliced

6 carrots, shredded
Milk or water to moisten
Salt and pepper to taste

Peel and slice raw potatoes into buttered baking dish, alternating with onions, carrots and hamburger. Add milk or water to moisten well and season the layers. Dot with butter and sprinkle with bread crumbs, if desired. Bake 1¼ hours in moderate oven. (Onions on top of hamburger will give a good flavor, finish with potatoes).

Agnes Lukso, Chicago, Ill.

SCALLOPED LIMA BEANS

3 cups cooked lima beans, about
   1⅓ cups dry lima beans
½ cup cheese, cut fine or
   coarsely grated
3 tablespoons flour

¼ teaspoon paprika
1 teaspoon salt
2 tablespoons chopped onion
2 cups tomatoes

Mix ingredients and pour into a buttered baking dish. Bake 25 minutes in moderate oven, 375°F.

Veronica Sofranko, Lovilia, Iowa

BAKED MACARONI

½ pound macaroni, cooked well and drained
¼ cup butter, melted
Add ¼ cup sifted flour
Add 1¼ cups warm milk, slowly to prevent lumping
Add ¼ pound grated cheese (American), reserve ¼ cup for top
1 teaspoon salt

Mix butter, flour and milk making a white sauce. Add cheese, salt and add to macaroni. Put in buttered baking dish and top with cheese. Bake 425°F for 30 minutes.

Helen Cross, Whiting, Ind.

MACARONI WITH TOMATOES

1 teaspoon chopped onion
1 tablespoon butter
1 tablespoon flour
1½ cups strained tomatoes

½ teaspoon salt
1 pint boiled macaroni
4 slices American cheese

Fry onion in butter until slightly colored, add flour; when well mixed add gradually the tomatoes, salt and cheese, making sauce. Put macaroni into buttered baking dish, pour over the sauce and bake with rest of meal, or set indicator at 350°F and bake for 20 minutes.

Barbara Bires, Pittsburgh, Pa.

MEATLESS CASSEROLE

2 cups diced potatoes
1½ cups sliced carrots
½ cup chopped onions

Cook altogether until done, then drain, and set aside the juice.

White Sauce made with 2 tablespoons butter and 2½ tablespoons flour, mix well until smooth, then gradually add one cup of milk. Add all or some of the above drained off juice to thin the white sauce. Pour the white sauce into the vegetables. Add one can flaked tuna and mix together, place into buttered casserole.

Dumplings: 1½ cups bisquick, ¾ cup milk. Mix the bisquick and milk, season a little to taste and drop dumplings on top of casserole. Bake 40 minutes. Serves 4.

Mary Skurka, Whiting, Ind.

MUSHROOM CASSEROLE

1 pound mushrooms	**2 cups milk**
4 tablespoons butter	**1 teaspoon salt**
2 tablespoons flour	**4 tablespoons cheese**
2 tablespoons onion	**⅓ cup bread crumbs**

Wash mushrooms clean, slice large ones. Cream butter and flour, add grated onion, milk and salt; cook over low flame until thick, about 5 minutes. Add drained fresh mushrooms that have been cooked in salted water; turn into buttered casserole. Sprinkle with well mixed grated cheese and crumbs. Bake in a slow oven, 300°F for 35 minutes.

Justine Kasovsky, Chicago, Ill.

MUSHROOM NOODLES

½ package noodles	**1 can water**
1 can mushroom soup	**Grated cheese**

Cook noodles in salted boiling water 15 minutes. Drain. Put in buttered casserole and add soup that had been stirred smooth, and mixed with water. Mix together and sprinkle cheese on top. Bake about one hour or one hour and 15 minutes in moderate slow oven, 325°F.

Margaret De Silva, Chicago, Ill.

POTATO AND EGG CASSEROLE

3 medium potatoes, cooked in jackets	**Butter**
4 hard boiled eggs, sliced	**Crackers or bread crumbs**
Salt to taste	**½ pint sour cream**

Peel potatoes and eggs. Butter casserole and sprinkle with bread or cracker crumbs. Slice potatoes in rings about ½ inch thick. Line bottom of casserole with potatoes. Add sliced eggs, dot with bits of butter, sprinkle with salt, then sprinkle with bread crumbs. Keep repeating this until casserole is filled. On top pour ½ pint sour cream and spread. Bake in moderate oven for 45 minutes.

Mary Timko, Munhall, Pa.

SCALLOPED CREAMED POTATOES

In a well greased 1½ quart casserole, place layers of well drained thinly sliced raw potatoes. (Boiled potatoes may be used). Sprinkle each layer with salt (using about 1½ teaspoons for entire amount) and pepper, finely cut pimiento strips and green onion tops. Pour small amount of cream sauce over them, and sprinkle with grated American cheese, using about ½ cupful altogether. Repeat until casserole is filled. Bake in a 400°F oven about 30 minutes, then reduce heat to 300°F and continue to bake about one more hour or until tender when tested, depending on the thickness of slices and quality of potatoes. It is better to allow about two hours, as these potatoes may stand for a while after they are done. Keep casserole covered for first part of cooking, removing last half hour or if they boil over. If top is not brown when potatoes are done, place under broiler for a few minutes and watch carefully to prevent burning. Serves eight.

Cream Sauce: Melt ¼ cup butter or other shortening, add ½ cup all-purpose flour and mix until smooth. Add 2 cups warm milk slowly, stirring constantly and cook until thick and smooth-about 5 minutes after it comes to a boil. Add about 1½ teaspoons salt toward end of cooking time. Thin with more milk if sauce appears to be too thick.

Frances L. Mizenko, Cleveland, Oh.

CASSEROLE BAKED POTATOES

8 medium sized raw potatoes
3 onions
Approximately 4 tablespoons butter or shortening
Salt and pepper to taste
Approximately 1½ tablespoons vinegar
Water or stock to cover (bouillon cubes may be used)

Peel and slice potatoes, and peel and slice onions; then arrange the sliced potatoes and onions in layers in a well buttered casserole, dotting each layer with butter. Sprinkle salt and pepper over each layer and pour enough water or stock mixed with the vinegar to cover well.

Cover casserole and bake for about 1½ hours in a moderate oven, 350°F. These potatoes are good with roast beef or lamb and may be prepared in the oven at the same time as the roast.

Ilona Valcicak, Benton Harbor, Mi.

SPINACH NOODLES

2 cups flour or more as needed
½ teaspoon salt
3 egg yolks
1 cup cooked, sieved spinach (fresh or frozen spinach is best)
Water if needed

Knead together well. Divide dough into four parts and knead each part. Roll thin and place to dry slightly. Place layers on top of each other with a thin layer of flour between them. Cut as you would noodles, wide, not fine. Serve with Tomato Friday Sauce and grated Parmesan and Roman cheeses.

Vincentian Sisters of Charity, Bedford, Oh.

SPANISH NOODLES

1 pound round steak, ground   **1 package of broad noodles**
1 cup celery, diced   **1 cup of canned tomatoes**
1 cup green peppers, diced   **1 onion**

Fry meat and onion in butter, add peppers and celery and let cook for while, then add tomatoes. Mix boiled noodles, and heat. Put in baking dish, dot with butter. Add little more tomato juice. Salt and pepper to taste. Bake about ½ hour.

Mary E. Grega, Cleveland, Oh.

SPAGHETTI CUSTARD

Heat 2½ cups milk, then add 1½ tablespoons butter and 1 cup chopped cheese, 2 teaspoons salt, ¼ teaspoon pepper. Mix well and pour this mixture over 3 slightly beaten eggs. Put 3 cups cooked spaghetti into buttered baking dish and pour the mixture over it and mix well. Stand the dish in pan of hot water and bake in moderate oven until the knife comes out clean after being tested, about 40 minutes.

Mrs. Joseph Hritz, Phoenixville, Pa.

SWEET POTATO CASSEROLE

3 large sweet potatoes   **4 tablespoons butter**
1 teaspoon salt   **8 marshmallows**
1 teaspoon cinnamon   **⅓ cup chopped nuts**
½ cup crushed pineapple, well
** drained**

Boil sweet potatoes until tender, peel and mash. Brown the butter and add to potatoes. Add remaining ingredients, mixing after each. Put in greased baking dish and bake 35 minutes in moderate oven, 350°F. Place 4 marshmallows on top, return to oven and brown lightly.

Theresa Sabol, Whiting, Ind.

SAUERKRAUT DISH *(Kolosvary Kapusta)*

1 pound beef and 1 pound pork stewed in 1 tablespoon butter and some paprika and 1 large onion.

Stew ¼ cup of rice in 1 tablespoon butter; diced medium sized onion and enough water to cook rice.

Cook 2 cans sauerkraut in 1 tablespoon butter; 1 large sliced onion and enough water to keep kraut thick. After kraut is cooked, sprinkle with a little flour and mix.

Into deep casserole, beginning with kraut mixture, put layers of each of the above three mixtures; one layer of kraut; then layer of meat and layer of rice. Do this until casserole is filled. Pour one pint of sour cream on top and spread. Bake in moderate oven for 40 minutes. Serve hot.

Mary Timko, Munhall, Pa.

RICE MILANESE

3 tablespoons olive oil
1 cup rice
Grated American cheese

Heat olive oil in a skillet. Add rice and stir constantly over medium flame until rice is just golden yellow, not brown. Remove immediately from heat. Add water or stock; season and pour into casserole. Cover and place in oven for one hour.

Before serving, grate American cheese over top and brown under broiler until cheese melts into rice. (Velveeta cheese is very good for this).

Serve with creamed eggs, chicken or fresh boiled pork slices in caper sauce. (A good substitute for potatoes).

Vincentian Sisters of Charity, Bedford, Oh.

CASSEROLE OF STEAK

1 pound cubed round steak	**2 small onions**
3 teaspoons shortening	**½ cup chopped celery**
2 cups boiling water	**4 cups tomatoes**
5 carrots	**1 chopped green pepper**
Salt and pepper to taste	**6 tablespoons uncooked rice**

Brown steak in shortening, place in buttered casserole. Add all other ingredients and mix. Cover and bake in moderate oven for 1¾ hours or until meat is tender. This may be made on top of stove if all other ingredients are combined after the steak has been browned. Simmer in a covered pan for almost an hour. Test and if steak is done remove and serve.

Margaret De Silva, Chicago, Ill.

SAVORY VEAL AND SPAGHETTI

2 pounds cubed veal steak
1 minced Bermuda onion
¼ pound butter
4 or 5 minced garlic cloves
1 minced green pepper
1 cup minced canned mushrooms,
  ½ pound fresh mushrooms

1 can tomato soup
2 tablespoons parmesan cheese
2 tablespoons worcestershire sauce
Salt to taste
½ pound spaghetti, cooked
  partially

Cook veal cut up in pieces, onion, pepper, mushrooms and garlic in butter until almost done. Add all other ingredients. Into a greased casserole dish place the almost

cooked spaghetti, then pour over the contents of the seasoned cooked meats and vegetables. Place in a moderate oven and bake covered until browned on top. This should take about 40 minutes.

Margaret Jurinak, Chicago, Ill.

BAKED BUCKWHEAT GRITS *(Krupova baba)*

½ pound buckwheat grits
8 medium potatoes
2 pounds pork shoulder, or left
  over roast beef or pork

Salt pork or ¾ cup bacon fat
3 onions
Salt and pepper to taste

Peel potatoes and cook until tender. Drain off water and save for later use. Mash potatoes and set aside. Cook meat in salted water until tender, drain off water and pour directly over grits. Cover the bowl and allow to stand for 10 minutes. If at the end of this period the grits are not split open, put on a low flame for a few minutes. Add the potato water, if necessary. Grits must be moist to split.

Cut meat into small pieces and add to grits.

Render salt pork or use shortening to sauté the thinly sliced onions. When brown add to the meat and grit mixture. Add the mashed potatoes and season. Blend thoroughly and turn into a greased tube pan. Bake about one hour in a moderate oven at about 350°F.

Left-over roasted meat may be used in this recipe. The meat in this case need not be boiled. The potato water is poured while hot over the grits. It is, however, important that enough shortening is used to make it moist and tasty.

Mary Mrena, Natrona, Pa.

- FISH CASSEROLES -

FISH AND CORN

¼ cup chopped onion	¼ teaspoon pepper
¼ cup chopped green pepper	1 cup milk
1½ tablespoons butter or margarine	2 beaten eggs
1 tablespoon flour	7 ounce can tuna
¾ teaspoon salt	1 cup drained, whole kernel corn

Cook onion and green pepper in butter until tender. Add flour and seasonings; blend. Gradually add milk. Cook over low heat until smooth and thick, stirring constantly. Remove from heat. Slowly stir into eggs. Add tuna and corn. Bake in greased 1 quart casserole or individual casseroles, in moderate oven, 325°F for 30 minutes. Serves 4.

Mary Skurka, Whiting, Ind.

CASSEROLE OF FISH AND NOODLES

8 ounce cooked noodles	2 tablespoons chopped green pepper
4 tablespoons butter	2 cups milk
2 tablespoons flour	2 cups cooked fish-salmon, tuna or halibut
4 tablespoons parsley	
½ cup chopped onion	

Cream butter and flour in top of double boiler. Add finely chopped onion, parsley and green pepper. Stir in milk. Cook until thick. Fold in the flaked fish. In bottom of baking dish place layer of cooked noodles. Pour over sauce and fish and cover with remaining noodles. Bake in moderate oven 350°F for 30 minutes.

Susan Galgan, Chicago, Ill.

CRAB CUSTARD

1 can or 1 cup flaked fresh crab meat	1 teaspoon paprika
3½ cups rich milk	½ teaspoon white pepper
1 teaspoon salt	1 teaspoon grated onion
¾ cup cracker crumbs	¼ teaspoon nutmeg
	4 eggs

Beat the eggs, add milk and seasonings, beat again and add the onion, cracker crumbs and flaked crab meat. Pour into individual buttered casseroles, or into a well buttered ring mold. Dot generously with butter on top, place in a pan of hot water. Bake in slow oven at about 350°F for about 40 or 45 minutes. The custard must be firmly set. Serve with the following sauce on page 281.

SAUCE

4 tablespoons butter
2½ tablespoons flour
1¾ cups milk
1 teaspoon salt
Dash of white pepper

¼ cup sherry wine
½ teaspoon worcestershire sauce
1 small can mushrooms, include
 liquor of same

Melt butter and remove from fire. Add the flour and stir until smoothly blended. Gradually add the milk. Return to the flame and stir until the sauce boils. Add seasonings and mushrooms. Place over a double boiler for one half hour. Just before serving add the sherry.

Catherine Otrembiak, Chicago, Ill.

TUNA-MUSHROOM CASSEROLE

8 ounce package potato chips, crushed
1 can tuna fish (7 ounce), flaked
1 can mushroom soup
½ small green pepper, chopped
2 tablespoons grated onion

Dilute soup with ⅔ can of water. Place ⅓ of crushed potato chips in casserole. Cover with layers of tuna fish, mushroom soup, green peppers, onions and potato chips. Repeat, ending with potato chips. Bake in moderate oven 350°F, 30 to 40 minutes.

Beatrice Pihulic, Hammond, Ind.

SCALLOPED TUNA AND NOODLES

1 can tuna fish
1 small can mushrooms
2 hard boiled eggs
1 small package noodles, cooked and drained

Mix all of the above ingredients together. Make a white sauce using about 1½ cups of milk and ½ can mushroom soup. Mix with tuna. Put in casserole and sprinkle crushed potato chips on top. Bake ½ hour at 350°F.

Helen Cross, Whiting, Ind.

TUNA NOODLE CASSEROLE

1 can tuna
1 can mushrooms
½ pound wide noodles
3 tablespoons butter

3 tablespoons flour
1½ cups milk
1 package Pabsett chesse

Melt butter, add flour and stir until smooth, add milk stirring constantly. Cook until thick, then add cheese and stir until cheese is melted. To the sauce add tuna, noodles and mushrooms. Mix and pour into casserole. Cover with grated cheese and bake about 30 minutes. (Left over cubed chicken maybe used instead of tuna fish).

Mary Kinsock, Whiting, Ind.

SALMON CHEESE CASSEROLE

1 tall can of salmon	**½ cup of milk**
¼ lb. American Cheese	**Biscuit mix**

Drain salmon and take out bone and skin. Arrange in the bottom of a greased baking dish in large pieces. Melt the cheese in the milk stir until smooth. Pour cheese sauce over the fish and place baking powder biscuits on top. Bake in a hot oven, 400°F until biscuits are done, 15 to 20 minutes.

Louise M. Yash, Cleveland, Oh.

PIZZA PIE

DOUGH

4 cups unsifted, unbleached all-purpose flour	**½ cup (scant) cooking oil**
2 teaspoons salt	**1½ cups hot water**
1 teaspoon sugar	**1 cake compressed yeast**

Put flour into large bowl and make a well in center. Add salt, sugar and oil. Have water hot enough so that when you add it next, it will be sufficiently warm to dissolve the yeast, which is added last of all, crumbled. Mix together and knead thoroughly until dough is smooth and does not stick to hands. Spread softened butter on top and let rise 2 hours, cover bowl with cloth. Dough should always be warm throughout the kneading process as well as in rising. When risen, punch down, divide dough in two and shape into balls. Let rise, covered, 1 hour longer on top of table. After second rising, roll out each ball to ½ inch thickness (either in circles or rectangles) and place on cookie sheet or broiler pan. Rub olive oil all over dough and spread topping in order given. Bake for 30 minutes in 375°F oven.

TOPPING

2 ounces olive oil

12 thin slices Mozzarella cheese

1 No.2 can tomatoes, strained and mashed, mixed with 1 cup thick grade tomato puree

8 tablespoons grated cheese (Lucatelli, Parmesan, or other Italian type cheese, such as for spaghetti)

2 teaspoons oregano

About 8 anchovy fillets, sliced or about 1½ pound Italian sausage, sliced

2 small onions, sliced, or 2 small cloves of garlic minced (optional)

Spread olive oil over top of each pizza dough. Lay on rest of topping in order given. This is enough topping for 2 pies. If making pizza for Friday meal, omit sausage. For any other time, omit anchovies. Pizza is just as good the second day. Simply reheat it.

Frances L. Mizenko, Cleveland, Oh.

Meats

TIME TABLE FOR ROASTING MEATS

Meats	Minutes Per Pound	Oven Temperature	Temperature on Thermometer
BEEF			
Standing Rib Roast			
Rare	16 to 18	325°F	140°F
Medium	20 to 22	325°F	160°F
Well done	27 to 30	325°F	170°F to 180°F
Bone and rolled roasts: add 15 minutes per pound			
VEAL			
Loin	30 to 35	300°F	170°F to 180°F
LAMB			
Leg	25 to 30	325°F	175°F to 180°F
Shoulder	25 to 30	325°F	175°F to 180°F
Loin	30 to 35	325°F	175°F to 180°F
Boned and rolled cuts: add 10 minutes per pound			
PORK			
Loin	35 to 40	325°F	185°F
(piece, 4 to 5 pounds)			
Loin, Whole	15 to 20	325°F	185°F
(12 to 15 pounds)			
Shoulder	35 to 40	325°F	185°F
Boned and rolled cuts: add 10 minutes per pound			
Ham, Fresh	30 to 35	325°F	180°F
FOWL			
Chicken	22 to 30	325°F	
Duck	20 to 25	325°F	
Goose	25 to 30	325°F	
Turkey	15 to 25	300°F	180°F

BROILING

STEAK

1 inch thick:

Rare	about 10 minutes
Medium	about 15 minutes
Well done	20 to 25 minutes

1½ inches thick:

Rare	about 15 minutes
Medium	about 20 minutes
Well done	25 to 30 minutes

BARBECUED BEEF ON BUN

1 pound ground beef
1 large chopped onion
1 chopped green pepper
2 tablespoons sugar
½ teaspoon cloves

1 tablespoon mustard
1 tablespoon vinegar
1 teaspoon salt
1 cup catchup

Brown meat in a tablespoon hot fat until it is crumbly, but not hard. Combine and add remaining ingredients. Cover and simmer gently for 30 minutes. Serve on toasted bun.

Beatrice Pihulic, Hammond, Ind.

BARBECUED BEEF

1 medium chopped onion
1 cup chopped celery
1 tablespoon melted shortening
1 tablespoon lemon juice
1 tablespoon white vinegar

½ cup cooked tomatoes
2 tablespoons brown sugar
1 cup catsup
1 teaspoon mustard
3 pounds ground beef

Brown onion and celery in shortening. Add seasonings and remaining ingredients, except meat, and simmer until some of the tomato juice evaporates. Place layer of beef in sauce pan, then layer of gravy. Simmer for 30 minutes.

Benedictine Slovak Sisters, Chicago, Ill.

BEEF 'N' BEAN BARBECUE

1 pound ground beef
¼ cup diced green pepper
½ cup diced celery
1 eight ounce can tomato sauce
½ cup water
1 clove garlic minced

2 tablespoons wine vinegar
1 teaspoon dry mustard
½ teaspoon thyme
1 tablespoon brown sugar
Salt and pepper
1 No.2 can pork and beans

Cook ground beef and vegetables in hot fat until vegetables are soft. Add tomato sauce, water, garlic, vinegar, mustard, thyme, brown sugar, and seasonings; blend well and simmer about 5 minutes. Pour meat mixture into 1½ quart casserole and cover with pork and beans. Bake in moderate oven (375°F), for 45 minutes. Serves 6.

Mary Skurka, Whiting, Ind.

SAVORY BEEF BAR·BE·CUE

1 chopped onion
2 tablespoons crisco
2 tablespoons vinegar
2 tablespoons sugar
4 tablespoons lemon juice
1 cup catsup
3 tablespoons worcestershire
  sauce

½ teaspoon prepared mustard
½ cup water
½ cup chopped celery
½ teaspoon paprika
½ teaspoon chili powder
Salt to taste
2 pounds ground beef

Sauté onion in hot fat. Add remaining ingredients, except meat, and simmer for 30 minutes over very low flame. Makes 2 cups of sauce. Brown meat in little fat, drain and add to sauce. Simmer about 15 minutes.

Ludmilla Cherney, Chicago, Ill.

CHILI CON CARNE

1½ pounds ground meat
2 large onions (cut into small
  pieces)
1 small stalk celery (cut small)
1 tablespoon salt

1 tablespoon chili powder
½ teaspoon pepper
2 eight ounce cans tomato sauce
1 No.2 can tomato juice
1 or 2 cans kidney beans

Fry meat until brown. Add onion celery and seasonings. Fry for 20 minutes. Add to a large sauce pan, tomato sauce and juice. Cook for 1 hour. Now add kidney beans and boil for 5 more minutes. Serve with oyster crackers.

Mary Skurka, Whiting, Ind.

CHILI CON CARNE

1 to 2 pounds beef
2 teaspoons chili powder
4 tablespoons suet, chopped
2 tablespoons flour

2 teaspoons salt
1½ quarts hot water
1 can red kidney beans

Cut the beef in small chunks (do not grind) add the chili powder, salt and flour. Mix thoroughly. Use a deep pot. Add meat mixture to hot fat, fry about 15 minutes, gradually add the hot water. Let simmer for 45 minutes or until meat is tender; add additional chili powder and salt to suit individual taste. Add the red kidney beans just before serving.

Mary Kollar, Olyphant, Pa.

TEXAS CHILI

1 pound dry chili or kidney
  beans
2 quarts boiling water
2 pounds ground beef
2 teaspoons chili powder

1 tablespoon salt
1 tablespoon lard
1 large onion, chopped
1 clove garlic, chopped
1 No. 1 can tomatoes

Let beans soak in water overnight, in the morning boil beans in 2 quarts of boiling water. Add a little salt and boil about one hour. Brown onion in lard, add ground beef, garlic, salt and chili powder and fry until meat is brown, mixing meanwhile (about 15 minutes). Add beans and tomatoes to meat and mix well. Cook slowly about half hour or until done.

Millie Bandor, Fort Worth, Tx.

HAMBURGER APRICOT RING

24 dried apricot halves
1 onion minced
2 tablespoons fat
1½ pounds beef chuck, ground

2 teaspoons Worcestershire
  sauce
1 cup soft bread crumbs
½ cup milk

Simmer apricot halves in water, for 5 minutes. Brown onion in fat; add the remaining ingredients. Drain the apricots and arrange in a greased ring mold. Add the meat mixture. Bake in a moderate oven. 325°F for 1½ hours.

Ella Vlasaty, Braddock, Pa.

BARBECUED HAMBURGER

Fry 2 pounds hamburger meat with as much onion and green pepper as desired, until nicely browned. Then add the following:

2 tablespoons vinegar
2 tablespoons brown sugar
1 small bottle catsup
1 teaspoon mustard

½ cup celery (if desired)
½ cup water
A little garlic or garlic salt,
  if desired

Simmer ½ hour, then serve between hamburger buns.

Mrs. Lissak, Chicago, Ill.

BARBECUED HAMBURGER

2 pounds ground meat
1 cup chopped onions
1 cup chopped celery
½ green pepper, minced
1 cup catsup
1 cup chili sauce
½ cup water

1 tablespoon salt
½ teaspoon pepper
1 tablespoon vinegar
1 small clove garlic, chopped
2 tablespoons Worcestershire
  sauce
2 tablespoons brown sugar

Brown the meat in hot fat. Add onion, celery, green pepper, garlic and salt. Simmer slowly with cover on for 15 minutes. Add catsup, chili sauce and water, combined with Worcestershire sauce, brown sugar and vinegar. Cook slowly for about 20 minutes.

Mary Skurka, Whiting, Ind.

HAMBURGER WITH PEAS

1 pound hamburger	**1 cup celery**
1 large onion	**Small can of peas**

Fry the onion in 1 tablespoon butter, and ½ teaspoon paprika, when onion is browned add the hamburger and celery, salt and pepper to taste. If necessary add the liquid from the peas. Pour the peas over the meat 15 minutes before serving.

Maria Talla, Binghampton, N. Y.

SAVORY HAMBURGER

1 pound ground beef	**1 green pepper**
¼ pound ground pork	**3 medium potatoes, sliced**
1 onion, cut fine	**1½ cups water**
1½ tablespoons cooking fat	**¼ cup cracker meal**
1 teaspoon salt	**1 egg**
¼ teaspoon pepper	**1 can tomato soup**
Pinch of paprika	

Mix beef, pork, salt and pepper, add onion, cracker meal and egg. Make hamburgers round and small. Fry on both sides about five minutes in the cooking fat. Add green pepper, sliced, add potatoes, water, tomato soup and paprika. Cook till potatoes are done.

Elizabeth Cerajewski, Whiting, Ind.

MEAT BALLS AND SPAGHETTI

1 small onion, chopped	**1 egg**
2 small cloves of garlic	**1 tablespoon chopped parsley**
½ pound ground steak	**¼ cup milk**
½ pound ground pork	**1 teaspoon salt**
1 cup moistened bread	

Mix all ingredients together. Form into small balls and brown in 3 tablespoons of oil or lard.

SAUCE
2 cans tomato paste
1 can tomatoes (small can)
1 can water

Cook slowly for 2½ hours. When done, cook 1 pound thick spaghetti, drain well. Pour sauce over same and sprinkle with ¼ pound grated parmesan cheese, fold in and mix lightly with meat balls.

Joliet, Ill.

EVERYDAY MEAT LOAF

⅔ cup dry bread crumbs
1 cup milk
1½ pounds ground beef
1 slightly beaten egg

¼ cup grated onion
1 teaspoon salt
⅛ teaspoon pepper

Soak bread crumbs in milk; add meat, egg, onions and seasonings; mix well. Form in 2 small loaves. Cover meat loaves with piquant sauce. You can also form into a single loaf in a 4¾ x 8¾ inch bread pan. Spread sauce over meat and bake 1 hour in 350°F oven. Serves 8.

Piquant sauce: Combine 3 tablespoons brown sugar, ¼ cup catsup, 1 teaspoon dry mustard and a little water.

Helen Cross, Whiting, Ind.

MEAT PASTRY ROLLS

CRUST
2 cups all purpose flour
⅔ cup Crisco
1 teaspoon salt
½ cup cold water

FILLING
2 pounds diced potatoes, raw
1 pound ground meat (¾ beef,
 ¼ pork)
1 large onion sliced
1 teaspoon salt, dash of pepper

Mix dough as for pie crust and divide into six parts. Roll each part into size of eight inch plate and fill with the meat filling; which has been mixed together in a large bowl. Place some of the filling in the middle of each rolled crust and add 1 teaspoon of Crisco, then fold up sides and prick holes with a fork on top of dough. Bake in oven until brown and done.

Ludmilla Cherney, Chicago, Ill.

PORCUPINE MEAT BALLS *(oven method)*

1 pound ground beef
⅓ cup rice, (uncooked)
½ cup chopped onion
½ teaspoon salt
Dash of pepper

2 tablespoons chopped parsley
1 egg
1½ teaspoons sage (may omit)
1 can condensed tomato soup

Wash the rice and mix with the ground meat. Add onion, seasonings, sage, parsley and egg, slightly beaten. Mix thoroughly. Form into balls (about 12-14 balls) and put into a deep baking dish. Heat the can of condensed tomato soup with 1 can of water and pour over meat balls in casserole, having the balls well covered. Place in a hot oven 375 to 400°F in a covered casserole. Bake 1 hour and 15 minutes. Serves 6 to 7.

Helen Cross, Whiting, Ind.

PORCUPINE MEAT BALLS *(Pressure Cooker Recipe)*

1 pound ground beef
½ cup uncooked rice
1 teaspoon salt
½ teaspoon pepper

1 tablespoon minced onion
1 small can tomato soup
½ cup water

Wash rice thoroughly. Combine meat, rice, salt, pepper, and onion. Shape into eight small balls. Heat tomato soup and water in cooker, drop meat balls in soup mixture. Place cover on cooker, allow steam to flow from vent pipe to release all air from cooker. Place indicator weight on vent pipe and cook 10 minutes with pointer at cook. Let pointer return to off position.

Anna Vrabel, Yokel-Piermont, NY

PORCUPINE MEATBALLS *(kettle method)*

1½ pounds ground beef
1 tablespoon salt
¼ teaspoon pepper
1 small minced onion
1 clove garlic

1 egg
½ cup precooked rice
1 can tomato soup
1 can water
1 small green pepper

Mix meat, salt, pepper, onion, garlic, rice and egg; form into balls. Put tomato soup, water and green pepper in a pan and bring to a boiling point, drop meat balls into this soup and boil slowly for 1 hour. Serve with mashed potatoes.

Mary Skurka, Whiting, Ind.

POTATO BEEFBURGERS

1 pound ground beef
1 medium potato
1 small onion

1 teaspoon salt
½ teaspoon pepper

Grate potato and onion into ground beef, add seasoning and make patties, fry on greased griddle.

Mary Schinsky, Los Angeles, Ca.

BEEF WITH SOUR CREAM AND MUSHROOMS

1 pound ground beef
½ pound fresh sliced mushrooms
Fry beef and mushrooms until
   brown

SAUCE
1 tablespoon butter
1 tablespoon flour
1 cup sour cream (½ pint)
1 teaspoon salt
Dash of pepper

Melt butter, add flour and blend, add sour cream stirring constantly. Pour meat into sauce and cook for several minutes. Serve over cooked noodles.

Mary Skurka, Whiting, Ind.

SAVORY CORNED BEEF

4 pounds corned beef
1 cup vinegar
1 cup water
1 cup brown sugar

4 cloves garlic
1 teaspoon caraway seed
1 teaspoon pepper
2 bay leaves

Place in pressure cooker, cook 30 minutes per pound (15 pound pressure) or by adding more water (covering meat), it may be boiled in a regular pot.

Mary Kollar, Olyphant, Pa.

CORNED BEEF

Select a piece of corned brisket, not too lean. Place in deep kettle and cover well with cold water. Bring to the boiling point. Pour off the water and again cover with cold water. Add to the water:

1 clove garlic
1 onion
½ teaspoon mixed spices

1 tablespoon sugar
1 tablespoon vinegar

Simmer gently until tender, allowing 20 to 30 minutes per pound. A 6 pound brisket will take approximately 3 hours of slow cooking. Cabbage and potatoes can be cooked in same kettle or cooked separately.

Irene Menzezoff, Flushing, NY

RIB ROAST OF BEEF

A rib roast may be either a standing roast, or a boned and rolled roast. A standing roast is easier to carve if the backbone is sawed from the rib bones. The roast should never be less than two ribs thick, otherwise it will tend to dry out too much in roasting process.

Wipe meat with clean damp cloth. Place on a rack in a roaster, with the fat side up. Insert the meat thermometer in the fleshiest portion without touching any bone. Salt and pepper may be added to the meat either before or after roasting. Roast uncovered according to the table and until the thermometer registers the required temperature. Do not add water or any other liquid.

When done, remove the roast from the pan and keep it hot while the gravy is being made from the drippings that remain in the pan. Skim off excess fat if necessary. Pour desired amount of hot water into pan and loosen drippings. Strain, measure and for each cup of liquid, add 1 tablespoon of cornstarch diluted in 2 tablespoons cold water. Cook until thick and then simmer about 5 minutes, seasoning while cooking, cornstarch, or if flour is used, maybe increased or decreased depending on thickness of gravy desired.

The flavor of a roast is enhanced if several medium-sized onions are peeled and halved and laid on the meat when it is put in the oven.

BEEF ROAST WITH LIMA BEANS

3½ pounds chuck roast
1 package dry lima beans
1 large onion, thinly sliced
1 small stalk of celery, diced fine

1 can tomatoes or catsup and
water mixed, enough liquid
to cover-season to taste

Soak the Lima Beans in hot water for one or two hours. Brown the meat on both sides and place in roasting pan. Slice onion and spread over the meat, add the celery and cover all with soaked lima beans. Then pour over the canned tomatoes or catsup and water mixed. Cover and place in a moderate oven preheated to 350 - 375°F, for about three to three and one-half hours. The last half hour, season, and be sure that the lima beans have had enough moisture to cook up tender, if so, uncover and allow to brown if not already brown at this stage.

Helen Kasza, Chicago, Ill.

BEEF POT ROAST WITH VEGETABLES AND NOODLES

(use dutch oven for this recipe)

Select a 4 pound beef pot roast, using blade, chuck, shoulder or rump. Heat dutch oven over medium flame and melt a small piece of suet in it. Wipe meat with damp cloth, dredge lightly with flour, and sprinkle with salt and pepper. Brown the roast on all sides in the hot fat. Add a medium sliced onion and cook with the meat. Cover and cook gently over a low heat. Add 1 cup water, reduce heat. Cook for 2 hours, turning meat occasionally. If desired, peeled, salted medium sized potatoes, carrots and onions may be added, the last hour of cooking. Remove meat and vegetables to a warm platter. Make a brown gravy, using the drippings in the pan, serve hot. Serve with hot buttered noodles. Serves 8.

Mary E. Grega, Cleveland, Oh.

SMOTHERED BEEF

3 pound beef rump	**2 tablespoons prepared mustard**
Flour	**1 teaspoon celery seed**
Salt and pepper	**1 cup strained canned tomatoes**
3 tablespoons lard	

Season the flour with salt and pepper. Roll meat in seasoned flour. Brown carefully on all sides in hot lard in a Dutch oven. Add other ingredients, cover and simmer for three hours or until meat is tender. Serve with noodles.

Ann Bronersky, Chicago, Ill.

SOUTHERN BEEF BARBECUE

This is a good recipe to use for left over roast beef. Small thin slices of beef are used. Use your favorite barbecue sauce or try a quickie made of:

2 cups tomato juice	**¼ teaspoon pepper**
1 tablespoon meat sauce	**2 tablespoons flour**
1 teaspoon celery salt	

Combine all the ingredients at once. Step-up the spices as desired. Spread about 2 cups of cooked rice in a baking pan and pour half the sauce over the rice. Spread slices of beef over the rice; then top with more sauce. Bake in moderate oven, 350°F for 20 to 30 minutes to heat and blend the flavors.

Courtesy Swift and Co., Chicago, Ill.

BROILING STEAKS

For broiling steaks always ask for thick slices. The best steaks are about 1½ to 2 inches thick. Wipe with a damp cloth and slash the fat edge of the steak to prevent curling, during the broiling. Heat the broiling oven and the broiling pan. Then rub the broiling pan with a piece of suet and place the steaks on same, the steaks should be rubbed with a clove of garlic before putting on pan. Adjust the pan so that the top of the steak is 2 to 4 inches from the heat source. Broil until one side is brown. Season. Turn with tongs to prevent piercing the meat. Broil the other side. Season. Serve at once on a heated platter. To test for doneness: Cut a slit in the steak near the bone and note the color. Oven for broiling may be set at 375°F and the oven door should be left partially opened during the broiling stage. A 2 inch steak will take about 10 minutes of broiling on each side. Thinner slices will take less time.

Daughters of St. Francis, Lacon, Ill.

APPETIZING STEAK

1½ pounds round or chuck
  steak about 1 inch thick
1½ cups flour
2 teaspoons baking powder
½ teaspoon salt

2 eggs, separated
1 cup milk
3 potatoes
3 onions
3 carrots

Season steak with salt and pepper and place in greased baking dish. Bake 30 minutes at 350°F uncovered. Add vegetables, cover and cook 30 minutes. Sift flour, baking powder and salt together. Add beaten egg yolks. Add milk and mix well. Fold in stiffly beaten egg whites. Pour over meat. Bake at 475°F, for 15 minutes longer.

Ella D. Vlasaty, Braddock, Pa.

BEEF ROLL-UPS

1½ pounds round steak cut in serving pieces
1 large onion chopped fine
4 slices bacon cut in two inch piece
3 tablespoons shortening or drippings

On each piece of meat place piece of bacon and ½ teaspoon onion grated, or chopped fine. Season with salt and pepper. Roll up and fasten with tooth picks. Brown thoroughly in a dutch oven in the drippings. Cover completely with water. Cook about 2 hours over low flame until tender. Season with salt and pepper. Thicken gravy with 1½ tablespoons cornstarch mixed with 2 tablespoons cold water. Mushrooms may be added to gravy.

Viola Matlon Brown, Whiting, Ind.

BEEF ROULADE

1½ pounds round steak half
  inch thick
Salt, pepper, paprika to taste
½ green pepper, minced

1 medium onion, minced
2 cloves garlic, minced
3 tablespoons butter
¼ cup fine bread crumbs

Cut steak into portions (6), pound well, sprinkle with salt, pepper and paprika. Combine green pepper, onion, garlic and crumbs. Place large spoonful of filling in center of each steak. Roll and tie with string to hold securely. Sauté in butter till tender, about 30 minutes. Serve with sauce.

Sauce: Sauté ½ pound mushrooms in 2 tablespoons butter till tender. Add salt to taste and 1 cup sour cream. Simmer 2 to 3 minutes.

Mrs. John Perko, Cleveland, Oh.

BEEF ROULDER

1½ pounds round steak	⅛ teaspoon pepper
Yolks of 2 hard-cooked eggs	1 teaspoon salt
2 tablespoons cream	2 tablespoons fat
1 medium chopped onion	1 tablespoon flour
2 sardines	1 cup light cream or top milk

Have the butcher cut the steak one-half inch thick. Pound the steak with a wooden mallet, cover with a dressing made as follows: Mash egg yolks and sardines to a paste. Add onion, 2 tablespoons cream, pepper and salt. Roll steak, fasten with toothpicks or tie with string. Cut in pieces 4 inches long. Heat fat in a pan, add rolls and brown on all sides. Cover and bake in moderate oven (350°F), for 1 hour. Add cream combined with flour and bake 10 minutes longer with the cover removed. Serve with the gravy.

Susan M. Mrazik, Homestead, Pa.

FILLED STEAKS *(For Anniversary Dinner)*

6 slices tenderize steak, 3 ounces each	1 onion, medium size
	1 tablespoon butter
½ pound ground pork	½ teaspoon black pepper
1 cup rice	2 teaspoons salt

Slice half of onion and sauté in ½ tablespoon butter until golden brown. Rinse rice in lukewarm water. Add ground pork, salt, pepper and onion. Mix together and blend well. Divide into 6 portions. Place a portion on each slice of steak and roll carefully and hold together with woodpins. Place in pan with ½ tablespoon butter and ½ of chopped onion. Simmer gently until done. When meat is done, remove. Add 1 tablespoon flour to the drippings for gravy. Cook until thick and season to taste. Serve steak with sweet potato puffs and fresh stringbeans.

Emily Kozak, Phoenixville, Pa.

ROLLED ROUND STEAK

2 pounds roundsteak	Onions
Bacon	4 tablespoons butter
Prepared mustard	2 cups hot water
Dill pickles	1 chicken bouillon cube

Have steak split to make two layers. Cut these layers into 3 x 6 inch strips. Spread mustard lightly on end of each strip and place on it a slice of dill pickle, 1 short strip of bacon and 1 slice onion. Roll and fasten with toothpick and roll in flour. Brown on all sides in butter. Add hot water. Cover and cook over low heat for 1½ hours. Before done, make a paste of flour and water and add bouillon cube.

Mary Skurka, Whiting, Ind.

STEAK, COUNTRY STYLE

2 pounds round steak
Flour
½ cup butter or margarine
2 medium onions, sliced
½ pound peeled mushrooms,
  sliced
½ cup water

1 teaspoon salt
2 tablespoons grated cheese
  (optional)
Dash of pepper
¼ teaspoon paprika
½ cup sour cream

Have steak cut into serving pieces or leave whole if preferred, dredge with flour seasoned with salt and pepper. Melt ¼ cup butter in a large skillet and add onions and mushrooms, cook until onions are tender and mushrooms are lightly browned. Remove onions and mushrooms from pan or push to the side, add the remaining ¼ cup butter and brown steak on both sides. Stir in the remaining ingredients, cover skillet and cook until meat is tender enough to cut with a fork. Serves 6.

Betty Hertko, Whiting, Ind.

SPANISH STEAK

Choose round steak, cut one-inch thick. Combine ½ cup flour, ½ teaspoon salt and ⅛ teaspoon pepper, and dredge the steak with the edge of a saucer until all flour is absorbed. Melt drippings or bacon in heavy sauce pan and brown the meat on all sides. Cover with a can of tomato soup, add slices of onion and green pepper rings. Cover closely and simmer for an hour or one and one-half hours. Serve in sauce.

Susan M. Mrazik, Homestead, Pa.

SPANISH STEAK AND RICE

1 large onion, sliced
2 tablespoons butter
1 pound round steak, cut in
  serving pieces

½ cup rice
1 can tomato soup diluted with
  2 cans water

Brown onions in butter. Remove onions and brown steak. Add tomato soup and two cans water. Wash rice. Add to steak. Add onion and season with salt and pepper. Simmer slowly until cooked.

Mary Skurka, Whiting, Ind.

SWISS STEAK

1 pound round steak	**1 small can tomato sauce**
1 green pepper	**Salt, pepper and flour**
1 large onion	

Cut steak into serving pieces. Pound as much flour into meat as it will take. Brown in fat. Add sliced onion and green pepper, add tomato sauce and enough water to cover (about 1 cup) more or less. Simmer in covered pan, slowly for one hour until tender.

Agnes Dvorscak, Whiting, Ind.

FRANKS

These Spanish hot dogs will make a fine luncheon dish. Cut 6 skinless frankfurters into thin slices. Cook 1 diced onion and ½ diced green pepper in 2 tablespoons butter. Do not brown. Add 1 cup canned tomatoes and simmer until part of tomato juice evaporates and the flavors blend. Add frankfurters and cook an additional 10 minutes. Thicken with flour blended in a small amount of water. Add sugar and seasonings. Serve on cooked noodles or rice.

Benedictine Slovak Sisters, Chicago, Ill.

WEINERS WITH TOMATOES AND GREEN PEPPERS

1 pound wieners	**6 fresh tomatoes or 1 can tomatoes**
1 onion, chopped	**Salt to taste**
6 green peppers	**Sugar to taste**

Fry onion in lard until browned, then pour into this the tomatoes, sliced green peppers, little salt and very little sugar to season, and let simmer over low heat until peppers are soft. Then add the wieners and cook all together until wieners are thoroughly warmed through.

Mary V. Haydu, Braddock, Pa.

CABBAGE ROLLS

1 pound ground beef	**1 head cabbage**
½ pound ground pork or veal	**2 tablespoons butter**
½ cup rice, partly cooked	**Salt, pepper and a dash of celery**
1 egg	**salt**

Buy a medium size head of cabbage, that is not firm. Remove core from whole head of cabbage with sharp knife. Scald or par-boil the cabbage in boiling salted water. Remove and allow to cool before handling. Then remove a few leaves at a time and trim down the thick ridge on back of leaves to make it easier for rolling.

Wash rice after partially cooked (cook about 10 minutes) in salted water, strain and run cold water through rice in strainer. At this stage the rice is about half cooked.

Sauté onion in butter until it becomes transparent. Combine with meat, egg, rice and seasonings, mix well. Spread each leaf (on the thick end) with meat mixture to about ¾ inch thickness, fold the two opposite sides and roll, starting with the thick end. Fasten with toothpicks. Place rolls in buttered casserole and pour over same a can of tomato soup diluted and bake covered at about 325°F, for about 2 hours or until browned and tender. These rolls may be cooked or baked in sauerkraut if preferred.

Daughters of St. Francis, Lacon, Ill.

HOLUBKY OR STUFFED CABBAGE ROLLS

1 large head cabbage	**1 pound ground beef**
1 cup shredded cabbage	**¾ teaspoon salt**
¾ cup uncooked rice	**½ teaspoon pepper**
½ cup diced onions	**½ cup sour cream**
¼ cup diced green pepper	**½ cup canned tomato soup**
¼ cup diced carrots	

Parboil head of cabbage, separate leaves and set aside. Mix together shredded cabbage, rice, onions, peppers, carrots, meat, salt and pepper. Form this mixture into loose (not too solid) rolls, leaving room for rice to expand. Wrap each roll in a cabbage leaf; fasten with toothpicks. Place into greased casserole, pouring over ½ cup water. Bake 90 minutes at 350°F. Stir cream and tomato soup together, pour over the cabbage rolls and bake an additional 30 minutes at 300°F. Serve piping hot.

Florence Ribovich, Hammond, Ind.

HOLUBKY

4 pound loose head cabbage	**½ cup rice cooked in boiling**
1 large can sauerkraut	**water about 8 minutes and**
1 medium can tomatoes	**drained**
1 slice pork shoulder, cut in	**1 egg**
pieces	**Salt and pepper to taste**
1 pound ground meat (beef and	
pork)	

Combine ground meat, rice, egg and seasoning. Core cabbage and parboil about 20 minutes covered. Separate leaves, when cool, stuff with meat mixture and roll up. In large kettle place a layer of sauerkraut, then a layer of cabbage rolls or Holubky, then a layer of tomatoes, then pieces of pork shoulder, seasoning as you go. When all is used cover to the top of the kettle with boiling water and cook over medium heat about 2½ hours.

Anna Matlon, Whiting, Ind.

HOLUBKY *(Stuffed Cabbage Leaves)*

1 small onion	Salt and pepper to taste
1 teaspoon lard	Loose cabbage leaves
1 pound ground beef	1 can sauerkraut
1 pound ground pork	1 can tomato soup
½ cup rice	

Brown onion in hot fat. Add beef, pork, rice and seasonings. Mix well. Cook separated cabbage leaves in boiling water for several minutes, until soft enough to roll. When cool, place 1 tablespoon of meat mixture on each leaf and roll. Take one-half of the sauerkraut and place in bottom of sauce pan, then cabbage rolls in layers, then the other half of the sauerkraut. Pour one can of tomato soup and enough water to cover. Cook slowly in covered saucepan about 1½ hours.

Joliet, Ill.

GOULASH

½ pound beef	½ green pepper, coarsely
½ pound pork	chopped
½ pound veal, cut in cubes	2 tablespoons or more paprika
2 tablespoons fat	1½ teaspoons salt
3 cups sliced onions	

Melt fat in heavy skillet. Add chopped onion and cook over low heat until lightly yellowed. Add paprika and blend well. Add meat, green pepper, salt, and about ½ cup water. Cover closely and simmer until meat is tender, about 1½ hours. Add a little more water, if needed, but mixture should not be overmoist when finished cooking. Makes 5-6 servings. Serve with hot boiled potatoes or fluffy steamed rice.

Florence Ribovich, Hammond, Ind.

ORAVSKY GOULASH

2 pounds beef or veal and pork	1½ teaspoons paprika
cut in 2 inch cubes	1 pound sauerkraut
1 teaspoon salt	1 tablespoon fat
1 tablespoon fat	1 cup thick sour cream
2 medium size onions, sliced	

Melt fat in heavy skillet. Add meat and cook, stirring occasionally until meat is lightly browned. Add the onion and continue cooking until onion is yellow and transparent. Add salt, paprika, and blend well. Add a small amount of boiling water, enough to cover half of meat. Cover and cook over low heat until the meat is tender, about 1½ hours.

In a separate sauce pan cook the kraut with 1 tablespoon butter and ¼ to ½ cup boiling water, about 15 minutes.

Add sauerkraut to meat and continue to cook for 15 minutes. This mixture should not contain too much liquid. If there seems to be too much, cook uncovered for a few minutes to evaporate some of it. Just before serving add 1 cup thick soured cream. Heat but do not cook further. Makes 6 to 8 servings.

Anna Gandy, Whiting, Ind.

STUFFED PEPPERS

1 pound ground meat (half beef and pork)
½ cup rice cooked in salted water about 8 minutes and drained
1 egg
Salt and pepper to taste
8 medium green peppers
1 large can tomato juice
1 can water
1 rounded tablespoon bacon drippings or fat
1 rounded tablespoon flour

In a large kettle brown the flour in the drippings. Pour in the tomato juice and water, salt and pepper to taste. Combine the meat, rice that was cooked in boiling water, egg and seasonings. Stuff the peppers which have been thoroughly cleaned. Place in boiling juice. Cook about 1½ hours over medium heat. If it is too thick, add water. If any meat is left over, shape into balls and place in juice to cook.

Anna Matlon, Whiting, Ind.

STUFFED PEPPERS

10 medium green bell peppers
½ pound ground beef
½ pound ground pork
½ cup rice
1 tablespoon butter
1 onion chopped fine

1 egg
Salt and pepper to taste
½ pint canned tomatoes
½ pint sour cream
4 tablespoons flour

Clean peppers, let stand about 5 minutes in boiling water. Brown onions in butter. Mix meat with onions, rice, egg, salt and pepper. Stuff into peppers and place in kettle. Pour tomatoes over peppers. Add about 1 tablespoon or more of salt and some pepper. Fill kettle with water until peppers are covered with liquid, simmer slowly for one hour. Remove peppers to another pan temporarily.

Mix 4 tablespoons flour with part of the sour cream. Add to the tomatoes in which the peppers have cooked. Stir well, then bring to a boil. Add rest of sour cream and the stuffed peppers. Be sure to blend the sour cream well before adding the stuffed peppers.

Maria Slosarcik, Gary, Ind.

- PORK -

ROAST LOIN OF PORK

3 to 4 pounds pork roast	**1 pared apple**
Salt and pepper to taste	**1 stalk celery**

Wipe the meat with a damp cloth and rub well with salt and pepper. Place, fat side up, on a rack in an open roasting pan. Arrange apple and celery over the pork. Roast in moderate oven, allowing 30 minutes to the pound and baste frequently with the drippings in the pan. Serve with brown gravy and apple sauce.

Veronica Radocha, Coaldale, Pa.

STUFFED ROAST CROWN OF PORK

Select a 6 or 8 pound loin of pork and have the butcher arrange it to form a crown. Prepare stuffing as follows:

2 cups cooked rice	**2 tablespoons drippings**
1 green pepper	**½ teaspoon sage**
1 pimiento	

To cooked rice add finely chopped green pepper and pimiento, drippings and sage, mix well. Put pork into roasting pan, fill cavity with stuffing, spread a piece of greased paper over pork and sear in a hot oven (450°F) 20 to 30 minutes, then reduce heat to moderate (350°F) and bake for 3½ hours, basting with 2 cups water during last half of roasting.

Mary Osadjan, Chicago, Ill.

BARBECUED PORK CHOPS

2 tablespoons fat	**1½ teaspoons salt**
2 cloves garlic, minced	**2 teaspoons chili powder**
1 large onion, sliced	**½ cup hot water**
½ cup lemon juice	**1 bay leaf**
1 can tomato soup	**Dash of thyme**
2 teaspoons prepared mustard	**6-8 loin pork chops, cut 1 inch thick**

Into hot fat, add garlic and onion. Sauté until tender. Then add all the remaining ingredients except the pork chops. Simmer for about 15 to 20 minutes. Place pork chops on grill or under oven broiler. When light brown on upper side, drench the chops with barbecued sauce and turn over to broil on other side. Brush with barbecue sauce and continue broiling. Turning every five or six minutes until well done. Any left over sauce may be heated and served with or over chops.

Betty Hertko, Whiting, Ind.

STUFFED BROILED PORK CHOPS

Dressing for 8 chops
½ cup finely chopped celery
¼ cup finely chopped onion
2 tablespoons shortening
3 small slices of dry toasted bread

¾ teaspoon salt
Pepper to taste
Pinch of sage or poultry seasoning
1 tablespoon green onion tops
**   or parsley**

Have butcher cut chops about 1 inch thick and make pocket for dressing. Sauté celery and onion in shortening for about 7 or 8 minutes and pour over the toast which has been soaked in cold water about 5 minutes and then squeezed dry. Add seasoning, onion tops or parsley. Stuff pockets with dressing, brush chops on both sides with melted butter or margarine, season with salt and pepper and sprinkle with light bread crumbs. Broil at 350°F, about 3 inches from heating element for 12 to 15 minutes on each side.

Frances L. Mizenko, Cleveland, Oh.

STUFFED PORK CHOPS

Four center cut pork chops, cut the thickness of two chops in one, cut pocket in the center of the meat section. Salt and pepper the meat and make filling.

Filling:
4 slices dry bread or toast, softened with water
3 slices bacon cut fine and fried with one small onion, very light brown
1 egg beaten
½ can mushrooms chopped fine, a little liver may be added if on
**   hand**
Salt, pepper, parsley and little sage.

Mix well the above ingredients and stuff the pork chops. Roll in bread crumbs and fry on both sides in shortening. Place on rack in roaster with about ¾ cup water in the bottom of the roaster. Put in moderate oven 350°F for 30 minutes. Very nice to serve company.

Mary Chromcik, Whiting, Ind.

SPANISH PORK CHOPS WITH RICE

1 cup rice	2 cans tomato juice
6 pork chops	2 tablespoons minced parsley
1 onion, sliced	2 tablespoons chopped celery

Wash rice thoroughly and boil in salted water for about 10 minutes. Drain. Brown pork chops in frying pan, then remove, add the onion and celery to the drippings and brown. Return the chops to the pan on top of the onion. Put a mound of rice on top of each chop. Pour the tomato juice around the chops and on top. Scatter the parsley over all and bake in a moderate oven, 350°F, for one hour. Yields 6 servings, 1 chop each.

Anna Lissy, Whiting, Ind.

PORK TENDERLOIN IN MUSHROOM SAUCE

1 pound pork tenderloin, frenched	1 can cream of mushroom soup
1 tablespoon butter or shortening	Salt and Pepper to taste

Brown floured frenched pork tenderloin in butter in heavy skillet. Turn and season. Pour over the cream of mushroom soup; cover and simmer until tender, about 1 hour. Check frequently and stir gently to prevent sticking. This may also be baked in the oven of moderate temperature for about 1 hour.

Mary Vevurka, Chicago, Ill.

PORK GOULASH (Seketina)

2 pounds pork	1 can sauerkraut
1 large onion	Season to taste
2 tablespoons shortening	

Brown the sliced onion in shortening, until golden brown. Add the pork cut up in cubes and sauté slowly for half hour. Then add sauerkraut and let simmer until meat is tender or bake in a moderate oven. Add water as needed to prevent burning.

Mary Ruzicka, Muskegon, Mi.

STUFFED SPARERIBS

2 pounds spareribs (one piece)	2 cups dried bread cubes
½ pound pork, ground	1 small can tomato sauce
½ pound beef, ground	1 clove garlic, chopped
3 eggs	1 tablespoon shortening
1 medium onion, chopped	Salt and pepper to taste

Brown onion. Moisten bread cubes in water, squeeze out water. Mix meat, onions, bread, eggs, garlic, salt and pepper. Lay spareribs flat. Spread meat mixture on top. Roll up. Melt shortening in roaster, place rolled spareribs into this melted shortening, then pour tomato sauce on top. Add about 3 tablespoons water, cover and roast in moderate oven at least 1 hour.

Maria Slosarcik, Gary, Ind.

SPARERIBS WITH VEGETABLE SAUCE

4 pounds spareribs	1 No. 2½ can red kidney beans
1 clove garlic, chopped fine	2 teaspoons salt
2 medium onions, chopped	½ teaspoon pepper
½ cup diced celery	1 can vegetable soup

Cut spareribs into serving pieces and place in kettle, add chopped garlic and rest of ingredients. Cover kettle tightly and simmer slowly until meat is tender, about 1½ hours. Serve with vegetable sauce poured over meat. (Serves 8.)

Sophie Marusak, Joliet, Ill.

BARBECUED SPARERIBS

Dice onion and brown in 2 tablespoons butter. Add:

2 tablespoons vinegar	Salt and pepper to taste
½ cup lemon juice	2 tablespoons brown sugar
1 teaspoon Worcestershlre sauce	1 small bottle catsup
	½ teaspoon mustard
2 cups chopped celery	½ cup water

Brown spareribs under broiler. Place ribs in roaster, pour sauce over them, and bake at least one hour, covered, and ½ hour uncovered. Use a moderate oven 350°F.

Clara Kucka, Whiting, Ind.

SPARERIBS AND LIMA BEANS

3 pounds spareribs	2 large onions
1 cup dried lima beans	1 cup apple cider
4 cups cold water	Salt and pepper

Soak lima beans in cold water for several hours. Drain, add 4 cups water and salt. Cover and cook slowly until beans are tender, about 1½ hours. Place a layer of lima beans in an oiled baking dish, season with grated or finely diced onion, add another layer of lima beans. Fill dish. Have spareribs cut into pieces for serving. Place on lima beans and pour the cider over all. Cook uncovered in a moderate oven (350°F) until spareribs are tender, about one hour.

Mary Osadjan, Chicago, Ill.

SPARERIBS AND PIGS FEET

1½ pounds spareribs
2 pigs feet
½ small head cabbage
1 pound, or large can
  sauerkraut
1 medium onion

1 teaspoon salt
¼ teaspoon pepper
1 tablespoon shortening
1 tablespoon bacon drippings
1 tablespoon flour

Cut spareribs in serving pieces, add pigs feet, 1 cup water, salt and pepper. Precook in pressure cooker about 15 minutes. Transfer to big kettle, add another cup water, cook about half hour. Cut cabbage, add to spareribs and add the sauerkraut. Brown 1 tablespoon shortening and the bacon drippings, and finely chopped onion. When light brown, add 1 tablespoon flour and mix till brown, pour into cabbage and sparerib mixture and cook about 20 minutes longer.

Elizabeth Cerajewski, Whiting, Ind.

JELLIED PIG'S FEET

4 pounds pigs feet (whole)
Water to cover
1 tablespoon salt
6 whole black peppers

1 whole onion (with skin)
1 clove chopped garlic
Paprika

Burn skin of pigs feet by holding over gas flame. This is optional. Wash well in warm water, then place in kettle and add enough water to cover well. Bring to a boil and skim. Lower heat and simmer slowly. Add garlic, salt, whole black pepper and onion, which has been sliced. Cook altogether until meat falls apart from the bones (about 5 or 6 hours). Strain and pour into dishes, add meat cut into pieces, and let stand over night in a cool place. Before serving sprinkle with paprika.

Mary Pataky, Whiting, Ind.

JELLIED PIG'S FEET

4 pigs feet, split
1 rounded tablespoon mixed
  whole spice

½ teaspoon salt
Clove of garlic
1 large onion

Cook all of the above ingredients together until tender 4 to 5 hours, or in pressure cooker for 30 minutes. Cool and remove the bones, then strain the liquid into bowls and add the cut up meat, set aside to jell. Serve cold.

Florence Ribovich, Hammond, Ind.

SAUERKRAUT STEW

1½ pounds pork	1 tablespoon flour
1 whole onion	¼ teaspoon salt
2 tablespoons shortening	1 tablespoon paprika
1 can sauerkraut	¼ cup milk

Put shortening into pan; add cut up onion, fry till light brown; add paprika; then add the meat and enough water to cover all, and cook for 1 hour. Add the sauerkraut to the meat and cook about 20 minutes longer. Into milk, add salt and flour, blend well then add to the meat and kraut mixture. Cook for another ten minutes and serve.

Ludmila Sacik, Ford City, Pa.

MAČANKA *(Pork Shoulder and Kidney in Brown Gravy)*

½ pound pork shoulder	1 onion
2 pork kidneys	1 tablespoon salt
6 cups water	

Cook slowly for 2 hours the day before. The next day prior to use; melt 3 heaping tablespoons lard in skillet, add ¾ cup of flour and 1 clove garlic, brown the flour, then add the minced garlic.

Now add the juice of meat to the browned flour. Make a gravy to a desired thickness. Add 3 tablespoons of vinegar. Use the meat from above juice, add it after cutting into small pieces and add to the gravy. Serve with homemade bread. This is an excellent Sunday brunch or luncheon dish.

Mary Skurka, Whiting, Ind.

BAKED HAM

Put into kettle a large uncooked ham (15 to 20 pounds). Cover with water, add one large onion, 3 cloves garlic and allow to come to boil. Then simmer or boil slowly for about 6 hours, or until tender. Let stand in water over night. In the morning remove from water and let stand on rack. Remove bone and tie ham, when cold it is ready to slice.

Rose Fedorko, Whiting, Ind.

SMOKED BAKED HAM

Wash well one ham, and rub into it brown sugar on all sides. Place in roaster, pour over it one can crushed pineapple and roast for about three hours. Baste once every hour and turn over in pan. After baking for 2½ hours, start testing to see if well done.

Veronica Radocha, Coaldale, Pa.

FRESH HAM BAKED

Purchase either half or a whole fresh ham. Wash thoroughly and salt well on all sides. Set aside for several hours. Pare two whole apples and add to the roaster with ham. Also add one large onion cut in slices, one carrot cut in pieces, add black pepper and bake in preheated oven at 375°F, for two or three hours, depending on size of ham. Turn meat over in pan as it is baking, about half hour intervals. Allow to bake only until tender. Serve hot.

Veronica Radocha, Coaldale, Pa.

BAKED HAM AND PINEAPPLE

2 slices 1 inch thick, ready
  cooked ham
6 slices pineapple

⅓ cup brown sugar
3 sweet potatoes, cooked, cut in
  half

Cut ham into 6 servings. Place in greased baking dish. Top each with pineapple. Fill pineapple centers with brown sugar. Top pineapple slice with sweet potato half. Bake uncovered at 325°F for 45 minutes. Serves 6.

Mary Skurka, Whiting, Ind.

BARBECUED HAM SANDWICHES

1 pound sliced baked or boiled
  ham
1 pound chopped ham
1 cup catsup

1 tablespoon brown sugar
Salt and pepper to taste
1 tablespoon vinegar
2 tablespoons water

Combine all ingredients except meat and cook in covered double boiler, about half hour. Add meat, heat well and serve between fresh split buns.

Anna Matava, Donora, Pa.

HAM A LA KING

2 cups boiled or baked ham
1 can mushrooms, or 1½ cups
  fresh mushrooms
5 tablespoons salad oil
2 tablespoons chopped pimientos
5 tablespoons chopped peppers

1 tablespoon capers
½ teaspoon salt
3 cups rich cream
2 tablespoons butter
2 yolks
Paprika

Brown the mushrooms for 5 minutes in the oil. Add the diced ham, capers, peppers and pimiento, then season with salt and paprika. Make a white sauce of the fat, flour and cream. Beat the egg yolks and add gradually to the white sauce. Add the ham mixture, mix thoroughly and serve on toast.

Mary Osadjan, Chicago, Ill.

HAM AND POTATOES AU GRATIN

1½ cups cooked ham, diced	3 tablespoons flour
3 cups cooked potatoes, diced	2 cups milk
4 tablespoons butter or margarine	Pepper to taste
1 small onion, minced	
½ cup cheddar or american cheese, diced	
2 tablespoons fine, dry bread or corn flake crumbs	

Put diced ham and potatoes in shallow, greased 1½ quart baking dish. Melt butter or margarine. Add onion and cook until golden. Blend in flour. Gradually add milk and cook, stirring until blended. Season with pepper to taste and add cheese. Stir until cheese melts. Pour over diced ham and potatoes. Sprinkle with crumbs. Bake in hot oven (400°F) 45 minutes or until slightly browned on top. Serve with tossed salad and hot rolls. Serves 4.

Donna Pesenko, Hammond, Ind.

HAM LOAF

1st PART	2nd PART
2 pounds ground pork	½ cup vinegar
1 pound ground beef	¼ cup water
1 pound smoked ham	½ cup brown sugar
1 cup milk	2 teaspoons dry mustard
1 cup bread crumbs	
2 eggs	

Mix thoroughly the ingredients in the first part and form into two loaves (pack firm), put into greased pan and pour over same the 2nd part that has been thoroughly mixed. Bake in 350°F oven for 1 hour.

Veronica Gluvna, Lorain, Oh.

COMPANY HAM LOAF

1 pound ground pork	2 cups bread crumbs
1 pound ground veal	2 eggs
1 pound ground smoked ham	1 cup milk

Mix the above ingredients and shape into 1 or 2 loaves. Bake from 1½ to 2 hours. While loaf is baking, make the following sauce:

⅔ cup vinegar	½ cup brown sugar
2 teaspoons dry mustard	

Pour off fat from loaf and pour over sauce. Lastly spread on the ham loaf.

Mary Kukuch, East Chicago, Ind.

UP SIDE DOWN HAM LOAF

1½ pounds ground beef
¾ pound ground ham
1½ cups milk
2 cups bread crumbs

2 eggs
½ teaspoon prepared mustard
4 slices pineapple

Mix altogether, except pineapple. Cut pineapple slices in half and lay in a border around the bottom of the loaf pan. Place half of maraschino cherry in the inside of half circle, and pack the ham mixture on top. Bake at 350°F about 1 hour. Serve hot or cold.

Emilia Krull, Whiting, Ind.

HAM AND SWEETS SCRAMBLE *(Yields 4 to 6 servings)*

3 cups chopped cooked ham
3 tablespoons chopped onion
¼ cup butter or margarine
2 tablespoons flour
½ cup pineapple juice

½ cup pineapple bits
⅓ cup brown sugar, firmly
  packed
3 cups sliced cooked sweet
  potatoes

Pan-fry onion in butter in a heavy skillet. Blend in flour. Add pineapple juice and cook until thickened. Stir in pineapple bits, brown sugar, and ham. Arrange sweet potatoes on top. Cover and simmer for 10 minutes. Serve hot.

Courtesy Swift and Co., Chicago, Ill.

NOTES ON BACON

Bacon should not be frozen since within a week the flavor of the fat may begin to show first stages of rancidity. So, wise buying, limited storage at 38 to 40°F, and proper cookery all contribute to the service of perfect bacon.

NEW COOKERY TRICK: Start cooking bacon without separating the slices. Just remove the number of slices in one piece and put the remaining section back in the refrigerator. Put the selected number of slices in a cold skillet and heat slowly. Turn and separate the slices as the heat loosens them. In this way the slices are not torn by trying to strip off the chilled slices.

Fry and turn and keep the heat low. A bit of burned bacon spoils the flavor. And, do not pour off the drippings during the cooking. This fat helps float the slices and makes possible complete browning of the entire slice without raw or burned spots. Also, more bacon can be fried at one time since the cooking depends on the heat of the melted fat rather than the heat of the bottom of the pan.

Remove each slice as it is cooked. Tongs are good for this. Drain on soft paper and keep the bacon hot until serving time.

OVEN BAKED BACON

When ½ pound or more bacon is desired for one meal, oven baking is a time saver. Heat the bacon in a hot oven (450°F) a minute or two. Then separate the slices and place each slice separately on a wire rack set in a baking pan. Bake in a hot oven (400°F) about 10 minutes or until as brown as desired. The bacon will brown on both sides without turning.

BROILED BACON

It is easy to broil bacon. Place on broiler pan, bring to a warm condition, then separate slices and broil slowly, allowing the fat to drip into bottom of broiler.

Courtesy of Swift and Co., Chicago, Ill.

BACON BEAN BAKE (Yield: four servings)

8 slices bacon
2 cups (No. 2 can) baked beans
¼ cup chopped onion
⅓ cup catsup

Mix beans, onion, and catsup in a 1 quart casserole. Top with bacon slices. Bake in a hot oven (400°F) about 50 minutes or until beans are hot and bacon is crisp. (The bacon slices should be laid in lattice style.)

Courtesy of Swift and Co., Chicago, Ill.

- VEAL -

VEAL ROAST

3 pounds roast of veal (leg or shoulder)
2 cups hot water
Pepper to taste
½ green pepper, chopped or sliced
2 teaspoons salt
3 strips of bacon

Place roast in a greased roaster with part of the hot water, season and roast in medium oven, occasionally baste with hot water and when partly roasted add the green pepper and spread the slices of bacon over top of roast. Continue to roast until tender. One cup of sour cream may be added to gravy.

Anna Vargocko, Joliet, Ill.

VEAL CUTLETS

Veal steak ½ inch thick
Salt and pepper
Well beaten egg to which add one tablespoon water
Bread crumbs
Tomato sauce
Swiss cheese

Cut veal into desired pieces and pound with meat tenderizer or with plate. Sprinkle with salt and pepper. Cover with bread crumbs, dip into egg, then cover with crumbs again. Let meat stand on waxed paper for about 30 minutes, turning it over several times while standing. Fry slowly in desired shortening until golden brown on one side, then fry second side. Place on a trivet, add ½ cup water to drippings; cover and cook slowly about 30 minutes or until tender, adding more water if it appears dry. Then pour a spoonful of tomato sauce on each cutlet and place a slice of Swiss cheese over it, sprinkle with salt, cover saucepan again and continue to cook very slowly about 10 minutes more; or meat may be placed in a baking sheet after the first steaming. Then pour tomato sauce and parmesan cheese over meat and bake in a 400°F oven, about 10 minutes.

Anna B. Yasso, Cleveland, Oh.

VEAL GOULASH

1 pound veal or other lean meat
Drippings
1 small onion
3 tablespoons flour

1½ cups boiling water
1 cup white turnips, diced
1 cup celery, diced
2 cups potatoes, diced

Cut veal in small pieces. Melt a tablespoon of drippings in frying pan, add veal and sauté till well browned, remove to casserole. Add 4 tablespoons drippings to pan and cook onions till slightly browned. Add to veal, cover and bake in moderate oven. An hour before serving add remaining vegetables. Bring to boil over fire and return to oven. Before serving, thicken liquid. Bake in 300°F oven for 3 hours.

Sophie Gometro, Nesquohoning, Pa.

CHOP SUEY

1¾ pounds veal and pork, cut
 in cubes
2 tablespoons lard
2 tablespoons molasses
8 medium onions, sliced
3 stalks celery, diced

½ bottle soy sauce
½ cup water
Salt and pepper to taste
2 small cans mushrooms
1 can bean sprouts (drained)

Brown meat cubes in lard. Add celery and water, cover and simmer five minutes. Meanwhile combine molasses, soy sauce, salt and pepper, blend until smooth. Stir into first mixture and again bring to boiling point with the well drained sprouts and onions. Add mushrooms.

Susan M. Mrazik, Homestead, Pa.

CHOP SUEY

1 pound veal	1 chicken bouillon cube
1 pound lean pork	1 tablespoon molasses
1 large stalk celery	1 tablespoon brown sugar
4 or 5 large onions	2 teaspoons salt
1 tablespoon chop suey sauce or	½ teaspoon pepper
Soy sauce	

Cut meat into small pieces. Place into skillet one teaspoon lard and when hot add the meat gradually and fry until brown.

Cut celery and onions in small pieces and place into a sauce pan. Add the browned meat and cover with 2 or 3 cups water. When meat and vegetables are tender then season and add soy sauce and bouillon cube. Simmer to blend the flavors then add the molasses and sugar, allow to simmer a while longer then thicken as follows:

Mix 3 tablespoons cornstarch, ⅔ cup of water. Add to the chop suey and boil for 5 minutes. Serve with rice or chow mein noodles.

Mary Skurka, Whiting, Ind.

MOCKED CHICKEN LEGS

3 pounds veal steak, sliced thin	Bread crumbs
1 pound pork shoulder or	1 beaten egg to which one
lamb steak	tablespoon water is added
Salt to taste	¼ cup shortening
Pepper and a little nutmeg	½ cup hot water
or marjoram	

Cut the pork or lamb steak into 2 inch pieces. Cut the veal steaks into long narrow strips, between 1 and 1½ inches wide. Place wooden skewer through a 2 inch piece of pork or lamb. Sprinkle with salt, pepper and other seasoning, and roll a long strip of veal steak over it. Be sure to roll it tightly, and at the same time shape it to look like a drum stick. Hold in place with toothpicks. Season and roll in bread crumbs, dip in egg, and roll again in bread crumbs. Let stand on waxed paper, turning occasionally, for about 30 minutes.

Place shortening into skillet and when hot add a few pieces to brown. Do not turn meat until browned, use a medium flame. When all the meat has been browned then add the hot water and mix well with the drippings. Place the meat in the skillet and cover. Allow to simmer slowly for 1½ to 2 hours. Thicken gravy with cornstarch or flour before serving, and season.

These mocked chicken legs may be turned into a buttered baking dish after browning. Place a little hot water 3 to 4 tablespoons on the bottom of the dish. Cover and bake in a moderate oven, 350°F. Once or twice during the baking make sure there is a little moisture in the baking dish. If dry add a little more hot water to keep meat from drying out. Serve with a gravy made from the drippings in the skillet by adding water and blending well. Thicken with cold water mixed with cornstarch. Cook 5 minutes and strain. Season. Yield: approximately 10 servings.

Justine Uhlarik, Chicago, Ill.

STUFFED VEAL BREAST

1 veal breast, weighing between 2 and 2½ pounds
12 slices white bread, two days old
½ pound veal, parboiled first then ground fine
1 egg

1 cup celery stalk, chopped fine
1 cup onion, chopped fine
¼ cup butter or margarine
Salt and pepper to taste
½ teaspoon marjoram, crushed fine

When purchasing a veal breast ask the butcher to make a pocket. Wash and wipe thoroughly. In 2 cups water, parboil the veal, drain, set aside the water for later use, and cool the meat. When cool grind the meat on a fine meat cutter. Into the ground meat add the bread cut into small cubes. Add the celery and onions that have been sautéed in the butter or margarine. Add the seasonings and egg. Mix thoroughly, if too dry, add a little water from veal. When mixture is ready, stuff the pocket cavity and sew up the ends. Place in a greased roaster and pour over same the balance or all of the water the veal was cooked in. Season the meat, and place over 3 strips of bacon crosswise. Place in oven preheated to 325°F and roast uncovered for 1 hour. Baste occasionally. Then add 1 sliced onion around the roast and cover the pan. Return to oven and continue roasting until meat is tender when pricked with a fork. Thicken gravy before serving.

Anna Krcha, Chicago, Ill.

STUFFED VEAL BREAST

1 veal breast, weighing between 2 and 2½ pounds
10 slices dry bread
½ pound ground beef or beef liver, ground or scrapped
1 egg

2 sticks celery including leaves
1 tablespoon soft butter
Salt and pepper to taste
Approximately half cup milk or water

Pour water over bread and allow to stand until bread is well puffed up. Drain off the water and squeeze out all the water in the bread. Place in a bowl, add to it the balance of ingredients. If liver is used be sure to remove all skin and vein before scraping or grinding. The amount of liquid is regulated according to the need. Some slices of bread are larger than others. Be sure the dressing is not watery. Fill cavity and sew up opening. Place in a roaster and bake in a moderate oven almost two hours, or until tender.

Anna Cmarik, Chicago, Ill.

VEAL BIRDS

1½ pounds veal steak   **½ pound sliced bacon**

Trim fat and gristle from meat, cut into small pieces, 2 x 4 inches. Salt and pepper only one side of each piece. Roll meat with salted side in. Wrap each piece with ½ strip of bacon and fasten toothpick. Place on skillet (no grease) and brown uncovered for about ½ hour or until dark brown. About 15 minutes on each side. Pour off excess bacon drippings, if any, leaving 2 tablespoons in pan. Pour 2 cups water over the birds, cover and simmer for about 1 hour or until tender. Remove birds onto plate and cover. Put 2 tablespoons flour into ½ cup water and make a smooth paste. Pour the paste slowly into the juice, stirring constantly. If too thick, add more water. Bring the gravy to a low boil, salt and pepper to taste. Submerge birds into the gravy, cover and let simmer for about 10 seconds more.

Mary Perhack, Whiting, Ind.

RISSOTO *(for 2)*

1½ pounds veal stew   **1 cup canned peas**
1 large onion, chopped fine   **¾ cup cooked rice**
2 tablespoons lard   **Salt, pepper, paprika to taste**

Brown onion in lard. Add cubed meat and brown. Add salt, pepper and paprika, stir to mix well. Add hot water to cover and simmer for 45 minutes. Add more water if needed. Cook rice till tender, add to meat together with canned peas, mix well and serve.

Mrs. John Perko, Cleveland, Oh.

JELLIED VEAL LOAF

2 pounds veal   **1 tablespoon gelatin**
1 onion   **2 tablespoons water**
1 stalk celery   **3 hard cooked eggs**
Stuffed green olives   **1 tablespoon salt**

Cut veal in small pieces, add onion, celery and seasoning. Cover with water. Cook until veal is tender and stock amounts to one cup. Grind meat mixture. Soak gelatin in two tablespoons of cold water and dissolve in boiling stock. Place layer of meat mixture in loaf pan; add three whole hard cooked shelled eggs and stuffed olives in rows; cover with the remaining meat mixture. Sliced eggs and olives may be laid on top of the loaf. Pour stock to which gelatin has been added over entire mixture. Chill in refrigerator. Cut loaf so eggs and olives are cut crosswise and in center of each slice.

Mary Osadjan, Chicago, Ill.

VEAL STEW WITH DUMPLINGS

1 pound veal, cut in cubes	1 bay leaf
2 cups hot water	1 teaspoon Worcestershire sauce
½ cup diced carrots	½ teaspoon salt
½ cup diced potatoes	Dash of pepper
¼ cup chopped celery	1 eight ounce can tomato sauce
¼ cup chopped onions	½ cup lima beans or peas

Roll meat in flour; brown in fat (hot). Add hot water; cook 1 hour. Add vegetables, bay leaf, worcestershire sauce, and seasonings; continue cooking 30 minutes. Add tomato sauce, bring to boiling; drop dumplings from spoon. Cover tightly and steam without lifting cover 12 to 15 minutes. Serves 4 to 5.

Dumplings; Sift 1 cup flour, ½ teaspoon salt and 1½ teaspoons baking powder, add ½ cup milk, and 2 tablespoons melted fat or salad oil to make soft dough.

Mary Salat, Chicago, Ill.

- LAMB -

SPRING LEG OF LAMB

Soak leg of lamb over night in a pan of brine (cold water, salt, black pepper), to which one clove of garlic has been added, 1 onion, ½ teaspoon thyme. In the morning, pour off brine, wash lamb and put into roaster, rub with salt, paprika and black pepper. Add one sliced onion and dot lamb with margarine. Add one cup water and roast until done. To brown, keep basting and uncover last ½ hour.

Ann Kuva, Indiana Harbor, Ind.

ROAST LEG OF LAMB

Wash leg of lamb, then salt and pepper same. Place in a roasting pan and add one teaspoon ground marjoram, one stick celery, one carrot, and one cup tomato juice. Bake in a preheated moderate oven (350°F) for two or three hours or until done. During process of roasting, baste occasionally.

Veronica Radocha, Coaldale, Pa.

LEG OF MUTTON

Wash the meat and place in roaster. On top of meat pour some olive oil (about 1 tablespoon), 1 clove of garlic well minced, ¼ teaspoon crushed marjoram, salt and pepper. Add 1 large can of tomatoes. Cover roaster and roast in a 350°F oven till meat is tender. This may take 2 to 3 hours. If roasting in a moderate oven it will not be necessary to add more liquid. Some pared potatoes may be added to roast, about 1 hour before meat is tender.

Mary V. Haydu, Braddock, Pa.

BROILED LAMB PATTIES

1½ pounds ground lamb	2 tablespoons chopped parsley
½ cup milk	1 tablespoon grated onion
½ cup bread crumbs	¼ teaspoon garlic salt
1 tablespoon bacon drippings	1 teaspoon salt

Mix ingredients together and shape into eight patties. Broil at 350°F. Place broiler pan three inches from flame. Broil 10 minutes, then turn, broil 5-10 minutes longer.

Ella Vlasaty, Braddock, Pa.

GRILLED LAMB CHOPS

Select 1 or 1½ inch thick loin chops with the kidneys attached. Place on a preheated broiler pan, and broil in oven with temperature set at 375°F, for about 10 minutes on each side. The chops should be about two inches or little more from flame. Season and serve immediately.

During broiling period oven door should be left partly opened.

Margaret Mihalik, Indiana Harbor, Ind.

LAMB STEW

3 pounds lamb shoulder, cut in serving pieces	Salt and pepper to taste
3 medium onions, sliced	1 teaspoon paprika
3 tablespoons shortening	2 cups tomatoes, fresh or canned
1 cup thick sour cream	½ cup minced parsley

Simmer the onions in the shortening until light brown. Add the well seasoned meat, and sear. Add about ¾ cup hot water, cover and cook slowly until meat is almost tender. Add tomatoes and continue cooking. Be sure to add water, if necessary, to prevent burning. Just before serving add the cream and parsley and cook a few minutes longer.

Margaret Mihalik, Indiana Harbor, Ind.

- MEAT SPECIALTIES -

FRESH SAUSAGE *(Frišne Klobasy)*

5 pound pork butt	2½ tablespoons salt
2 pounds leg of veal	1 teaspoon pepper
5 yards casings	1 clove garlic, chopped
½ teaspoon caraway seed	2 cups cold water

Grind meat in coarse grinder and mix well with other ingredients. Wash casings thoroughly and stuff them with meat mixture. Place in refrigerator or cold place until ready to cook. Cook 30 to 40 minutes.

Anna Stanek, Whiting, Ind.

HOME MADE PORK SAUSAGE *(Klobasy)*

10 pounds lean pork shoulder, chopped or ground fine	1 tablespoon black pepper
	4 tablespoons salt
3 cloves garlic, chopped fine	1 quart water

Combine meat, garlic and seasonings. Add water and mix thoroughly. Cut casings to desired length. Run water through before stuffing. Cook with sauer kraut and spareribs. Serve hot.

George Kochis, Whiting, Ind.

POTATO SAUSAGE *(Bobrovecke Droby)*

½ peck potatoes (Idaho)	2 medium onions
½ pound beef casings	1 teaspoon marjoram
½ pound bacon	½ teaspoon peppermint leaves
1 pound pork shoulder	crushed
2 tablespoons salt	

Cook pork shoulder in small pan, with enough water to cover, for 15 to 20 minutes. Cut bacon in small cubes, place in pan and fry until golden brown. Add ground onions and fry 5 minutes longer. Pare and quarter potatoes; keep in cold water until ready for use. Grind pork shoulder and potatoes with medium cutter, add simmered bacon, onion, salt, pepper, marjoram and dried peppermint leaves. Add the water the meat cooked in and mix well. Have casings clean and fill them any desired length. (I always place the casings under the faucet and let the water run through, and cut them 24 inches, then I proceed to fill.) Place the sausages in boiling water, lower heat, and cook slowly for one hour. Remove from heat and cool. To use as a delicious side dish, fry sausages on both sides in a little fat. Also, this filling can be baked in a loaf pan like a pudding, by adding three tablespoons of flour.

Anna Stanek, Whiting, Ind.

JATERNICKY *(Slovak Meat and Rice Sausage)*

8 large onions
1 pound lard
2 pounds pork hearts
1 pound pork liver
3 pounds pork lungs or plucks
3 pounds pork shoulder

4 tablespoons black pepper
2 tablespoons marjoram
Salt to taste
1 pound pork casings
6 pounds rice

Cook rice in hot salted water till done. Cook all meat, cool, then grind meat and mix well with rice. Fry onions in lard, add to rice and meat mixture, mix thoroughly and stuff into pork casings. This recipe is for a large amount, if for five or six people, make ⅓ of this recipe.

Margaret Marko, Whiting, Ind.

HEARTS *(Beef, Veal or Pork)*

2 medium hearts
2 tablespoons chopped onion
3 tablespoons fat
¾ teaspoon salt
¼ teaspoon celery salt

1 sixteen ounce can consomme
2 whole cloves
3 whole black peppers
1 bay leaf

Clean hearts and cut into small pieces. Lightly brown onion in fat. Roll heart pieces in flour and brown, then add the consomme and 1 can water. Add seasonings and cook about 1½ hours over low flame, stir occasionally. More water can be added if needed. Keep tightly covered.

Mary Salata, Chicago, Ill.

BREADED LIVER AND ONIONS

Peal off outer membrane, then dip liver in egg and milk mixture, then in cracker crumbs and fry quickly on both sides until brown. Set aside when all the liver is browned. Fry 1 or 2 onions until lightly brown, then put a layer of onions, a layer of liver etc., cover and simmer over low flame until tender

Mary Salata, Chicago, Ill.

LIVER IN CREAM

2 pounds calf's liver
2 cups milk
Salt and pepper

2 onions, chopped
1 cup cream
¼ cup butter

Slice liver, place in a shallow dish and add milk. Cover and place in refrigerator for 12 hours. Remove liver, drain. Season and roll lightly in flour. Brown onions in butter. Remove and fry liver on both sides quickly in same butter. Reduce heat, add onions and cream to cover and simmer for 15 minutes.

Mary Osadjan, Chicago, Ill.

CHICKEN LIVERS AND RICE

2 tablespoons butter	1 cup rice
1 large onion, chopped	1 teaspoon salt
3 chicken livers, chopped	4 cups water
½ cup water	

Sauté onions in butter until brown. Add chicken livers and ½ cup of water, simmer for 5 minutes. Wash rice well, and add 4 cups of water. Boil 10 minutes. Add chicken livers to rice. Simmer covered, until rice is done. Season with salt and pepper.

Mary Skurka, Whiting, Ind.

STUFFED SUMMER SQUASH

Take 1 long narrow summer squash, wash and peel carefully, cut off ends. Remove center with spoon, by scooping out enough pulp to leave a one inch rind without breaking through. Then fill cavity with the following filling:

FILLING	2 teaspoon, minced parsley
1 pound ground meat	1 cup cooked rice
Salt and Pepper to taste	¼ teaspoon crushed marjoram
1 small onion, grated	1 egg slightly beaten

Mix above ingredients thoroughly and stuff the squash cavity.

Into a greased roaster place a layer of canned tomatoes, or pour into bottom of the roaster 1 can tomato soup diluted with ½ cup of milk. Add salt and 2 teaspoons sugar, 1 tablespoon grated onion, and mix. On this bedding, place the filled squash. Lay 3 strips of bacon over the top and place into moderate oven, 350°F, for about ½ hour. Cover and lower heat to 325°F, and continue baking until squash is tender.

When finished carefully lift with pancake turners or large spoons under each end of squash, and place on platter without breaking if possible. Place roaster on top of burner and thicken gravy with 1 tablespoon of flour and about ½ cup of milk, well blended and free of lumps. Simmer a few minutes and serve in gravy dish. Serve with potatoes and salad and you will have a tasty luncheon.

Anna Krcha, Chicago, Ill.

TORTILLA FOR ENCHILADAS

½ cup white cornmeal	1½ cups all purpose flour
1 teaspoon salt	1 cup hot water

Put cornmeal and hot water in bottom of mixing bowl, let soak and stand until cool. Then add rest of the ingredients. Mix and make dough of consistency to be rolled out. Divide dough into small balls. Roll each ball thin and round the size of bottom of the frying pan, cook each side until light brown and bubbly.

The less grease used the better.

Warm tortilla in little oil in frying pan, next chop onion, thin slice cheddar cheese, some pieces of chicken or roast and lettuce. Place mixture in middle of tortilla, season to taste with salt and pepper, roll and eat while warm.

If you wish you may cook the onion in little margarine.

Mary Kollar, Olyphant, Pa.

EASTER BREAD LOAF WITH MEAT (Velkonočna Hlavka)

3 pounds veal

(Some cooks boil a calf's head, then scrape off the meat and grind.) Boil the veal and grind it, when cooled slightly. Cover to keep warm. Into a cup place 1 cake of yeast, mix it with about ¼ cup warm milk and 1 to 2 tablespoons of sugar, allow this to stand in warm place to rise. Separate 18 eggs, beat the egg yolks.

Place the warm ground veal into a bowl, add the beaten egg yolks, salt to taste, pinch of pepper and a little ground cloves. Then mix in the risen yeast sponge, add 1 cup of bread crumbs, ½ cup of sifted flour and mix well. Then fold in the well beaten egg whites. The dough should be thick enough so that a wooden spoon will stand upright in the dough. If dough looks thick, add a little milk to make it thinner. Set this dough in a warm place to rise. Then mix again and put the dough into pans which have been well buttered and spread with bread crumbs, to prevent sticking to pans. Allow to rise in a warm place, then brush with beaten egg that has been diluted with a little milk and bake in oven at 350°F for about 1 hour. Cool and remove from pans.

Mary V. Haydu, Braddock, Pa.

EGG DUMPLINGS FOR FRICASSE

1 egg
2 cups flour

1¼ cups milk or water
½ teaspoon salt

Combine all ingredients, and if necessary, add more liquid. The dough should be soft and beaten well until it becomes elastic, then drop by one-half teaspoons into boiling salted water. Cook for 5 to 7 minutes, or until all rise to top of water. Drain well. Serve with gravy or mixed with melted brown butter.

- POULTRY -

SOUTHERN FRIED CHICKEN

1 fryer
4 carrots
2 tablespoons butter

1 celery heart
Salt and pepper to taste

Soak chicken in milk 4 hours, then wipe good and dry. Melt butter, add carrots and celery, let simmer till light brown, then add chicken and allow to cook in pan until nice and brown. Add salt and pepper to taste. You will find this style of chicken very good and should be accompanied with Southern Hot Biscuits served with honey.

Irene Galos, Warrenville, Ill.

BOILED ITALIAN CHICKEN

Chicken halves
Buttermilk
Salt, pepper, garlic salt and accent

Flour
Sweet paprika

Select very small chicken halves. Wash in cold water, but DO NOT SOAK. Marinate in buttermilk for about one hour. Then shake off the excess buttermilk and season each half on both sides with salt, white pepper, little garlic salt and accent - sprinkling lightly.

Arrange halves in well greased shallow pan. Sprinkle tops of chicken halves with flour and sweet paprika. Bake at 325°F for about 1½ hours or little longer, depending on degrees of tenderness desired. Baste very frequently with the following sauce (chicken should be golden brown):

¼ cup margarine - part olive oil
½ cup water or chicken stock
2 medium chopped onions

1 tablespoon lemon juice
2 tablespoons orange juice

Cook onions in margarine until yellow then add other ingredients and simmer together. Do not cover chicken except with wet paper if necessary. After removing the chicken add a little more water to the pan to make about a cup of thin gravy and spoon over chicken before serving.

Vincentian Sisters of Charity, Bedford, Oh.

CHICKEN PAPRIKAS

4 pound chicken
1 tablespoon butter
1 tablespoon sweet paprika
Sprinkle of sharp cayenne pepper

1 small onion
1 pint sour cream
Salt to taste

Take the butter and onion and set on medium flame to brown a little, add the sweet paprika and dash of cayenne pepper, then add cut up chicken in small portions and stew slowly till well done.

Then take one pint sour cream, mix in 1 tablespoon flour and stir into chicken when done, do not boil, just stir lightly and simmer slowly until it thickens slightly.

Mary Janovcik, Cleveland, Oh.

CHICKEN PAPRIKAS

Heat 1 tablespoon lard and equal amount of butter, add three sliced onions, and simmer to light brown. Cut chicken in pieces; place in hot shortening. Salt to taste and cover to simmer in its own juice, then keep adding hot water for gravy. Add 4 bay leaves, ½ teaspoon sharp red pepper. When chicken is about tender, add 1 cup sour cream. Do not cook too much after cream is added. Lastly add 1 tablespoon flour blended in cold water until smooth, add to gravy. Cook about 5 minutes and serve.

Mary E. Grega, Cleveland, Oh.

STEWED CHICKEN

1½ tablespoons cooking fat	**¼ teaspoon pepper**
1 tablespoon butter	**1 cup warm water**
1 medium onion	**1 cup cold water**
1 teaspoon salt	**1 tablespoon flour**

Cut chicken into serving pieces. Heat cooking fat and butter; cut up the onion and brown. Add chicken, pepper and salt. Cook chicken slowly until light brown, add ½ cup warm water, put cover on and let cook for about 20 minutes, then add another ½ cup warm water and let cook until tender. Blend well 1 tablespoon flour and 1 cup water and pour over chicken. Cook until it thickens. Serve with mashed potatoes.

Elizabeth Cerajewski, Whiting, Ind.

CHOP SUEY (Chicken or Pork)

1 green pepper	**2 cups sliced onion**
1 cup pork or chicken, sliced thin	**1 teaspoon sugar**
	1 teaspoon salt
1 - 4 ounce can mushrooms	**3 teaspoons soya sauce**
2 tablespoons oil or shortening	**1 can bean sprouts, drained**
2 cups thinly sliced celery	**1 teaspoon cornstarch**

Heat shortening or oil in pan until very hot. Add meat and fry for 2 minutes, add salt and mix; then add 2 teaspoons soya sauce and mix; then add celery, onion and green pepper and mix; then add bean sprouts and mushrooms and the rest of the ingredients and mix thoroughly. Then take 1 teaspoon corn starch and 1 teaspoon soya sauce in a little cold water, mix well and add to chop suey. Stir until gravy reaches desired consistency. Serve with steaming hot rice. Makes 3 to 4 servings.

Mary Kollar, Olymphant, Pa.

BUTTER-CRISP CHICKEN

Fried chicken makes ideal party fare whether served hot or cold. Serve the crusty fried chicken pieces on your handsomest platter on the buffet table. Make it easy for your guests to identify their favorite pieces by arranging- the dark meat pieces on one side of the help-your-self platter and white meat portions on the other side. Serve the wings, back, and the bonier pieces if you wish, or plan extra amounts of chicken when purchasing in order to save these bonier pieces for another day service for family. A large jellied fruit salad, buttery hot rolls and good coffee are the perfect companion foods for the chicken.

Fried chicken for a crowd is easy to prepare as Butter-crisp or Oven-easy Fried Chicken.

Butter-crisp Chicken may be browned and stored in the refrigerator for final cooking in a swathing of butter in a moderate oven. These last minutes before serving cause the hostess no worry.

5 - 2-pound ready-to-cook chickens	**1 teaspoon pepper**
4 cups flour	**3 tablespoons paprika**
2 tablespoons salt	**2 pounds shortening**
	½ pound butter or margarine

Cut chickens into serving pieces. Rinse in cold water, drain well. Put flour, salt, pepper, and paprika in a large paper bag. Shake 3 or 4 pieces of chicken in the bag at a time to coat thoroughly. Heat enough shortening in a heavy skillet to make a layer ¾ inch deep. Place chicken in hot shortening. Brown on both sides. Place chicken, one layer deep, in a shallow baking pan. Brush chicken generously with melted butter. Bake in a moderate oven (350°F) until tender, about 30 to 40 minutes. Baste with melted butter after 15 minutes of baking. If chicken cannot be served at once, reduce oven heat. Brush chicken with more melted butter. Yields 20 servings.

Courtesy of Swift and Co., Chicago, Ill.

OVEN-EASY CHICKEN

Oven-easy Fried Chicken eliminates all pre-browning in a skillet. A large pan and a dependable oven make this a good method to use when cooking for a crowd.

5 - 2 pound ready-to-cook chickens	**1 teaspoon pepper**
4 cups flour	**3 tablespoons paprika**
2 tablespoons salt	**1 pound butter or margarine**

Mix flour, salt, pepper, and paprika in a large paper bag. Melt butter in a shallow baking pan in a hot oven (400°F). Shake 3 or 4 pieces of chicken in the bag at a time to coat thoroughly. Remove baking pan from oven and place chicken, skin side down, in a single layer. Bake in a hot oven (400°F) for 30 minutes. Turn chicken. Bake another 30 minutes, or until tender. If chicken cannot be served at once, reduce oven heat. Brush chicken with more melted butter. Yields 20 servings.

Courtesy of Swift and Co., Chicago, Ill.

CHICKEN HAWAIIAN

Put Chicken Hawaiian on your next bridge luncheon menu. It's an intriguing service of the favorite fried chicken which dresses up boneless chicken breasts in a piquant sauce. Serve the browned, crispy coated chicken on toast topped with the sauce and slivered almonds. A platter of the chicken and asparagus spears makes tempting luncheon fare. Yields 4 servings.

2 chicken breasts
Finely sieved bread crumbs
Fat for frying
2 tablespoons lemon juice
¼ teaspoon curry powder (optional)
4 slices toast

1 egg, slightly beaten
1 teaspoon salt
1 cup pineapple juice
1 tablespoon cornstarch
1 tablespoon sugar
Slivered almonds

Split breasts in half. Remove bones, keeping meat in one piece. Dip in egg. Roll in bread crumbs. Season with salt. Pan-fry in ¼ inch hot fat in a heavy skillet until brown. Remove fat from pan. Combine juices, cornstarch, curry, and sugar. Pour over chicken. Cover. Cook slowly 20 to 25 minutes. Serve on toast. Top with slivered almonds.

Courtesy of Swift and Co., Chicago, Ill.

TURKEY

1st Step: If a frozen bird is purchased it will be necessary to thaw the bird, remove pin feathers, singe and wash thoroughly. Remove the kidney and lung tissues embedded inside on either side of backbone. Cut off the oil sack at the back. Wash inside of turkey, thoroughly with cold water and dry. Store in refrigerator until ready for use.

If the turkey is not fully drawn when purchased, then request the butcher to draw same, and if possible ask him to remove the leg tendons, cut off the feet, remove crop from back. An incision should be made down center back of the neck skin, so the skin may be pulled away from the neck. Then the neck is cut off close to the body. The crop and wind pipe will be removed from this opening. The oil sack at the back should be cut away. The bird should be washed thoroughly with cold running water. After the lungs and kidneys have been removed, wash thoroughly the inside of the turkey and dry. The bird then may be placed in the refrigerator until ready for use.

2nd step: Remove the bird from the refrigerator at least two hours before ready to stuff. Just before stuffing allow hot water to run through the inside of the bird and well between the thighs. Make stuffing and fill the cavity of the neck end lightly; fold skin over the back, and hold it in place with a steel skewer. Fill body from lower end, again make sure you do not pack, but fill lightly, so there is room for expansion. Fasten this opening with steel skewers or sew up with a heavy thread. If skewers are used place them across the opening at regular intervals. Then with a heavy twine (store twine) bring the skin edges together by "lacing" the twine around the pins. Truss the bird by folding the wings to form a triangle, and thus catch the wings under the back of the bird. It may be necessary to hold the wings in position with a metal skewer, securing each wing with the skewer. Tie a cord around lower end of each drumstick, to prevent the muscle and skin from drawing away from the leg bone during roasting. Push drumstick close to body (be careful, not too tightly), then tie the legs by the end to the tail piece. Pull the string firmly and in shape. The bird is now ready for the roasting pan and should go immediately into the oven.

3rd step-ROASTING: Weigh stuffed bird after it has been trussed and estimate total time of cooking. Lay the stuffed trussed bird on a heavy rack in an open pan. Brush skin thoroughly with melted shortening. Cover top of bird with a soft muslin cloth or a double thickness of cheese cloth that has been well saturated with melted shortening. If the cloth is first wet and then dipped in the shortening it will accept the fat more readily. Place bird on the side and set in oven preheated at either 300°F or 325°F, depending on size and age of bird. Then turn bird on other side and roast, when brown on this side, place the bird for the last ⅓ of the time to roast on the back with breast side up. Baste thoroughly the breast or place bacon strips over same to keep from drying out. The bird may be basted with fat from the pan and right over the cloth covering same. If bird is not browned well, then remove the cloth the last hour of roasting. Always make sure the bird is placed into oven with thighs first, or the heavy part of the bird goes to the rear of the oven.

Note: After serving, remove the stuffing from the cavities and refrigerate both bird and stuffing. Reheat only that portion of stuffing that is to be used. Use the stuffing within four days.

If stuffing is made of giblets, sausage or other meats, be sure to cook before adding to stuffing. If left over broth is used in stuffing, be sure it was not refrigerated over 24 hours, and be sure it was thoroughly chilled.

Large birds may be best roasted unstuffed, and the stuffing may be baked separately in a separate pan. This for birds over 22 pounds.

TURKEY DRESSING

This is enough dressing to fill a cavity and front opening of a 25 pound bird.

1 loaf, more or less, white bread. Do not remove crusts.
Toast, butter lightly, and cut into ½ inch cubes
1 cup finely chopped parsley
¾ cup minced onions
½ cup butter or oleomargarine, part drippings

Cook in shortening onions, and parsley for about five minutes over medium heat. Add to cubed bread. Then add the following seasoning:

1 teaspoon sage	**1 teaspoon pepper**
Salt to taste	**1 to 2 teaspoons accent**

Mix all ingredients lightly but well. Wipe turkey dry inside and stuff, but do not pack the dressing. Always bake the turkey uncovered in a pan with low sides. Baste it frequently and cover only with wet delicatessen paper.

Vincentian Sisters of Charity, Bedford, Oh.

ROAST DUCK

Duck is prepared for roasting in the same manner as chicken, except that little or no trussing is necessary. Wash the bird and cut off the neck. Sprinkle the inside with salt, and fill the cavity with favorite stuffing. Sew up the opening and truss or tie. Place in roasting pan with about 1 cup hot water for basting. If duck is very fat, start it in a very hot oven for about twenty minutes. Then reduce the temperature to 325°F and continue roasting, basting frequently. The fat from the pan should be poured off occasionally and the basting done with hot water or fruit juice, rather than with the fat in the pan.

SPICED FRUIT DRESSING FOR DUCK

3 cups toasted bread cubes	3 tablespoons chopped onion
1 orange rind, grated	¼ teaspoon ground cloves
1 teaspoon grated lemon rind	¼ teaspoon ground ginger
½ cup cubed oranges	1 teaspoon salt
3 cups cubed apples	⅛ teaspoon pepper

Combine all ingredients and fill body cavity without packing. This recipe makes enough dressing for a 4 pound duck (drawn).

RABBIT FRY (Man's meal)

1 minced onion, medium sized	2 cups "still' white wine
1 tablespoon minced parsley	1 cup vinegar
6 whole black peppers	1 tablespoon salt

Skin, clean and cut up the rabbit in serving portions. Prepare a marinade with the above ingredients, then pour over the rabbit in a large earthenware crock. Cover and let stand for twenty-four hours. Keep the crock in a cool place. When ready to fry, combine 1 cup of flour, 2 tablespoons of paprika, 2 teaspoons pepper and 2 teaspoons salt. Place in paper bag. Lift out the meat from the marinade, pat dry and drop one piece at a time into the paper bag and shake vigorously. Heat one pound of lard in a heavy skillet until hot, but not smoking. Drop rabbit pieces into the hot lard one by one and brown thoroughly on each side. Remove from skillet onto a cookie sheet which is covered with heavy brown paper. Place in a 250°F oven for 15 to 25 minutes. Serve with mashed potatoes.

Mary Kollar, Olyphant, Pa.

VENISON WITH GRAVY

Wash and salt the meat. Prepare a marinade as follows: 1 part vinegar to 3 parts of water, with sliced onions, carrots, celery, parsley and allspice. Marinate the meat in this for two or three days. On the third day remove some of the liquid. Place the meat into the oven to roast, using the remaining liquid when necessary. When meat is done, make a gravy with sour cream.

- FISH -

CRAB DELIGHT

2 tablespoons chopped green
    pepper
2 tablespoons butter
2 tablespoons flour
½ teaspoon dry mustard
¼ teaspoon salt
½ teaspoon worcestershire sauce
Pinch of cayenne

1 cup strained tomatoes
1 cup grated processed cheese
1 egg, slightly beaten
¾ cup milk, scalded
1 cup flaked crabmeat
¼ cup chopped pimiento
Toast or patty shells

Cook green pepper in butter for three minutes. Add flour and mix until smooth. Combine seasonings, tomatoes, cheese and egg, add to the first mixture. Cook in top of double boiler for 10 minutes. Add scalded milk slowly, stirring constantly. Add crabmeat and pimiento and just heat through. Serve on toast or patty shells. Serves four.

Anna K. Hruskovich, Whiting, Ind.

DEVILED CRAB

1 medium onion, chopped fine
2 tablespoons celery
1 tablespoon green pepper
1 pimiento (canned), minced
Salt and pepper to taste
1 can crab meat

1 teaspoon dry mustard
1 teaspoon worcestershire sauce
1 hard boiled egg, chopped
1 egg
1 tablespoon bread crumbs

Combine onion, celery, green pepper and pimiento. Chop fine and sauté in hot fat, until cooked through, but not browned. Then combine dry mustard, salt, pepper, worcestershire sauce and hard boiled egg. Combine the two mixtures, and raw egg and the bread crumbs. Chill well, then mold into patties. Just before serving dip into beaten egg and bread crumbs and fry. Serve with salad. Fresh or canned Tuna, Lobster or Shrimp, may be substituted for the crabmeat.

Mary Kollar, Olyphant, Pa.

CODFISH BALLS

2 cups raw potatoes
1 cup shredded salt codfish
1 teaspoon butter

⅛ teaspoon pepper
Dash of celery salt
1 egg

Cut potatoes into small pieces; place in a deep sauce pan and cover with cold water; add fish and boil until potatoes are tender. Remove from fire and drain. Add butter and seasonings and beat well with fork. Beat the eggs and gradually add to the mixture and allow to stand until cool. Drop by tablespoons into hot fat 1 inch deep, fry until golden brown. Drain on brown paper; serve immediately, garnish with parsley.

Virginia Harar, Chicago, Ill.

TO FRY FISH

The flavor of all fried fish is enhanced by adding sliced raw onion to the cleaned, salted fish. Fish should be salted for at least an hour before frying. An over night salting is even better. Do not use the onion from the fish. Frying in butter gives the best flavor, but butter burns easily. It is adviseable to use half butter and half shortening, unless fish is watched very carefully.

BAKED FISH

Pike or other fish, cut into
   serving pieces
Salt and pepper to taste
1 sliced onion
1 egg, slightly beaten

1 tablespoon water
Flour for dredging
1 cup bread crumbs
½ cup butter or half butter and
   half other shortening

Add onion to fish, season with salt and pepper, keep in refrigerator over night. Wipe fish dry and dredge in flour. Thin the beaten egg with water, then dip fish in egg and roll in bread crumbs. Fry in butter, or other shortening until brown. Place in baking pan and bake about 25 minutes in 350°F oven. Garnish with lemon slices and parsley.

Justine Kasovsky, Chicago, Ill.

PAPRIKA FISH

4 pound fish
¼ to ½ cup butter or shortening
2 large onions, sliced
½ teaspoon pepper

1 cup top milk or cream
2 tablespoons paprika
Few grains garlic salt

Use bass, small haddock, mackerel, snapper or kingfish. Cut fish in thick steaks or fillets. Use either a roasting or baking pan, depending on the size of fish. Melt butter or other shortening, add sliced onions and sauté until light yellow. Place in bottom of baking dish and place fish over the onions. Beat the cream or top of milk lightly with the paprika, salt, pepper and garlic salt, and pour over the fish. Place in a moderate oven (375°F) and bake, basting frequently. Fillets may take 20 to 25 minutes to bake, large steaks may take 30 to 35 minutes. Remove fish to service dish and strain sauce over fish. Sprinkle with a little chopped parsley and serve with boiled potatoes, that have been sprinkled with parsley and dredged with melted butter.

Florence Hovanec, Whiting, Ind.

FISH IN TOMATO SAUCE

Split six herring (fresh) or any other fish, as lake trout, white fish etc., using less fish if larger in size, and lay open in greased baking dish or casserole. Salt and brush with melted fat. For 15 minutes bake in 350°F oven. Then pour over the following hot sauce and bake 15 to 20 minutes additionally.

Tomato Sauce: Sauté one tablespoon chopped onion in one tablespoon shortening. When onion is tender blend in one tablespoon flour, stir until slightly yellow, then add one cup tomatoes. Season with 1 teaspoon salt and few grains pepper. A dash of nutmeg or marjoram may be added. Simmer together for about 5 minutes. Serves 6.

Mary Vevurka, Indiana Harbor, Ind.

BAKED STUFFED HADDOCK FILLETS

2 fillets of haddock
Lemon juice
1 cup bread crumbs
⅔ cup milk

¼ cup melted butter
¼ pound mushrooms, peeled
Salt and pepper

Place one fillet on greased baking dish, brush with lemon juice, sprinkle with salt and pepper. Mix bread crumbs with melted butter. Reserve half the crumbs and to remainder add chopped mushrooms, ½ teaspoon salt, and dash of pepper. Put the stuffing on the fillet of fish, cover with the other fillet. Brush with melted butter or fat, pour milk over the top. Brown quickly at 450°F, then reduce heat to 350°F and bake for 25 minutes, basting frequently. Then sprinkle with salt and the reserved crumbs and bake until crumbs are brown.

Anna Matava, Donora, Pa.

TUNA NEW ORLEANS

1-6½ oz. can chunk tuna
1 can cream of celery soup
1 fresh tomato, quartered
½ cup chopped green pepper

1 - 6 oz. can of mushrooms
1 tablespoon chopped onion
2 tablespoons butter

Sauté quartered tomato, green pepper, mushrooms and onion in butter for 5 minutes. Add cream of celery soup. Heat for 5 minutes. Add tuna and heat another 5 minutes. Serve over hot rice or toast points.

Donna Pesenko, Hammond, Ind.

HERRING FILLETS IN CUSTARD

Buy fresh herring and remove heads and tails and center bone. Wash thoroughly. Place into a buttered shallow casserole or baking dish (7½ x 12 x 1½) a layer of herring fillets, sprinkle with salt and pepper, grate a little onion over same, then pour over it the following: Beat one egg, and pour into it 1½ cups milk and season lightly. Over top sprinkle either paprika or little nutmeg and set to bake, until custard is set, approximately 30 minutes. Remove with pancake turner in squares to serving dish and serve hot.

A thicker custard may be made with 2 eggs instead of one.

When fish is placed in baking dish, place the skin side down.

Loretta Kasovsky, Chicago, Ill.

PICKLED HERRING

3 whole salt herrings
2 large onions, sliced
1 cup vinegar

4 peppercorns
6 whole allspice
1 teaspoon sugar

Soak herrings in cold water for at least 24 hours. Change water every 8 hours or more often. Save the milch from herrings. Skin and remove bones, if you wish, and cut each herring into pieces for serving. Arrange a layer of onions in deep dish and a layer of herring and top with onions. Boil vinegar and cool. Rub milch through fine sieve, mix with vinegar, sugar and spices and pour over the herring and onions.

Mary Vevurka, Indiana Harbor, Ind.

SALMON BAKED WITH CREAMETTES

1 cup sour cream
¼ cup butter

1 box of Creamettes
1 large can salmon

Cook Creamettes until tender, add salt. Drain and place in baking dish, buttered. Cover Creamettes with drained, flaked salmon, add salt, pepper and pour cream and melted butter over all. Bake in 400°F oven, for 20 to 30 minutes.

Anna Kolena, Chicago, Ill.

SALMON LOAF WITH EGG SAUCE

½ cup rice
3 tablespoons butter
4 tablespoons flour
½ teaspoon salt
Dash of pepper
2 cups milk

2 tablespoons chopped green
  pepper
4 tablespoons chopped celery
1 No. 2 can pink salmon
1 egg beaten
1 teaspoon minced parsley

Cook rice for 5 minutes only in 3 cups of rapidly boiled salted water. Drain. Melt 2 tablespoons of the butter, blend in flour, salt, pepper and add milk. Cook with constant stirring until thickened. Add celery, green pepper and parsley and continue cooking over hot water about 10 minutes. Remove skin from salmon and flake. Combine with rice, beaten egg and white sauce. Turn into buttered bread pan, pat top until smooth and level, dot with rest of butter, and bake in moderate oven 325°F for 45 minutes. Yields about 5 servings. Serve with egg sauce.

EGG SAUCE

2 tablespoons butter	½ teaspoon salt
2 tablespoons flour	Dash of pepper
1½ cups milk	½ teaspoon horseradish
2 hard cooked eggs	1 teaspoon lemon juice

Melt butter, blend in flour and add milk slowly, stirring well. Cook directly over flame until sauce boils, stirring constantly; then lower flame and simmer for 5 minutes. Remove from stove, add salt, pepper, horseradish, lemon juice and one of the eggs sliced. Use second egg, also sliced for garnishing. Yield 1½ cups. This salmon loaf with egg sauce is a fine dish for bridge or company luncheon.

Anna Krcha, Chicago, Ill.

SALMON LOAF

1 large can salmon	¼ teaspoon salt
½ cup bread crumbs	2 tablespoons grated onions
½ cup catsup, mixed with water	¼ teaspoon nutmeg or marjoram
2 eggs	

Mix well the above ingredients. The amount of catsup used depends on how much one likes tomato flavor - be sure to thin out the catsup with water. Bake in a buttered casserole or bread pan, in a moderate oven about 35 to 45 minutes, or until nicely brown.

Ann Grapenthin, Chicago, Ill.

BAKED SHRIMP

1 pound uncooked shrimp	3 tablespoons chopped parsley
2 eggs, well beaten	¼ cup grated sharp cheese
½ cup fine dry bread or cracker crumbs	1 small clove minced garlic
	Salt and pepper to taste
1 large onion chopped fine	One 8 ounce can tomato sauce
¼ cup butter, melted	

Directions continued on page 341.

Peel off shells and remove black vein from shrimp. Dip in eggs and bread crumbs. Place in buttered shallow baking dish. Saute onion in butter until lightly browned. Sprinkle over shrimp. Top with parsley and cheese. Mix garlic, salt and pepper with tomato sauce and pour over all. Bake in moderate oven 350°F for 30 minutes.

Agnes Lukso, Chicago, Ill.

SAVORY SHRIMP STUFFED GREEN PEPPERS

6 green peppers, even in size
1½ cups cooked rice
1½ cups cooked shrimp
¼ teaspoon pepper
½ clove garlic, minced
1 cup boiling water
⅓ cup tomato paste

2 teaspoon curry powder
1 cup chopped fresh tomatoes
1 cup bread crumbs
¼ cup butter, melted
1 teaspoon grated onion
1 teaspoon salt

Cut a thin slice from stem end of peppers and remove seeds. Place peppers in pan, add boiling water, cover and steam 5 minutes. Combine cooked rice and chopped cooked shrimp. Mix with onion, salt, pepper, garlic, curry powder, tomato paste and chopped fresh tomatoes. Stand drained peppers in standard size muffin cups. Fill peppers with shrimp mixture and top with buttered crumbs. Bake in moderate oven 375°F for 20 minutes. Serve immediately.

Anna Kolena, Chicago, Ill.

STUFFED WHITE FISH

3 pound white fish
2 medium sized onions
2 eggs, beaten
Salt and pepper to taste
½ teaspoon celery salt

2 teaspoons chopped parsley
¾ cup bread crumbs (or use
   enough bread cubes to make
   a firm filling)

Clean fish thoroughly and remove head. Pull skin off of the fish, being careful not to tear it. Remove meat from bones and put through grinder with the onions. Add the eggs. Season and add bread crumbs or bread cubes, mix thoroughly. Fill skin of fish with the mixture, making it look natural. Place on a well buttered baking dish and bake in a 375°F oven. Occasionally spread melted butter over top and just before finished sprinkle lightly with paprika. Remove to platter and serve at once.

Note the filling must not be watery, if not thick enough, or firm enough, add more onions and bread crumbs. The seasoning should be used in good measure for best flavor.

STUFFING FOR ANY FISH

Quantity of ingredients will depend on amount needed. Sauté in butter onions, add a few thin slices of garlic, or few grains of garlic salt, add chopped fine parsley. When onions are slightly brown, add a little water and cover to cook through the onions and parsley, add seasonings and mix with bread cubes. Add beaten egg or eggs, depending on amount needed. Mix well and use in fish as stuffing by just flapping over the loose skins, keep in position with two or three toothpicks, and bake in a buttered baking dish, in moderate oven for about 40 minutes.

This filling may be spread over fillets of fish and topped with other fillets, season the fish, then pour over the top either catsup mixed with a little water to keep dressing moist, or plain milk. Bake in moderate oven, from 35 to 40 minutes.

Katarina Labash, Chicago, Ill.

- MEAT ACCOMPANIMENTS -

FRIED APPLES

1 apple　　　　　　　　**¼ teaspoon sugar**
1 beaten egg　　　　　　**1½ tablespoons shortening**
¼ teaspoon cinnamon

Core apple, and cut into ¼ inch thick slices. Dip in egg, sprinkle with sugar and cinnamon. Fry slowly in shortening until brown and tender.

Mary Ruzicka, Muskegon, Mi.

APPLES WITH HORSERADISH

4 tart apples, peeled
4 to 5 tablespoons prepared horseradish
¾ teaspoon sugar

Grate apples into bowl containing horseradish and sugar. Blend while grating to prevent discoloration of apples. Taste, if too tart or strong, add a little more sugar.

Emily Jurinak, Chicago, Ill.

SPICED APPLESAUCE

1 quart cooked sweetened apples, strained
3 tablespoons red cinnamon candies
2 tablespoons grated orange rind and juice
1 teaspoon lemon juice
1 teaspoon lemon rind
1 teaspoon cinnamon

While the applesauce is still hot, add the cinnamon candies, grated orange and lemon rind, orange and lemon juice. Mix thoroughly and add cinnamon. Mix again, and bring to a boil and simmer until candies are dissolved. Cool and serve as meat accompaniment.

Catherine Otrembiak, Chicago, Ill.

BEET HORSERADISH

1 pound boiled beets
2 ounces fresh horseradish
2 tablespoons vinegar
1 teaspoon sugar
1 teaspoon salt
Pinch of pepper
½ cup water

Grate beets and horseradish. Combine vinegar, sugar, salt, pepper and water. Bring to a boil. Pour over grated beets and horseradish. Mix thoroughly. Store in jar in refrigerator and serve with meats.

Sophie Kaminsky, Whiting, Ind.

CRANBERRY SAUCE

1 pound cranberries
1½ cups sugar
1 cup water

Boil water and sugar together for 5 minutes. Add cranberries and boil for 5 minutes more. Put through a strainer. Pour into a mold and let stand until firm.

Josephine Leslie, Whiting, Ind.

PEARS IN CREME DE MENTHE

Drain juice from can of pear halves. Pour over them ¼ cup lemon juice and ¼ cup of Creme de Menthe. Let this stand on ice for about 2 hours. This makes and excellent garnish and dish for a lamb dinner.

Vincentian Sisters of Charity, Bedford, Oh.

FRIED PRUNES

25 to 30 prunes
25 to 30 almonds, blanched
BATTER
2 well beaten eggs
1 tablespoon sugar
Salt to taste
1 teaspoon baking powder
Flour, enough to make a runny
  batter
¾ cup milk

Soak prunes over night. Remove the pit, making as small a hole as possible, fill the center with a nut meat. Make a batter by adding sugar and salt to the beaten eggs. Sift flour and baking powder together. Gradually add flour mixture alternately with the milk to the beaten eggs. Beat until smooth. Drop a prune into the batter and lift out with a tablespoon of the batter. Drop into a frying pan with some butter. (Since butter burns easily, some shortening may be added to the butter). Enough batter should be used with each prune to make a small cake batter all around the prune. Turn to brown on both sides. Serve hot with roast pork dinner.

Catherine Otrembiak, Chicago, Ill.

- SAUCES -

BASIC SAUCE

2 tablespoons butter	1 cup soup stock, meat
2 tablespoons flour	or vegetable
4 tablespoons cream or top of milk	Salt and Pepper to taste

Heat butter, blend in flour until smooth. Allow to brown slightly for flavor, and add soup stock gradually, constantly stirring. Soup stock should be cold, if not, then add a little cold water first. After sauce is smooth and free of all lumps, bring to a boiling point. Then lower heat, and cook for three minutes. Add cream and seasoning, when well blended and heated through, remove from flame and serve.

CAPER SAUCE

Add two tablespoons capers to each cup white sauce or to the above basic sauce.

EGG SAUCE

Add hot basic sauce to two slightly beaten egg yolks. Beat thoroughly.

DILL SAUCE

Add one tablespoon or more freshly chopped dill to each cup of basic sauce. Do not boil after addition of dill as it will lose its color and aroma.

MUSHROOM SAUCE

Add ½ cup chopped, sautéed or cooked mushrooms to each cup of basic sauce.

PARSLEY SAUCE

Add two tablespoons minced parsley to each cup of basic sauce, cook slightly, just enough to soften the greens. These sauces are popular in the Slovak kitchens. A little variety from the white sauce commonly used in America.

Helen Kocan, Whiting, Ill.

BROWN ONION SAUCE *(Cibulový Privarok)*

4 tablespoons shortening	Salt and pepper to taste
1 tablespoon sugar	3 tablespoons flour
1½ large onion, sliced	½ teaspoon minced chives
1¾ cups stock or bouillon	(optional)

Melt fat and add sugar, cook until brown. Add onions, stirring steadily to brown evenly. Add flour and continue to stir until well blended and browned. Add the cold stock gradually to prevent lumping. When sauce is smooth add the seasoning and cook for 10 minutes over low flame. Press through a strainer and reheat. Add the chives. Makes about 1 cup sauce.

Katherine Labash, Chicago, Ill.

SAUCE FOR BAKED FISH

1 onion, chopped	3 slices American cheese
1 tablespoon butter	1½ cups milk
1 tablespoon flour	

Melt butter, add onion and flour, brown. Add cheese and milk. Cook until cheese is melted and sauce is thick, pour over fish, put in oven and bake for 20 minutes.

Barbara Bires, Pittsburgh, Pa.

CAPER SAUCE FOB LAMB

Use the broth in which the lamb has been boiled. Make a paste with butter and flour, enough for the desired amount of sauce. Let brown only very slightly, then add hot broth, enough to make a sauce the consistency of thin white sauce. Just before serving add ¼ cup drained capers.

Do not boil gravy with the capers. This spoils the flavor of both the capers and the sauce.

For boiled pork; use broth in which pork has been boiled.

Vincentian Sisters of Charity, Bedford, Oh.

NECK BONE SPAGHETTI SAUCE

2½ to 3 pounds neck bones
1 large can of tomatoes
1 small can tomato sauce

1 clove of garlic
Salt, sugar and pepper

Wash the neck bones, and brown them in a skillet in about 1½ tablespoons lard. Then transfer the neck bones to a deep pot, add the tomatoes and the tomato sauce and add about 1 cup water. Puncture the garlic clove and add that to the pot, adding seasonings according to taste. Cover and let simmer for about 3 to 3½ hours. The meat will fall off the bones, and the bones then can be removed. This leaves a little of the meat in your sauce which makes it very delicious. Serve on your macaroni or elbow macaroni. You may use grated cheese over the sauce.

Irene Van Offelen, Chicago, Ill.

RAISIN SAUCE

1 cup raisins
6 cloves
1 cup water
⅔ cup brown sugar
1 teaspoon cornstarch
½ teaspoon cinnamon

¼ teaspoon salt
Dash of pepper
1 tablespoon vinegar
¼ teaspoon Wocestershire sauce
1 tablespoon butter

Wash raisins. Cook slowly with cloves and water for 10 minutes. Mix together sugar, cornstarch, cinnamon, salt and pepper. Add to raisins and cook stirring constantly until slightly thickened. Add vinegar, sauce and butter stirring constantly until blended. Serve hot on baked ham.

Elizabeth Dedinsky, Whiting, Ind.

TARTAR SAUCE

2 hard cooked egg yolks
Salt and pepper to taste

Mix the two hard cooked egg yolks until quite smooth and free from lumps. Salt and pepper to taste.

1 cup of olive oil
1 tablespoon chopped green onion tops
3 to 6 tablespoons white vinegar
2 tablespoons mayonnaise

Gradually beat in 1 cup olive oil with 3 to 6 tablespoons white vinegar. Add the very finely chopped green onion tops with the mayonnaise to the egg yolk mixture and beat until very smooth. This can be served hot or cold. Good for appetizer sauce. Excellent with scallops, fish, shrimp or cold cuts and cold chicken.

Vincentian Sisters of Charity, Bedford, Oh.

TOMATO SAUCE

Heat shortening or oil in a sauce pan, when hot add about ½ pound ground beef, which has been mixed with an egg, salt and pepper. Stir until browned. Then add can of tomatoes, chopped parsley, small can tomato paste, and small clove of garlic. Let all this simmer for about three hours.

This sauce is good for Macaroni, Spaghetti and Baked Egg Plant.

Maria V. Haydu, Braddock, Pa.

TOMATO SAUCE

Use fresh or canned tomatoes, boil, then strain or put through sieve. Make a thickening agent by browning flour in butter or shortening, adding a little cold water, enough to make a smooth paste, add salt, pepper and sugar to taste and mix with the tomato. Cook a few minutes and be sure it is free of lumps. Use with boiled meats or roasts. This gravy or sauce is somewhat thick, but smooth. A little garlic may be added or celery salt if desired.

Helen Kasza, Chicago, Ill.

TOMATO FRIDAY SAUCE

1 clove garlic, minced
1 onion, minced
¼ cup oleomargarine, or butter, or part olive oil

Cook together about five minutes the above ingredients, then add:

1 can tomato paste
1 No.2 can tomatoes
½ cup water

Cook for 1 hour, allowing it to simmer. Season with salt, little pepper, a lump of raw butter, ¼ cup sherry at the most.

Vincentian Sisters of Charity, Bedford, Oh.

CHOW CHOW FISH SAUCE

1 large bottle chow chow, chopped fine
½ cup chili sauce
1½ cups mayonnaise

6 hard cooked eggs, riced
1 tablespoon minced parsley
1 tablespoon minced green pepper

Combine above ingredients and serve over fish.

Ann Grapenthin, Chicago, Ill.

CUCUMBER SAUCE FOR FISH

Peeled and grated 1 large cucumber
1 cup mayonnaise
1 tablespoon minced chives or grated onion
1 tablespoon lemon juice
½ teaspoon prepared mustard

Prepare the cucumber, and combine with mayonnaise and other ingredients. This goes well with fish molds and Mousse made of salmon.

Margaret Mihalik, Indiana Harbar, Ind.

SAUCE FOR CRABMEAT COCKTAIL

2 tablespoons horseradish
1 cup chili sauce
Juice of ½ lemon
Salt

1 teaspoon Worestershire sauce
Few drops Tobasco sauce
Chopped celery

Mix and use in proportion to amount of crabmeat.

Ann Hruskovich, Whiting, Ind.

Pastry

BUTTER PIE SHELL

1 cup flour	⅛ teaspoon salt
1 tablespoon sugar	½ cup butter, or margarine

Combine all the above ingredients. Bake at 300°F for 45 minutes to 1 hour. Cool and fill with any filling.

Clara Kucka, Whiting, Ind.

HOT WATER PIE CRUST

3 cups flour, sifted	½ cup boiling water
1 cup plus 1 tablespoon lard (have lard at room temperature)	2 teaspoons salt

Put lard in rather large bowl. Pour boiling water over it. Stir with fork, add flour and salt all at once. Keep mixing only with fork. Do not press or squeeze, just pick up all particles of flour. Put in refrigerator, then use as needed.

Helen Cross, Whiting, Ind.

PIE PASTRY

2 cups sifted all-purpose flour	⅔ cup shortening
1 teaspoon salt	5 to 6 tablespoons cold water

Sift flour and salt together, cut shortening into flour with pastry blender or 2 knives. Then gradually add cold water, handling as little as possible.

This dough can be used at once or covered and kept in refrigerator. Makes one 2-crust pie or 2 quick pastry shells.

Veronica Radocha, Coaldale, Pa.

FLAKY PIE PASTRY

2 cups sifted flour	¼ teaspoon salt
1 cup shortening	About 5 tablespoons ice water

Sift flour and salt together and cut in shortening with 2 knives or pastry blender, until you have many particles of shortening which are surrounded and separated by flour, like peas of various sizes. Add ice water a little at a time, using only enough to hold dough together. Just squeeze the dough together. Do not mix.

Divide the dough into 2 parts, a larger part for the bottom crust. When you roll the top crust do not flour the top heavily, but lightly or just roll under waxed paper.

The board may be well floured. Place carefully on filled pie, sprinkle sparingly but evenly with milk and lightly with sugar. Brown quickly but finish pie at a lower temperature so as to cook the fruit but not burn the crust.

Vincentian Sisters of Charity, Bedford, Oh.

ANGEL PIE

4 egg whites
½ teaspoon cream of tartar

Beat well until eggs are stiff, add cream of tartar and then add 1 cup sugar gradually until it's like marshmallow cream. Bake 1 hour in 275°F oven. Let cool.

Filling: One package lemon pie filling. Prepare according to directions on package. Cover with ½ pint whipping cream. Cool 4 hours in refrigerator before serving.

Mary Salat, Chicago, Ill.

APPLE BUTTER TARTS

1 recipe pastry
½ cup sugar
1 tablespoon cornstarch
½ cup water
1 cup apple butter

1 teaspoon grated lemon rind
½ cup raisins
2 egg yolks
2 egg whites
2 tablespoons sugar

Mix sugar and cornstarch, add water, apple butter, lemon rind and raisins. Cook in double boiler until thickened. Add beaten egg yolks. Cook 10 minutes. Roll pastry to ⅛ inch thickness. Cut in rounds 3 inches in diameter. Bake at 450°F until delicately browned. Spread filling between layers of pastry and over top. Cover with meringue using 2 egg whites and 2 tablespoons sugar. Bake at 325°F for 10 minutes.

Ella D. Vlasaty, Braddock, Pa.

APPLE PIE

2 large apples, pared and
** cooked soft**
1 egg yolk
1 cup sugar

Piece of butter size of egg
1 teaspoon flour
1 teaspoon lemon juice

Mash well cooked apples. Add well beaten egg yolk. Add sugar, butter, flour and lemon juice. Mix well and pour into rich pie crust. Bake in quick oven. Serve with whipped cream.

Bernadette Evans, Homestead, Pa.

SOUR CREAM APPLE PIE DELUXE

¾ cup sugar
2 tablespoons flour
⅛ teaspoon salt
1 cup dairy sour cream
½ teaspoon vanilla
2 cups finely cut, pared tart apples
1 egg, well beaten
1 9-inch pie shell, unbaked

TOPPING
⅓ cup sugar
⅓ cup flour
1 teaspoon cinnamon
¼ cup butter

Sift sugar, flour and salt together. Add cream, egg and vanilla and mix until smooth. Fold in apples. Place in pie shell. Bake in hot oven 425°F for 15 minutes. Lower heat to 350°F and bake 30 minutes longer. Blend sugar, flour, cinnamon and butter and sprinkle top. Return to oven and bake at 350°F, 15 minutes longer. Upon removing pie from oven, put immediately in refrigerator until cool.

Helen Kalata, Chicago, Ill.

APRICOT TARTS

½ cup butter
2 cups flour

2 packages cream cheese
1 large can apricots

Rub butter into flour, then add cheese, work until the dough is soft. Roll out and cut into squares. Put one apricot on each square and fold ends together. Put on cookie sheet and bake in moderate oven about 30 minutes. When done, sprinkle with cinnamon and powdered sugar.

Susan Galgan, Chicago, Ill.

BUTTERMILK PIE

Orange Pastry: Any plain pastry recipe

Use orange juice instead of water and add ¼ teaspoon orange rind (grated) and one tablespoon sugar, line a 10 inch pie tin.

FILLING
1 cup sugar
3 tablespoons flour
4 tablespoons butter, melted

¼ teaspoon salt
3 eggs
2 cups buttermilk

Mix sugar, flour and gradually add egg yolks and buttermilk. Stir until smooth, then add melted butter and stir well. Fold in stiffly beaten egg whites and pour into pastry lined pan. Bake in hot oven 450°F for a moment and then reduce heat to 350°F, bake for 45 minutes.

Mary Jeanne Galos, Warrenville, Ill.

DIFFERENT CHERRY PIE

½ cup cherry juice
½ cup water
1 cup sugar
3 tablespoons cornstarch

⅛ teaspoon salt
2 cups pitted cherries
1 - 8-inch baked pastry shell
¾ cup grated American cheese

Combine juice, water, sugar, cornstarch and salt; heat to boiling and cook until thick. Remove from heat and add cherries. Cool. Pour into cooled baked pastry shell which has been sprinkled with cheese. Chill. Serve with whipped cream. Serves 6.

Mary Skurka, Whiting, Ind.

CHOCOLATE CHIP PIE

24 marshmallows
¼ cup milk
½ pint whipping cream
2 - 1-ounce squares baking
   chocolate, grated fine

CRUST
24 graham crackers, crushed
⅓ cup melted shortening, or
   butter
¼ cup sugar

Crush graham crackers. Mix with sugar and melted butter. Press evenly and firmly around sides and bottom of pie pan. Chill.

Cook marshmallows with milk over boiling water, stir until combined. Cool. Whip cream until stiff. Fold in grated chocolate and cooled marshmallow mixture. Pour into pie shell and chill until firm. Garnish with part of the grated chocolate. Chill in refrigerator till ready to serve. Yield: One nine inch pie.

Leona Zientara, Whiting, Ind.

COCONUT CUSTARD PIE

1½ cups fresh coconut
1 pint milk
3 eggs
¾ cup sugar

¼ teaspoon salt
1 teaspoon vanilla
¼ teaspoon nutmeg

Beat whole eggs, gradually add sugar, then add milk, salt, vanilla, coconut and nutmeg. Pour into unbaked pastry shell and bake in moderate oven about 30 minutes, or until custard is firm.

Veronica Radocha, Coaldale, Pa.

CUSTARD PIE

4 eggs, beaten
⅔ cup sugar
½ teaspoon salt

¼ teaspoon nutmeg
2⅔ cups milk
1 teaspoon vanilla

Beat eggs and beat in sugar, salt, nutmeg. Add lukewarm milk. Beat well, add vanilla. Pour into pastry lined pan. Bake 30 to 35 minutes at 350°F, then 15 minutes at 325°F. Bake just until a silver knife inserted into side of filling comes out clean.

Helen Cross, Whiting, Ind.

GRAHAM CRACKER PIE

20 Graham crackers
⅓ cup sugar

Roll and crush graham crackers and mix with sugar. Save about 2 tablespoons for the top of pie. Add 2 tablespoons Crisco and cold water to the graham cracker mixture to make a paste like dough. Line pie plate. Bake 14 minutes at 375°F.

CUSTARD FILLING

1 pint scalded milk
2 egg yolks
⅔ cup sugar

¼ cup flour
Pinch of salt
1 teaspoon vanilla

Mix egg yolks, sugar and flour, add milk and cook over low flame, stirring constantly. Add salt and vanilla. When crust is cool, fill with custard filling. Beat the egg whites until stiff and add 3 tablespoons sugar. When stiffly beaten, spread over custard. Sprinkle with the reserved graham cracker crumbs and bake about 10 minutes in 375°F oven.

Katherine Dymsia, Braddock, Pa.

LEMON CHEESE CAKE PIE

3 - 3-ounce packages cream cheese
2 tablespoons butter
½ cup sugar
1 whole egg
2 tablespoons flour

⅔ cup milk
¼ cup fresh lemon juice
2 tablespoons grated lemon rind
1 graham cracker crust, 8-inch

Cream the cheese and butter, add sugar and whole egg. Mix well. Add flour, then milk, stir in lemon juice and rind. Pour into unbaked graham cracker pie shell. Sprinkle with crumbs. Bake 35 minutes in moderate oven 350°F. Chill and serve.

Graham Cracker Crust: Crush graham crackers to make 1¼ cups fine crumbs. Add ⅓ cup sugar and ⅓ cup melted butter. Mix well. Reserve ¼ cup of mixture for topping. Press remainder on bottom and sides of 8-inch pie plate. Chill until set.

Beatrice Pihulic, Hammond, Ind.

LEMON CHIFFON PIE

Pastry-Makes one 2 crust 9-inch pie or two 9-inch pie shells

2¼ cups sifted flour **¾ cup crisco**
1 teaspoon salt **¼ cup water**

All measurements level. Sift flour with salt into bowl. Remove ⅓ cup flour. Cut Crisco into remaining flour with pastry blender, fork or two knives, until pieces are the size of small peas. Mix ¼ cup water with the ⅓ cup flour to form paste. Add flour paste to mixture. Mix and shape into a ball, divide dough into two parts. Roll and place in pans. Prick closely. Bake shell in hot oven 425°F, 12 to 15 minutes, or until brown. Cool shells before filling.

FILLING

4 beaten egg yolks **¼ cup cold water**
½ cup sugar **1 teaspoon grated lemon rind**
½ cup lemon juice **½ cup sugar**
½ teaspoon salt **4 stiffly beaten egg whites**
1 tablespoon unflavored gelatin **½ cup heavy cream, whipped**

Combine egg yolks, ½ cup sugar, lemon juice and salt; cook in double boiler until thick, beating constantly with beater. Add gelatin softened in cold water, stir until gelatin dissolves. Add lemon rind and cool, until partially set. Beat remaining ½ cup sugar into egg whites and fold into cooled mixture. Pour into cooled baked shell. Chill until firm. Spread with sweetened whipped cream before serving.

Clara Kucka, Whiting, Ind.

LEMON MERINGUE PIE

2 cups sifted pastry flour
½ teaspoon salt
½ cup cold shortening

2 tablespoons cold water
1 tablespoon cold milk

Sift together, flour and salt 4 times. Mix shortening into flour and salt with blender until mixture has shortening in pieces about size of peas. Stir milk and water into mixture with fork. Gather together dough with fork and roll out on lightly floured pastry board. Place pastry in pie pan and prick with fork. Bake at 450°F for about 15 minutes. Cool.

FILLING FOR LEMON PIE

1½ cups sugar
3 tablespoons flour
4 tablespoons cornstarch
½ teaspoon salt
2½ cups hot water

3 egg yolks, slightly beaten
Juice of 2 lemons
Grated rind of 1 lemon
2 teaspoons butter

Mix together sugar, flour, cornstarch and salt. Stir mixture into hot water. Cook over direct heat until mixture is thick. Beat egg yolks slightly and stir into cornstarch mixture, slowly, stirring constantly. Return to heat for 1 minute, stirring constantly. Remove from heat and stir in lemon juice, rind and butter. Mix well. Cool entirely before adding to cool pie shell. Make meringue by beating 3 egg whites until stiff and dry. Gradually beat in 6 tablespoons sugar and 2 teaspoons lemon juice. Now pour cooled filling into cooled pastry and top with meringue. Bake at 325°F for 20 minutes.

Anna B. Russell, Cleveland, Oh.

LEMON FILLING FOR PIE

1 cup sugar
3 tablespoons flour
½ teaspoon salt
2 egg yolks

Juice of 1 lemon
1 tablespoon butter
1½ cups sweet cream

Mix well the sugar, flour, salt, egg yolks, juice and cream together. Beat the whites of the eggs stiffly and then mix this into the first mixture. Have your baked pie shell ready. Pour this mixture into the pie and put into the oven to bake 400°F, for about 12 minutes, and then lower the heat gradually, and bake a little more.

Martina Gereg, Lorain, Oh.

LEMON-PINEAPPLE CHIFFON PIE

1 package lemon jello
¼ cup sugar
1 cup boiling water
1 can crushed pineapple (small can)

1 large can carnation evaporated milk (thoroughly chilled)
1 package Knox gelatin (plain)
2 - 9-inch backed pie crusts

Dissolve Lemon Jello in 1 cup of hot water, add sugar and chill slightly, not until stiff. Add crushed pineapple and Knox gelatin dissolved in small amount of water. Keep chilled until milk is whipped. Whip Carnation milk with beater until stiff, add Jello and pineapple mixture, pour into 2 baked shells, chill in refrigerator. Top or spread pie with whipped cream. Delicious.

Susan Matuscak, Cleveland, Oh.

MAGIC LEMON MERINGUE PIE

1⅓ cups sweetened condensed milk (1 can)
½ cup lemon juice
Grated rind of 1 lemon or ¼ teaspoon lemon extract
2 eggs
2 tablespoons sugar
1 baked pie shell

Blend together the condensed milk, lemon juice, grated rind and egg yolks. Pour into an 8-inch baked pastry shell or graham cracker crust. Cover with a meringue made by beating the egg whites until stiff and gradually add sugar. Bake until brown in moderate oven 350°F. Chill before serving.

Maria Proskac, Coaldale, Pa.

MILE HIGH PIE

1 tablespoon plain gelatin
¼ cup cold water
½ cup sugar
½ teaspoon salt

4 egg yolks
½ cup crushed pineapple
½ cup sugar
4 egg whites

Soften gelatin in cold water. Mix ½ cup sugar, salt, yolks and pineapple in top of double boiler. Cook mixture until it coats spoon. Remove from stove. Add softened gelatin to mixture and stir until gelatin is dissolved. Let cool slightly until thickened. Beat whites very stiff. Add ½ cup sugar. Carefully fold egg mixture in with egg whites. Pour into baked pie shell. Put in refrigerator to set. Should be chilled at least ½ hour before serving. Top with whipped cream.

Anna Matava, Donora, Pa.

NESSELRODE PIE

1 tablespoon unflavored gelatin
¼ cup cold water
2 cups light cream
2 eggs, separated
Pinch of salt
¼ cup, plus 6 tablespoons
  granulated sugar

1½ teaspoons rum flavoring, or
  1 tablespoon rum
1 baked 9-inch pie shell
Whipping cream
Chocolate shavings

Soak gelatin in cold water five minutes. Scald cream in top of double boiler. Beat egg yolks with fork and stir in salt and ¼ cup of sugar. Add cream slowly to eggs. Return to double boiler and cook, stirring constantly, until slightly thickened (about five minutes). Remove from heat, add gelatin and stir until dissolved. Pour into bowl and chill until custard begins to thicken. Beat egg whites stiff. Add remaining 6 tablespoons sugar gradually and beat until very stiff. Pour into baked pie shell and place in refrigerator to set. Just before serving decorate with whipped cream. Shave baking chocolate and sprinkle over top.

Beatrice Pihulic, Hammond, Ind.

PECAN PIE

1 cup corn syrup
3 eggs
1 cup brown sugar
⅛ teaspoon salt

¼ cup butter, or margarine
1 teaspoon vanilla
1 cup pecans

Beat eggs. Add remaining ingredients, adding melted butter last. Pour into unbaked pie shell over the pecans. Bake in 350°F oven 50 to 60 minutes.

Marcella Halloran, Streator, Ill.

PINEAPPLE WHIPPED CREAM PIE

2¼ cups crushed pineapple,
  canned
¾ cup granulated sugar
1 tablespoon butter
½ teaspoon salt

1½ heaping tablespoons cornstarch,
  dilute in 1½ tablespoons
  cold water
3 egg yolks, slightly beaten
½ pint or more whipping cream
3 tablespoons sugar

Cook pineapple, sugar, butter, salt till its very hot, put in diluted cornstarch, stir constantly to prevent lumping, when thick, but not stiff, put in yolks stirring constantly so eggs won't cook up or curdle. Cook only 2 or 3 minutes until clear and thick. Cool. Pour filling to very edge of baked shell. Spread on sweetened whipped cream. (Keeps good next day if in cold place).

Mary Osadjan, Chicago, Ill.

PINEAPPLE-PEACH PIE

1 package frozen peaches,
   drained
1 package pineapple
½ pound cream cheese
3 eggs

½ cup sugar
1 teaspoon almond flavor
1 cup sour cream
2 tablespoons sugar
1 teaspoon brandy or sherry wine

Thaw out peaches and mix with eggs, cream cheese and sugar, and almond flavor. Line pie plate with pie dough and pour mixture into this pie plate. Bake in oven 375°F for about 20 minutes. When cooled take 1 cup sour cream, 2 tablespoons sugar, 1 tablespoon brandy, mix well these ingredients and put on baked pie and bake again for 15 minutes. Put pineapple on top of pie to garnish.

Maria Cervenak, Cleveland, Oh.

PRUNE PIE

1½ pounds prunes
⅓ cup sugar
4 teaspoons cornstarch

3 cups cereal cream
6 egg yolks
3 teaspoons vanilla

Soak prunes over night.

Boil prunes. Pit and mash through a colander. Combine with sugar mixed with cornstarch, slightly beaten egg yolks, cereal cream and vanilla. Mix together and pour into unbaked pie crust. Bake ¾ hour in a moderate oven, or until firm when tested. Cool and top with whipped cream. Makes two 7-inch pies.

Susan Chizmark, Joliet, Ill.

CRUSTLESS PUMPKIN PIE

2 tablespoons butter
½ cup brown sugar
3 eggs, separated
½ teaspoon salt
1 cup pumpkin

½ cup top milk
2 tablespoons flour
1 teaspoon cinnamon
Pinch of each: ginger, cloves
   and nutmeg

Cream butter and sugar. Add egg yolks, beat. Add flour with spices and salt, then milk, mixed with the pumpkin. Fold in stiffly beaten egg whites. Bake in a deep pie pan at 300°F or 325°F for one hour.

Chill. Serve cold with caramel sauce, whipped spiced cream or just plain. Chilling develops the flavor. This pie has a custard bottom and a light tender pudding on top when it is baked.

Vincentian Sisters of Charity, Bedford, Oh.

RHUBARB CREAM PIE

1½ cups sugar	2 beaten eggs
3 tablespoons flour	3 cups cut rhubarb
½ teaspoon nutmeg	1 recipe pasty
1 tablespoon butter	

Blend sugar, flour, nutmeg and butter. Add eggs, beat smooth. Pour mixture over rhubarb in 9-inch pastry lined pie pan. Make lattice top crust. Bake in hot oven 450°F for 10 minutes, then in 350°F oven for 30 minutes.

Florence Hovanec, Whiting, Ind.

STRAWBERRY FILLING FOR PIE

1 quart strawberries
2 cups sugar
¼ cup corn starch

Boil until thick. Decorate top of pie with whipped cream.

Maria Zibrida, Chicago, Ill.

GLAZED FRESH STRAWBERRY PIE

1. Make crust dough. Pierce the pastry well with a fork before baking crust at 400°F.

2. Put aside a cup of small strawberries to make a glaze for pie. Shortly before dinner, fill the crust with the rest of your quart of plump and juicy berries, the nicest you can find.

3. For glaze, cook 1 cup berries, ¾ cup sugar, 1 cup water for 5 minutes. Strain. Add 2½ teaspoons cornstarch mixed with ¼ cup sugar and ⅛ teaspoon salt. Add a few drops of red coloring. Cook until thick. Cool.

Helen Cross, Whiting, Ill.

STRAWBERRY CHIFFON PIE

1 tablespoon gelatin	1 tablespoon lemon juice
½ cup cold water	1 egg white
½ cup sugar	⅔ cup whipping cream
1½ cups crushed strawberries	Large vanilla wafers

Put gelatin in top of double boiler, add ¼ cup cold water. Let stand 5 minutes. Add sugar and remaining water. Stir over boiling water until gelatin and sugar have dissolved. Remove from flame, add the crushed strawberries and lemon juice. Cool mixture until it starts to congeal. Beat until foamy. Fold in stiffly beaten egg white and whipped cream. Line 8-inch pie plate with vanilla wafers and fill with strawberry mixture. Garnish with whole berries. Chill and serve.

Maria Proskac, Coaldale, Pa.

STRAWBERRY CHIFFON PIE

1½ cups crushed strawberries   1 tablespoon unflavored gelatin
¾ cup sugar   ¼ cup cold water
2 or 3 tablespoons lemon juice   1 cup heavy cream, whipped

Combine berries, sugar and lemon juice. Let stand 30 minutes. Soften gelatin in cold water and dissolve over hot water. Add to fruit mixture and chill until partially set. Fold in whipped cream. Pour into graham cracker crust.

Graham cracker crust: Crush 12 graham crackers (1½ cups crumbs), add ⅓ cup sugar and ½ cup melted butter or shortening. Mix well. Press firmly in greased 8-inch pie pan. Chill until set. Fill.

Mary Skurka, Whiting, Ind.

STRAWBERRY PINEAPPLE PIE

½ cup sugar   Hot water
½ cup flour   3 egg yolks
¼ teaspoon salt   2 tablespoons butter
1 No. 2 can crushed pineapple   9-inch baked pie shell
  (2½ cups)   1 pint strawberries

Combine sugar, flour and salt. Drain syrup from pineapple, measure syrup. Add enough hot water to make 1⅔ cups, add to sugar mixture, stirring constantly, cover. Cook 15 minutes. Beat egg yolks, add hot custard slowly. Cook over hot water 5 minutes. Add pineapple and butter, stir until butter melts. Cool. Pour into baked pie shell. Wash strawberries, hull, halve largest berries; arrange on pie. Mash smaller berries for glaze.

Strawberry glaze: Mash about ½ to ⅔ cup strawberries. Add ½ cup light corn syrup. Cook until berries are soft. Press through a sieve. Mix 1½ tablespoons cornstarch with 1 tablespoon water; add to strawberry syrup. Cook until thickened, stirring constantly. Add 1 teaspoon lemon juice. Tint with red food coloring. Cool slightly before pouring on pie.

Vern Jadrnak, Gary, Ind.

WHIPPED CREAM PIE

Prepare one pie shell or make individual tart shells; diced fruit or berries, whipped cream, sweetened and flavored with vanilla. Prepare pie crust, bake and chill. Just before ready to serve, turn sweetened drained fruit into the pie shell. Cover the top generously with whipped cream.

Anna Janega, Lansford, Pa.

MOLDED PASTRY HORN SHELLS *(Trubky Trdelniky)*

4 cups all purpose flour
1 pound butter
3 tablespoons sugar

4 egg yolks
1 pint sour cream

Sift dry ingredients, cut in butter with a knife or pie blender, until size of peas. Add egg yolks and sour cream, blending well, but lightly after each addition. Knead gently a few seconds on covered and floured board. Shape into a long loaf about 12 inches long. Cover with wax paper and place in refrigerator over night. In morning divide loaf into 4 equal parts. Roll out each piece and cut into 1½ inch wide strips. Have Cannoli forms or small horns well washed and dried. Roll strip on form, sealing open laps by pressing gently. Beat up an egg or use remaining egg whites and brush on the molded horns, being careful not to get egg on the mold, which would cause horns to stick. Place on greased cookie pan one inch apart. Bake at 350°F for 20 minutes. Slide off tins and let cool. Yield 28-30 horns.

FILLING
1 quart heavy whipping cream
2 tablespoons powdered sugar
1¼ teaspoon vanilla

Beat well until peaks form. Do not over-beat. Add other ingredients and beat enough to mix. Fill the horns and sprinkle lightly with powdered sugar before serving.

Veronica Radocha, Coaldale, Pa.

Salads

- GELATIN SALADS -

JELLIED APPLESAUCE

2 teaspoons plain gelatin
2 tablespoons water
2 cups thick strained applesauce
¼ cup sugar

¼ teaspoon nutmeg
1 teaspoon lemon juice
Red coloring

Soften gelatin in cold water, heat applesauce, sugar and spices together. Add gelatin and stir until dissolved. Add lemon juice and a drop or two of vegetable coloring. Pour into individual molds and chill until firm. Serve with pork or fowl. May be served as a dessert topped with whipped cream.

Helen Kalata, Chicago, Ill.

APPLE MALLOW SALAD

1 package strawberry Jello
1 cup hot water
8 marshmallows

1 No. 2 can applesauce (2 cups)
2 tablespoons mayonnaise

Dissolve Jello in hot water. Add marshmallows and stir until dissolved. Add applesauce. Mix well. Blend in mayonnaise. Pour into mold and chill.

Mary Salata, Chicago, Ill.

APRICOT NECTAR MOLD

1 package lemon gelatin
½ cup grated carrots

2 cups hot apricot nectar
½ cup pineapple, diced

Dissolve gelatin in hot apricot nectar. Chill until thick and syrupy. Fold in carrots and pineapple. Turn into mold and chill until firm.

Theresa Sabol, Whiting, Ind.

APRICOT RING MOLD SALAD

2 tablespoons gelatin
½ cup cold water
2 cups apricot nectar
Dash of salt
3 tablespoons lemon juice
1 cup crushed pineapple
½ cup salad dressing
2 - 3-ounce packages, cream cheese

1 cup chopped celery
½ cup chopped pecans
2 teaspoons gelatin
¼ cup cold water
Lettuce
Salad dressing
Canned apricots, halves
Halves of pineapple slices

Soften the tablespoon of gelatin in the ½ cup cold water, dissolve over hot water and add to the apricot nectar blended with salt and lemon juice. Chill when the mixture begins to thicken, fold in crushed pineapple. Pour half the mixture into an 8½-inch ring mold which has been brushed with salad oil. Chill until firm.

Blend salad dressing into cream cheese, add celery and pecans. Soften two teaspoons gelatin in ¼ cup cold water. Dissolve over hot water and add to cheese mixture. Spread over firm apricot layer. Chill until firm. Pour remaining apricot aspic over cream cheese layer and chill again. When firm, unmold on crisp lettuce. Fill center leaves with salad dressing. Surround mold with apricots and pineapple.

Betty Hertko, Whiting, Ind.

ASPARAGUS AND TOMATO SALAD

1 package lemon Jello
1 pint warm water
18 canned asparagus tips
2 medium tomatoes

½ teaspoon salt
4 teaspoons vinegar
½ teaspoon scraped onion
¼ teaspoon Worcestershire sauce

Dissolve Jello in warm water. Chill until slightly thickened. Trim asparagus to height of molds. Cut one tomato into thin wedges, arranged alternately. Dice remaining asparagus and tomato and combine with remaining ingredients; fold at once into slightly thickened Jello. Fill molds and chill until firm. Unmold on crisp lettuce. Garnish with mayonnaise. Serves 6.

Anna B. Russell, Cleveland, Oh.

PINEAPPLE CREAM CHEESE MOLD

2 packages lemon flavored gelatin
2 cups boiling water
2 teaspoons plain gelatin, combined with ¼ cup cold water
2 cups pineapple juice
1 No. 2½ can of crushed pineapple, thoroughly drained
½ teaspoon orange, or ½ teaspoon green coloring
5-3-ounce packages cream cheese (keep cheese in refrigerator
   until needed)

Pour the boiling water over lemon gelatin. Then at once add the combined plain gelatin and water which has stood until thick. Next add pineapple juice and coloring. Mix thoroughly and let stand in a cold place until slightly congealed. Beat cream cheese with wooden spoon or electric mixer until of medium consistency. Do not permit it to become warm. Add the gelatin mixture to the creamed cheese slowly using electric mixer and continue to beat until thoroughly blended. Let this mixture stand in ice water until of medium consistency. Last fold pineapple into it. Pour into a well oiled ring mold that measures 10x2½ inches and allow it to stand in refrigerator for 7 or 8 hours, or longer, until firm. (This recipe may be cut in half and poured into a smaller mold. Any style mold may be used. Serves 15.)

Theresa Krasula, Chicago, Ill.

JELLIED PINEAPPLE SALAD

1 package lemon Jello	½ cup cream, whipped
1¾ cups boiling water	1 tablespoon mayonnaise
½ pound marshmallows	1 small can crushed pineapple
1 package cream cheese	Grated American cheese

Dissolve Jello and add marshmallows in water. When marshmallows are soft but not entirely melted, add the pineapple, which has been drained. Let stand until set. Mix cream cheese and mayonnaise and add whipped cream. Spread on top of gelatin mixture. Let set. When ready to serve, grate cheese on top.

Florence Hovanec, Whiting, Ind.

MOLDED HEALTH SALAD

1 package lemon flavored gelatin	Grated rind of ½ orange
3 tablespoons vinegar	1 cup shredded raw cabbage
1½ cups hot water	1 cup shredded raw carrots
Juice of one lemon	1 cup chopped, cooked beets
Juice of one orange	½ cup celery

Dissolve gelatin in the hot water. Stir in vinegar. Chill until syrupy. Sprinkle fruit juices and grated rind over shredded vegetables and add to gelatin. Turn into molds and chill.

J. Kasovsky, Chicago, Ill.

PORT AND CHERRY MOLD

2 packages cherry or strawberry gelatin
2 cups hot water
2 cups port wine or wine and fruit juice
3 cups drained canned bing sweet cherries

Dissolve gelatin in the hot water. Add wine or wine and fruit juice. Use the juice from the cherries. Chill until slightly congealed, then fold in cherries. Turn into a ring mold or other form and chill until firm. Serve with a dressing made by combining equal parts of mayonnaise and whipped cream and fold in several tablespoons of chopped toasted almonds.

Mary Kovacik, Whiting, Ind.

PINEAPPLE SALAD MOLD

2 packages of red or green jello
1½ cups hot water
Dissolve Jello in hot water

Into dissolved jello add ½ pint sour cream and 1 small can crushed pineapple with juice of same. Stir well to blend thoroughly. Pour into a mold and place in refrigerator until set. This is excellent as a salad with roasts or fowl.

Margaret Czabala, Chicago, Ill.

RAINBOW SALAD LOAF

GREEN LAYER

1 package lime gelatin
1 cup hot water

½ cup ice water
1 cup crushed pineapple

Dissolve gelatin in hot water. Add ice water and chill until thick. Fold in crushed pineapple. Pour into a 4x9 loaf pan. Chill until firm. Pour second layer on top.

YELLOW LAYER

1 package lemon gelatin
1 cup hot water
½ cup ice water

¾ cup finely grated carrots
1 tablespoon lemon juice

Dissolve gelatin in hot water. Add ice water and chill until thick. Fold in carrots and lemon juice, carefully pour oven green layer. Chill until firm. Add third layer.

RED LAYER

1 package cherry gelatin
1 cup hot water
½ cup ice water

⅔ cup finely cut celery
1 sweet pickle, finely cut

Dissolve gelatin in hot water. Add ice water. Chill until slightly thick. Fold in celery and pickle, carefully pour over yellow layer. Chill until firm. When entire loaf is firm, unmold on plate or tray. Frost entire loaf with cream cheese frosting.

FROSTING

3 small packages cream cheese
¼ cup mayonnaise

Allow cream cheese to soften in a warm room. Add mayonnaise and mix thoroughly.

Mrs. A. Grapenthin, Chicago, Ill.

FROZEN STRAWBERRY CHEESE SALAD

1 - 16-ounce package frozen strawberries
1 carton cottage cheese
1 cup whipping cream

Partially defrost strawberries and combine with cottage cheese. Fold in whipped cream and place in mold to freeze. Defrost approximately 20 minutes before serving. Top with whipped cream and maraschino cherry.

Mary Schinsky, North Hollywood, Ca.

24 HOUR SALAD

4 egg yolks
½ cup sugar
Juice of 1 lemon

1 teaspoon butter
1 cup sweet cream, or evaporated milk

Cook all but lemon juice until thick, when cooled add lemon juice. Add the following and let stand over night.

1 cup cream, whipped
½ pound diced marshmallows

1 large can white cherries, pitted
1 large can diced pineapple

Add almonds or pecans just before serving.

Rose Leslie, Whiting, Ind.

BING CHERRY SALAD

1 No. 2 can sliced pineapple
1 package cherry-flavored
** gelatin**
1 - 3-ounce package cream cheese
2 to 3 tablespoons cream, or
** top milk**

1 No. 2 can Bing cherries, pitted
⅓ cup lemon juice
1 package orange-flavored gelatin
½ cup sliced, stuffed olives

Drain pineapple and add enough water to pineapple syrup to make 1½ cups. Heat to boiling and dissolve cherry gelatin in hot liquid. Chill until partially set and add pineapple slices cut in ⅛ inch pieces. Pour into oiled 8-inch square pan; chill until firm. Soften cheese with cream. Spread over gelatin and chill until firm.

Drain cherries and add water and lemon juice to cherry syrup to make 1¾ cups liquid. Heat liquid to boiling and dissolve orange gelatin in hot liquid. Chill until partially set. Add cherries and olives and spread over cheese. Chill until firm. Cut in squares to serve. Serves nine.

Beatrice Pihulic, Hammond, Ind.

BING CHERRY SALAD

1 box Jello, dissolved in ½ cup hot water
1 cup bing cherry juice (from canned cherries)
¼ cup port wine
3 tablespoon lemon juice

Fill molds with pitted Bing cherries and cover with the above jello mixture. Chill. Unmold on lettuce and garnish with cheese, cottage cheese or cream cheese.

Vincentian Sisters of Charity, Bedford, Oh.

CRANBERRY AND ORANGE MOLD

1 pound cranberries   **2 cups sugar**
2 small oranges   **2 packages lemon Jello**

Grind raw cranberries and the whole unpeeled oranges together. Then add the sugar. Let stand for 15 minutes, in the meantime make jello and let it cool until almost stiff, then add the cranberry mixture and mix together very well, pour into ring mold and chill until firm. Turn over on platter and fill center with lettuce or parsley greens for decoration. Very colorful.

Anna Kochis Jr., Hammond, Ind.

CRANBERRY MOLD

COMBINE:
1 cup ground raw cranberries
1 cup ground unpared raw apples
1 cup sugar

DISSOLVE:
1 package lemon flavored gelatin in 1 cup hot water

Add 1 cup pineapple syrup; chill until partially set. Add cranberry-apple mixture, ½ cup seeded Tokay grapes halved and ¼ cup broken walnut meats. Pour into six individual molds, chill until firm. Unmold cranberry salads on 6 pineapple slices on crisp lettuce. Pass mayonnaise. Serves six.

Anna K. Hruskovich, Whiting, Ind.

COOL-AS-A-CUCUMBER SALAD

Looks cool, tastes cool-delicious with a big dinner

1 package lime-flavored gelatin	1 cup heavy sour cream, whipped
¾ cup hot water	or 1 cup mayonnaise
¼ cup lemon juice	1 cup chopped, unpeeled
1 teaspoon onion juice	cucumber

Dissolve gelatin in hot water. Add lemon juice and onion juice. Chill until partially set. Fold in cream and cucumbers. Pour into 6 oiled individual molds and chill until firm. Unmold on crisp lettuce. Garnish with tomato wedges.

Theresa Krasula, Chicago, Ill.

FROZEN FRUIT SALAD

2 cups diced pineapple	8 tablespoons powdered sugar
24 maraschino cherries, cut in	2 packages cream cheese
pieces	½ cup mayonnaise
24 marshmallows, cut	½ pint whipping cream

Mix the pineapple, cherries, marshmallows with powdered sugar and let stand for awhile. Meanwhile cream the cheese with mayonnaise. Fold in whipping cream and mix together with fruit mixture. Place in freezing tray and freeze at highest temperature until firm. This should be made about 6 to 8 hours before serving. Serves 8.

Florence Hovanec, Whiting, Ind.

FROZEN FRUIT SALAD

1 pint cream	1 teaspoon powdered sugar
1½ cups cut up fruit (any kind)	1 tablespoon instantaneous
¾ cup mayonnaise	gelatin
Lettuce	2 tablespoons cold water

Soak gelatin in cold water, melt it over steam and beat it into the mayonnaise. Add powdered sugar to the cream and whip it, then combine with mayonnaise. Stir in the cut up fruit. Pack and freeze. The mayonnaise may be omitted and served separately.

Ann Hook, Munhall, Pa.

FROSTED LIME-WALNUT SALAD

1 package lime gelatin	½ cup finely sliced celery
1 cup boiling water	1 tablespoon chopped pimiento
1 No.2 can crushed pineapple	½ cup chopped walnuts
1 cup small curd cottage cheese	

Dissolve gelatin in boiling water, cool till syrupy. Stir in remaining ingredients. Mold in 8-inch pan rinsed in cold water.

Frosting: When salad is firm, unmold or leave in pan. Frost top with 1 package (3 ounce) cream cheese mixed with 1 tablespoon mayonnaise and 1 teaspoon lemon juice. Decorate with maraschino cherries, water-cress and walnut halves. Makes 6 to 9 servings.

Louise Zaremba, Joliet, Ill.

LIME JELLO SALAD

2 packages lime Jello
1 carton well drained cottage cheese

1 small can crushed pineapple
¼ cup chopped walnuts

Make jello and let cool till just a little stiff, then add the drained cottage cheese and pineapple that also has been well drained. Mix together and add chopped walnuts, pour into square pan, and chill until very stiff. Serve on lettuce. Should be made day before you want to use it for best results.

Anna Kochis, Jr., Hammond, Ind.

LIME HORSERADISH MOLD

1 package lime gelatin
¼ cup horseradish
½ tablespoon Knox gelatin
⅛ teaspoon salt

2½ cups water, hot
1 tablespoon grated onion
⅛ cup cold water
½ jar cottage cheese (6 ounces)

Add lime gelatin to hot water, add salt. Add Knox gelatin combined with ⅛ cup cold water and remelted over hot water stirring until dissolved. Chill until it begins to thicken. Add horseradish, cottage cheese and onion. Pour into oiled ring mold and chill until firm. Serves 6.

Theresa Sabol, Whiting, Ind.

LIME PEAR MOLD

2 packages lime gelatin
1 No. 2½ can pear halves

Prepare according to direction on box. Place pear halves tops down in ring mold. Pour gelatin over pears and set. Unmold on endive or lettuce and fill center of ring with cottage cheese.

Clara Kucka, Whiting, Ind.

MANHATTAN SPECIAL SALAD

1 package lemon Jello
1 pint warm water
¾ cup diced tart apples
½ cup diced celery, salted

¼ cup broken walnut meats
½ teaspoon salt
4 teaspoons vinegar
Cream cheese balls

Dissolve jello in warm water. Chill until slightly thickened. Combine apples, celery, nuts, salt and vinegar; fold at once into slightly thickened jello. Turn into individual molds. Chill until firm. Unmold on crisp lettuce; garnish with water cress and cheese balls. Serve with mayonnaise. Serves 6. Nuts may be omitted in this recipe, if desired.

Anna B. Russell, Cleveland, Ohio

COOL MELON SALAD

1 package lime Jello
1 pint warm water

1½ cups cantaloupe, or honey
dew melon, cut in ½-inch balls

Dissolve jello in warm water. Chill. When slightly thickened, fold in melon balls. Turn into mold. Chill until firm. Unmold on crisp lettuce and garnish with mayonnaise or serve plain as dessert. Use only firm, ripe sweet melon.

Anna B. Russell, Cleveland, Ohio

MINTED PEAR SALAD

1 cup sugar
1 cup hot water
2 teaspoons gelatin
2 tablespoons cold water

¼ cup mint leaves
Green vegetable coloring
Firm, ripe Bartlett pears

Bring the sugar and hot water to a boiling point. Stir until sugar is dissolved, then boil five minutes. Soften the gelatin in cold water. Combine the two mixtures and stir until the gelatin is dissolved. Add the mint and let stand five minutes. Strain and add just enough coloring to tint a delicate green. Wipe peel, core and halve the pears. Arrange in serving dish, pour gelatin mixture over and chill. Serve very cold.

Vincentian Sisters of Charity, Bedford, Oh.

PEAR, CHEESE AND PINEAPPLE SALAD

1 package cherry Jello
1 package lemon Jello
1 package lime Jello
6 pear halves and juice
6 maraschino cherries

1 cup whipping cream
8 ounce package cream cheese
1 No. 2 can crushed pineapple
and juice

This is a three-layer salad to be made in two bread pans or three small loaf pans.

1st layer: Dissolve package of cherry jello in one cup of boiling water and add one cup of pear juice. Place pear halves in pan face down with cherry in middle of each pear. (Three in each pan down center). Pour jello over pears and put in refrigerator to jell.

2nd layer: Dissolve lemon jello in one cup of boiling water and add one cup of cold water. Let thicken in refrigerator. Whip one cup of whipping cream and fold in jello. Add cheese which has been left at room temperature. Pour over red layer and allow to chill until set.

3rd layer: Dissolve lime jello in one cup of boiling water and add one cup of pineapple juice. Add crushed pineapple and pour over cheese layer. Chill until set. When unmolded, the red layer will be on top, the white in the center and the green at the bottom. Will make 18 to 20 servings.

Anna K. Hruskovich, Whiting, Ind.

- VEGETABLE AND FRUIT SALADS -

SALAD SUPREME

1 package Philadelphia cream cheese (½ pound size)
½ cup mayonnaise
1 No. 2 can crushed pineapple, drained
1 bottle cherries, diced
½ pint whipped cream, to which add ¼ cup powdered sugar
1 teaspoon salt

Soften cheese with a little mayonnaise, little at a time. Add pineapple, cherries, fold in whipped cream. Place in a tray and freeze overnight in refrigerator. Slice, place on lettuce leaf. Serve with nut bread, crackers, or small hot buttered rolls. Yield: 12 servings.

Susan M. Mrazek, Homestead, Pa.

COTTAGE CHEESE SALAD

1 cup cottage cheese	**1 teaspoon salt**
2 cups cooked rice	**3 tablespoons celery, minced**
1 cup peas	**3 tablespoons chopped onion**
4 tablespoons pimiento	**4 tablespoons tart relish**

Combine ingredients lightly, chill. Serve on lettuce with French dressing or mayonnaise.

Anna B. Russell, Cleveland, Oh.

KIDNEY BEAN SALAD

2 cans kidney beans
1 cup onions, chopped
1 cup celery, chopped
1 cup carrots, shredded

Juice of one lemon
2 tablespoons olive or peanut oil
½ cup mayonnaise
½ teaspoon salt

Combine and mix well, beans, onions, celery and carrots. Blend oil, lemon juice and mayonnaise, add to the bean mixture. Season with salt. Garnish with parsley and two hard boiled eggs.

Theresa Hanuska, Lake Worth, Fl.

KIDNEY BEAN SALAD

2 large cans kidney beans
2 hard boiled eggs
½ cup chopped celery

6 or 8 sweet pickles cut in small
    pieces
Mayonnaise to suit taste
Salt and pepper

Rinse kidney beans in cold water and drain. Add chopped eggs, celery and pickles, small onion if desired, adds very good taste. Blend together with salad dressing. Serve cold.

Clara Kucka, Whiting, Ind.

KIDNEY BEAN SALAD

1 can kidney beans
½ cup celery, diced
¼ cup sweet pickles, diced

Onion juice from small onion
Cooked salad dressing

Drain the beans and rinse with cold water, remove water. Add remaining ingredients and mix with salad dressing.

LIMA BEAN SALAD

1 can of lima beans
½ pound bacon
1 onion, chopped
1 green pepper, diced
1 tablespoon flour
2 teaspoons seasoned salt

½ teaspoon salt
¼ teaspoon pepper
2 teaspoons worcestershire sauce
2 tablespoons brown sugar
2½ cups tomatoes

Cook bacon in large skillet until crisp, remove bacon and drain. Add onion and pepper to fat in pan and cook 5 minutes. Blend in flour, seasoning and sugar. Add tomatoes and simmer (uncovered) for 10 minutes. Add beans and heat. Mix in bacon which has been broken into small pieces.

Mary Markovich, Whiting, Ind.

ENDIVE AND POTATO SALAD

Wash and cut a head of endive into small pieces, set aside. Cut up four slices of bacon into small pieces and fry with 1 large onion till soft. Add ¼ cup vinegar, ½ cup water, salt and pepper, 3 tablespoons sugar and simmer for 5 minutes. When ready to serve pour over endive and cut up 3 large cooked potatoes and toss lightly with endive and serve.

Mrs. J. Hritz, Phoenixville, Pa.

POTATO SALAD

6 medium sized potatoes
1 large onion
3 eggs, hard boiled

Boil potatoes in jackets, when cold peel and slice. Add thinly sliced onion and dice the hard boiled eggs, pour over all a boiled dressing.

DRESSING
½ cup vinegar   **1 tablespoon salt**
2 eggs, well beaten   **1 tablespoon butter**

Cook until thick. (Can also be used for cabbage).

Leona Chabala, Nokomis, Ill.

DUTCH POTATO SALAD

8 boiled potatoes   **½ cup vinegar, diluted with**
1 stalk celery, diced   **½ cup cold water**
2 hard cooked eggs, sliced   **¼ teaspoon dry mustard**
1 onion, minced   **¼ teaspoon pepper**
1 tablespoon minced parsley **½ teaspoon salt**
2 eggs, well beaten   **4 slices bacon, sliced**
1 cup sugar

Dice potatoes, add celery, sliced eggs and onion. Fry bacon crisp and brown; beat eggs, add sugar, spices and vinegar and water. Mix well. Pour egg mixture into the hot bacon and stir until mixture thickens (10 minutes). Pour over potatoes, mix and toss lightly. Cool and serve.

Mary Kollar, Olyphant, Pa.

HOT POTATO SALAD

6 new potatoes
1 small onion, minced
¾ teaspoon salt
¼ cup sour cream

6 slices uncooked bacon, sliced
¼ cup vinegar
Dash of pepper
Watercress

Boil potatoes in skins, peel and slice. Fry bacon until crisp. Remove bacon from fat and brown onion in bacon fat. Add vinegar, salt, pepper and sour cream; add potatoes and bacon. Serve hot, garnish with watercress.

Anna Hook, Munhall, Pa.

MOLDED POTATO SALAD

Lemon gelatin mixture: 2 tablespoons granulated gelatin (Knox) soaked in ½ cup cold water for a few minutes and melted over hot water; add to:

1 cup warm water
2 tablespoons lemon juice
1 teaspoon salt

1 tablespoon sugar
Stir until dissolved

Place about one inch of above lemon gelatin mixture in bottom of ring mold, when nearly set arrange a design of radish roses with slices of sweet pickle for leaves, or stuffed olive design and egg slices.

Into balance of lemon gelatin fold in the following:

1 cup mayonnaise or miracle
  whip
4 cups diced cold potatoes
  (not Idaho's)

¼ cup parsley, chopped
¼ cup green pepper, chopped
¼ cup pimiento, cut in pieces
½ cup cream, whipped

Fill mold and chill overnight, unmold, fill center with a few lettuce leaves holding olives and radish roses. Arrange sliced cheese or cold meats or both around mold.

Justine Kasovsky, Chicago, Ill.

SOUR CREAM POTATO SALAD

6 medium potatoes, cooked and
  sliced (about 5 cups)
½ cup sliced cucumber
1 small onion, minced
4 ribs celery, diced
Salt and pepper

4 slices crisp bacon
3 hard cooked eggs
¾ cup sour cream
2 tablespoons mayonnaise
2 tablespoons vinegar

Combine potatoes, cucumber, onion, celery, salt and pepper to taste. Remove yolks from eggs and dice whites. Combine with potato mixture. Add crisp bacon. Mash yolks and combine with the sour cream, mayonnaise and vinegar. Mix well and pour over potato mixture. Toss lightly. Chill. Sprinkle with paprika before serving.

Mary Pataky, Whiting, Ind.

SPRING SALAD

2 cups cooked peas
2 cups cooked green beans
French or Roquefort dressing
Watercress

6 cooked cauliflowerets
2 tomatoes, peeled and sliced
1 head lettuce
Radish roses

Marinate vegetables in French dressing separately and chill for one hour. Line salad bowl with outside leaves of lettuce and place 4 lettuce cups around center of bowl. Fill each with one of the vegetables, and garnish center of bowl with water cress and radish roses.

Ann Hook, Munhall, Pa.

TOMATO ASPIC WITH GRATED CHEESE

1 pint tomato juice
1 tablespoon gelatin, soaked in ¼ cup cold tomato juice
1 tablespoon lemon juice
1 tablespoon grated cheese (any make) for every mold
Salt and sugar to taste

Heat pint of tomato juice, add and dissolve ¼ cup of gelatin and cold tomato juice. Add lemon juice, salt and sugar to taste.

Pour into molds and top each mold with a tablespoon of grated cheese. The cheese will blend with the aspic. Chill. Serve garnished with egg slices and black olives.

Vincentian Sisters of Charity, Bedford, Oh.

CAESAR SALAD

½ cup garlic flavored salad oil
¼ teaspoon salt
Few grains of pepper
1 tablespoon Worcestershire sauce
1 raw egg

½ cup lemon juice
1 head lettuce
1 head endive
1 bunch watercress
¼ cup grated parmesan cheese
1 pint crisp croutons

Place 1 or 2 garlic buds into ½ cup salad oil and let stand several hours. Remove garlic. To the oil, add salt and pepper and sauce. Break crisp salad greens into salad bowl; add cheese. Pour over the oil. Break egg, pour lemon juice over egg and toss all together. Add croutons and toss again. Serve at once. This salad may be made at the table.

Mary Buca, Chicago, Ill.

QUICK CRANBERRY SALAD

2 cups raw cranberries, ground   **2 apples, diced**
2 oranges, ground   **8 marshmallows, cut up**

Combine together and add 1 cup sugar. Let stand in refrigerator and use on lettuce leaf any time.

Mary Fedor, Streator, Ill.

NUT AND APPLE SALAD

4 diced apples   **Lettuce**
¾ cup pineapple cream   **2 tablespoons lemon juice**
  dressing   **¾ cup salted almonds**

Combine apples, lemon juice and dressing. Arrange on lettuce. Garnish with almonds.

Ann Hook, Munhall, Pa.

PINEAPPLE SALAD AND DRESSING

1 No. 2½ can pineapple chunks
10 marshmallows, cut
½ cup English walnuts, broken in pieces

Heat juice of pineapple to a boil. Mix 2 eggs, 2 tablespoons of corn starch, 3 tablespoons sugar, pour hot juice over it and beat. Put back on stove and cook a few minutes, beat and pour over marshmallows, pineapple and nuts.

Veronica Sofranko, Lovilia, Iowa

WALDORF SALAD

2 cups diced, pared pears or   **½ cup mayonnaise**
  1 cup each of diced pears and   **1 cup thinly sliced celery**
  unpared red apples   **½ cup coarsely chopped walnuts**
2 tablespoons lemon juice   **Lettuce**
1 teaspoon granulated sugar

Toss fruit with lemon juice, sugar, 1 tablespoon mayonnaise. Just before serving, add celery, walnuts, rest of mayonnaise. Toss. Serve on lettuce, sprinkle with French dressing.

Mary Uhely, Los Angeles, Ca.

- MEAT, CHICKEN AND FISH SALADS -

CHICKEN AND TOMATO SALAD

½ cup diced, cooked chicken
¾ cup diced, cucumber
6 tomatoes
Cauliflower buds

¼ cup mayonnaise
¼ cup chopped nuts
Lettuce
Parsley

Scald, peel and chill the medium sized tomatoes. Scoop out the inside of the tomatoes. Remove seeds from the pulp. Chill the ingredients and when ready to serve, mix cucumber, chicken, tomato pulp and the nuts with mayonnaise. Add salt to taste. Fill the tomatoes. Arrange on lettuce leaves. Garnish with mayonnaise and decorate each tomato top with parsley and cauliflower buds.

Ann Hook, Munhall, Pa.

HAM SALAD

¾ cup baked or boiled ham,
   ground
1 large onion, chopped fine

1 egg, boiled and chopped
¼ cup green pepper, chopped
¼ cup mayonnaise

Combine above ingredients and mix well.

Anna J. Korman, Chicago, Ill.

HAM, TONGUE AND CABBAGE SALAD

1 head cabbage
1 cup diced cold tongue
1 sweet red pepper, chopped
1 cup mayonnaise

1 green pepper, chopped
1 cup diced, cold, cooked ham
½ onion, chopped

Shred cabbage as for cole slaw. Add next 5 ingredients and blend mayonnaise with cabbage mixture. Sugar and salt may be added if desired.

Ann Hook, Munhall, Pa.

HEARTY MEAT SALAD

1 cup chopped celery
1½ cups diced apples
1½ cups shredded carrots
1 cup cooked peas
1 green pepper, chopped
2 cups cubed pork, or luncheon
   meat, or chicken

1 cup mayonnaise, or salad
   dressing
¼ teaspoon pepper
½ teaspoon salt

Combine ingredients and chill thoroughly. Serve in lettuce cups or tomato cups.

Betty Hertko, Whiting, Ind.

CRAB MEAT SALAD

1 can crab meat	4 sweet pickles
1 or 2 cups sea shells, macaroni	1 apple, diced
3 hard boiled eggs, sliced	Salt, pepper, paprika
1 cup celery, diced	Desired amount mayonnaise

Cook sea shells until tender. Add remaining ingredients together, combine with sea shells. Serve on leaf of lettuce. Serves 6.

Mary Skurka, Whiting, Ind.

LOBSTER SALAD

1½ cups diced lobster meat	Mayonnaise
½ cup diced celery	Lettuce
Vinegar to taste	

Cut the meat into pieces of convenient size for eating. Sprinkle a very small amount of vinegar over the lobster. Keep the celery crisp until time to use. Mix the lobster and celery together, stir enough mayonnaise to moisten and flavor. Arrange the salad on center of a bed of crisp white lettuce bordered with green lettuce leaves. Pour on the remainder of mayonnaise.

Ann Hook, Munhall, Pa.

PASADENA SALAD

¾ cup shrimp (1 small can)	Salt and pepper
1½ cups celery	1 teaspoon tarragon vinegar
½ cup radishes	½ cup mayonnaise
½ cup peas	¼ cup nuts

Cut shrimp in small pieces. Slice radishes and celery. Combine shrimp and vegetables. Add salt and pepper. Put into salad bowl. Add vinegar and spread mayonnaise over top. Sprinkle with chopped nuts and garnish with hearts of lettuce or parsley.

Mary Beno, Cleveland, Oh.

TUNA FISH SALAD

1 small can tuna fish
½ cup cooked rice
¼ cup chopped green pepper

¼ cup chopped celery
2 hard cooked eggs, sliced
Mayonnaise

Mix Tuna fish, rice, green pepper, celery and hard cooked eggs together, add enough mayonnaise to hold together. Chill, place on lettuce leaves and serve.

For Variation - When tomatoes are in season cut tomato in four sections ¾ way through and scoop out some of the pulp and fill center with tuna mixture. Very good for luncheons. Serve with crackers.

Anna Kochis, Jr., Hammond, Ind.

- SALAD DRESSINGS -

COOKED SALAD DRESSING

½ cup vinegar from sweet
** pickles**
2 tablespoons sugar
¼ teaspoon salt

½ teaspoon mustard
1 egg
1 tablespoon flour

Mix dry ingredients in upper part of double boiler. Add the beaten egg gradually to make smooth mixture and add vinegar. Cook over hot water until thick, stirring constantly. Cool. Add to salad.

Martha Weissman

CUCUMBER DRESSING

2 tablespoons finely chopped,
** cucumbers**
2 tablespoons vinegar
½ cup mayonnaise
¼ cup chili sauce

¼ teaspoon salt
1 tablespoon finely chopped celery
1 tablespoon finely chopped
** green pepper**
1 teaspoon finely grated onion

Mix cucumber with vinegar and salt. Let stand for at least an hour. Fold in mayonnaise and remaining ingredients. This will serve four.

FRUIT SALAD DRESSING

2 tablespoons melted butter
2 tablespoons sifted bread flour
½ cup granulated sugar
2 egg yolks
½ cup pineapple juice
¼ teaspoon salt (less may be used)

2 egg whites
2 tablespoons sugar
1¼ cups lukewarm, strained
   pineapple juice
1 cup whipping cream (optional)

Combine melted butter and flour; mix until smooth. Then add ½ cup sugar and the egg yolks combined with ½ cup pineapple juice, add salt. Mix thoroughly. To the egg whites, beaten to a medium consistency, add 2 tablespoons granulated sugar and beat only until blended. Blend egg whites gently into first mixture and add slowly the lukewarm strained pineapple juice. Cook in upper part of double boiler or in heavy saucepan until thick and smooth, stirring constantly. Let simmer several minutes. Watch carefully that it does not curdle, keeping flame low. (If it curdles, beat a few seconds with egg beater). Allow mixture to become cold, and then if desired fold in whipping cream that has been whipped to a medium consistency. Serve very cold.

HONEY LEMON DRESSING

¼ cup lemon juice
⅓ cup honey

Few grains of nutmeg
Dash of salt

Combine ingredients in covered jar and shake well.

LIME FRENCH DRESSING

6 tablespoons salad oil
2 tablespoons lime juice
¼ teaspoon salt

1 teaspoon powdered sugar
¼ teaspoon paprika

Measure all ingredients into bottle or jar and shake well.

Justine Kasovsky, Chicago, Ill.

MAYONNAISE (DELICIOUS FOR FRUITS)

1 cup Eagle brand milk
2 egg yolks
2 tablespoons dry mustard
⅛ teaspoon salt

¼ pound melted butter
½ cup vinegar
2 egg whites, beaten stiff

Melt butter, add milk, egg yolks and salt. Add little vinegar to mustard to make a smooth paste and add remainder vinegar to other ingredients and last fold in beaten egg whites.

To vary flavor for salads use lemon juice, salad oil, pickle juice, sour cream or chili sauce.

Katherine Dymsia, Braddock, Pa.

MAYONNAISE DRESSING

2 eggs, slightly beaten
1 teaspoon flour
1 teaspoon dry mustard
Add pinch of salt

¾ cup vinegar
¼ cup water
½ cup sugar, scant

Cook until it thickens, then add lump of butter, size of an egg. Beat well. Makes 1 pint of dressing.

Veronica Sofranko, Lovilia, Iowa

NO OIL SALAD DRESSING

⅓ cup sugar
1 teaspoon dry mustard
1 teaspoon salt
½ teaspoon paprika
¼ teaspoon pepper

1 can tomato soup
⅓ cup vinegar
1 tablespoon Worcestershire sauce
1 tablespoon finely minced onion
1 clove finely minced garlic

Combine dry ingredients, add vinegar slowly, then tomato soup, onion and garlic. Store in refrigerator and use when needed.

Mary Uhely, Los Angeles, Ca.

PINEAPPLE DRESSING

½ cup olive oil
½ teaspoon salt
1 teaspoon sugar

¼ cup pineapple juice
Few grains cayenne

Combine all ingredients and shake well before using. Makes about 1 cup.

SALAD DRESSING

1 cup milk
3 eggs, beaten
3 tablespoons sugar
1½ tablespoons flour

1 tablespoon dry mustard
1 teaspoon salt
½ cup vinegar
Lump of butter

Put dry ingredients together and mix well, then beaten eggs and milk. Add vinegar and butter last. Boil in double boiler, mix constantly until thick and done. Add sour cream if desired.

Mary A. Sosko, Homestead, Pa.

STAY SLIM SALAD DRESSING

Chili sauce can be used for salad dressing. Many prefer it to dressings containing oil. It is excellent for those who do not wish to gain weight, or those who wish to avoid rich and fatty foods.

Justine Kasovsky, Chicago, Ill.

RED CABBAGE SLAW

1 medium head red cabbage	2 tablespoons honey
1 dill pickle	3 tablespoons oil
1 medium spanish onion	1 teaspoon salt
3 tablespoons lemon juice	½ teaspoon black pepper

Grate or cut fine the cabbage, mix into it the chopped pickle and chopped onion. Blend together the lemon juice, honey, oil and seasoning and add to cabbage. Mix well and serve chilled.

Mary Pilat, Chicago, Ill.

Sandwiches

SANDWICHES

Bread for sandwiches should be at least a day old and of firm texture. Slice with a very sharp knife thick, or thin slices with a sawing motion. The slicing of bread should be done ahead of time. The butter should be soft and creamed and spread thinly and evenly. If fancy cutters are used, shape before spreading. To keep sandwiches fresh, wrap in moisture-proof paper, then in damp towel or napkin and place in refrigerator. Lettuce, sliced tomato, cucumber, and bacon are best added just before serving.

There are many types of sandwiches, some of which may be served hot, some cold-on plain bread, fancy bread, on toast or between sliced roll; open-faced, double or triple decked, pinwheel and loaf or layer sandwich. The pinwheel and the loaf or layer sandwich may be prepared in advance and sliced before serving.

Sliced fillings should be arranged to fit the sandwich and may in turn be topped with crisp lettuce. Salad dressing maybe used to moisten and to hold together the ingredients for chopped or minced fillings.

Whatever the filling is, if it is minced, the one thing to remember is that it must be well mixed to make it easy to spread and attractive to serve. If meat or cheese is used, the filling should be thinly sliced to make it easy to eat. For a substantial sandwich, several layers of thinly sliced meat are better than one thick slice.

HOT AND COLD SANDWICHES

Note: All recipes are individual, unless otherwise indicated.

Bacon and Tomato Sandwich

Broil 3 slices of bacon and arrange between slices of toast with crisp lettuce and sliced tomato.

Chicken Sandwich

Using hot sliced chicken. Place a slice of bread, unbuttered, in the center of a hot plate. Cover with a slice of chicken, pouring over all a gravy from chicken stock. Garnish with a strip of dill pickle.

Cottage Cheese and Marmalade Sandwich

Use brown bread. Spread one slice generously with well-drained cottage cheese, seasoned with salt, pepper and onion juice. Top with lettuce. Spread another slice of bread with orange marmalade and place on top. Cut into four triangular sections and garnish with a small slice of tomato, topped with a slice of hard-cooked egg, again topped with a slice of stuffed olive.

Ham and Swiss Cheese Sandwich

Spread slice of white or rye bread with butter. Place a thin slice of ham on bread, over this spread chopped chutney, chow-chow, or piccalilli, then thinly sliced Swiss Cheese. Top with second slice of bread.

Sunday Supper Sandwiches

Combine one 6-ounce can tuna fish, flaked. 2 tablespoons each, chopped onion, chopped pickle, and mayonnaise. Split 6 round flat buns; butter and spread with tuna-fish mixture. Top with slice of cheese. Broil 3 minutes or until cheese melts.

Club or Three Decker Sandwich

These are made of three slices of bread which may be plain, toasted, buttered, or spread with a creamed savory butter. Serve cold or hot. They may be cut into halves, diagonally, in thirds or quarters. Cover the first slice of bread with a spread or filling, top with a second slice of bread. Then another spread of filling and finally top with a third slice of bread. Gently press together, then cut as indicated above. When cut in quarters, they maybe held together with toothpicks.

Chicken-Bacon and Tongue-Tomato on Whole Wheat

Lower layer. Sliced chicken topped with broiled bacon. Second layer. Sliced tongue, tomato slices and lettuce leaves.

Crab Meat Mayonnaise, Tomato and Egg Salad, Cress on Toast

Lower layer. Crab meat dressed with mayonnaise, then topped with tomato slices. Second layer. Egg salad topped with water cress.

Pinwheel Sandwiches

Use fresh bread. Cut thin slices the long way of loaf, trim crusts, and spread with softened butter and filling. Starting at one end, roll the slice and seal the open edge with creamed butter. Wrap in moisture-proof paper, chill and cut in slices. If bread tends to break when rolling, wrap slice in damp cloth until it becomes slightly moist.

QUANTITY SANDWICH FILLINGS

Note: 1 cup of filling will be sufficient for about 6 sandwiches. The bread or toast used for spreading these fillings may be spread first with either plain butter or one of the savory butters.

Chicken Filling

Pass through the food chopper enough cold cooked chicken to make ½ cup, with 3 olives, a strip of green pepper and 2 hard-boiled eggs. Add 2 teaspoons of chili sauce, 3 tablespoons of mayonnaise and few drops worcestershire sauce. Blend thoroughly.

Crab Meat Filling

To 1 cup flaked cooked or canned crabmeat add ⅓ cup of finely minced celery, few drops of onion juice, ⅓ cup mayonnaise, with salt and pepper to taste. Chill before using. Any preferred bread or toast. Lobster, shrimp, tuna fish and salmon filling may be similarly prepared.

Egg Mayonnaise Filling

To the finely chopped whites of 6 hard-cooked eggs add the yolks pressed through a sieve. Season and moisten with mayonnaise. Use Graham bread.

Liver and Bacon Filling

Broil 9 slices of bacon and ¼ pound beef liver. Pass both through food chopper with a slice of onion. Add salt, pepper, and 1 teaspoon worcestershire sauce. Blend thoroughly.

Prune and Nut Filling

To ½ cup of sieved prune pulp add 1 teaspoon of lemon juice and ½ cup ground nut-meats with a few drops of almond extract (optional).

Roquefort Cheese Filling

Combine ½ cup Roquefort cheese, ½ cup American cheese and 1 teaspoon worcestershire sauce. Season highly with pepper, lightly with salt.

VARIOUS FILLINGS FOR SANDWICHES

Chopped chicken, ham and pickle

Chopped ham, green pepper and egg

Chopped date and cream cheese

Grated pineapple, cream cheese and nut

Sardine, chopped egg and mayonnaise

Crab meat, minced celery mixed with salad dressing and water cress

Peanut butter, pimento and sliced cucumber

Cold pork, chopped sweet pickle, salad dressing and lettuce

Tuna fish salad with broiled bacon

Soups

BEEF SOUP

1½ pounds chuck and soup bone	2 tablespoons canned tomatoes
3 stalks celery or 4 to 5 sprigs parsley	¼ cup lima beans
1 onion	1 small clove garlic
2 carrots	6 whole peppercorns
1 small potato	Pepper and salt to taste

Wash meat and bone. Place in soup kettle and add about 1½ quarts of water. Bring to a boil and slowly simmer for 1 hour. Remove scum. Add vegetables, except the greens (which should boil with this soup only for one-half hour). At this point salt to taste, add peppercorns and pepper, continue boiling until meat is tender. Then pour ½ cup cold water into the soup to settle it. Meanwhile boil noodles in salted water and drain. Place in soup tureen, strain the soup over them and serve.

Justina Uhlarik, Chicago, Ill.

GROUND BEEF SOUP

1 pound ground beef	¼ teaspoon black pepper
10 cups water	1 tablespoon salt
1 cup diced celery	3 tablespoons tomato
1 cup diced carrots	½ cup rice
1 medium onion, diced	

Place the ground beef in cold water, stir and bring to a boil. Skim the soup and add diced vegetables and tomato. Season and cook slowly for 1½ hours. Add rice and cook 45 minutes longer. Serves 6 to 8.

Anna Stanek, Whiting, Indiana

BEET SOUP

1 bunch young beets	Juice of 1 lemon
1 cup sour cream	Salt and sugar to taste

Peel and wash beets, then cut in small cubes or grate them on a coarse grater and boil in 1 quart of water until soft. Add lemon juice, sugar and salt to taste. Boil 5 minutes longer, then stir in sour cream, mix well and serve either hot or cold. If a creamier soup is preferred, add 2 beaten egg yolks to the cream.

CARAWAY SEED SOUP

1 tablespoon caraway seeds	1 tablespoon butter
4 cups water	1 tablespoon flour
Salt to taste	1 cup cold water

Simmer caraway seeds in salted water for 10 minutes. Brown flour in melted butter, stir in cold water and bring to a boil. Add to caraway seed water, bring to a boil and strain.

Sophie Gresko, Whiting, Ind.

CHICKEN SOUP

4 to 5 pound chicken	5 peppercorns
3 to 4 quarts cold water	1 teaspoon salt
1 onion	¼ teaspoon pepper
2 stalks celery, or ¼ cup celery root, diced	1 tablespoon canned tomatoes

Singe, clean, wash thoroughly and cut up chicken into serving portions. Add water and simmer slowly about 2 hours, then add vegetables and cook 1 hour longer. Skim thoroughly during cooking for a clear soup.

Justina Fiala, Chicago, Ill.

CHICKEN VEGETABLE SOUP WITH DUMPLINGS

1 small spring chicken	Parsley and celery, chopped
1 onion	1 green pepper
3 tablespoons melted butter	1 tomato
½ teaspoon pepper	2 carrots
1 tablespoon salt	6 cups water
1 tablespoon paprika	½ cup rice
2 cups water	
1 kohlrabi, or small head of cabbage	

Sauté onion in butter until golden brown. Add chicken cut in serving pieces, (legs and breast save for frying). Add diced vegetables, seasonings and 2 cups of water. Simmer gently for about ½ hour, or until chicken and vegetables are done. To the 6 cups of water, add rice, bring to a boil, add dumplings and continue to boil until the rice is cooked. Combine chicken and vegetables to the dumplings and rice and serve.

Dumplings: Scrape chicken liver, add ½ teaspoon salt, 1 egg and enough flour to make a soft dough. Drop by teaspoonfuls into the boiling rice.

Mary A. Bosko, Homestead, Pa.

CLAM CHOWDER

1 dozen clams	1 large onion
3 ounces salt pork	1 teaspoon thyme
2 quarts boiling water	5 chowder crackers
3 large potatoes	Salt and pepper to taste
1 can tomatoes	

Cut pork in small pieces and brown. Dice potatoes, cut onions into small pieces. Add water, seasoning and boil 1 hour. Now add juice of clams and boil ½ hour. Add chopped clams and boil 20 minutes longer. Dust with paprika. Serve with crackers.

EGG SOUP

2 tablespoons butter	5 whole black peppers
4 tablespoons flour	5 eggs
3 bay leaves	1 tablespoon vinegar
6 cups water	Salt to taste

Melt butter, add flour and brown. Add the water and stir until well blended. Add bay leaves, peppers and salt. Cook about 30 minutes simmering slowly. Just before soup is ready to serve, drop whole egg, one at a time into the soup and allow to cook about 5 minutes. Add vinegar. Serve with whole boiled potatoes.

Theresa Paunicka, Whiting, Ind.

FISH CHOWDER

Use the heads, backbones with what flesh adheres, or use small whole fish, that have been washed and cleaned well. Place in a pan and cover with water. Let cook until meat may be easily removed from bones. Drain and save liquid. Separate the fish meat from the bones, and to each 1½ cups cooked fish add 1 medium sized onion, chopped medium fine, 2 potatoes, diced, 1 carrot, 1 tablespoon butter, a dash of black pepper and salt to taste. A piece of bay leaf or more may be added and several whole black peppers. Add the strained liquid to the fish and vegetables and simmer until vegetables are tender. Stir into this about ½ cup milk. If soup needs thickening add 1 tablespoon of flour to milk and stir into the soup.

Pauline Knapcik, Chicago, Ill.

HAM BONE PEA SOUP

1 ham bone	2½ quarts water
¾ pound split peas	1 cup milk
1 stalk celery	1 tablespoon flour
1 sprig parsley	1 tablespoon butter
2 onions	

Cover ham bone with water and add the peas, celery and parsley. Simmer until peas are soft enough to put through sieve. Fry the onion in enough butter to brown slightly and add to soup, simmer for another half hour. Then in skillet melt the tablespoon of butter and add the flour, stir until flour is well browned, add enough cold water to make a smooth sauce and add to the soup, stir in thoroughly. Add the cup of milk and cook another 2 minutes or until all ingredients are well blended. Serve with grated cheese or croutons. If preferred, peas may be left whole, unsieved.

Daughters of St. Francis, Lacon, Ill.

KOHLRABI SOUP

Remove leaves from kohlrabi and peel. Cut into small cubes or slices and put into saucepan. Add water to cover the vegetables, add salt to taste and boil for a minute or two, then lower the flame and simmer in uncovered pan until tender, approximately 40 minutes. Be sure there is enough water in pan to keep the vegetables well immersed. Make a brown sauce of 1 tablespoon or more of shortening, and equal amount of flour, stir until nicely browned, then add about ¼ cup cold water and blend well, allow to simmer for a minute then add to the kohlrabi. Into ½ cup of rich milk or cream add 1 tablespoon flour and blend well. Add to kohlrabi, and simmer for a few minutes, but do not boil. Season to taste and serve.

Justine Kasovsky, Chicago, Ill.

LIMA BEAN SOUP

1 cup dry lima beans	2 tablespoons butter
1 cup tomatoes, canned	4 tablespoons flour
1 cup potatoes, diced	1½ teaspoons salt
1 onion, cut fine	¼ teaspoon pepper
1 cup carrots, diced	1 quart water
1 cup celery, diced	

Soak lima beans in 2 quarts of water 1 hour. Cook till almost tender. Add the vegetables and the seasoning and cook till vegetables are done. Melt butter, add flour and brown, add to soup and stir until blended. Boil 5 minutes.

Dorothy Sabol, Whiting, Ind.

LIMA BEAN VEGETABLE SOUP *(With Meat Stock)*

¾ cup lima beans
3 quarts water
1 cup celery, diced
1 cup carrots, diced
1 large size onion, diced
1 soup bone, chuck

1 can No.2 tomatoes
½ clove garlic
¼ teaspoon caraway seeds
¼ teaspoon black pepper
1 tablespoon salt
2 cups potatoes, diced

Soak the beans for about 2 hours. Place soup bone into water and bring to a boil. Skim and add the lima beans and vegetables. Cook together slowly with the garlic, caraway seeds and seasonings for about 2 hours. Then add the potatoes and cook until done. Serves 6 to 8 people.

Anna Stanek, Whiting, Ind.

MEATLESS VEGETABLE SOUP

1 cup dry lima beans
½ cup rice
1 cup diced celery
1 cup diced carrots

3 onions, diced
4 quarts water
4 tablespoons butter
1 bay leaf

Boil lima beans about 1 hour, then remove skins, add rice, boil slowly with lima beans, add balance of vegetables and butter, simmer until done. Add salt and pepper to taste. (About 2 hours in all).

Anita Jambor, McKeesrocks, Pa.

FRESH MUSHROOM SOUP *(Sour)*

1 pound fresh mushrooms
1 tablespoon butter
1 teaspoon flour

Sauerkraut juice to taste
Salt and pepper to taste
1 teaspoon finely chopped onion

Wash mushrooms and cook in 1 quart of water until tender. Strain. (Save water). Run mushrooms through food chopper. Add sauerkraut juice to mushroom water. Salt and pepper and bring to a boil.

Brown flour in butter until light brown, add onion and brown. Add ¼ cup water and bring to a boil and stir. Strain. Add to contents along with mushrooms and simmer for a couple of minutes.

Sophie Gresko, Whiting, Ind.

- SOUP ADDITIONS -

EGG DROPS (PAPCUN)

½ cup flour
1 whole egg

½ teaspoon salt
1 tablespoon water

Mix ingredients, then knead well. Grate dough, while grating, dip dough into flour to keep from sticking. Cook in salted boiling water for three minutes. Pour cold water over drops, then strain. Serve in any soup.

Sophie Gresko, Whiting, Ind.

EGG DROPS

2 well beaten eggs
¼ teaspoon salt

1 tablespoon water
½ cup flour

Mix ingredients in a bowl and stir until smooth. Pour slowly from end of spoon into boiling soup that has been strained, or into a clear broth and boil two or three minutes. If poured from a considerable height, shape of drops will be improved.

Pauline Knapcik, Chicago, Ill.

FARINA SOUP DUMPLINGS (HALUŠKY)

2 slices white bread
1 egg
1 tablespoon shortening

2 or 3 tablespoons farina
¼ teaspoon salt
Flour, enough to form soft
   dumplings

Soak and squeeze the bread in water. Add egg, shortening, farina, salt and enough flour to bind the ingredients. Blend well, then cut with fork into small pieces and into the soup. Cook slowly for 15 minutes. The dumplings expand while cooking. Serve with any soup.

Martina Gereg, Lorain, Oh.

EGG NOODLES

1 cup flour
2 whole eggs
1 teaspoon salt

Sift flour on bread board. Add eggs and salt. Knead until the dough is very smooth. Sprinkle flour on the board and over the top of the dough. Roll out very thin. Sprinkle a little flour over the dough, fold in half, then cut into two inch wide strips. Cut strips very thin. Dry on bread board. To store, place in cellophane bag. Cook in boiling water for two minutes the amount of noodles desired. Rinse in cold water.

Lorraine Theresa Gresko, Guadalajara, Mexico

FARINA SOUP DUMPLINGS

1 egg
1 tablespoon cold water
½ teaspoon salt, or less

Pepper to taste
1 teaspoon flour mixed with 5
   tablespoons farina

Slightly beat egg, add water and seasonings. Blend well, gradually add flour and farina mixture, beating while adding. When smooth, beat a few minutes longer to incorporate air into mixture. Drop from fork into boiling soup, lower heat and cook for about eight minutes, set aside for a few minutes, then serve hot in soup plates. The dumpling mixture is not too thick, but thick enough to drop easily from fork. The size of dumplings desired are regulated with the fork.

Margaret Czabala, Chicago, Ill.

LIVER DUMPLINGS FOR SOUP

1 slice liver
1 onion
Parsley
Celery
1 tablespoon water

2 eggs
1 teaspoon butter
Flour
Salt and pepper to taste

Grind liver, onion, parsley and celery. Add water, eggs, seasonings and enough flour to make small balls, or drop from teaspoon into soup. Add butter and mix well. Drop from spoon into soup and cook about fifteen minutes.

Barbara Bires, Pittsburgh, Pa.

CHICKEN LIVER DUMPLINGS

Chicken livers from about 3
   chickens
1 cup bread crumbs
3 tablespoons flour

1 medium size onion
1 teaspoon salt
Dash of pepper
1 egg

Put chicken livers through a grinder. Chop onion fine and add to pureed livers. Add bread crumbs, flour, salt, pepper and egg. Mix thoroughly. Drop from teaspoon into about 2 quarts of chicken soup, bring to a boil. This will make 6 servings.

Mary Andrechick, Woodbridge, NJ.

LIVER DUMPLINGS *(PECIENKOVE HALUŠKI)*

½ pound liver, beef or pork
¼ pound salt pork or fat
   from pork
1 medium size onion
1 slice dry bread

1 large egg
1½ cups flour
1 teaspoon salt
⅛ teaspoon baking powder
Pepper to taste

Put meat and onion through food chopper, then run through the slice of bread. Add egg, flour, salt, pepper and baking powder. Mix thoroughly, if too stiff, add a little water. Drop from teaspoon into boiling beef broth and cook twenty minutes.

Veronica Latchney, Detroit, Mich.

POTATO DROPS

1 cup flour　　　　　　　　**1 medium grated, raw potato**
1 egg　　　　　　　　　　　**Water, if needed**
Salt

Combine and mix all ingredients, then knead very well. Roll out thin, cut in triangles and cook in salted boiling water. Rinse in cold water and strain. Very tasty with beef soup.

Sophie Gresko, Whiting, Ind.

VEAL FILLING FOR SOUP PIROSHKY

Dough-Pirohy recipe page 92

Veal filling is made as follows: Cook in salted water, ½ pound veal until tender, remove from liquid, grind or chop fine. Melt about 1 tablespoon butter in a skillet, brown slightly, add veal and stir to keep from burning. Add finely chopped parsley, salt and pepper to taste. Cook together about two minutes. The piroshky triangles are made small, not over two inches long. Place a little veal filling on triangle, fold and seal edges. Drop into boiling salted water and cook until piroshky come to the top of the water, continue cooking for another three minutes. Drain. Place in soup plates, about 5 or 6 and pour hot soup over same.

Helen Kocan, Whiting, Ind.

LENTIL SOUP

½ pound lentils　　　　　　**Salt and pepper to taste**
½ cup chopped celery　　　　**½ cup strained tomatoes**
1 large onion, chopped　　　**7 cups cold water**
2 tablespoons flour

Cover lentils with plenty of cold water and let stand overnight. Drain and add 7 cups cold water, cook slowly about two hours. Sauté onion and celery in hot fat, then add flour. Blend and cook for a few minutes then add to the cooked lentils. Season with salt and pepper, add the tomatoes and cook about 10 minutes. Serve hot.

POTATO SOUP

3 medium potatoes, diced	2 quarts water
1 stalk celery, diced	3 tablespoons butter
2 onions sliced thin	2 tablespoons flour
2 diced carrots	1 cup top milk
1 sprig finely chopped parsley	Salt and pepper to taste

Cover vegetables with water, add seasonings and cook until tender. Heat butter until light brown, stir into it the flour and keep stirring until flour is browned. Add about ½ cup cold water and blend until smooth, then gradually add the milk, stirring constantly to keep from lumps. Add to soup and cook a few minutes to blend thoroughly. Serve with chopped parsley.

CREAM OF TOMATO SOUP

3½ cups fresh or canned tomatoes	3 tablespoons flour
¼ cup chopped onion	½ teaspoon sugar
2 tablespoons butter or margarine	3 cups milk, scalded
	1 teaspoon salt

Cook the tomatoes and onion together for 20 minutes. If fresh tomatoes are used, about 10 minutes for canned tomatoes. Press through sieve. Melt butter and blend in the flour and sugar. Gradually add the cooled sieved tomatoes. Cook over low heat, stirring constantly, until thickened. Gradually add the scalded milk, stirring constantly. Reheat but do not boil. Season to taste with salt. Serve at once. Serves 6.

Vegetables

VEGETABLE COOKING HINTS

Water soaks out vitamins and minerals. Cook vegetables in as little water as possible (about 1-inch), and use left-over liquids from vegetables for soups, sauces and hot dishes. Steaming is an excellent way to prepare vegetables. Save valuable vitamins and minerals by cooking vegetables and fruits whole with outer covering left on.

Soda used in cooking vegetables destroys some vitamins. Don't shell or shred vegetables, or squeeze out fruit juices, until just before you are ready to use them.

The outer green leaves of lettuce are richer in vitamins than the inner ones. Shred them for salads and sandwiches. Leaves and outer stalks of celery are tasty in soups, hot dishes, etc.

Dice and cook cauliflower ribs and serve as a separate vegetable.

SAVORY GREEN BEANS

4 strips bacon	1 teaspoon salt
2 medium onions, chopped fine	¼ teaspoon pepper
1 pound green beans, cut	½ cup water
3 tomatoes, skinned and chopped	½ clove garlic

Fry bacon until crisp and remove from pan. Add onions and chopped garlic and sauté until lightly brown. Add beans cut in one inch pieces or cut diagonally, tomatoes, seasonings and water. Cover pan, bring to boiling point, then lower heat and cook until beans are tender. Add bacon and serve immediately.

Mary Vevurka, Chicago, Ill.

STEWED CABBAGE

1 small head cabbage, shredded	1 tablespoon vinegar
1 onion	1 tablespoon flour
2 tablespoon butter	¼ cup water
3 tablespoons catsup	Salt and pepper

Brown onion in butter. Add water. Add shredded cabbage. Add salt and pepper to taste. Add catsup. Simmer slowly, stirring occasionally, about ¾ hour, or until cabbage is done. Add vinegar and flour, bring to a boil and serve.

Maria Slosarcik, Gary, Ind.

SWEET-SOUR CABBAGE

6 cups shredded cabbage
⅓ cup sweet or sour cream
2 tablespoons vinegar
2 tablespoons sugar

½ teaspoon salt
Pepper to taste
1 teaspoon butter

Cook shredded cabbage in small amount of water until just tender, from 5 to 7 minutes. Drain if necessary, then combine with cream, vinegar, butter and seasonings that have been mixed together. Heat through for about a minute and serve immediately.

Virginia Harar, Chicago, Ill.

BAKED CARROT RING (FILLED WITH GREEN BEANS)

1 tablespoon onion
2 tablespoons green pepper
4 tablespoons parsley
¼ cup water
2 cups cooked carrots

1 cup soft bread crumbs
2 eggs
1 teaspoon salt
1 cup thick white sauce
1 teaspoon baking powder

Boil finely chopped vegetables in water 3 minutes. Add to mashed carrots, bread crumbs, unbeaten egg yolks and salt. Beat egg whites until frothy, add baking powder and beat until stiff and creamy. Fold into carrot mixture. Butter ring mold thoroughly and line with sifted bread crumbs. Then pour in carrot mixture. Bake in slow oven 300°F about 1¼ hour or until set and baked through. Unmold unto platter and fill center with well drained, seasoned green beans.

CARROT RING

1 pound carrots, grated with
  small shredder (grated finely)
1 green pepper, shredded or cut
  small
1 cup milk, poured into 3 eggs,
  beaten

1½ tablespoons melted butter
½ teaspoon salt
1 teaspoon sugar
Pepper to taste
½ cup blanched chopped
  almonds (optional)

Combine milk, eggs, seasoning, sugar and melted butter; add balance of ingredients. Bake in well greased or buttered ring mold 45 to 50 minutes in 325°F oven, set in pan of water. Remove from oven. Allow to set a few minutes, unmold and fill center with buttered peas or other vegetable of different color.

Gertrude Kolar, Chicago, Ill.

CAULIFLOWER IN SOUR CREAM

Select white cauliflower with no discoloration. Remove outer leaves. Wash in cool water until clean; cook cauliflower in little salted water until just tender. You may cook in milk to keep cauliflower white. Drain and put in baking dish, put pieces of butter over and sprinkle bread crumbs over top. Pour over sour cream and bake in oven until browned.

Anna Dzurovcak, Hammond, Ind.

BROILED SHEEP'S HEAD MUSHROOM (Peceni Kotrc)

Wash the mushroom thoroughly, slice and allow to stand in salt water for about one hour. Drain and place in pan with enough water to cover. Bring to a boil and allow to simmer for about half hour. Drain and dry a bit. Set slices on a baking sheet and place under broiler at about 375°F. Place a dot of butter on each slice before broiling. Serve hot.

Anna Cmarik, Chicago, Ill.

FRIED SLICED GREEN TOMATOES

Slice green tomatoes about ½ inch thick. Dip in batter that has been made of egg, flour and salt. A little water, not over a tablespoon may be added to the egg. When batter is smooth, dip the slices and drop into deep fat to fry until golden brown. Or fry in butter, if preferred.

Anna Cmarik, Chicago, Ill.

CREAMED CUCUMBERS

Two medium sized cucumbers peeled and cut into pieces or slices, cook in hot water slowly until cucumber is tender and transparent looking. Drain and mix into one cup or more white sauce which has been salted, and season with a little pepper and a slice or two of garlic. Just a little garlic for flavor. Serve while hot on whole wheat toast. For a variation, a little grated cheese may be added. (People that cannot eat raw cucumber can eat it this way.)

Justine Kasovsky, Chicago, Ill.

QUICK FROZEN CORN ON COB

1. Select ears of young, firm, fresh-picked corn

2. Blanch (scald) for 7 minutes

3. Drain-and cool thoroughly

4. Place enough ears for one meal in freezer bag

5. Tie or seal securely

6. When cold store in deep-freeze

BAKED CORN ON THE COB

1. Remove ears from freezer bag

2. Place in baking dish or aluminum foil

3. Bake in hot oven for 20-25 minutes (uncovered)

4. Brown under broiler flame for 2 minutes

5. Serve immediately

Helen Mathews, Gary, Ind.

CREAMED ENDIVE OR DANDELION

Wash thoroughly 1 to 2 pounds endive or dandelion. Cook in covered kettle with plenty of salt, until tender. Drain. Chop up 5 strips of bacon with 2 tablespoons minced onion and fry until soft. In a bowl mix:

1 heaping tablespoon flour　　**2 tablespoons water**
2 tablespoons sugar　　**⅓ cup vinegar**
1 egg, beaten　　**Salt**

Mix well and pour over browned bacon and onion, stir constantly. Cook until thickened. Pour over greens and mix well. Garnish with sliced hard boiled eggs.

Mrs. J. Hritz, Phoenixville, Pa.

PARMESAN CAULIFLOWER

Separate cauliflower into flowerettes. Cover with boiling water. Cook uncovered until tender about 20 minutes. Drain well. Turn into serving dish; season with salt, pepper, a dash of nutmeg and melted butter. Sprinkle with finely chopped parsley and parmesan cheese.

Anna Cmarik, Chicago, Ill.

CUCUMBERS IN SOUR CREAM

1 medium size cucumber,　　**1½ teaspoons sugar**
　sliced thin　　**1 tablespoon vinegar**
1 small onion, sliced very thin　　**½ cup or more sour cream**
½ teaspoon salt　　**1 tablespoon green onion tops,**
Pinch of pepper　　**cut in ½ inch pieces**
2 dashes of paprika

Slice cucumber and onion. Combine all other ingredients and pour over cucumber and onion. Cover and chill about 15 minutes before serving. This dressing may be used on cole slaw or other salad vegetables.

Justine Kasovsky, Chicago, Ill.

BAKED EGG PLANT

Pare, clean and cut egg plant into quarter inch thick slices. Salt the slices and let stand for about an hour. Squeeze out the water from the salted egg plant. Then dip the egg plant first in flour, then the beaten egg, and last into the bread crumbs. Let stand about half hour, then fry in deep fat till golden brown.

Butter a baking dish or a casserole, then put a layer of the fried egg plant, top with a layer of tomato sauce, little grated cheese then again a layer of the egg plant and so on till you have used the egg plant and tomato sauce. Top with grated cheese and bake in an oven 350°F for about an hour.

Mary V. Haydu, Braddock, Pa.

FRENCH FRIED-EGG PLANT

1 medium size egg plant, peeled
1 cup sifted pastry flour
1 teaspoon salt
¼ teaspoon baking powder
1 teaspoon sugar
⅔ cup milk, scant
2 eggs, well beaten
Shortening or oil for deep
 fat frying

Cut egg plant in strips 2 inches long and ½ inch thick. Sprinkle with salt, dip in batter, made by combining the flour, baking powder, salt and sugar with the milk and eggs. Deep fry at 375°F a few pieces at a time until they are golden brown. Drain and serve at once. Serves 8.

Anna B. Russell, Cleveland, Oh.

KOHLRABI IN HOLLANDAISE SAUCE

When kohlrabi have been cooked tender, drain and put into deep dish, cover with sauce and sprinkle with chives or parsley.

HOLLANDAISE SAUCE

2 tablespoons butter
1 tablespoon flour
2 tablespoons tarragon vinegar
Yolk of 1 egg
¾ cup water
1 tablespoon grated onion
¼ teaspoon celery salt
1 teaspoon salt
Dash of white pepper

Put butter in sauce pan, when melted add flour and stir until smooth; add onion and cold water and stir until thick; beat yolk of egg until light, add seasoning and vinegar. Then add to the butter and flour mixture. Remove from fire at once and beat until thick. Pour over kohlrabi. Plain vinegar may be used in this recipe, but tarragon vinegar gives a better flavor.

Anne B. Cmarik, Chicago, Ill.

SHEEP'S HEAD MUSHROOM *(Barana hlava: kotrc)*

Clean thoroughly. Slice ¼ inch thick and soak in salt water for 1 hour. Drain, dry in clean cloth, then dip first in flour, then in egg and milk mixture, then in cracker crumbs. Fry in deep fat until brown. Serve.

Mary Fedor, Streator, Ill.

RICE WITH GIBLETS

1 onion	**½ cup rice**
2 tablespoons butter	**Giblets**
1 cup celery	**Salt and pepper**
½ can whole tomatoes	

Cut up onion and sauté in butter until golden brown, add chopped giblets and a little water, salt and pepper to taste, simmer until almost tender, add more water if necessary, add diced celery, cook about 10 minutes. Cook rice separately, add to chicken giblets with tomatoes. (Add a little sugar, if tomatoes are sour.) Heat through.

Mary Kubik

RICE

½ cup rice	**1 red or green pepper, chopped**
2 tablespoons butter	**1 teaspoon salt**
2 onions	**½ teaspoon pepper**
1 cup strained tomatoes	**1 cup water**
1 clove garlic	

Wash rice thoroughly, place in frying pan with butter or bacon fat, add onion and the garlic minced fine. Let fry a few minutes, add rest of the ingredients with one cup of water. Cook slowly about one hour and as water evaporates, add more to keep from burning, until rice is tender.

Elizabeth Lipovsky, Bethlehem, Pa.

SWEET POTATO MOUNDS

Cook sweet potatoes (yams) until tender, peel and mash, add a little orange juice (about ½ orange), dash of mace or ¼ teaspoon of nutmeg, butter, salt and white pepper to taste. Form into balls around marshmallow; roll in crushed cornflakes. (These may be prepared ahead of time and covered with waxed paper and place in refrigerator until time for baking). Arrange on a buttered cookie sheet and bake in 350°F oven until heated through. Stale marshmallows will stay in shape better.

Loretta Kasovsky, Chicago, Ill.

SWEET POTATOES

Steam sweet potatoes in skins until more than half done. Allow potatoes to get cold, then peel and slice. Place in buttered casserole or baking dish and cover with melted butter and honey. Sprinkle a little salt over all and bake in oven to brown.

Margaret De Silva, Chicago, Ill.

SWEET POTATO PUDDING

6 medium sized sweet potatoes	3 tablespoons butter
6 tablespoons milk	½ teaspoon salt
¼ teaspoon nutmeg	¼ pound marshmallows

Wash and pare potatoes. drop into boiling water. cook gently until tender, about 35 minutes, (or cook in peel and pare after cooked). Drain, mash, add milk, butter and salt and nutmeg. Whip until well mixed. Turn into greased casserole; cover with a layer of marshmallows. Place in a moderate oven 350°F until marshmallows are toasted, about 25 minutes.

Agnes Pilch, Chicago, Ill.

VOLCANO POTATOES

4 medium size potatoes, baked	3 slices American cheese, cubed
½ teaspoon salt	2 tablespoons milk
1 tablespoon butter	

Wash potatoes and bake, when done, while still hot cut length-wise, scoop out into bowl. Mash and combine with ingredients, refill skin shells and put in broiler and brown.

Ann Kuva, Indiana Harbor, Ind.

BAKED POTATOES WITH CHEESE AND ONIONS

Grated American cheese may be added to the scooped out baked potato pulp that has been whipped up with cream and butter. Season and add chopped green onions.

Theresa Bugel, Chicago, Ill.

BAKED POTATOES WITH HERBS

4 large potatoes	**HERBS**
3 tablespoons butter	½ teaspoon minced thyme
3 tablespoons cream	½ teaspoon finely chopped parsley
Salt and pepper to taste	½ teaspoon finely chopped chives or green onion tops

Wash well or scrub potatoes, dry and grease with a little oil or shortening, to keep skins moist. When potatoes are baked, cut a slice from the long side of each potato and scoop out the inside. Mash the potato pulp and mix with butter and cream until fluffy. Then season and add the herbs. Refill potato skins and reheat in oven.

Theresa Bugel, Chicago, Ill.

SOUR POTATOES *(kysle zemiaky)*

4 tablespoons bacon fat	½ lemon rind, grated
3 tablespoons flour	Pinch of thyme
1 medium sliced onion	Pinch of marjoram
1 cup stock or boullion	½ bay leaf
5 or 6 large cooked potatoes	Vinegar to taste (1 or 2
2 teaspoons chopped parsley or	tablespoons)
parsley flakes	

Melt bacon fat in large frying pan. If bacon fat is not handy, render few slices of bacon, and chop the bacon into the sauce, but use the bacon fat. Into the fat add flour and chopped onions or sliced onions, and brown well. Add cold stock and stir well to make a smooth sauce. Add all seasonings except vinegar. Reduce to low heat and cook five minutes. Add sliced or cubed potatoes and the vinegar. Cook for about 15 minutes. Taste for additional seasoning or vinegar. Remove bay leaf before serving. Excellent if served with hot, cold or broiled meats. If preferred, the thyme, marjoram and lemon rind may be left out and a dash of garlic salt added.

Daughters of St. Francis, Lacon, Ill.

POTATOES AND SPINACH

Cut 9 medium potatoes into small pieces about 1½ inches square and place in sauce pan. Put in just enough water so the potatoes would boil. On the potatoes put the cleaned cut spinach (1½ pounds). Do not cover the spinach with water. The steam from the boiling potatoes and the excess water on the spinach will take care of it. Cook about 20 or 25 minutes.

If there is too much water in the saucepan when the potatoes and spinach are boiled, drain off. Add butter and very little milk, salt to taste and beat well.

Benedictine Slovak Sisters, Chicago, Ill.

SAUTÉED SAUERKRAUT

¼ cup butter or drippings, sauté in it ½ cup sliced onions. Sauté the contents of one No.3 can kraut (washed). Cover the pot and cook the kraut until it is hot.

ADD:

2 tablespoons brown sugar　　　**1 tablespoon vinegar**
1 teaspoon caraway seed, or　　**Cook slowly for 15 minutes**
　3 to 4 whole cloves

Margaret Lissak, Berwyn, Ill.

STUFFED RED TOMATOES

Cut slice off top of tomatoes and save. Scoop out insides with teaspoon. Mix 1 pound ground meat with ½ cup cooked rice, 1 tablespoon chopped onion, 1 egg, salt and pepper. Fill scooped out tomatoes and cover with sliced top. Put top side down in pan and add about 1 inch of water. Bake about ¾ hour until cooked. Brown flour in lard and add to cooked and strained tomato pulp and add enough sugar to sweeten, cook until thick. When ready to serve, pour over stuffed tomatoes.

Mary Salat, Chicago, Ill.

MASHED YELLOW TURNIPS

Cut peeled yellow turnip into cubes (about 1 inch). Cover with boiling salted water and cook until tender. Drain off water and shake pot over gas flame, to dry out as much water as possible. This is important because the turnips would be soggy and watery instead of fluffy.

Mash turnips, then force through ricer to get out all the lumps or put them in the electric mixer.

Add a small lump of raw butter and about 2 or 3 tablespoons of browned butter, salt to taste and a little black pepper which is important in turnips.

Keep turnips piping hot over boiling water. Serve with a speck of black pepper sprinkled over the top.

To dress them up, the mashed turnips can be packed into a wet mould and then turned out on a platter and topped off with parsley and a red pimento cut plain or fancy.

Serve with roast turkey, chicken or creamed tuna.

Vincentian Sisters of Charity, Bedford, Oh.

RICE WITH MUSHROOMS

½ cup rice
2 tablespoons shortening
2 onions
1 medium sized can mushrooms
1 cup celery
1 cup water, or more

1 red or green pepper, chopped
1 giblet, 1 heart, 1 liver of any
  fowl
1 teaspoon salt
½ teaspoon pepper

Place shortening in frying pan and when melted, sauté the finely chopped giblet, heart and liver for a few minutes. Then add the thinly sliced onion and finely cut celery and mushrooms. Allow to sauté for a few minutes or until turning brown. Add water, rice and other ingredients. Cover and allow to simmer slowly about one hour, and as water evaporates, add more to keep from burning. Occasionally stir to keep from sticking to pan.

If dry mushrooms are used-soak about 5 minutes, then bring to a boil and simmer for a few minutes. Drain, saving the water to add to the rice mixture. Saute the mushrooms, (cut finely) with the onions.

Mary Mrena, Natrona, Pa.

STRING BEANS WITH POTATOES *(Fazula zo zemiakmi na kislo)*

½ pound green string beans
3 medium sized potatoes
Few sprigs of dill
1 small onion
2 tablespoons lard, bacon drippings or chicken fat

2 tablespoons flour
Salt and pepper to taste
Vinegar or ⅓ cup sour cream

Clean the beans and cut into short pieces, dice the potatoes and put to cook in about two quarts of water. Allow to simmer about 20 or 25 minutes until vegetables are tender. Add the minced dill the last few minutes of cooking.

Sauté the sliced onion in the shortening, until delicately browned, stir in gradually the flour and keep stirring until lightly browned, blend in a little juice from beans to make a smooth paste. Add this into the mixture. Then make a paste of additional 1½ tablespoons flour and about 3 cup sweet or sour cream. If sweet cream is used, add a little vinegar, and stir this into the simmering bean soup. Allow to cook a few minutes until thoroughly blended, but do not boil.

Makes a nice Friday luncheon dish.

Irene Van Offelen, Chicago, Ill.

Miscellaneous

- HOUSEHOLD HINTS, TRICKS AND SUGGESTIONS -

To keep silver shining bright, place in pan, sprinkle with laundry starch so each piece is well covered. Store away and when needed, the silver will be bright and ready for use.

Helen Butas, Bellaire, Oh.

White furniture can be cleaned with a solution of baking soda and warm water. Use 1 teaspoon baking soda to 1 pint of water. Dry thoroughly.

Clean windows with a cloth dampened with glycerine.

If the chamois used for window polishing and other household uses becomes stiff, wash it in sudsy lukewarm water to which 1 teaspoon olive oil has been added. This will soften it considerably.

When washing dishes on which fish has been served, add a piece of cut lemon to the water. This will remove all fish odors and give a new brilliance to china.

Turn a lemon rind inside out and rub your discolored bread or meat boards. Wash with warm water and dry.

Coffee and tea stains may be removed by using glycerine.

Remove mildew by washing in hot suds, moisten with lemon juice and salt and dry in the sun. If mildew persists, try bleaching with hydrogen peroxide.

Mustard stains may be removed by saturating the spots with warm glycerine when washing in soap suds to which a small amount of alcohol has been added. If stain persists, apply oxalic acid (10 percent solution), rinse, follow with rinse of ammonia water.

Remove very soiled lines on collars, cuffs, etc., with an abrasive hand soap; it's easier on the material than a brush.

Rub lipstick or rouge stains with Vaseline. Wash in hot suds. If stains remain, bleach with peroxide; do not use soap first, it may set the stains.

Iron rust may be removed by soaking in oxalic acid solution. When the stain has disappeared, apply a weak ammonia solution and rinse well. Dry in the sun.

Lace edgings may be kept in a crisp state by adding a little sugar to warm water and dipping the clean lace in same.

Blankets and all Woolens - Choose a soap that is mild and pure for washing. Do not rub soap into woolens. Fill the washer with warm, not hot, water to within an inch of the water line and add enough soap to maintain a good layer of suds throughout the washing process. Always remove blankets or other woolens before draining water. Rinse in 2 or 3 waters of the same temperature as the washing water. Borax (half a cup to the tub) or a little soap may be added to the last rinse to soften the water. Dry blankets out of doors, preferably on a clear, warm day when the wind is not too strong. Blankets with striped borders that may "run" should be hung on the line with the stripes vertical, so that if the colors do "run" they will not streak the body of the blankets. When dry, fold and put away in a mothproof container.

Wash sweaters separately, preferably by hand. Trace an outline lightly with pencil on plain paper before washing. Wash as for woolens. Size to outline after rinsing, by placing on flat surface and stretching sweater back to original size. Never hang sweaters over a line or on a hanger to dry.

General Cooking Hints

Baking spilled over in the oven creates smoke and an odor. Both can be checked by sprinkling some table salt thereon.

Brown sugar which has become hard and lumpy, place in a bread box or refrigerator for a few days to soften.

Cream pie or custard will not become watery if milk is scalded before using.

Cream which is hard to whip will whip quickly by adding a few drops of lemon juice.

Custards will not curdle so readily if a tablespoon of flour mixed with sugar is added.

If roasting a large fresh ham, par-boil it first for one hour slowly. Then use garlic salt on it, then roast for 1½ hours or until done. This will give a good flavor.

When frying fish a little vinegar heated in a pan, will kill the odor of fish.

Gravy thickening, sauces, etc., can be made smooth by using a small jar with a tight lid. Put the mixture of milk or water and flour into the jar and shake well until all lumps disappear.

Milk, in being boiled, frequently sticks to the pan. To prevent this, rinse the pan in hot water before using.

Pancakes can be cooked without smoke or odor by rubbing the griddle with a small bag of salt, which will also prevent the cakes from sticking to the iron. This is equally effective on waffle iron.

Rice will be whiter and fluffier if a teaspoon of lemon juice is added to the water while cooking.

Spaghetti or Macaroni frequently boil over when cooking. This can be prevented by adding a tablespoon of cooking oil or lard to the water.

Sweet potatoes and apples will not turn black if placed in salt water immediately after peeling.

Spinach should be cooked in open kettle with no water. Cook slowly until juice is drawn, then quickly. The color will be bright dark green.

When cooking shrimp add a few caraway seeds to the water to kill the odor while cooking the shrimp.

A good hint - If a person cannot ride without getting sick, try chewing on whole olives, they make you thirsty, but will keep your stomach in place.

RENDERING LEAF LARD

Skin the leaf lard and cut into small pieces. Put one cup of water in a large kettle, add cubed lard. Place over a low flame to melt slowly, and stirring frequently to prevent scorching. Simmer until all the fat has melted from the skin, then remove the cracklings with a skimmer. Add one tablespoon of salt, or a little more, to settle fat. When clear, strain through a coarse cotton cloth into jars or crocks. This same method may be used for pork backs.

Anna Romanick, Chicago, Ill.

CRACKLING BISCUITS

1 cup milk
¼ cup sugar
1½ teaspoons salt
1 cake yeast
½ cup warm water

1 egg
4 cups flour
2 cups cracklings (left overs from
   leaf lard rendering)

Scald milk, add sugar and salt. Let cool until lukewarm. Dissolve yeast in warm water. Beat egg, add flour, milk, yeast and cracklings. Knead until smooth. Let rise until double in bulk. Roll out on floured board to ¼ inch thickness. Cut with large glass or biscuit cutter. Place on greased cookie sheet. Brush with beaten egg. Let rise until doubled in size. Bake at 375°F for twenty minutes, or until brown.

Joanne Stoffel, Chicago, Ill.

- NUTRITION -

Balanced Meals

A safe rule for providing well-balanced meals is to select and include foods from the 7 basic groups. In addition to the Basic 7, eat any other foods you want.

Seven Basic Groups

GROUP ONE - Green and yellow vegetables, some raw, some cooked, frozen or canned.

GROUP TWO - Oranges, tomatoes, grapefruit, or raw cabbage or salad greens.

GROUP THREE - Potatoes and other vegetables and fruits, raw, dried, cooked, frozen or canned.

GROUP FOUR - Milk and milk products, fluid, evaporated, dried milk, or cheese.

GROUP FIVE - Meat, poultry, fish or eggs, or dried beans, peas, nuts, or peanut butter.

GROUP SIX - Bread, flour, and cereals. Natural whole-grain, or enriched.

GROUP SEVEN-Butter and fortified margarine (with added vitamin A).

Serve a wide variety of foods. Have a list of menus for balanced meals. This will be a helpful guide in insuring good nutrition in the meals.

Variety In Meals

While it is important to select well-balanced food, it is also important to assemble food into well-planned, well-cooked and attractively served meals.

QUANTITIES REQUIRED FOR 50

Food	Serving Per Person	Order
Bread- 3 lb. loaves	1 to 2 slices	2 to 4 loaves
BEVERAGES		
Coffee	1 cup	1 to 1¼ lb.
Cocoa	1 cup	8 ounces
Tea, Hot	1 cup	2½ ounces
Iced	1 glass	3 ounces
DAIRY PRODUCTS		
Butter	1 pat	1 lb.
Coffee Cream	2 teaspoons	1½ quarts
Cheese	1½ ounces	4¾ lbs.
Ice Cream	No. 12 dipper	2 gallons
SUGAR		
Granulated	1½ teaspoons	¾ lb.
Loaf	1½ cubes	1½ lbs.
MEATS		
Ground meat, patties	3 ounces	12½ lbs.
Meat Loaf	3 ounces	10 lbs.
Pork Chops	1 each (3 or 4 to 1 lb.)	12½ to 15 lbs.
Ham, smoked with bone	2 ounces	20 lbs.
Turkey, dressed weight	2½ ounces	39 to 40 lbs.
RELISHES		
Celery curls 2½ inches	1 piece	2 medium stalks
Olives, green	3 to 4	2 quarts
Pickles, 3 inches	½ pickle	1½ quarts
VEGETABLES		
Allow 3 ounces per person	3 ounces	9½ lbs.
Head Lettuce		8 to 10 heads
Lettuce for garnish		4 to 5 heads
Potatoes, Mashed	5 ounce portions	18 lbs.
Brown	3½ to 4½ ounces	18 to 20 lbs.
Scalloped	5 ounces	14 lbs.
Sweet potatoes	4½ to 5 ounces	20 to 22 lbs.
PUDDINGS, Soft		
Cornstarch	½ cup	6 to 7 quarts
Tapioca, etc.	½ cup	6 to 7 quarts

Food	Serving Per Person	Order
SALAD DRESSING		
French	¾ to 1 teaspoon	1 qt. to 1½ qts.
Mayonnaise	1 to 1½ teaspoons	1½ qt. to 2 qts.
SALADS		
Cole Slaw, etc.	½ cup	6 quarts
Potato Salad (main course)	1 cup	12 quarts
Fish or Meat Salad (main course)	⅔ cup	8 quarts

SANDWICHES
(Estimate for Quantity Buying)

BREAD

1 pound loaf white bread yields 17 ⅝-inch slices without end crusts.

1 pound loaf white bread (thin slices) yields 23 ½-inch slices without end crusts.

2 pound loaf white bread (Pullman) yields 28 ½-inch slices without end crusts.

1 pound loaf whole wheat bread yields 16 ⅝-inch slices without end crusts.

1 pound loaf rye bread yields 19 ⅝-inch slices without end crusts.

MEAT

Corned Beef, cooked, 1 pound sufficient for 8 to 10 sandwiches.

Ham (baked or boiled) 1 pound sliced as purchased, has about 16 thin slices.

1 slice (1 ounce) sufficient for 1 sandwich.

2 slices (2 ounces) sufficient for a generous sandwich.

3 slices (3 ounces) makes a generous serving of ham for a meal.

Summer Sausage, 1 pound sliced as purchased, has about 18 slices.

- CONTENTS OF CANS: VEGETABLES & JUICES -

One #2 can of vegetables yields 5 servings of about ½ cup each.

One #2½ can of vegetables yields 7 servings of about ½ cup each.

One #10 can of vegetables yields 25 servings of about ½ cup each.

One #5 can (46 or 47 ounces) of juice yields 12 servings of about ½ cup each.

FROZEN VEGETABLES

Twelve, 12 ounce packages frozen vegetables will yield 50 servings.

COFFEE (URN METHOD)

Coffee, ground, for 50 servings, 1½ pounds; for 100 servings, 3 pounds.

Water, freshly drawn, for 50 servings, 3 gallons and 3 quarts; for 100 servings, 7½ gallons.

METHOD:
1. Fill jacket of urn with water until glass gauge registers about ¾ full.
2. Heat the water to the boiling point, but avoid boiling.
3. Replenish water whenever gauge shows less than ½ full.
4. Pour coffee into wet urn bag or basket and pour or siphon freshly boiling water evenly over the coffee.
5. Cover and let water drip completely through once.
6. If urn bag is used, pour ½ of the coffee brew back over grounds to give a full extraction and a clear brew. Remove bag or basket as any seepage from grounds impairs the delicacy of flavor and aroma.

NOTE: Coffee grounds will absorb about 2 quarts water. Make coffee just before using as it deteriorates on standing.

COFFEE (KETTLE METHOD)

COFFEE, ground, for 25 servings, ½ pound; for 50 servings, 1½ pounds.

WATER, freshly drawn, for 50 servings, 3 gallons and 3 quarts; for 50 servings, 7½ gallons.

METHOD:
1. Place coffee in a sack large enough to permit free circulation, (any cloth bag may be used that is not too heavy) of water and allowing expansion of coffee.
2. Tie the bag with a cord of sufficient length to fasten to the handle of the container. This facilitates removal of the bag from the hot brew.
3. Pour freshly drawn water into a large kettle; heat to boiling point.
4. Place coffee bag in boiling water; tie cord to handle of kettle. Reduce heat to keep water below the boiling point. Coffee must always be kept below the boiling point.
5. Submerge the bag with a stick or paddle; push up and down to force the water through the grounds.
6. Cover kettle; brew 12 to 15 minutes.
7. Lift bag; drain thoroughly in kettle. Remove bag entirely.
8. Serve coffee at once.

NOTE: Remove coffee grounds from bags immediately after they are taken from the brew. Wash bags thoroughly, without soap, in cold water and place in pan of cold water until used again. Keep the bags wet all the time they are not in use, if used constantly. Replace the bag with a new one about once a week.

FRUIT PUNCH FOR GROUPS

6 pounds sugar
4 quarts tea (10 tablespoons
green tea)
9 cups orange juice

1 pint bottle cherry, raspberry
or pineapple syrup
6 quarts White Rock
8 quarts ginger ale
4 cups lemon juice

Pour hot tea on sugar. When cool add orange and lemon juice and syrup. Pour some of this on cake of ice or cubes and just before serving add, one bottle at a time, of ginger ale and White Rock. Few slices of orange adds to appearance. Liquor may be added. Makes about 81 cups or 324 sherbet glass servings.

Anna Krcha, Chicago, Ill.

SPICED TEA

6 quarts boiling water
5 teaspoons Orange Pekoe Tea
1 teaspoon ground cinnamon
1 teaspoon ground cloves

1 quart orange juice
Juice of 3 lemons
1 pound sugar

Place the tea and spices in a cheesecloth bag. Let the bag stand in the boiling water from 3 to 5 minutes. Remove bag from water and kettle from the flame. Add other ingredients.

Anna Krcha, Chicago, Ill.

- MEATS -

SAVORY MEAT LOAF FOR 50

3 cups milk
3 cups fine dry bread crumbs
9 pounds ground beef
3 pounds ground pork
3 tablespoons salt

1½ teaspoons pepper
2 tablespoons onion Juice
2 tablespoons lemon juice
1 tablespoon poultry seasoning
2 tablespoons minced parsley

Scald milk; add to bread crumbs. Combine with meat and seasonings; mix thoroughly. Pat into 6 loaf pans, 9½x4¼ inches. Bake in a moderate oven, 350°F one hour. Serve with Tomato Sauce.

TOMATO SAUCE

Small piece bay leaf
¾ cup minced celery leaves
⅔ cup flour
2 No. 2½ cans tomatoes

⅔ cup butter or margarine
1 onion
1½ teaspoons salt
½ teaspoon pepper

Add bay leaf, celery leaves and minced onion to tomatoes; simmer 10 minutes; strain. Melt butter or margarine in saucepan; stir in flour and seasonings. Add strained tomatoes gradually. Cook stirring constantly until mixture thickens; reduce heat and cook 10 minutes. Allow about 2 tablespoons sauce per serving.

K. Labash, Chicago, Ill.

BARBECUED SPARERIBS FOR 50

25 pounds spareribs

Cut spareribs into half pound serving portions. Place in single layers in shallow roasting pans. Cover and bake in moderate oven for 1 hour. Cover with barbecue sauce and bake uncovered for 1 hour, or until tender, basting once or twice.

BARBECUE SAUCE

12 eight ounce cans tomato sauce
1½ cups vinegar
3 tablespoons chili powder
1 cup sugar
Few drops Tobasco sauce

4 tablespoons Worcestershire
sauce
2 cups minced onion
1½ cups minced green pepper
1 teaspoon pepper
2 tablespoons salt

Add all ingredients to tomato sauce. Stir until well mixed.

HAMBURGER WITH SPAGHETTI FOR 50

3 pounds spaghetti
8 pounds hamburger
8 small onions
1 cup drippings

2 teaspoons pepper
8 No. 2 cans tomatoes
1 quart buttered bread crumbs
4 tablespoons salt

Cook spaghetti in boiling salted water until tender; drain. Brown meat and minced onion in drippings; add seasonings, tomatoes and spaghetti. Turn into baking pans, cover with buttered bread crumbs. Bake in a moderately slow oven for 30 minutes.

POTATO SALAD FOR 50

2 tablespoons salt
½ teaspoon pepper
15 pounds potatoes, cooked and
diced
6 cups diced celery

3 cups green peppers (chopped),
or 3 cups pickles, (chopped), or
3 cups stuffed olives (chopped)
1 cup minced onion
1½ dozen eggs, hard-cooked
1½ quarts salad dressing

Add salt and pepper to cold potatoes; mix with prepared vegetables. (Note, green peppers may be used, or chopped pickles, or chopped stuffed olives in addition to celery and onion). Add chopped eggs and salad dressing. Toss lightly together. This recipe allows ⅔ cup per serving.

GERMAN POTATO SALAD FOR 50

1½ pounds bacon
15 pounds potatoes, cooked
**   and diced**
2 tablespoons salt
1 teaspoon pepper

¾ cup flour
1½ cups vinegar
6 cups water
1 cup onion

Cook diced bacon over low flame until crisp. Add bacon to potatoes. To bacon fat, add salt, pepper and flour, mix well. Stir in vinegar and water. Cook until thick. Add thinly sliced onion. Pour hot over either hot or cold potatoes. Allowing ⅔ cup per serving.

ROZKY

1 pound butter
1 pound flour
¾ cup water

Juice of 1 lemon
3 egg yolks, well beaten

Take one-half of the flour and mix with the butter as in making pie crust.

Take remaining one-half of flour and mix with water, lemon juice and egg yolks. Knead for 20 minutes, or until bubbles form. Roll out on floured board to one-half inch thickness. Place mixture of flour and butter in the center of the rolled dough, and fold in half, then again in half. Place in refrigerator for 2 hours. Take dough out of refrigerator and roll out once, fold and put back in refrigerator for 1 hour. Repeat rolling and place in refrigerator for 30 minutes. Remove dough from refrigerator, place on floured board and divide into three parts. Roll out one part at a time to an eighth of an inch thickness. Cut into 3 inch squares. On one corner place favorite filling and roll top edge to bottom. Press open corners together, so filling will not escape. Bake on cookie sheets or thin baking pans (ungreased) in a 400°F oven for about 10 to 15 minutes.

Anna Stanek, Whiting, Ind.

BASIC RULES FOR TABLE SETTING

Basic rules are created as a guide, and not necessarily followed rigidly. In setting any table, the aims should include ease of serving the food, convenience of flatware arrangement for eating purposes, a centerpiece and a well balanced table. With the proper atmosphere established at the table, eating becomes an enjoyable experience and not a mere task that must be done three times a day. Food that is haphazardly thrown on unmatched plates on a cluttered table certainly does not appeal to the eye.

The decoration need not be elaborate. A simple centerpiece, a dish of fruit, a few flowers, or a figurine or two. A few fresh flowers, for example, when placed on a breakfast table, will not only make the food taste better, but make the entire morning seem brighter.

1. For formal dinners: Use all-over cloth of white damask or lace. For informal dinners and luncheons: Lace or linen mats or runners. For breakfast: Gay, colorful mats of cloths.

2. Place napkins, folded in squares or rectangles, at the left of the forks, open corner nearest to the plate. If no food is on the plates when the guests are seated, the napkin (folded) may be laid on the empty plate.

3. Place silver I-inch from edge of table in straight line. Place no more than 3 pieces of silver on each side of plate.

4. Place all forks, except cocktail fork, at left of plate with prongs up. Cocktail fork is placed on plate or at extreme right. Knives and spoons at right of plate.

5. Flat silver should be arranged at each place in the order of its use for the various courses, so guests may use the outside pieces on each side first. When salad accompanies main course, dinner fork may be used for both meat course and salad.

6. At informal dinners, dessert silver is usually on the table at beginning of the meal. For more formal service, dessert silver is brought on with the dessert.

7. Table decorations should usually be below eye level, except candles, whose flame should be well above it.

8. Place water glass or goblet just above point of knife - bread and butter plate just above the forks. Place small butter spreader across butter plate, either parallel to edge of table or in line with rest of silver.

How To Serve

1. It is correct to remove and place all dishes from the right, but foods passed must be offered from the left so the guest may use his right hand in serving himself.

2. Always serve coffee and tea, fill water glasses from the right.

3. Just before serving dessert, clear table of everything except centerpiece. Remove crumbs with folded napkin and small plate. Dessert silver may then be put in place or served directly on individual dessert plates.

WEDDING ANNIVERSARIES

First .... Paper
Second .... Cotton
Third .... Leather
Fourth .... Books
Fifth .... Wooden
Sixth .... Iron
Seventh .... Copper
Eighth .... Electric
Ninth .... Pottery
Tenth .... Tin
Eleventh .... Steel
Twelfth .... Silk or Linen
Thirteenth .... Lace
Fourteenth .... Ivory
Fifteenth .... Crystal
Twentieth .... China
Twenty-Fifth .... Silver
Thirtieth .... Pearl
Thirty-Fifth .... Coral or Jade
Fortieth .... Ruby
Forty-Fifth .... Sapphire
Fiftieth .... Gold
Fifty-Fifth .... Emerald
Seventy-Fifth .... Diamond

- WEIGHTS AND MEASURES -

3 teaspoons = 1 tablespoon

4 tablespoons = ¼ cup

5⅓ tablespoons = ⅓ cup

8 tablespoons = ½ cup

10⅔ tablespoons = ⅔ cup

12 tablespoons = ¾ cup

16 tablespoons = 1 cup

2 tablespoons =1 liquid ounce

1 cup = ½ pint

2 cups = 1 pint

4 cups = 1 quart

4 quarts = 1 gallon

8 quarts = 1 peck

4 pecks = 1 bushel

2 tablespoons fat = 1 ounce

½ cup fat = ¼ pound or 1 stick

1 cup fat = ½ pound

2 cups fat = 1 pound

2¼ cups granulated sugar = 1 pound

2¼ cups firmly packed brown sugar = 1 pound

1⅓ cups firmly packed brown sugar = 1 cup granulated sugar

3½ cups confectioners' sugar = 1 pound

4 cups sifted all-purpose flour = 1 pound

4½ cups sifted cake flour = 1 pound

1 cup, less 2 tablespoons, sifted all-purpose flour = 1 cup sifted
 cake flour

1 tablespoon cornstarch = 2 tablespoons flour

5 cups rye flour = 1 pound

3¾ cups whole wheat flour = 1 pound

4 cups cocoa = 1 pound

2⅔ cup coconut = 1½ pound carton

1 medium lemon = 3 tablespoons juice

16 marshmallows = ¼ pound

6 cups cooked macaroni = 8 oz. package

7 cups cooked noodles = 8 oz. package

NUTS - 1 cup chopped = ¼ pound
        3½ cups almonds = 1 pound
        3½ cups pecans = 1 pound
        3 cups walnuts, (broken) = 1 pound
RAISINS - 3¼ cups seeded = 15 oz. package
        3 cups seedless = 15 oz. package
2⅓ cup rice = 1 pound
5 cups grated American cheese = 1 pound
6⅔ tablespoons cream cheese = 1 - 3-ounce package
11 finely crumbled graham crackers = 1 cup
4 coarsely crumbled zweiback =1 cup
9 finely crumbled zweiback = 1 cup
1⅓ tablespoons vinegar or 1½ tablespoons lemon juice and sweet
  milk to make 1 cup = 1 cup sour milk
½ cup evaporated milk and ½ cup water = 1 cup milk
Grated peel of lemon = 1½ teaspoons
12 to 14 egg yolks = 1 cup
8 to 10 egg whites = 1 cup

- SUBSTITUTION OF INGREDIENTS IN COOKING -

CHOCOLATE AND COCOA: ¼ cup cocoa, plus ½ tablespoon shortening is approximately equal to 1 square of chocolate. In substituting cocoa for chocolate in cakes, the amount of flour must be reduced.

BROWN AND WHITE SUGARS: Usually may be used interchangeably, measure for measure. Brown sugar should be firmly packed.

CAKE FLOUR AND ALL-PURPOSE FLOUR: Cake flour must not be used for breads and rolls, as it does not contain enough gluten. To substitute all-purpose flour for cake flour in cakes and cookies, measure one cup, remove 2 tablespoons from the cup, replace with 2 tablespoons cornstarch. The resulting product is likely to be less moist than if made with cake flour.

The following guide will be helpful in determining the size of pans for any recipes:

A cake with shortening containing 2 cups of flour may be baked in -
    a. 2 layer-cake pans 9 inches in diameter or 8 inches square
    b. 1 loaf pan 4x8 inches
    c. 1 sheet pan 8x9 inches and 2 inches deep

C

CAKES - FROSTINGS - FILLINGS

Pages 103 - 160

CAKES FOR OCCASIONS

CANDIES

Pages 162 - 169

CANNING - PRESERVING

Pages 172 - 185

JELLIES, MARMALADES, PRESERVES

RELISHES

CANNED VEGETABLES

PICKLING

COOKIES

Pages 189 - 220

DESSERTS

Pages 222 - 226

CUSTARDS

FROZEN AND GELATIN DESSERTS

CAKE AND PUDDING DESSERTS

TORTES

STRUDELS AND STRUDEL FILLINGS

SAUCES FOR PUDDING DESSERTS

EGGS, CHEESE & CASSE- ROLES Pages 268 - 283

EGGS

CHEESE

MISCELLANEOUS CASSEROLES

FISH CASSEROLES

MEAT - FISH - FOWL

Pages 286 - 348

PASTRY

Pages 350 - 362

SALADS
Pages 364 - 384

MEAT, CHICKEN AND FISH SALADS

GELATIN SALADS

SALAD DRESSINGS

SANDWICHES
Pages 386 - 389

HOT AND COLD SANDWICHES

VEGETABLE AND FRUIT SALADS

QUANTITY SANDWICH FILLINGS

SOUPS & SOUP ADDITIONS
Pages 392 - 400

SOUPS

SOUP ADDITIONS

VEGETABLES
Pages 402 - 411

MISCELLANEOUS
Pages 414 - 427

QUANTITIES REQUIRED FOR 50

Quantity Recipes